TASHKENT

PITT SERIES IN RUSSIAN AND EAST EUROPEAN STUDIES
Jonathan Harris, Editor

CENTRAL EURASIA IN CONTEXT
Douglas Northrop, Editor

Tashkent

 ## FORGING A SOVIET CITY, 1930–1966

PAUL STRONSKI

UNIVERSITY OF PITTSBURGH PRESS

Published by the University of Pittsburgh Press, Pittsburgh, Pa., 15260
Copyright © 2010, University of Pittsburgh Press
All rights reserved
Manufactured in the United States of America
Printed on acid-free paper
10 9 8 7 6 5 4 3 2 1

Library of Congress Cataloging-in-Publication Data

Stronski, Paul.

Tashkent : forging a Soviet city, 1930–1966 / Paul Stronski.

p.   cm. —   (Pitt series in Russian and East European studies) (Central Eurasia in context)

Includes bibliographical references and index.

ISBN 978-0-8229-4394-5 (hardcover : alk. paper) — ISBN 978-0-8229-6113-0 (pbk. : alk. paper)

1. City planning—Uzbekistan—Tashkent—History—20th century. 2. City planning—Political aspects—Uzbekistan—Tashkent—History—20th century. 3. Social change—Uzbekistan—Tashkent—History—20th century. 4. Architecture—Uzbekistan—Tashkent—History—20th century. 5. Urban renewal—Uzbekistan—Tashkent—History—20th century. 6. Tashkent (Uzbekistan)—History—20th century. 7. Tashkent (Uzbekistan)—Social conditions—20th century. 8. Tashkent (Uzbekistan)—Ethnic relations—History—20th century. 9. City planning—Soviet Union—Case studies. 10. Social change—Soviet Union—Case studies.   I. Title.

HT169.U92T375 2010

307.1'21609587—dc22   2010020948

CONTENTS

PREFACE AND ACKNOWLEDGMENTS

This study draws mostly on archival sources in Tashkent and Moscow. In Uzbekistan, I used collections of the Uzbek SSR branch of the State Planning Agency, the Uzbek Writers and Architects Unions, the Plenipotentiary of the Evacuation of the Sovnarkom of the Uzbek SSR, and other republic-level organizations from the Central State Archive of the Republic of Uzbekistan (O'zRMDA). At the Tashkent City Archive (TShDA), I used collections from the Tashkent City Council (Gorispolkom), the archives of various Tashkent industrial factories, and the City Architectural Bureau. Documents from Tashkent Oblast Archive (TVDA) concern Tashkent Oblast Council (Oblispolkom) documents, while the Ministry of Health and urban planning agencies were the focus of my work at the Central State Archive for Scientific-Technical and Medical Documentation of the Republic of Uzbekistan (O'zRI-TTHMDA). Party-level documents in the manuscript are mostly from Russian archives, as scholars cannot gain access to the Presidential Archives of the Republic of Uzbekistan. In Moscow, material from the following institutions was incorporated into this study: the Russian State Archive of Social and Political History (RGASPI) and the Russian State Archive of Contemporary History (RGANI) for documents from the Central Committee of the Communist Party of the Soviet Union, the Russian State Archive of Art and Literature (RGALI) for materials for union-level organizations of art, literature, and architecture, and the Russian State Archive (GARF) for information from the Procurator General (Office of the Public Prosecutor) of the Soviet Union, the NKVD, GULAG special settlements, and the Supreme Soviet. Additional information on urban planning and statistics came from the Russian State Archive of Economics (RGAE). In the United States, I consulted collections at the Hoover

Institution, the New York Public Library, and the Library of Congress. The majority of archival sources for this period of Tashkent history are in Russian, with some limited Uzbek-language material. When it existed, however, Uzbek-language material most often came from the Tashkent City Archive. Information from published Uzbek-language sources—newspapers, travel guides, Uzbek-language publications of the era, and current monographs— has also been incorporated into this study.

Party communiqués, NKVD reports, and documents from the Procurator General add insights into the general mood of the population and the difficulties that officials had in implementing state and Party decrees or in sculpting new identities across the Soviet Union. However, I read these reports largely as documents that were produced by elite officials for specific purposes. The authorities who wrote to Party and state security organizations had precise concerns that they sought to highlight, often revealing institutional agendas or personal biases against Soviet ethno-national groups or social classes. In addition, these documents often concentrate on what went wrong in the Soviet state, not necessarily on the successes of specific policies or proposals. So, while some documents convey instances of large-scale resistance to Soviet initiatives, others show how, for better or worse, local residents began to accommodate and adapt the new urban infrastructure of Tashkent to their own lives, even if some of their actions did not always seem ideologically correct. On the other hand, newspapers clearly conveyed the official interpretation of Soviet achievements; they helped to create the image of the type of society and city that Soviet leaders envisioned for Tashkent. Hence, they, too, are vital for improving our understanding of how the Soviet regime strove to fashion urban areas and modern citizens. Newspaper articles occasionally attacked the Sovietization process in Uzbekistan but almost exclusively focused on the inability of city leaders or local institutions to bring about social change. Therefore, while it celebrated Soviet Tashkent, the official press also exposed a great deal of information on the difficulties that the state encountered in forging this socialist city and new Soviet identities for its residents.

Memoir sources have been interwoven into the text of this story. While memoirs are problematic sources due to the passage of time between the events and writing, they add to our understanding of daily life during a time of tremendous difficulty for the Soviet people. They also provide a glimpse into the reality of life that Party documents do not. Many more Russian-language memoirs have been preserved. As a result, these sources often reveal Russo-centric biases, particularly in their orientalist descriptions of the Central Asian lifestyle and culture, but they nonetheless provide a sense of the collective mood and societal fears of the time. They also expose basic assumptions about the social status and ethnic hierarchies of various groups within the Soviet state.

For practical purposes I have chosen to use common English spellings for all place names to avoid the political and nationalistic implications of using either Uzbek or Russian spellings. While I recognize that most of the English place names have been derived from the Russian, not the Uzbek, they are more commonly recognized as places in Central Asia by the English-reading public. I considered using both Uzbek and Russian spellings but decided against this approach as it was cumbersome and did not suit the topic of creating Soviet spaces, a process that attempted to create a common identity, not a dual one. For simplicity, I usually refer to prominent Uzbeks with the common English-language spelling of their names. With three alphabet changes in the Uzbek language in the past one hundred years, there simply are too many transliterations from which to choose. I decided that the most commonly used English-language variants would provide the text with more consistency, although I have provided a list of currently accepted Uzbek-language equivalents for many of the names that appear in the text. At times, I also differentiate Tashkent residents by race or ethnicity. To denote Muslim (or formerly Muslim) residents, I most often use the term "Uzbek Tashkenter." I also use the terms "indigenous resident," "Central Asian Tashkenter," or "Central Asian Soviet citizen." These latter usages at times can connote residents of other Central Asian ethnic groups (mostly Kazakhs or Tajiks), although I do identify Kazakhs, Tajiks, or Turkmen as such when these distinctions are important. Distinct ethnic groups in the region, such as the Bukharan Jews or Soviet Korean population, are usually identified as such. For the sake of clarity, Russian, Ashkenazi Jewish, Ukrainian, and other Tashkenters of European background usually become "Russian Tashkenters" or "Russian-speaking Tashkenters." When necessary, however, I differentiate between Russians, Ukrainians, Ashkenazi Jews, Poles, Tatars, or ethnic Germans in Tashkent in order to highlight ethnic dynamics, nationality politics, and social hierarchies in the city.

Many people and institutions assisted me in completing this manuscript. I am grateful for the support I received from the History Department and the Center for Russian, East European, and Eurasian Studies (CREEES) at Stanford, which provided me with funding throughout my graduate studies. I also received funding for overseas research from the Research Scholar Exchange Program (RSEP) through the American Councils for International Education (ACTR/ACCELS), the National Security Education Program (NSEP) David L. Boren Graduate International Fellowship, and the Graduate Research Opportunity (GRO) Fellowship through the Stanford University School of Humanities and Sciences.

My graduate school advisor, Amir Weiner, allowed me to focus on the non-Russian regions of the Soviet Union and remained supportive throughout. Norman Naimark, an inspiring scholar and teacher, offered advice and encouragement both during and after graduate school. Terence Emmons helped me conceive of this project, and Robert Crews took over for him and provided close readings, perceptive comments, and support. Doug Northrop of the University of Michigan and an anonymous reader provided valuable insights and guidance that helped me refine the manuscript. Adeeb Khalid provided tremendous guidance as I figured out how to conduct archival research in Uzbekistan. Likewise, Michael Share of the University of Hong Kong listened to my arguments and provided helpful research assistance in both Moscow and Hong Kong.

Molly Molloy, Linda Wheeler, and the staff of the Hoover Institution Library at Stanford tracked down obscure primary sources, and Irina Barnes, Mary Dakin, and the late Rosemary Schnoor provided invaluable assistance and friendship at CREEES. In Uzbekistan, Dilorom Alimova and Dono Ziiaeva of the Institute of History provided me with institutional support. Mirzohid Rahimov of the Institute of History and Manzura Umurzaqova, formerly of ACTR/ACCELS, consistently helped me cut bureaucratic red tape. The staffs of the Uzbek Central State Archive, Tashkent City Archive, and Tashkent Oblast Archive, the Uzbek Central State Archive for Documentation of Medical and Scientific Institutes, and the Navoi Library assisted me in many ways, as did the numerous intellectually supportive individuals I encountered in Tashkent. Of course, any errors or misinterpretations in this work are my responsibility, not theirs.

In Moscow, the archivists and librarians of the State Archive of the Russian Federation, the Russian State Archive of Art and Literature, the Russian State Archive for Social and Political History, the Russian State Archive of Economics, the Russian State Archive of Contemporary History, and the Moscow Historical Library provided valuable help. Marina Nestyeva, Yuri and Sveta Grigoriev, and "Tyota Nina" and Vera Gelman opened their homes to me and offered valuable insights on the Soviet experience. In Tashkent, the Niyazov and Anvar families were most hospitable. Matluba Anvar encouraged me to delve into gender in my study and shared her own work to pique my interest. Beth Kolko, Alanna Shaikh, Dave Hunsicker, Kevin Dean, Mamura Azizova, and Munira Azzout provided camaraderie and intellectual debates. Alanna Shaikh deserves special mention for reading and editing this entire project at various stages. Dave Hunsicker and Mamura Azizova provided essential assistance with the Uzbek language.

I am also grateful to Caitlin Murdoch, Ann Livschiz, Steve Barnes, Andy Jenks, Mikolaj Kunicki, and Kim Warren, all fellow graduates of Stanford, who provided me with an intellectual home and good friendships for many years. In Hong Kong, Dawn Schrepel, Shawn Baxter, Angie Baker, Ed Howard, Matthew Tyson, Dale Kreisher, and Adam Murray provided diversion and interesting political debate. Laura and Patrick Ellsworth helped me tighten the manuscript. Now, in Washington, DC, they continue to play similar roles, as do Dan Flaherty, Erin Crowe, Susan Feinberg, Robert Krikorian, Matthew Ouimet, and others in the Office of Russian and Eurasian Analysis. I particularly appreciate John Parker's help in both finishing this project and figuring out the clearance process for this book. Because I now work for the Department of State, I also want to make clear that the views expressed in this book are my own and do not reflect those of the U.S. Department of State or the U.S. government.

I would also like to acknowledge the influence of Suzi Novak, an excellent high school teacher, and of Marcia Morris and David Andrews at Georgetown University. I am also grateful to Jim Smith, of the American International Health Alliance, who sent me on an extended trip to Central Asia in 1995, when I became intrigued about how socialism had transformed the region.

Finally, my brothers, James and Neil Stronski, and their families—Theresa, Patty, Emily, Keelin, Isabel, Patrick, Luke and Caroline—always provided me with a refuge. My grandmother, Bea Dwyer, unfortunately did not live to see me complete this project but she would have read every word. My parents, Victor and Margaret Stronski, let me get on a plane to Central Asia shortly after September 11, 2001. I apologize for putting them through that, but I hope they are happy with the results. It is to them that I dedicate this book.

NAMES AND TERMS

Frequently Used Uzbek Names

Common English Spelling	Contemporary Uzbek Variant
Hujum Abdullah-Khojaeva	Hujum Abdulloh-Xo'jayeva
Bakhri Akhmedova	Bahri Ahmadova
Yuldash Akhunbabaev	Yo'ldosh Oxunboboyev
Tashpulat Aslankulov	Toshpo'lat Aslonqulov
Abdullah Babakhanov	Abdulloh Boboxonov
Gafur Gulom	G'ofur G'ulom
Akmal Ikramov	Akmal Ikromov
Tulkinoi Kadyrova	To'lqinoy Qodirova
Tamara Khanum	Tamara Xonum
Fayzullah Khojaev	Fayzulla Xo'jayev
Sodik Khusainov	Sodiq Husaynov
Nureddin Mukhitdinov	Nuriddin Muhiddinov
Usta-Shirin Muradov	Usta-Shirin Murodov
Alisher Navoi	Alisher Navoiy
Khamid Olimjon	Hamid Olimjon
Khanifa Pulatova	Hanifa Po'latova
Sobir Rakhimov	Sobir Rahimov
Sharaf Rashidov	Sharof Rashidov
Shaakhmed Shamakhmudov	Shoahmad Shomahmudov
Fatima Yuldashbaeva	Fatima Yo'ldoshboyeva
Usman Yusupov	Usmon Yusupov
Halema Yusupova	Halima Yusupova

Central Asian and Soviet Acronyms and Terms

Amir Timur (Tamerlane): fourteenth-century conqueror of Central Asia and founder of the Timurid Empire

Anders Army: the Polish armed forces that regrouped outside of Tashkent. Under the command of Wladyslaw Anders, this army-in-exile consisted largely of Polish citizens who were released from the gulag and eventually made their way through Central Asia and into Persia, where they joined British forces in the Middle East.

Ankhor: the canal that divided the Central Asian and European sections of Tashkent

arba: a traditional donkey cart

aryk: a small irrigation canal

Basmachi: indigenous Central Asian rebels who fought against Soviet rule

bey: a wealthy or landowning peasant

blat: a system of personal connections in the Soviet Union that allowed one special privileges

byt': Russian word for traditional cultures and ways of life

evakopunkt: evacuation point or registration area for Soviet wartime evacuees

fabkom: Communist Party committee for a factory

GKO: Russian acronym for the Soviet wartime State Defense Committee

Gorispolkom: the executive committee of a city soviet

Gorkom: a city Communist Party committee

Gosplan: the state economic planning agency of the Soviet Union

GULAG: Russian acronym for the Main Administration of Corrective Labor Camps; also (in lowercase) a generic term for a Soviet forced labor camp

hauz: a traditional Central Asian water collection pond that also functions as a meeting place

hovle: traditional single-story private house with an enclosed courtyard

hujum: the campaign in Central Asia for women's liberation and unveiling; literally means "attack"

ichkari: women's section of a traditional home

Informburo: Information Bureau of the Communist Party

ispolkom: executive committee of a soviet

Jadids: late-nineteenth- and early-twentieth-century Muslim reformers

khanate: a political entity ruled by a khan

kibitka: derogatory Russian word for an Uzbek mud-brick home

kishlak: an Uzbek village

kolkhoz: collective farm

kombinat: an industrial or factory complex

Komsomol: Communist Youth League

kul'turnost': the Soviet concept of being highly cultured and possessing proper manners

madrasa: Islamic secondary school

mahalla: traditional Central Asian community neighborhood

Mosoblproekt: Moscow Oblast Planning Organization, a prominent urban planning agency

Navoi: a fifteenth-century Central Asian poet

nikoh: a religious wedding ceremony

NKVD: People's Commissariat for Internal Affairs, the precursor to the KGB

Obkom: the oblast Communist Party committee

oblast': province or country

paranji: veil worn by Uzbek women

Pravda Vostoka: main Russian-language newspaper of the Uzbek SSR

Qizil O'zbekiston: main Uzbek-language newspaper of the Uzbek SSR

raikom: district-level Communist Party committee

Sovnarkom: Council of the People's Commissars

Stakhanovite: elite Soviet worker who set records in fulfilling production plans

sunnat toi: traditional circumcision ceremony

tabib: traditional healer

tashkari: men's section of a traditional home

Tashgorproekt: Tashkent City Planning Organization

Tashselmash: Tashkent Agricultural Machinery Factory

Uzplanproekt: Uzbek SSR planning organization

Uzpromproekt: Uzbek SSR industrial planning organization

Uzselproekt: Uzbek SSR agricultural planning organization

voenkomat: the office that drafted men for service, organized military reserves, and performed military functions at the local level

voentorg: a trade supply organization/store for the military and their families

vozhd': the supreme leader, a common term that usually referred to Stalin

ZAGS: acronym for the Soviet bureau that registered marriages

TASHKENT

INTRODUCTION

> Collapsing houses, torture chambers, open-pit fires, dampness, bitter
> winter cold, and an unenviable downtrodden life—that is the path
> of our enemies. New, well-equipped homes, ovens, wooden floors,
> phonographs, beds with springs, and electricity—this is the path of the
> Communist Party.
>
> —Usman Yusupov, November 1938

On September 17, 1939, *Pravda Vostoka* declared that the construction of
the Great Fergana Canal fulfilled the "centuries-long" dream of supplying
the people of Central Asia with water. The Soviet government's investment
in the region, the expansion of the local transportation infrastructure, and
the "voluntary" and "heroic" efforts of thousands of ordinary Uzbek Soviet
citizens transformed a former Russian colony into a "flowering garden" and
the center of Soviet life in Asia. According to Usman Yusupov, first secretary of the Central Committee of the Communist Party of Uzbekistan,
the canal presaged the future prosperity of the region: "Each Soviet village
will no longer have a *hauz,* from which people drink water with worms,
but proper drainage canals will now flow to make [the entire region] flour-
ish."[1] The new canal exemplified the Stalinist state's abiding concern for its
Central Asian citizens and its ability to guide them into the modern age and
to socialism. Officially, Soviet power had removed water, the source of life,
from the hands of the "feudal-*bey* landlords," who previously had forced

Asians into poverty, hunger, and flight. The revolution reorganized social and economic relations in Central Asia, and all citizens of the region—Uzbeks in particular—gained from the abundant harvests of fruits, vegetables, and cotton that this new Soviet infrastructure produced.

The centerpiece of this "flourishing garden" was to be the modern city of Tashkent. The Uzbek capital, the largest urban area in Central Asia, also received water in the summer of 1939 as a result of the construction of Komsomol Lake, which was in the center of the city and fed by a canal. Located in the newly established Stalin Park of Culture, the lake was built by the "voluntary" efforts of Tashkent's Komsomol members. The park replaced a purportedly ramshackle, dusty, and barren Uzbek *mahalla* (traditional neighborhood) with a monument to Soviet progress. The desert city's workers gained a lakeside resort complete with wide sandy beaches, clean water, cascading fountains, and competitive swimming and boating areas. Its grand opening in June 1939 was a much-touted Soviet holiday for Tashkent residents.[2] By all published accounts, the Soviet state was rapidly transforming the physical environment of the city for the benefit of its residents. Tashkent in official Soviet discourse was becoming the center of Soviet Asia and a symbol of the prosperity, abundance, and progress that the socialist system provided to the region.

A little more than a decade later, Russian writer Viktor Vitkovich described an even more impressive vision of the city as a budding urban metropolis with Soviet cars racing up and down brand-new asphalt streets as trams and trolleybuses delivered Central Asian commuters to multistory office blocks and factories. He saw Tashkent as "so advanced" that it was no longer uniquely Central Asian, that it instead resembled numerous other state-of-the-art urban centers across the globe with its new schools, hospitals, industrial enterprises, and suburban areas. He portrayed Tashkent's main thoroughfare, Navoi Street, as a clean and boisterous place where "office workers carry portfolios; school boys hop along, textbooks tucked under their belts; ice-cream vendors push handcarts. A truck waters the street and a momentary rainbow comes into being in the sunlight. There is as much pulsating life as in any Soviet capital."[3] In Vitkovich's account, Soviet Central Asia is depicted as well on its way toward modernity, with the technological achievement of Tashkent—paved roads, automobiles, and mechanized public transportation—all helping the Uzbek people ride toward the future of communism. Soviet propagandists and Party officials argued that Uzbekistan, under the leadership of the Communist Party, was transitioning from a backward Asian colony into a twentieth-century industrial state with new urban spaces that showcased the "liberation" and "prosperity" of the Uzbek people under socialism. Tashkent had become both the "flower" and the "factory" of Soviet Uzbekistan—a model urban center that contained all the important markers of economic development that socialism would spur across all of Asia in the years to come. The Sovietization model of Tashkent reportedly had universal applications, and the new Uzbek capital soon would help spark a global revolution to bring socialism to towns and cities across Uzbekistan, Central Asia, and beyond.

In this regional study, the transformation of the social and physical landscape of Central Asia and the Soviet Union is viewed through the prism of the city of Tashkent, the multiethnic capital of the former Uzbek Soviet Socialist Republic (Uzbek SSR) and now of independent Uzbekistan. Such a view addresses two topics largely overlooked in existing literature of Soviet history: urbanism and the Central Asian experience during the 1930s to the 1960s, the middle period of Soviet power.[4] Tashkent provides an interesting focus because it is outside the core Slavic republics of the Soviet Union and because Soviet officials—Party leaders in Moscow and Tashkent, city planners, architects, and factory directors—embarked on a massive effort to create a socialist urban center in Asia at a time of revolutionary change. This effort had a significant impact on the everyday lives of Tashkent residents, primarily Uzbeks and Russians, but also Kazakh, Tajik, Jewish, Tatar, and countless other ethno-national groups that either lived in the region or arrived there during the Soviet era. As material from local, national, and Communist Party archives as well as extensive published sources show, the drive to make Central Asia "socialist" was part of a broader campaign of rebuilding cities to create a new socialist society and to transform an ethnically diverse population into "new Soviet men and women." Communist Party leaders in Moscow and city officials in Tashkent sought to create a carefully planned urban space by destroying public reminders of the non-Soviet past (e.g., mosques, single-family houses, and traditionally narrow streets) and replacing them with architecturally elaborate theaters, apartment buildings, modern factories, and hospitals—all allegedly built for the benefit of the people of Uzbekistan. The residents of the city responded in multiple ways, with some resisting the destruction of their hometown, others actively accepting the new urban areas, and the majority gradually adapting to the changing environment of the new Soviet Central Asia in which they lived, often trying to fuse some traditional practices or customs with the new Soviet culture that was taking root in Tashkent.

While transforming the Uzbek capital was outwardly about city development, Soviet urban renewal campaigns had a much more important purpose, namely, bringing about the breakdown of traditional social relations and increasing the state's ability to monitor its citizens. Building a "Soviet city" was not the end goal in itself but the means to change the society it housed. New socialist cities were to provide Soviet Uzbek citizens with unique urban areas that the state deemed superior to those anywhere else in the world, particularly in the colonial and postcolonial societies of Asia and the Middle East, allegedly because of socialism's ability to plan and monitor the development of all sectors of the economy, from industry and agriculture to urban growth and population migration. In turn, this extensive planning would create the optimal environment for building ideologically and physically healthy citizens of the Soviet state, who could participate in socially productive labor, appreciate high culture, and willingly lay down their lives for socialism. Creating an ideal modern capital for the Uzbek SSR was as much about creating a vision of the new Uzbek Soviet national identity as it was about building streets, establishing new schools, installing plumbing, or improving the living standards of this distant outpost of socialism in Asia, which grew into one of the larger and more important urban centers in the Soviet Union over the course of the twentieth century.

Creating Uzbekistan

Soviet officials created or, to use Benedict Anderson's term, "imagined" Uzbekistan, just as they imagined and then created a variety of other ethnic and national groups.[5] Sovietization in Central Asia, whether it concerned Soviet-style education, public health campaigns in the Uzbek capital, or the construction of an apartment building, was meant to "modernize," "civilize," and "free" the Uzbek people from the allegedly negative aspects of their past and push them into a happy Soviet future. Architects and urban planners sought to create a new city and, in the process, a new Soviet Uzbek national identity. This project included the creation of an urban center that combined twentieth-century building designs with purported local and ethno-national architectural details. In a time of global decolonization, these efforts in Central Asia underscored the fact that the Soviet regime strove to "solve" ethnic discrimination by providing formerly colonized minorities with cities that mirrored the prosperity of Russia, but with minor allowances for cultural differences. In short, political and cultural leaders in Moscow and Tashkent developed their views of Uzbek national identity and tied this identity closely to the image of a prosperous Soviet state. To show that the Soviet Union had moved beyond colonial oppression and was heading toward communism, Soviet officials were determined to build the modern urban infrastructure that was needed to establish a socialist society and create ideologically sound Soviet citizens in the Central Asian desert.

However, the socialist experience in Central Asia remains an under-studied topic. Until recently, scholars focused on the ability of Central Asians to resist Sovietization and paid less attention to how Central Asian identities changed under Soviet rule, a surprising oversight considering that the Uzbek SSR and its four Central Asian neighbors supported the Soviet state to its very end, long after anti-Soviet independence movements had developed in the Caucasus region, the Baltics, and even in Russia itself.[6] In fact, the multiethnic population of Tashkent reacted to, adapted, and ultimately helped to shape these efforts during times of intense turmoil in Soviet history as the state experienced rapid industrialization, World War II, postwar Stalinism, de-Stalinization, and the dawn of the Brezhnev era. A variety of themes runs through this history, ranging from city planning, migration, industry, education, health care, and cultural affairs, demonstrating that the effort to create new cities touched a wide variety of daily activities. The Soviet system gradually gained a support base in the region, particularly during times when the top-down pressure of Stalinism decreased—temporarily during World War II and more noticeably in the late 1950s, after Stalin's death, when Uzbeks interacted more closely with the Soviet institutions that had taken root in the city.

In 1924, Soviet officials divided Central Asia into individual republics and established a territory called the Uzbek Soviet Socialist Republic. As Francine Hirsch has shown, they created images of the new Uzbek ethnos, declared the language that local residents spoke to be "Uzbek," and then revised the Uzbek alphabet three times in the first three decades of Soviet rule—from Arabic to Latin and finally to Cyrillic.[7] Simultaneously, Soviet historians—initially, most of them Russian—began to create an Uzbek historical narrative to fill in the region's "national content." Party officials initiated a campaign to transform Navoi, a fifteenth-century Central Asian poet who wrote in both Turkic and Persian, into the Uzbek national literary figure.[8] Soviet propaganda in Uzbekistan frequently included mention of the heroism of the struggle against the Basmachis, the anti-Soviet Central Asian rebels who were finally defeated in the mountains of Central Asia in 1931. Concurrently, public health specialists and Party leaders criticized pre-existing Central Asian cultural or historical traditions, particularly the purported low status of women, high illiteracy rates, poor health standards, the strong influence of Islam, and "barbaric" local customs—polygamy, underage marriage, and circumcision. All of these "backward" traits were eventually to be overcome through rational Soviet science, the creation of modern health-care and education systems, and productive factory labor. While in some ways this creation of new national groups began as a top-down process initiated by Party leaders in Moscow, recent archivally based studies indicate that new national identities and cultural traditions were much more the result of a complex negotiation between indigenous residents on the ground in Central Asia and top Party ideologists sent out from Russia to help construct socialism in the region.[9]

In creating the Uzbek SSR, Soviet officials also selected a capital city and began to conceive of what "Soviet Uzbek" architecture should look like. Architects and artists studied the building traditions of Central Asia, declared most of them "backward," and then postulated how they could "improve" local building designs with modern Soviet technology. In categorizing Uzbek cities, Soviet urban planners painted a picture of traditional Central Asian towns as primitive, unhealthy, and uncomfortable, echoing sentiments expressed by European officials across colonized Asia. In fact, Soviet architects and city officials spoke negatively of the disorder of the winding streets of the Old Town sections of Tashkent to such an extent that the dust in these streets and the one-story "mud" homes along them became the defining characteristics of historic Central Asian urban centers. Propaganda portrayed these traditional homes with their enclosed courtyards as prisons for women. Soviet officials also decreed the community *hauz* to be a breeding ground for disease. By the early 1930s, the Soviet regime celebrated a few achievements of Uzbek history—Navoi and the defeat of the Basmachi rebels—but was busy belittling almost everything else. Party officials identified negative traditions that were to be excised from Soviet life in Central Asia, while simultaneously inventing new ones that would help create a new socialist identity for the region.

Although Soviet policies introduced to Central Asia a number of features unique to socialist societies, in many ways they continued the project launched by the tsarist regimes, which also viewed traditional Central Asian society as stagnant and resistant to change. Soviet leaders in Uzbekistan decreed that the revolution liberated Central Asians from colonial oppression and imperialism, but their efforts to "enlighten" the local population, their goals of creating a modern European-style urban environment in Central Asia, and their propagandistic use of the region's transformation to showcase state power remind one of similar programs of late-nineteenth-century Russian administrators in the newly conquered territories of Turkestan. In Central Asia and the Russian Empire as a whole, these similarities show that certain ideas about cities, urban life, and the means of ruling urban spaces spanned the revolutionary divide, despite the clear ideological break of 1917.

Furthermore, in "inventing" Soviet Uzbekistan, government bureaucrats, Party leaders, and architects put much effort into reconstructing Tashkent so that it would fit their ideologically inspired images of what a "capital city" needed to look like, just as their imperial predecessors had emphasized the need for a European-style urban center in Central Asia.[10] As the focal point of the Soviet system in Asia, Tashkent was to be like Moscow—an immensely powerful political, economic, and cultural center that could act as the "capital" for international socialism. As a result, state officials, city planners, and mapmakers closely followed the Moscow example throughout the Soviet era in the way in which they built the socialist system in Central Asia. They needed Tashkent to look like a contemporary capital city of the "liberated" Uzbek SSR, just as the Soviet capital was the political and symbolic heart of socialism for the entire "liberated" working class of the former tsarist empire and beyond.

Tashkent was of particular importance to the Soviet regime as a symbol of socialism and a beacon of hope for Asian peoples who lived under Western colonial domination. In many ways, Tashkent, the largest city in Central Asia, was to become Moscow's "shining star" in the East and an example of the adaptability of Soviet-style socialism. With the new city of "Soviet Tashkent," Moscow was hoping to show Asia and the Middle East the "light" of socialism and help spread its revolutionary ideology around the globe. This creation of a model socialist city in Asia was an important goal of all Soviet leaders immediately upon the establishment of the Uzbek SSR in 1924, but it grew in importance during the cold war, when the Soviet Union and United States competed intensely for influence in the decolonizing world. It is thus appropriate to examine the transformation of this multiethnic Central Asian city in a broad context of twentieth-century European, colonial, and postcolonial trends in the planning of both cities and societies and the distinct path laid out under this authoritarian socialist system. This transformation included European socialists' efforts to bring "enlightenment" to oppressed classes and peoples of the world, which was one aspect of broader twentieth-century attempts to create ideal citizens in modern states. Tashkent was effectively a city situated at the crossroads of colonialism and an ultra-centralized socialist state. Given this situation, it was a rapidly changing place that was both Central Asian and Soviet (i.e., "modern"), even when Party leaders did not always identify it as such or when local residents tried to preserve some aspect of their family or community customs in their new Soviet lives, often using the state's own laws and regulations. This history of Sovietization in Central Asia is neither a simple case of a Soviet identity being imposed on the region from Moscow through Russification nor simply an example of popular resistance to this process from the residents of Tashkent. Through urban planning, among other programs, the multiethnic Soviet state sought to create common identities for Central Asia's diverse inhabitants and, at the same time, to concentrate power and decision making around Moscow. With great difficulty, that regime over time successfully fused Soviet and regional identities through the gradual interaction—both positive and negative—of the population with political and cultural institutions of the city, even if the ultimate creation of a Soviet Uzbek identity was not exactly what Soviet planners originally had in mind. However, since Uzbeks were among the most stalwart supporters of the Soviet regime during the late *glasnost'* era, Soviet cultural mentalities and allegiances certainly took root in the region and proved to endure for a long time.

The utopian ideals of the Soviet regime promised enormous benefits: improved standards of living, racial and ethnic equality, liberation from colonial oppression, economic prosperity, industrial growth, expansion of water resources, and educational or socioeconomic opportunities for individual citizens. However, the regime's ideological stress on industrial development, its uncompromising faith in Marxist theories of development, its desire for total control over the population, and its bureaucratic inefficiency complicated efforts to build an ideal capital city. Exploring the ways in which Soviet officials sought to transform Central Asian urban society and the level of success they achieved also invites an evaluation of the success of this epic campaign, particularly because these utopian ideals of socialist urbanization led to a tremendous displacement of the Tashkent population and a reordering of urban space, thus introducing stresses into urban life, including hunger, disease, overcrowding, and deteriorating sanitary conditions. Furthermore, in promoting a socialist vision for Central Asian cities, Soviet officials—many of whom were based in Russia—aimed to reorient traditional community structures toward new Soviet ideals but often ignored the importance of the home, causing many residents—and even some city officials and urban designers in Moscow—to view the urban transformation plans as assaults on local neighborhoods and cultures or, to use the term coined by J. Douglas Porteous and Sandra Smith, as a form of "domicide," all in the name of building for the public good and the Soviet future.[11]

Tashkent in Pre-Soviet History

Thousands of miles from Moscow, Uzbekistan is situated in the middle of the Kyzyl Kum (Red Sand) desert. The region experiences a continental climate, with long, hot summers and shorter but frequently cold and rainy or snowy winters. Two main rivers, the Syr Darya and Amu Darya, run through the region to the Aral Sea. Central Asia bore religious and cultural influences from Buddhism, shamanism, and Zoroastrianism until the Arab conquest in the seventh and eighth centuries led to the conversion of the region's inhabitants to Islam. Pre-Islamic influences remain important aspects of popular religious belief and practices in Central Asia. Genghis Khan and the Mongol Empire seized much of Central Asia in the thirteenth century before the Mongol invasion of Russia. These conquests began a pattern of constant migration into and across Central Asia. Although Uzbekistan has a predominantly Sunni Muslim population, trade routes (as well as tsarist and Soviet migration policies that brought in deportees and voluntary migrants) led a variety of other ethnic and religious groups, including Jews, Orthodox Christians, Poles, Koreans, Armenians, Tatars, and Germans, to Tashkent.

For much of Central Asia's history, the cities of Bukhara and Samarkand, now in independent Uzbekistan, dominated the region, while Tashkent was a minor commercial town. Bukhara was an important site of Islamic learning, and Samarkand was a political, economic, and cultural center on the Silk Road trade route. Samarkand also served as the seat of the Timurid Empire, ruled at the peak of its power by Amir Timur (or Tamerlane, 1369–1405). Both Samarkand and Bukhara have strong Persian influences in language, culture, and ethnic makeup, a fact that is reflected in their Soviet and post-Soviet populations. The Islamic architecture of the region, particularly in Samarkand, with its main square (Registan), the astronomer Ulug Beg's observatory, and *madrasas* on the Registan, became symbols of the Timurid Empire's power and scientific achievements. Samarkand later served as an important comparison point for Soviet artists and building designers when creating "Soviet-Uzbek" architecture. From the seventeenth to nineteenth centuries, the region was dominated by three local powers: the emirate of Bukhara, the khanate of Khiva, and the khanate of Kokand.[12] Russian perceptions of cruel and repressive rulers in these cities grew in the nineteenth and twentieth centuries, but the symbolism of glorious Samarkand and Bukhara, two of the Islamic world's greatest cities, lingered the Soviet era.

For most of the pre-Soviet modern period, Tashkent was a small trading center. The Russian conquest of Turkestan in 1865 spurred the growth of the city, as Jeff Sahadeo has shown.[13] Russian armies seized the town from the Kokand khanate in that year, making it the center of the tsarist regime in Central Asia and reorienting the region toward Moscow and thus to European culture, philosophies, and ideologies. Imperial administrators quickly set up a military fortress, and the region grew in political and economic importance to become the de facto capital of Russian Central Asia. This growth brought in large numbers of migrants from Russia—exiles, peasants, soldiers, railroad and textile workers, and government bureaucrats—who lived in European-style settlements built alongside the traditional Central Asian ethnic city. From Tashkent, Russian armies gradually moved on Samarkand, Kokand, Bukhara, and Khiva, the latter two becoming protectorates of the tsarist state. The establishment of Russian Central Asia was accomplished in ten years and was undertaken largely for economic and foreign policy reasons to demonstrate Russia's status as an imperial power.[14] Robert Crews has examined how the tsarist regime successfully penetrated Muslim communities in the region, showing that the state used Islam to build support among the local population and involved them more actively in the mechanisms of empire. As such, he also explores the ways in which the indigenous population in Central Asian in turn used the state to solve local disputes, settle religious disagreements, and shore up family relationships.[15]

Russian influences likewise brought Western political ideas to the region, including revolutionary ideologies. Until recently, Western scholars largely viewed the communist revolutionary era in Tashkent as a European affair, with railway workers and soldiers fighting for Soviet power and reforms. However, historians have argued that there was considerable support for a revolutionary change among indigenous peoples, specifically among the Jadids, a group of intellectuals who attempted to bring about Muslim cultural reform, as Adeeb Khalid has shown.[16] The revolution and the subsequent Russian civil war brought chaos to Central Asia, with an out-migration of some Russian settlers, followed by an influx of refugees to Tashkent because of the war and the famine that was ravaging some areas of Russia. After the Bolsheviks won the civil war and after the creation of national borders in Central Asia in 1924, Tashkent lost some of its symbolic importance, particularly after Soviet officials designated the historically Central Asian Samarkand, not the more Russian city of Tashkent, as the first capital city of the newly established Uzbek SSR. In the first ten years of Bolshevik rule, the state largely held off making a direct assault on the city of Tashkent and on many local cultural or social institutions. By 1930, however, re-imagining Uzbek cities took central stage when the more modern and industrial Tashkent regained its official claim as the political center of the republic, a symbol of the Soviet Union's march toward the future and toward communism and a sign that attitudes toward Uzbekistan and its inhabitants were changing quickly.

The study of Central Asia is a relatively new field in the West. Until recently, scholarship focused largely on the cultural and literary traditions of Uzbekistan and Central Asia or on the influence and, at times, the "threat" of Islam to the Soviet state. Little attention was paid to the topic of Sovietization, except to show how it was a form of Russian/Soviet domination and Russification of the region.[17] Furthermore, some Western scholarship focuses too specifically on individual Central Asian peoples and makes little effort to place the socialist experience in Central Asia in the broader context of Soviet and world history. This problem continues, with post-Soviet nationalist historiography in Uzbekistan too often dwelling on the victimization of Uzbeks in the Soviet era but not on their role in the creation and functioning of the Soviet system, the establishment of Soviet-Uzbek identities, and the participation of Uzbeks in some of the darkest crimes of socialism in the twentieth century.[18] On the other hand, Soviet literature often simply reiterates the "achievements" of the Soviet era but adds little to our understanding of the difficulties of bringing about major transformations, the hardship caused by such rapid changes, or the ways in which local and state officials interacted to create the new Soviet society in the region.[19]

In the subfield of Soviet Central Asian studies, Gregory Massell argued in the 1970s that Marxist-Leninist ideology was particularly important to the Soviet regime in Central Asia but that it needed adaptation to suit the local environment. Massell explains that because the region lacked an indigenous working class that could support socialism, Soviet leaders attempted to build support for the Soviet project among women, the "surrogate proletariat," who, like the workers of Europe in Marxist ideology, possessed the lowest status in Central Asian cultural and economic life. Through a forced and violent female unveiling campaign, called *hujum* (which means "attack" in Uzbek), Central Asian women were to gain liberation from the traditional family and Islamic social structure and become the building blocks upon which a new Soviet culture would be created.[20] This campaign was an attempt to destroy traditional social norms and to replace them with a new and "modern" Soviet society, an early example of the regime's efforts at social engineering. Two recent studies using newly accessible archival data have picked up on Massell's arguments. Marianne Kamp focuses on the policies toward and perceptions of Central Asian women mostly before the direct assault on the veil in the late 1920s, while Douglas Northrop follows the women's liberation movement and popular resistance to the hujum campaign through the 1930s to show how violence became a critical component of Stalinist rule in the region.[21] He notes high levels of resistance at the height of Stalinist violence but a more gradual accommodation to Soviet norms over time, particularly during World War II. In many ways, the war years helped solidify allegiances and a sense of loyalty between Uzbeks and the Soviet state, no matter whether one was fighting on the front lines, working in a Soviet factory, or trying to relieve the hunger and suffering of so many desperate war evacuees and refugees who found themselves in the Tashkent region. With the all-encompassing effort to defend the Soviet Union against the Nazis, Central Asian and Soviet identities began to merge more tightly and Soviet citizens in Tashkent gradually gained a greater understanding of socialism and a bigger stake in the success and longevity of the Soviet project in the region, even if its policies and bureaucratic inefficiencies contributed to the tremendous suffering.

Shoshana Keller has concentrated on Soviet attempts to eradicate Islam, and she places these efforts in a local as well as in a broader context of Soviet antireligious campaigns.[22] Other studies have looked at Soviet attempts to "modernize" Central Asia and other less "developed" regions of the Soviet Union, either through bringing "Soviet" (i.e., European)-style health care to Central Asia, constructing the Turksib railroad through the region, or building socialism through various projects in the arctic north, all of which were part of the general campaign at transforming indigenous peoples by replacing traditional cultures with "modern" Soviet ones. These studies, however, generally focus on the early years of Soviet rule without thorough examination of World War II, a cataclysmic global event that fundamentally transformed this region, as it did much of the world.[23]

The topic of urbanism in Soviet history has also gained momentum recently, with historians beginning to look beyond high culture, elite politics, the terror, collectivization, and industrialization. The traditional neglect of this topic is surprising considering that urbanization was a natural outcome of Stalin's policies of modernizing and eradicating Islam and that Soviet officials used economic and social planning to control urban life. Stephen Kotkin's study of the city of Magnitogorsk demonstrates how the Soviet experiment was an exercise aimed toward an overall enlightenment and explores how Party leaders, factory workers, and local officials went about building a new Soviet culture in the city through industrialization.[24] However, Magnitogorsk, a city that was built from scratch in the Soviet era, was not representative of most Soviet urban environments that had preexisting cultures and infrastructures with which Soviet power had to contend. Although the city had many non-Russian workers, it was still located in an ethnically Slavic region, so Kotkin's study thus gives little indication of how Sovietization occurred in an ethnic republic and of the cultural dislocation it caused in a minority region, particularly one that was not predominantly Orthodox Christian.[25] Also, Kotkin does not follow the story of Magnitogorsk through the trauma of World War II, when men went off to the front to die for socialism and women and children moved in greater numbers onto the factory floor, thereby transforming gender and family dynamics, a process that can be seen as a fundamental turning point in the solidification of Soviet values and identities in Central Asia as a whole.[26]

Indeed, archival research on Tashkent indicates that city planning was an ever-changing interaction between central authorities, republic-level officials, and local Tashkent planners to develop images of both the Soviet state and Uzbekistan that were "modern" and "progressive."[27] Building Soviet Tashkent was neither a strictly "top-down" nor "bottom-up" process. Local officials and residents themselves participated in this effort to shape local identities and the urban environment, often responding to events either on the ground in Tashkent or in distant parts of the Soviet Union that could indicate fundamental changes in the direction of society. Soviet planners also gradually had to acknowledge the importance of city residents, who, despite Soviet ideology's belief in the transformative power of rational planning, were not always rational beings and did not necessarily act as Soviet urban planners and Party officials believed they would or should. Moreover, residents' actions, complaints, and innovative responses to the problems that arose in this major Soviet city at times hampered official attempts to create a model multiethnic socialist urban space in Central Asia as Tashkenters themselves tried to put their own stamp onto this massive redevelopment project.

Urban studies must look beyond the conventional boundaries of Soviet history, particularly the revolution, World War II, the Stalin-Khrushchev break, and the cold war. These arbitrary divisions limit our ability to see the continuities, particularly in Central Asia, between these periods of Soviet history.[28] In fact, examining the history of Soviet Central Asia by studying Tashkent shows that Stalinism was a central component of both the Uzbek Soviet experience in the twentieth century and the urban planning apparatus, just it was throughout the Soviet world. The Stalinist system lasted well beyond the death of Stalin. Although the Stalinist stress on building grand public structures lost influence during the Khrushchev and Brezhnev eras, the construction of model cities, with beautiful city centers, ethno-national motifs, and, in Tashkent, maximum decorative use of water, continued to the end of the Soviet era and beyond, as did the authorities' strong desire to mold, shape, monitor, and control the lives and habits of Soviet citizens.

Although Tashkent was never touched by German bombs, World War II had a tremendous influence on the Sovietization process in the Uzbek capital. Its urban layout and ethnic makeup were fundamentally altered by the millions of refugees who came through the city during the war years. While Stalingrad, Kiev, and Minsk were all completely destroyed, the Soviet cities of Central Asia and Siberia experienced rapid industrial, economic, and population growth during these years. Studying how this city managed its unexpected wartime development is essential to our understanding of how local governing structures and planning agencies responded to the conflict. Instead of rational planning—the mantra of Soviet urban design—city officials responded to crisis after crisis to guarantee the survival of the Soviet Union, even if its clumsy response to the war across the board could not guarantee the survival of scores of Soviet citizens. In Central Asia, the rapid wartime industrialization exposed the uneven prewar economic development of the Soviet Union because the region lacked the infrastructure (both physical infrastructure and trained employees) for military industrial production. Unable to handle all the city's needs, Party officials decreed which institutions and people were useful enough to the war effort to assist and left the majority to fend for themselves, silently showing that Soviet officials had created hierarchies of importance among institutions, cultures, political priorities, and socioeconomic and ethnic groups.

An awareness of the impact of the war on urban societies is likewise necessary for understanding the social and economic development of the Soviet Union during the cold war. Scholars must examine how Soviet cities on the home front both incorporated this growth and regularized these four years of unprecedented industrial development. In many ways, the early postwar liberalization and sheer necessity enabled city planners to reinterpret traditional Uzbek architecture, neighborhoods (*mahallas*), and local lifestyles, ultimately calling for the adaptation—not the destruction—of Central Asian towns. However, the more open interpretations of Soviet cultural norms fell victim to the rise of late-Stalinist architecture at the end of the 1940s. Because of constantly changing decrees from Moscow, construction was delayed or executed in an uncoordinated—perhaps even chaotic—fashion. As a result, the Soviet citizens of Tashkent, who identified much more closely with the socialist system after the war and desperately hoped for a higher standard of living after the Nazi-Soviet conflict, did not see much improvement in their lives in the early postwar years, despite the sacrifices they had made between 1941 and 1945.

It is important to consider how urban planners in the Khrushchev and Brezhnev eras promoted the idealized image of a victorious multiethnic state while concurrently dealing with the pressing problems of postwar Soviet life, a time of extreme economic hardship. Central Asian cities were fast becoming symbols of the Soviet Union's global aspirations, with Tashkent, the largest urban center in the region, serving as de facto ambassador to the postcolonial world. The earthquake that hit Tashkent in 1966 caused a slight delay in the push to display the city as a model of postcolonial socialism. That natural disaster damaged large parts of the city but conveniently provided planners with the blank slate that would allow them to transform the Uzbek capital into a truly "high modern" city that would showcase socialism in Asia. They went on to create the contemporary urban landscape that forms the backbone of Tashkent today. In doing so, planners gave birth to a new myth of Tashkent as a socialist "city reborn," one that persisted for the remainder of the cold war—and beyond.

A CITY TO BE TRANSFORMED

> The city consisted of "two parts [which] are so distinct and so unlike that a visitor may sometimes walk a considerable distance without meeting a Russian in one or a native in the other. European Taskend (Tashkent) is but of yesterday—Asiatic Tashkend of more than a thousand summers."
>
> —Henry Lansdell, 1887

In the early 1930s, European and American writers, artists, and journalists traveled across Soviet Central Asia to chronicle the tremendous economic and social transformations that were occurring in the region—from the vast campaigns to divert Central Asian rivers to the efforts to transform the landscapes of towns and cities across the region. One of these visitors, Joshua Kunitz, later wrote of the dynamism of Soviet Central Asia in contrast to its alleged backwardness. For Kunitz, Central Asia was a place where people had "lived for centuries in unchanging primitive conditions, [where] the only means of locomotion was the ass or the camel," and where the traditional "Central Asian village was a symbol of darkness, filth, and disease."[1] In stark orientalist language, this visitor—who clearly was positively inclined toward the Soviet project—underscored common perceptions in the European mindset of the "primitive" East, a place where local inhabitants were in desperate need of European knowledge, technology, and even social, economic, political, and ideological structures.

Although he often used the rhetoric of colonialism in his writings, Kunitz was not an advocate of this traditional European form of domination in Asia but a staunch defender of socialist ideology and its universality. Like so many others—Russians, Westerners, and even some Central Asians—Kunitz had deep faith in the adaptability of socialism to reach beyond its European origins to help jump-start entire societies along the path of Soviet-style progress and move away from imperial models of governance. He argued that the revolutionary changes in Central Asia during the 1920s and 1930s were leading to a full-blown renaissance of local cultures and lifestyles, with indigenous residents being the primary beneficiaries of socialist rule. Having been liberated from the oppressive regimes of Central Asian emirs and tsarist rulers by the revolution, the Uzbeks—and other ethnic groups across the region—were quickly advancing toward modernity under the guidance of the Communist Party, through the help of the Russian people and with the assistance of Soviet innovation. Using the imagery of socialist modernization, he described the magnetic force that Soviet technology reportedly held for the residents of Central Asia:

One can well imagine the tremendous fascination that a tractor, a motor truck, an airplane, a hydro-electric plant, or a locomotive holds for the Central Asian peasant. He is awed by it, but he is drawn to it. He is suspicious of its novelty, but lured by the advantages it offers. All the Bolshevik had to do was to bring these things to the attention of the peasant and they spoke for themselves. All that was necessary was to organize a couple of modern state farms, several machine and tractor stations, and to electrify a few villages, and no amount of political bungling could counteract the power of such propaganda.[2]

Kunitz saw Soviet technology and rationality as having the transformative power to pull indigenous residents out of their allegedly backward past and push them toward the socialist future and ultimately to communism. For this traveler to Uzbekistan, the Sovietization of Central Asia was a symbol of progress, a reaction to European colonialism, and part of the natural course of history. In the early 1930s, however, Soviet Uzbekistan was still very much a work in progress, with a society in turmoil and Central Asians just beginning to take more active roles in the socialist modernization projects that were occurring in their cities, towns, villages, and collective farms.

But if Kunitz's depiction of Tashkent was the public image of the city in the 1930s, what was the reality of life in Central Asia that residents faced in these early years of socialist power? What was unique about this Central Asian urban space and what were its major flaws that Soviet power sought to change? The following portrayal provides an overview of Tashkent before its Stalinist transformation, addresses these questions, and explores how Soviet officials initially attempted to transform the city in the early years of Soviet power. It does so by looking at the volumes of literature that were published by Russian imperial and Soviet administrators, residents, and European travelers who visited Tashkent and Central Asia in the nineteenth and early twentieth centuries. These accounts—government reports, academic articles, and travel accounts written by tsarist bureaucrats, city planners, and others in pre-revolutionary Central Asia—colored Russian perceptions of the region, many of which spanned the revolutionary and colonial divides and survived long into the Soviet era. Soviet responses to these views often used similar language and voiced similar perceptions, despite the official change in ideology.

Furthermore, by examining relevant architectural journals and secondary literature, it is possible to trace the development of the city from its early days as a military outpost to the tsarist regime's efforts to remake it into a European-style urban space. By tracing that development, we can also determine the extent to which Soviet urban renewal projects in Central Asia were founded upon the pre-revolutionary and Russian imperial endeavor of creating "Europe" in the distant desert, even though post-revolutionary administrators and urban planners in fact had much larger goals. This pre-history of Stalinist Tashkent demonstrates that the Russian imperial and Soviet urban renewal projects were parts of a common European endeavor to promote modernity and enlightenment, and it provides critical background for understanding the city that Soviet officials attempted to craft into a model socialist urban space, from the height of Stalinism to the dawn of the Brezhnev era.

Images and Realities of Pre-Soviet Tashkent

Tashkent traditionally was—and in many ways still is—the center of Russian life in Central Asia. Conquered by the Russians in 1865, the city served as a military, political, and economic center for Russian Turkestan.[3] Under continuous military administration, the city drew large numbers of ethnic Russians and Russian speakers from the European parts of the empire, starting with military officers and tsarist administrators, as Jeff Sahadeo has shown.[4] Economic, political, and religious migrants eventually followed, especially after the construction of the railroad at the turn of the twentieth century. By the time of the Russian revolution, the city included Russian political and economic elites, soldiers, political and religious exiles, railroad workers, merchant traders, peasant migrants, and refugees who had fled famine and war.[5] All of these migrant groups lived alongside a larger population of indigenous Central Asians, many of whom were drawn to the increasingly magnetic city of Tashkent in the hope of gaining economic opportunities. By 1917, Tashkent was rapidly becoming an island of European migrants within a large sea of indigenous Central Asians.

After Russian forces captured the Central Asian town of Tashkent from the Kokand khanate, Russian imperial administrators sought to build a European-style urban space on the eastern edge of the existing Muslim settlement. This new Russian city began as a military outpost and became the most important administrative, trading, and transportation center of Central Asia and quite possibly of the entire Russian East. The newly acquired territories in Central Asia had economic and military importance for the tsarist state, largely due to their role in reducing Russia's dependency on foreign cotton. Central Asia increased the economic independence of the tsarist state, whose textile industry had been badly hurt by the U.S. civil war and the resulting global shortage of cotton. Most importantly, however, these new Central Asian lands transformed the Russian state into a true European-style empire with a vast and diverse Asian possession of its own. Acquiring such an empire was part of the tsarist effort to be considered an equal to Britain and France in the late-nineteenth-century international arena.

In an effort to play the nineteenth-century "empire game," the tsarist regime strove to bring European civilization to Central Asia, just like its Western European counterparts had done in Africa, India, and Indochina.[6] But, as scholars have shown, this process did not initially include active Russification or the conversion of locals to Christianity. Instead, General Konstantin von Kaufman, the first governor-general of Turkestan, initiated a policy of noninterference in local Muslim and traditional life, while Russian officials built a European-style city for themselves.[7] Russia was certainly not as strong or as rich as Britain in terms of its ability to conquer, administer, and transform distant lands. As a result, tsarist administrators initially were willing to leave Central Asian urban areas largely untouched. This move seemed logical to Russian generals and imperial-era officials, who believed that the Muslim residents of these territories would quickly recognize the "superiority" of Russian rule and follow Russian colonizers into "modernity" after seeing European technology and culture on display in the new city of Tashkent. Russian imperial bureaucrats, following their British and French counterparts in Asia, emphasized the power of rationally arranged spaces to remake and "civilize" the population at large. As Robert Crews and Jeff Sahadeo have shown, urban planning was an important component of this project. In the imperial era, Russian officials in Central Asia perceived rationally planned streets and urban spaces as signs of the superiority of Russian/European culture, which stood in contrast to the reportedly chaotic urban spaces of the Muslim world. As a result, Russian administrators went on a building spree in Tashkent, designing and constructing schools, a library, Christian churches, medical facilities, museums, and Western-style gardens in the new "Russian" section of the city, all to showcase the Russian/Western lifestyle for the indigenous population.[8] Tsarist bureaucrats argued that these construction projects reordered the desert landscape of Tashkent and would impress local residents—Russian and Muslim—with the power and scientific advancement of the tsarist state.[9] This perception of a rationally planned urban environment influenced the creation and administration of Russian Tashkent for much of the imperial period, laying the historical groundwork for a subsequent Soviet belief that orderly and modern urban spaces had the power to transform the residents who lived and worked in them.

Instead of transforming the Muslim residents of Central Asia immediately, Russian administrators and urban planners chose to construct their new society, "Russian Central Asia," on empty land alongside the pre-existing city. One reason for this decision was that it was easier, cheaper, and less problematic to build next to the existing settlement rather than on top of it, which would have forced the eviction of indigenous residents—a task that Soviet planners would later struggle to carry out over a period of many years. In the strict racialist order of nineteenth-century colonialism, building on top of or among the old neighborhoods also would have put Russians and Central Asian Tashkenters in considerable proximity to each other, a concern voiced by many European travelers and residents in nineteenth-century Central Asia. The idea of instead creating a spatial separation between ethnic and racial groups within colonial cities was an important tool of imperial rule in the region and elsewhere in the colonial world, as Paul Rabinow and Gwendolyn Wright have shown for cities of the French empire. This spatial separation allowed for constant comparisons between local ("inferior") and Russian ("advanced") cultures. Consequently, Tashkent developed into a "dual city," with a modern European area growing near a traditional Asian town and a canal, the Ankhor, as the all-important symbolic border that separated the two communities. Tashkent's two cities subsequently developed alongside each other, with each major ethnic group living in insular sections of the town, a trend that again mirrored other colonial urbanization projects in Asia and Africa.[10] In creating imperial Tashkent, arguably one of the first "colonial"-style cities of the tsarist empire, Russian officials clearly looked to established European models of empire building and administration.

In the popular mindset of many nineteenth-century Russian residents (again mimicking typical European conceptions of colonial spaces), Tashkent was also a city that lacked modern conveniences. Central Asians were portrayed in travel literature and memoirs as primitive and unchanging in comparison to Europeans, with whom the Russians in Tashkent identified themselves. This European self-perception allowed many Russian Tashkenters to view their new town as an isolated European settlement surrounded by "uncivilized" Asia and "backward" Asians. Memoir accounts from this era convey the feeling that Russian administrators and residents sensed they were in danger from hostile native inhabitants, the harsh climate, infectious diseases, or the sheer distance from the metropole, despite the fact that there was no clear geographic division—such as an ocean or large mountain range—between where the Russian state ended and the Russian Empire began. One memoir by Count Konstantin Pahlen, for example, noted the monotony of the journey from Russia to Turkestan and the delays travelers endured due to mechanical problems with trains and railroad tracks. Unlike traditional memoirs of the Western European colonial experience, which included long sea journeys, the Russian trek to Central Asia appeared more like the American narratives of westward expansion, with their common themes of long and occasionally gruesome journeys across a harsh terrain and, at times, less-than-friendly encounters with indigenous residents. Nonetheless, these Russian travelers gradually moved through the Eurasian landmass toward Tashkent to help expand the Russian state's hold on new territory and push modern Russian/European civilization across the continent.

A common theme of this memoir literature was Tashkent's geographic distance from the core of the Russian Empire. However, upon entering the safety and comfort of urban Tashkent, memoirists often viewed the city as a welcome refuge of civilization but one whose position was unstable because of the unpredictable indigenous population nearby. Pahlen wrote that the train station was "packed tight with a surging crowd of natives from every Asiatic tribe and race. . . . No limitations were placed on the numbers on the platform and the whole seething mass of humanity spills over the lines."[11] In his memoir, one can identify an underlying fear of the indigenous population and the fact that Central Asians surrounded the "cultured" Russian city of Tashkent. This theme of Europeans being at the mercy of and possibly overcome by "Asian masses" proliferated in published accounts of the period and was reinforced in the art and literature of the time. Asia was a "dangerous" and "primitive" continent with a threatening culture and potentially hostile natives. Russians—due to the unique geographic position of their country as a Eurasian landmass bordering both Germany and China—expressed this threat very sharply, as exemplified in Alexander Blok's famous poem, *The Scythians* (1918).[12] Russia, as the bridge between Europe and Asia, was presented as pivotal for defending European culture and Europeans from the perceived barbarism, disease, and instability that Asia could inflict on the West. In the late tsarist period, Tashkent was viewed as an important outpost in Russia's effort to quell the Asian threat, an effort that allowed Russians to perceive their country as an important player in Europe's increasingly globalized role. Russians, like westward-bound Americans and European colonists, justified the eastward expansion of the state as part of their fate—necessary to protect Russia's core as well as to bring enlightened culture to the region. With such a teleological viewpoint, the move into Central Asia was part of the course and destiny of European—including Russian—history.

This expansionist mission often was complicated by the physical illnesses that struck many imperial Russian and European visitors, who later recalled fighting off exotic disease-carrying insects and enduring extreme temperatures in both summer and winter. Fears of the local environment, local diseases, and local residents were frequent tropes in memoirs of the Russian imperial project in Central Asia.[13] In this manner, as Edward Said has demonstrated for Western European perceptions of the Asian "other," the Russian memoir and travel literature of Central Asia highlighted differences between the modern Russian and backward Muslim areas to underscore Russian dominance and superiority in its relationship to Central Asia and to justify tsarist rule in the region.[14] Life might have been harsh, uncomfortable, and even dangerous in Tashkent, but the Russians, as representatives of European culture, perceived themselves as having the capacity and moral imperative to improve Asia, even if the Asian residents of Turkestan did not desire, recognize the need for, or, in the end, derive much positive impact from this intervention. This coexistence between European culture in the Russian city and Asian traditions in the Muslim quarter also allowed Russian administrators, ethnographers, and memoirists to create a hierarchy of civilizations in Tashkent in which Russian culture took precedence over local traditions. Thus, promoters of Russian culture were on an equal footing with other European cultures that were attempting to dominate Asia, Africa, and other parts of the colonial world and also with the United States, which was concluding its transcontinental march toward the Pacific.[15] This hierarchy of cultures and lifestyles would remain an important factor in Tashkent throughout the nineteenth and twentieth centuries.

In fact, Russian imperial accounts of visits to the region frequently implied that Russian civilization was in a constant battle with indigenous cultures and the local geography. Tsarist officials and their Soviet successors lamented the disorder of Central Asian settlements. They focused their criticisms on narrow streets, crooked alleyways, and dead-end pathways. For Europeans, the Old City was an incomprehensible maze that was difficult to navigate and could easily lead one to become lost and disoriented.[16] Furthermore, making comparisons to a supposedly clean and healthy European environment, visitors described traditional Central Asian regions of the city as having piles of rotting garbage, frequent dust storms, extreme temperatures, and dirty water, as if such conditions somehow did not exist in the rapidly industrializing cities of nineteenth-century Russia. According to one Russian administrator, the Asian "population of Tashkent . . . lives in unthinkable filth. . . . The houses consist of mud huts, without stoves or windows, and are barely held together by handfuls of clay. They wash down their food with repulsive water from the canals on the street."[17] Henry Lansdell, another visitor, remarked on the prevalence of guinea worms in the water supply of Central Asian cities and on local residents' propensity to drink from stagnant pools.[18] Treatment of those infected by the worm consisted of having a "native specialist, usually barbers, insert a needle under the worm and one end is drawn out by the fingers of the right hand, whilst those of the left press the affected part, the operation lasting from one to five minutes. Russian medical men wind off the animal on a reel . . . till the whole [worm,] commonly three, but sometimes (according to one physician) seven feet in length[,] is extracted."[19] As Usman Yusupov's comment in 1938 suggests (see chapter 1's epigraph), this image of filthy water and waterborne parasitic illness was imprinted in the minds of Europeans and Russians in the region. It became a literary mechanism through which they viewed Central Asian society, and it was one that lasted well into the Soviet era.[20]

In the imperial period, however, these reports indicated to the reading public that the problem with Central Asians was not only their ignorance of waterborne diseases but also the fact that their treatment for such illnesses was itself unsanitary and usually performed by barbers or other individuals with no medical training. What the region required for its improvement was technology and education, which Russian rule, at least rhetorically, was to provide.[21] Memoirists disdained local health-care traditions, which they identified as arising from the backwardness of local Muslims, who looked to Islam and local healers (tabibs), not to medical science, for health care.[22] In the eyes of many Russian or European residents, Central Asian inhabitants of Tashkent suffered from poor health care and a lack of knowledge about basic sanitation and were in need of help, or so many memoirists implied. This image of unsanitary conditions and health care provided by untrained specialists became an important tool for explaining how indigenous Central Asians could work to "improve" themselves for years to come. In addition, it justified the Russian role in Central Asia, once again providing imperial administrators with the belief that they could help the local residents along the teleological march toward modern (i.e., European) life.

The Tashkent Russian Model

In contrast, Russian travel accounts speak of the European sections of Tashkent as clean and sanitary, with adequate water supplies—circumstances that were allegedly the direct result of technological innovation and modern urban design. Gardens with flowers and fruit trees were established throughout the new sections of the city for the pleasure, relaxation, and health of the Tashkent Russian elite.[23] These areas were intended to transform the harsh climate of the region and improve the ability of Russian residents to withstand the extremely hot Central Asian summer. In fact, city construction plans for tsarist Tashkent followed general Western European norms, with the gardens and rest areas designed to maximize fresh air— uncontaminated by Asian residents—for the city's European population. At the same time, urban renewal projects belittled locals for their supposed inability to create a healthy urban environment.[24]

Imperial planners quickly moved to create a miniature version of a European city in the distant desert. The streets of the Russian section of Tashkent were designed along a radial grid to bring European order to "less developed" Asia. Imperial Tashkent's symmetrical layout was typical of newly built Russian cities of the era, such as Vernyi (later known as Alma-Ata and now Almaty), and even resembled the plan of the Russian city of Tver, which served as a model in Russian urban planning books of the nineteenth century.[25] New Tashkent was developed around Cathedral Square, with the Cathedral of the Transfiguration of the Savior at its center. The cathedral and its bell tower—built in Byzantine style and designed by Petersburg-trained architects A. I. Razanov and Wilhelm Geintsel'man—reportedly dominated the skyline in a city that consisted largely of one-story mud-brick structures. The "White House," the home of the governor-general, complemented the cathedral, creating a square that was the administrative and spiritual heart of the city.[26] The square formed a major meeting point for the New City and was a prominent site on military parade routes because it was a symbol of Russian power in Central Asia.[27] Near the square, planners located classical/neoclassical–style buildings, including the palace of the exiled Prince Nikolai Konstantinovich and a women's gymnasium.[28]

A secondary center of the new Russian city revolved around a circular park, from which Tashkent's new streets radiated outward. This site, Konstantinov Square, included a monument to Governor-General von Kaufman. The park was surrounded by a teachers' academy, the Tashkent branch of the state bank, and other European-style structures, all of which resembled prominent buildings of nineteenth-century Moscow.[29] An observatory, Catholic and Protestant churches, a Western-style market, and a tram system were built along the streets of the city to make Russian Tashkent a symbol of progress in the desert, complete with markers of the political, spiritual, commercial, and scientific power of the tsarist state.[30] The architectural styles of the Russian buildings—Byzantine, classical, and Gothic (the Catholic cathedral)—evoked mighty empires and eras of the European past and allowed imperial planners to co-opt the entire European experience in designing and then constructing their outpost in the Central Asian desert. Planners began with Greece and Rome but included Byzantium (the Orthodox cathedral), the Enlightenment (an observatory), capitalism (banks), and the rise of technology (trams) in their design for imperial Tashkent. The belief that societies were advancing toward something called "modernity" was clearly evident in the symbols of Russian power and in the way in which imperial planners recreated the history of European development through architecture, with Russia being a prominent part of that broad European vision. This urban design theoretically permitted residents to travel from the "darkness" of the old Tashkent to the "light" of the new city all in one day, enticing the local population to make the rapid jump from the past into the future.

Since indigenous residents were portrayed in literature and government documents as incapable of moving toward modernity on their own, imperial rule was seen by urban planners and administrators as capable of speeding up the development of Central Asia. Russians were deemed able to transform the local physical environment, or at least the parts of Central Asia where they lived, while indigenous residents were not. In tsarist Tashkent, Central Asian residents allegedly were stuck in the past, while the new European inhabitants were marching toward the future of the Russian Empire, according to the Russian bureaucratic mindset. But, in the imperial period, it was these Russian officials who decided what was modern and it was Slavs who went about bringing this modernity to Tashkent. Little effort was put forth and little desire was even expressed to involve locals in this process, with the state largely content to leave indigenous Tashkenters on the sidelines of this rapid modernization scheme. With the mixture of architectural styles, Russian Tashkent became a city of symbols in which the physical space of the "new city" sought to demonstrate Russian superiority and dominance to local residents, to Russian bureaucrats, and to Russia's rivals in Europe.

Despots and Deviancy

Tsarist administrators argued that imperial rule not only brought civilization to the region but also liberated local residents from the harsh rule of Central Asian despots. In the late 1800s, Europeans of all stripes learned from newspapers and published travel narratives about the torture inflicted on British servicemen during expeditions to Central Asia.[31] Russians heard similar orientalist stories of cruelty against both travelers and the indigenous population of Bukhara and Khiva. Count Pahlen informed the Russian reading public of the "frightened appearance of Bukharan natives," who met horrible ends in the underground dungeons of Bukhara.[32] Russian intellectuals learned that Central Asian ruling elites, whether they were khans, mullahs, or wealthy *beys* (landlords), used their power to enslave and impoverish Muslims. Officially, Russian rule in Turkestan was supposed to end the slave trade in the region and banish extreme forms of punishment. This "liberation" from Central Asian despotism enabled the tsarist state to present itself as an enlightened European power.[33] Interestingly, only a short time after Russia freed its own serfs, emancipation in Central Asia became a primary motif in the justification of Russia's presence in the region, and it was promoted to both domestic and foreign audiences.[34]

Furthermore, visitors frequently disdained local cultural traditions, including early marriage and polygamy, as proof of the superiority of Russian and European values. The early marriage of girls, often before the onset of puberty, was identified as leading to disease, infertility, and birth defects among indigenous Central Asians.[35] Negative perceptions of Central Asian lives also existed in the Russian mindset due to published accounts of degenerate behavior among native inhabitants of the region. Russians and Europeans read stories of not only underage marriage but also rampant drug use and young boys who danced for the rich in teahouses and at palaces of the Central Asian elite, thereby underscoring orientalist conceptions of deviant cultural and social practices among Central Asians.[36] Russian travelers presented Central Asian society as combining despotic, unhygienic, and immoral behavior, a descriptive pattern that dated from the tsarist era but would persist long after the demise of the Romanov dynasty. Concurrently, travelers projected these images against the purported civilizing project of Russian rule, conveniently represented by the modern and clean sections of Russian Tashkent—a technique that was used throughout the colonized world to justify the expansion of European states into Asia or Africa.[37]

Once again, these efforts to promote a Slavic environment in Tashkent were more about portraying Russian power and superiority to fellow Russians and other Europeans than about improving the daily lives of Central Asian Tashkenters. However, the Russian state did not ignore the indigenous population. In fact, as Robert Crews has demonstrated, the tsarist regime successfully penetrated Muslim communities across the Russian Empire and used Islam to help buttress support for the regime among its diverse Muslim population. Through engagement with Central Asian elites and the preservation of Islamic law, the Russian state became intrinsically involved in many local Central Asian issues, disputes, and rivalries in its effort to build, secure, and expand its empire in Central Asia.[38]

Nevertheless, despite using Islam to gain the support of Muslim populations and criticizing local traditions that they deemed primitive, some Russian administrators in the region admitted knowing little about Central Asian social norms or customs. They blamed their lack of knowledge on the fact that it was difficult for them to break out of the European environment of the new Tashkent. Such people instead depended largely on local elites who functioned in both worlds to help translate and interpret customary Central Asian life for them. In fact, life in the indigenous settlements of Central Asia was mysterious to all outsiders, as seen from an American diplomat-adventurer's trip across the Ankhor Canal. To visit a Muslim home in the Old Town of Tashkent, this diplomat walked through a labyrinth of narrow streets. He noted that his destination consisted of a drab wall with a small door that opened to the street, underscoring the notion of Central Asian urban spaces as desolate, barren, and closed off to outside influences. After entering, he remarked that the home itself was a maze. He claimed that he had to traverse two courtyards before arriving at the *tashkari* or men's section of the house. The women's quarters, or *ichkari,* which he did not see, were through yet another narrow passageway.[39] Clearly, Western accounts of Central Asian lives created the impression that the inner sanctum of the Central Asian family was far removed from modern society and, therefore, hard for outsiders to explore, understand, or transform. Even to those who ventured across the Ankhor Canal to the other world of Tashkent, Central Asian lives were off limits, with houses hidden on narrow and barren streets and with Muslim women allegedly isolated inside the home and out of touch with the larger world around them—notions of the Central Asian city that persisted well into the twentieth century. Many memoirists believed that civilization and modernity were clearly what Central Asia needed. At the same time, however, their works revealed that they did not have enough knowledge of local conditions or the needs and desires of local residents to help bring about these changes.

While Russian Tashkent was deemed superior to the Central Asian section of the city, it also had its negative side. It was a beautiful and easily mapped urban space, with straight avenues, efficient transportation, and modern standards of sanitation. But, as Russian Tashkent grew, so did its social problems. Famine in the 1890s accelerated migration to Tashkent, with hungry Russian peasants arriving in the Tashkent region in search of a better life. The railroad brought workers to Central Asia, as did burgeoning cotton processing plants and alcohol distilleries. These new residents were not the model Russians that the colonial project sought to highlight but members of the underclass of that society. The arrival of political exiles and of a non-Russian European population, particularly Polish political prisoners and soldiers, also caused concern for the city's administrators as class, ethnic, and religious fissures developed in opposition to the image of Tashkent as a unified and cultured colonial city.[40] Tashkent was no longer a city of elite generals and Russian imperial administrators; it was experiencing a massive in-migration of peasants and others—some from distant parts of the empire—a process that was repeated in countless cities across late-nineteenth-century Russia and Europe.

As Sahadeo has shown, one example of the resulting increase in social problems was the evolution of the Voskresenskii Market, established a short distance from Cathedral Square. The market was meant to provide goods to the Russian population in a cleaner environment than that of the typical Central Asian bazaar. This Russian-style shopping arcade was European Tashkent's answer to the bustle, haggling, and dirt of the Central Asian marketplace. However, it quickly devolved into a place for drinking, prostitution, robbery, and violence. No longer a model of European cleanliness, it grew into a shantytown for poor and criminal elements in the center of the Russian city. Its orderly and sanitary trading conditions deteriorated into urban squalor.[41] The Russian modernization campaign in Turkestan, meant to "civilize" Muslims and showcase the power of the tsarist regime, could, and often did, produce unintended consequences. By the early twentieth century, Tashkent was not simply an ideal colonial Russian city; instead, it was beginning to resemble many other urban areas across Russia itself.

As imperial power collapsed, Tashkent's problems only increased. The Central Asian uprising in 1916, the strains of World War I, and an increasing shortage of food further undermined support for the autocracy. When the February Revolution and October Revolution swept away the tsarist regime, the region was pushed into even more chaos.[42] War refugees sought safety in Central Asia, causing the city to become a haven for an odd array of foreign diplomats, starving Austrian prisoners of war, and the desperately poor, many of whom arrived in Central Asia with visions of Tashkent as the "City of Bread," a place with ample food supplies.[43] Their hopes were in vain. The imperial attempt to create a model Russian city in Asia quickly ended with the Bolshevik revolution and the Russian civil war, which brought further upheaval to Central Asia as well as the entire Russian Empire.

The Revolution and Early Soviet Plans for Tashkent

Defending their hold on power during the revolution, the Bolsheviks immediately grasped the importance of altering the symbols of rule in Central Asia. Due to a lack of resources, however, the initial efforts at remaking "Bolshevik Tashkent" consisted of smashing the monuments to tsarist autocratic rule. Konstantinov Square, the secondary center of Tashkent, was renamed Revolution Square, and the statue of Governor-General von Kaufman was replaced with a simple obelisk to the fallen Bolsheviks of the revolution.[44] In the initial years of Soviet rule, before the transformation of Cathedral Square into Red (also known as Lenin) Square, this newly named Revolution Square served as a site for Tashkent citizens to celebrate the new regime. Furthermore, Soviet power was not content to leave the Old City without symbols of the revolution. As a result, a monument to the leader of the Russian revolution was placed in Old Dzhuva Square, a prominent gathering area in the Central Asian section of the city, to mark the death of Lenin in 1924.[45] The Lenin Monument put a public stamp of Sovietness on Tashkent's Old City, an early and clear indication that the new regime would not be content to leave the native settlement and its residents as they were.

After the revolution, with the British intervention, the Russian civil war, the Basmachi revolt, and a tenuous alliance with the cultural reformist Jadids, Tashkent's new rulers struggled to consolidate their hold on the region and delayed a direct attack against Islam and local traditions. By the mid-1920s, and after the establishment of the Uzbek SSR in 1924, the campaign against traditional mores (byt') intensified, as did efforts to create an Uzbek national identity.[46] However, attempts to decrease the impact of Islam and transform native traditions met with difficulty, as Central Asia's local communists often remained unaware of the goals of the Soviet transformation and frequently tried to combine their identities as both Muslims and communists, a phenomenon that would prove lasting. Creating a new mindset among Tashkenters—Russian and Central Asian alike—clearly was more difficult than seizing power.[47] State-sponsored violence remained a constant presence in these efforts to solidify power, forge new identities, and create new social norms in the early years of Soviet power.

In the late 1920s, Soviet rule shut down most religious and non-Soviet educational institutions and converted mosques, churches, and madrasas to secular use. The Cathedral of the Transfiguration of the Savior served as a museum until its demolition in 1932. An unfinished Catholic cathedral—built to serve the city's pre-revolutionary Polish migrant population—survived physical destruction by becoming a medical training school and then a storage facility. Mosques in the Old City were converted into workers' clubs, women's centers, or "red teahouses." Madrasas commonly became Soviet schools, although Soviet propaganda noted that the conversion of these buildings demanded much effort to make them "clean" and "sanitary"—again a holdover in the conceptions of unhygienic Central Asian physical spaces. This image of traditional buildings in Central Asia as "being filthy" persisted over the revolutionary divide, while the European-style palace of Prince Nikolai Konstantinovich notably survived the violent onslaughts against symbols of the past. Converted into a pioneer youth club, it in fact outlasted the Soviet era.[48] However, the majority of these early efforts at making a post-revolutionary Tashkent consisted of the small-scale transformation of individual buildings, not an all-out campaign to destroy the old and remake the urban landscape of the city.

As the Soviet Union consolidated its hold on power, it had neither the time nor the resources for elaborate urban development plans. For most of the first two decades of Soviet rule, large-scale reconstruction projects for Tashkent remained on paper. In 1924, planners developed the initial Soviet urban renewal proposal for the city: the "Plan for the regulation of part of the New City of Tashkent." This project, drafted by G. M. Svaricheskii and G. P. Bauer, left the pre-Soviet city center as it was and focused instead on transforming "shantytown" worker areas on the edges of the New City. In this sense, transforming urban space did not differ much from the imperial-era city plans that focused on building up the newer and more Russian sections of the city. Housing complexes for industrial workers were to be a main aspect of this new vision of the city.[49] The workers, for whom the revolution was fought, were to be the prime beneficiaries of this plan, not the Uzbek residents of the city, whom the revolution officially liberated from colonial oppression. The Svaricheskii/Bauer project, however, was never implemented because the focus on transforming Soviet Central Asian cities shifted to Samarkand, which was designated the first capital of the Uzbek SSR in 1924.

For Tashkent at this time, much of the urban planning effort remained focused on individual factory buildings and attempts to expand the electricity grid around the city. Planning for and constructing hydroelectric plants throughout the Tashkent region were important elements in the effort to transform urban life. Samarkand in the 1920s was to be the political and social center for the new Uzbek SSR, while Tashkent continued on its path toward becoming the most industrialized city in the region. Although far from the industrial heartland of the Soviet Union, Uzbekistan was by no means excluded from the large-scale Soviet electrification programs of the late 1920s, which gained priority over the creation of idealized urban spaces. Furthermore, with efforts to rapidly increase cotton production in Central Asia, much effort was put to developing irrigation infrastructure and establishing agricultural machinery production and repair facilities in the region, the first of which opened in 1931 as the Tashkent Agricultural Machinery Factory (Tashselmash).[50] The Soviet regime clearly pushed to develop new factories in Tashkent at this time. Still, as the economic resources it chose to develop suggest, Soviet planners from the start focused the Uzbek SSR's economy on agriculture or industries that were tied directly to agriculture, such as cotton or food processing. Tashkent, although the "modern" center of Uzbekistan, clearly was not envisioned as a prime industrial engine of the larger Soviet state but was destined to play a supporting role in providing and processing the raw materials that the super-industrial socialist state would need.

Tashkent's reconstruction increased in importance in the following decade, with urban planning resuming at a fast pace in Tashkent once the city regained its status as the Uzbek capital in 1930. To respond to rapid urbanization, the Central Asian Construction Institute was established in the city in 1930, staffed by professors trained in Moscow, Leningrad, and Kiev. Abdullah Babakhanov, who in 1934 was one of the first to graduate from this institute, became a prominent Uzbek architect, serving as head architect of the Tashkent City Planning Agency from 1938 to 1944 and chair of the Uzbek Architects' Union at various times from the 1940s to the 1960s.[51] He was one of the early beneficiaries of the Stalinist revolution and quickly rose to a position of power during the purges, when the original Soviet Uzbek guard was swept away. To help facilitate urban planning in Uzbekistan, four new planning organizations (Uzplanproekt, Uzprompro-ekt, Uzselproekt, and the Architectural Planning Department of Tashkent) were established in 1934, as was the Uzbek branch of the Architects' Union.

While these new agencies planned for all of Uzbekistan, they were based in Tashkent and used Tashkent as their primary drawing board for imagining the future of socialism in Central Asia.[52]

Furthermore, shortly before Tashkent regained its status as the capital and most important urban center in Central Asia, the city's two main regions, the Russian quarter (the New City) and the Uzbek settlement (the Old City), were unified politically and administratively into one large urban center.[53] Colonialism, with the political, social, and economic inequalities that the city's geographic segregation implied, had allegedly come to an end with this symbolic urban unification. There was no longer a "Russian Tashkent" and a "Central Asian Tashkent." There was simply a "Soviet Tashkent." At this time, Soviet officials also changed course and demanded greater participation of all groups in Tashkent society. The Central Asian part of the city—and the Uzbek population of Tashkent—could no longer be left out of the urban redevelopment plan. The mandate to incorporate everyone into the new Tashkent became even more evident when Soviet officials began working to promote female liberation and counter the dominant Islamic culture in the early 1930s, as Douglas Northrop and Marianne Kamp have each shown in their studies of the *hujum,* the campaign to force the women of Central Asia to take off their veils.[54] To help create a new plan that would focus on the Asian sections of the city, the Uzbek Central Committee of the Communist Party organized the Bureau for the Replanning of Central Asian Cities, led by a Moscow-trained engineer, Alexander Sil'chenkov. This bureau was tasked with designing an urban space that would not only break down the symbolic barriers in a still largely segregated city but also bring about fundamental changes to the ways in which local residents lived and interacted with each other and with the organs of the Soviet state. Reflecting trends of his time, Sil'chenkov designed an experimental and modernist urban center that supposedly would bring together Old and New Tashkent into one socialist whole. Although the plan was vague as to the manner in which this symbolic unity was to be achieved, Sil'chenkov's declared goal was to transform the Uzbek capital's distinct neighborhoods to support modern industry, help improve public health, and give all residents access to the cultural, educational, and political institutions of socialism. If successful, this plan would then be adopted for Samarkand, Bukhara, Fergana, and a whole slew of smaller cities and towns throughout the region.

Equally important, however, was the fact that Sil'chenkov's design reflected broader planning trends in the Soviet Union in the late 1920s, a time when the debates over utopian architecture created an active intellectual atmosphere among city planners throughout the country. These debates suggest that Tashkent urbanism should not be seen in a vacuum and must be placed in the context of broader Soviet—and even international—trends in urban design. Sil'chenkov's design for Tashkent reflected the early Soviet trend toward modernism. Like other experimental city planners, Sil'chenkov saw his mission as that of transforming both the urban landscape and the structure of life in the Uzbek capital.[55] Building new cities was not the prime goal of these early urban renewal efforts, but changing the society within them certainly was.[56] Soviet planners began to praise the introduction of rationally ordered spaces in the refashioning of existing cities and the building of new ones. The "evolutionary" nature of most cities was deemed not applicable to a socialist society, which, lacking private property, gave the state enormous power over urban development. On the other hand, socialist planning also would allow for the creation of ideal urban environments with strict controls over population and industrial growth in order to forge a socialist society of the future. These new types of cities and the residents who lived within them would not be dependent on market influences or religious beliefs as they had in the past. They now would depend solely on socialist ideology. Soviet planners aimed to use cities to reorder social relations, foster economic development, and provide for the needs of residents—food, housing, and recreation space—whether they were located in Soviet Europe or Soviet Asia.

These renovated urban spaces would be places where industry and technology officially could be used for the benefit of the state and its people. Therefore, these early urban plans and architectural designs focused on making technological advances in construction and on showcasing the scientific achievements in the city. The architecture of the past—Byzantine, Greek, and Roman designs as well as the dilapidated homes of the oppressed classes—were to be removed and replaced by modern structures that stressed functionality, efficiency, and modernity, hence the razing of the Cathedral of the Transfiguration of the Savior and the residence of the former governor-general.[57] Tashkent in the early 1930s remained a city of symbols, but these symbols now had to be thoroughly modern and industrial.

These debates raged on in Tashkent, as they did elsewhere in the Soviet Union. And, once again, the Uzbek settlements of the region were denigrated for being the epitome of nonrational spaces, with the official conversation often reviving the arguments of the tsarist period about the "backwardness" of winding streets and the dark interiors of enclosed homes. Soviet scholars and administrators of the time equated such structures with the primitive nature of the pre-Soviet past of the Asian republics. Having visited Turkmenistan and Uzbekistan, the Soviet ethnographer P. Pavlenko reiterated pre-revolutionary complaints that Central Asian settlements grew up in random fashion and lacked order.[58] In his 1933 book, *Puteshestvie v Turkmenistane* (Travels in Turkmenistan), Pavlenko remarked that the pre-revolutionary state did nothing to improve the conditions of life for native inhabitants of Central Asia because the tsarist state was not interested in the "outskirts" of the empire. Instead, he accused the previous regime of focusing exclusively on ethnic Russian areas. He particularly criticized imperial urban planners for creating "new cities" for Russian colonizers in Central Asia, while leaving their Central Asian subjects untouched by modernity. Pavlenko held that the socialist state now possessed the power and the desire to transform all areas of Central Asian society.[59] Having liberated the region from colonial and local forms of oppression, the Soviet Union now needed to showcase the development and advancement of these former colonial areas as equal members in the Soviet Union. Party officials argued that Tashkent (and the Uzbek SSR) could not be left as a "half-modern/half-premodern" space with its residents stuck somewhere between the two. They now argued that reconstruction plans had to change every sector of society and every region of Central Asia in order to symbolize and help bring about the bright Soviet future in Asia. This was a significant development from pre-Soviet urbanism, with its symbolic focus on building up the image of Russian modernity in Asia.

In the early 1930s, a variety of urban planners, ethnographers, and political figures attempted to implement this Soviet transformation by bringing "modern" urban infrastructure into Uzbekistan. Sil'chenkov's vision for the Uzbek capital was clearly that of an experimental city, one that sought to transform every resident's way of life. Sil'chenkov foresaw moving the city center from the traditionally Russian section toward the Old City. Like his imperial predecessor, he believed the Old City was a region where crime, disease, and traditional cultural norms festered. But, unlike tsarist administrators, he proposed completely depopulating the area and destroying the existing Uzbek settlements, replacing them with a large urban park—a symbol of fresh air, modernity, and cleanliness. By expanding the Bozsu irrigation canal, Soviet technology would help supply this park on the western side of the city with ample supplies of water. The dry and dusty wasteland of Old Tashkent was to be turned into a lush "green" area; Soviet power would give Uzbek Tashkenters the gardens that previously only the Russian elite possessed.[60] Furthermore, Sil'chenkov proposed moving the administrative center to the former Old City, symbolically transferring the reins of power from the traditionally Russian quarter to the Central Asian section of the city. Officials of the Soviet regime reacted to their perceptions of imperial-era discrimination that allegedly had led to the neglect of the Central Asian residents of Turkestan. However, while focusing on creating a large park and administrative center to transform the Old City and the lives of its residents, Sil'chenkov's proposal did not address the pressing problem of where they could relocate the thousands of people who would be displaced. Creating a park—a Soviet symbol of light, fresh air, and rejuvenation—was presented as a panacea to alleged Central Asian backwardness and the past colonial oppression that the revolution had purportedly reversed. However, practical solutions for housing large extended Uzbek families—who would be forced from their old homes—were not discussed, a common oversight during the Soviet era as planners busily developed and adapted their utopian designs for Central Asian urban spaces.

Leading city planners of the time were actively proposing new forms of housing in Russia and elsewhere that would transform family and gender relations through communal living.[61] Following these trends, Sil'chenkov proposed incorporating the communal lifestyle into the housing structure of his New Tashkent. He collaborated closely with Stepan Nikolaevich Polupanov, an architect of constructivist buildings who arrived in Uzbekistan in the late 1920s. A graduate of the Kharkov Artistic-Construction Institute, Polupanov enjoyed a long career in Tashkent city planning, although he had begun his career designing "Soviet Kharkov," then the capital of Soviet Ukraine, before moving to Central Asia. As a planner of the capital of Ukraine, the second most important republic in the Soviet Union, Polupanov was thoroughly steeped in the Soviet architectural movements, particularly the constructivist movement, and he came to Tashkent to replicate it. Like many other technical and industrial experts of the 1930s, he moved to Uzbekistan with a mission to build modernity and expand socialism to the distant reaches of the Soviet Union. Seeking to bring the latest theories of urbanization to the region and aiming to create a constructivist city in Central Asia, he helped tie Tashkent's urbanization to broader visions of twentieth-century city planning. He proposed that new housing communes be essential parts of Uzbekistan's future, just as they were to be necessary components of the cities of Russia and Ukraine.[62] As an Architects' Union member and professor of architecture in Tashkent, Polupanov designed these model communes for Tashkent and Samarkand based on those planned for Moscow and other Russian cities. All of these structures stressed the importance of functionality and new visions of gender and family relationships. Tashkent was at the forefront of official efforts to adapt the utopian ideologies of socialism to everyday life, a particularly challenging task for those in the non-European republics of the Soviet Union.

Polupanov proposed that in these new housing structures the tasks of daily life (cooking, cleaning, and laundry) would be performed communally, thereby symbolically liberating women from domestic chores and enabling them to participate in society on a broader scale. On-site children's nurseries were envisioned to promote female participation in the workplace, thereby increasing state control over the rearing of young citizens and over family life, although Polupanov's design did not take into account the need for expanding nursery facilities to accommodate the large number of children Uzbek families had. The vision of the new Soviet Uzbek family structure was clearly evident in Polupanov's design, but the building blocks for achieving it were largely neglected, a situation that foreshadowed some of the problems that Soviet architects and urban planners would face for years to come. However, since reordering the housing structures was meant to transform the Soviet family and limit the influence of pre-Soviet, traditional, or religious beliefs in the socialist society, Polupanov's housing communes were described as the wave of the Uzbek future, particularly because they would help free Uzbek women from the confines of the *ichkari*.[63] In this sense, the commune proposal can be viewed as a supplement to the forced unveiling campaign, the *hujum*. Taking off the veil was to be the initial public break from traditional Central Asian society that a woman could make; moving into a new type of housing structure would constitute the next level of women's liberation. Both physically and symbolically, destroying the traditional Central Asian home was part of the campaign to transform Uzbek women and the Uzbek family and to solidify state control over the lives of Tashkenters, particularly the city's Central Asian inhabitants. Polupanov's proposal for alternative housing received early support in the effort to alter the physical and social environment of Tashkent because it made the city less specifically Asian—dark, dirty, and oppressive to women—and more uniformly Soviet—light, liberating, and transformative.[64]

However, with Uzbek society in such turmoil over the *hujum* campaign, it proved difficult to get residents, particularly indigenous Central Asians, to move into such revolutionary structures. The new housing complexes that were constructed remained inhabited by the Russian population, many of whom had migrated to the region and had thus already been detached from their traditional homes, families, and community support networks and therefore more urgently needed places to live. This tendency of Russian and other migrants to move willingly into new housing compounds was repeated numerous times throughout the Soviet era as planners struggled to create a vision for Soviet housing—and then implement it in an orderly fashion—and finally entice Uzbeks to make the jump from traditional neighborhoods. However, the fact that Uzbek homes were subject to bulldozing while Russian migrants had little to lose from the destruction of Tashkent's existing settlements naturally meant that the city's Russians supported and received the benefits of the urban transformation program more often than their Uzbek neighbors.

Beyond housing, the Sil'chenkov plan for Soviet Tashkent preserved the radial grid of the Russian section of the city and incorporated the traditional European-style urban center. Sil'chenkov envisioned connecting the Russian town to the new park in the former Old City by expanding and widening the existing Shaikhtanur Street, which was briefly renamed Ikramov Street after Akmal Ikramov, the first secretary of the Uzbek Communist Party until his death in the 1937 purges. It was later named Navoi Street after the fifteenth-century Central Asian poet, the name it holds to this day. This broad avenue would become the main thoroughfare of the Uzbek capital, replacing the native settlement's narrow streets and winding pathways, which had been deemed unsuitable for modern life. A circular street pattern was proposed to radiate from the new park, which would serve as a parade ground for pageantry that would symbolize and glorify Soviet power.[65] A constructivist's dream, Sil'chenkov's Tashkent was a modern city of geometric forms. His proposal sought to replace the "premodern" section with an ultra-contemporary space. In effect, Sil'chenkov's proposal aimed to build a large garden space to symbolize a break with the supposed poverty and famine of the past. This new Tashkent "garden" would enable Central Asians to "escape" the squalid environment of traditional Central Asian settlements and would provide them with a "clean" and "sanitary" space, like Russian settlers purportedly possessed in the tsarist period, in which to begin their march toward socialism and modernity.

While Sil'chenkov was the principal planner of this design, Polupanov's role in creating Soviet Uzbek cities became tremendously important, particularly in filling in the details of how individual streets and buildings were to be planned and constructed. In addition to the housing communes, Polupanov designed the constructivist Gosbank building in the city of Andijan and the "Government House" for Tashkent's Red Square in 1930—buildings that were important parts of the early effort to Sovietize Central Asia. His project for the administrative center of the Uzbek capital transformed the existing Cathedral Square, a mark of imperial rule, into a constructivist monument to Soviet power. The cathedral was razed, while portions of the White House, the former residence of the governor-general of Turkestan, were incorporated into the new construction, which was considerably larger and extended the length of the newly named Red Square.[66] The classical design of the original White House was subsumed into the modernist vision for the new building, which was striking in its simplicity. Its basic concept consisted of a long corridor to which offices and meeting rooms were attached, but on only one side of the building. It was a functional structure that served a specific purpose: government administration. Similar to general movements in construction and architecture, Polupanov's design for the Government House had little aesthetic detail, instead focusing on technological and scientific achievement to reflect the future of an ultramodern and industrial Soviet society. The facility also included a meeting hall for a thousand people, again with little decorative detail. In 1933, the complex was completed with the addition of a monument to Lenin and two "tribunal-type" stages for use on official holidays and celebrations.

Unfortunately for Polupanov, these projects were completed just as constructivist ideas were purged from Soviet architecture. In fact, by the mid-1930s, modernist structures that celebrated functionality and the advancements of technology were no longer perceived as the future of Soviet urban design. Instead, the Soviet state began to embrace the symbolic traditions of the recent Russian past, particularly classicism, to evoke the greatness and promise of Soviet society. Just as its imperial predecessor had done, the Stalinist state began to co-opt the symbolic legacy of Greece and Rome and deemed that the functional designs of the 1920s no longer suited the desired image of socialism.[67] Polupanov quickly altered the outer appearance of his newly constructed building in Tashkent's Red Square. In 1935, he was forced to change its façade by adding columns to its front to make it more "monumental." Along the Ankhor Canal, located just behind the building, an existing narrow street was widened to set the building apart from the surrounding area. A granite pedestal was placed under the Lenin Monument to make it more imposing to spectators on the square.[68] These additions to Tashkent's Red Square purportedly enhanced the beauty of the city's main administrative building, one of the tallest (three stories) and most significant structures in Tashkent. Most importantly, the complex was located at the site where military or athletic parades—the Soviet version of royal pageantry—would culminate. Creating the proper architectural look for this building was politically vital for the Soviet regime.

In this sense, one sees that Polupanov was adept at quickly recognizing and responding to new ideological trends in Soviet urban design, an ability that would serve him well for the next twenty years. His architectural—and political—skills allowed him to become a frequent contributor and survivor of the Tashkent urban scene for years to come, continually adapting his buildings and architectural plans to go alongside the ever-changing visions proposed for Soviet Tashkent.

One of those later plans, proposed in 1933, called for the architectural "unification" of the Old and New Cities, although this new redevelopment plan again lacked detail showing how this unification would occur. N. N. Semenov, the designer of this proposal, called for an increase in parkland and an expansion of irrigation canals to improve the health of city residents and to showcase the power of Soviet technology to transform a barren desert into a lush landscape. Structures near the former Voskresenskii Market in the earlier New City area were to be removed, and a small park, named Theater Square, would take their place, although a theater was not completed until 1948.[69] This and other green spaces symbolically liberated the city from the squalor of pre-revolutionary capitalism and colonialism. The Old City was to benefit most from this plan, at least on paper. The Semenov proposal envisioned moving the administrative center of Tashkent westward along Ikramov Street (i.e., Navoi Street) toward the Old Town, which would not be depopulated to make way for a garden, as Sil'chenkov wanted, but was to be developed with industry and educational institutions. Semenov developed this plan during the height of the industrialization campaign; he knew that Central Asian Tashkenters needed more than flowers to bring about their transformation into modern Soviet citizens. Industrial institutions, interspersed with gardens, were necessary to help create the machines and the people the Soviet Union wanted to build socialism. Thus, he included factories in the development plans for the traditionally Uzbek sections of the city to facilitate the movement of indigenous residents into socially productive industrial labor and, ultimately, into Soviet society.

The introduction of modern industry and other symbols of Soviet progress into the Old Town was seen as having a transformative effect on the region. It was easier to build up the area than it was to depopulate it, as Sil'chenkov had proposed. Also, by placing industry in the midst of the local population, the state symbolically gave residents the key to modern socialist life and the possibility of gaining greater status in Soviet society by becoming workers. If the socialist revolution liberated Uzbeks from colonialism and provided them with their own Soviet republic, they would also need markers of industry to help propel them into the communist future and thus serve as the symbol of socialism's hope on the Asian continent. Semenov's proposal conveyed the notion that Uzbeks were no longer just distant imperial subjects; the presence of industry in the Old Town of Tashkent symbolized that Soviet power now provided them and other minority ethnic groups with equal economic and social opportunities. Despite these plans for the industrialization of the Old City, however, the actual construction in the city at the time occurred elsewhere. Slightly to the east, in what was the Russian town, the Tashselmash factory went up, and to the south, the Tashkent Textile Kombinat appeared, along with its socialist village, which included housing, schools, and public health facilities. These structures were all located much closer to the newer sections of the city than to the center of Old Tashkent. Despite calls for transforming the formerly Muslim section of Tashkent, innovative buildings, industrial expansion, and the establishment of educational institutions—all Soviet markers of progress—developed much more rapidly on the Russian side of the city.[70] The Soviet Union created impressive programs to transform the region and wanted to implement them quickly. However, the need for fast results mandated that the new symbols of Soviet industry be placed in areas containing the infrastructure needed to support modern production (electricity, water, public transportation) or on empty land, where such infrastructure could be installed quickly. This lack of major investment in the Uzbek quarter would haunt Soviet urbanization campaigns in Tashkent for years to come; the pronouncement of reconstruction plans in Moscow and actual construction in Tashkent often proceeded in opposite directions.

Moscow's Ambassador in the East

Soviet propaganda hailed Tashkent as the "beacon" of Soviet power in the East that would light the socialist path to prosperity for neighboring peoples of Asia. Urban planners and Party officials recognized that Tashkent, the largest city in Central Asia, would become a model city for the entire region. Like Moscow, it was a "laboratory" where Soviet urban designers were poised to conduct some of their most valuable experiments on the Soviet population. If successful, the building of Soviet Tashkent would be replicated across Central Asia in Bukhara, Samarkand, Namangan, Andijan, and, if possible, Beijing, Kabul, or Tehran. The public image of postrevolutionary Tashkent was vitally important to the Soviet state, which held that the Uzbeks had been liberated from colonial subjugation by the revolution and now were building a just society. They, not a wealthy khan or the distant tsar, were officially in charge. Tashkent, in the words of Yusupov, needed to become Moscow's shining star in Asia to reflect these changes and to call the "oppressed peoples" of the colonial world to follow their Soviet Uzbek brothers and sisters on the road to socialism.[71]

Yet planners changed course once again and decreed in the late 1930s that Tashkent's reconstruction should follow closely the example of Moscow. The Moscow ideal was itself undergoing a fundamental transformation at this time, however, with wide new boulevards, monumental architecture, and a metro system that was both efficient and beautiful. Urban planners in the Soviet Union viewed pre-revolutionary Moscow—epitomized by the winding "labyrinth" of streets in the Kitai Gorod section of the city—as the opposite of a rationally arranged and modern Soviet capital. In fact, although Tashkent's Old City was seen as the embodiment of backwardness, the arguments against Kitai Gorod, one of the oldest sections of Moscow, were remarkably similar to those used against the traditionally Muslim sections of the Uzbek capital. Lazar Kaganovich, who spearheaded the reconstruction efforts in the Soviet capital, criticized Moscow's historical city center for its lack of order and the haphazard placement of houses, which allegedly resulted from private owners' desire to place buildings wherever they saw fit.[72] Soviet reconstruction efforts, in effect, removed this problem because architects no longer needed to accommodate their designs to private interests and urban planners in the Soviet Union knew they had only one official customer to please—the state. Socialism theoretically provided architects with a blank slate upon which to build new cities. Soviet power nationalized the land and gave state planners the ability to refashion the entire urban area, not just small parts of it, as was the case before the revolution.

For the Stalinist reconstruction of Moscow, Kaganovich determined that the main streets of the capital should be both straightened and widened. He also mandated the removal of one-story wooden buildings that interfered with the "unified vision" of the city.[73] Main avenues of the city were to be at least forty meters wide, ostensibly to improve "circulation" or traffic flow.[74] At the plenum of the Architects' Union in 1938, Professor A. E. Stramentov stated that wide streets also were necessary to protect the population because the fire brigade could neither travel to nor fight fires effectively on narrow roads. Furthermore, Stramentov noted the need to create avenues that would allow for demonstrations and public parades without causing traffic delays or blocking the flow of goods and people throughout the city.[75] Using biological analogies of roads serving as veins and traffic and people being the lifeblood of the urban environment, Soviet planners referred to cities as "living organisms."[76] All "blockages" in a city's artery system had to be eliminated for aesthetic, safety, and economic reasons. While these ideas originated in Moscow, they were intended to be replicated across the Soviet Union. By knocking down pre-Soviet buildings, straightening streets, and creating large urban spaces with structures of neoclassical design, the regime made symbolic moves away from the past to create an "open" and "healthy" environment for the Soviet people.

Furthermore, single-family homes, commercial centers, and other buildings that represented the old regime were to be removed from Moscow, often with the claim that they did not fit into or even that they impeded the new architectural unity of the socialist urban environment. As such, planners spoke of the need to design entire "city ensembles," not just individual buildings. If planners had not done so already, markers of the past had to be removed from the urban body as if they were cancerous growths that threatened the survival of Soviet cities. Symbols of the previous regime— whether they were GUM (the shopping arcade along Red Square that Kaganovich condemned), private palaces, or the enclosed homes of Tashkent— became prime candidates for demolition across the Soviet Union.[77]

Modern public transportation was also seen as a central aspect of a city's development, and the city's transport systems shifted from the streets to underground tunnels or to the rivers and canals. In Tashkent, the continued reliance on animal-drawn transportation, with all of its inefficiencies and sanitary problems, was a blot on the Uzbek capital. Vasili Stribezhev, a construction worker who arrived in Tashkent from provincial Voronezh in the late 1930s, recalls being shocked at the wide use of camel caravans and wooden donkey carts as transportation in the city. Trucks to carry equipment, construction supplies, and produce throughout the city were in short supply, leaving animal transport as a vital method for moving goods around the capital of the Uzbek SSR. Although writing his account for the archives in 1991, he and other Russians mockingly referred to Tashkent in the 1930s as a city of "asses," certainly not the image of modernity that socialist rule was to bring.[78] Nevertheless, these words convey negative stereotypes of the city and its residents as well as a sense of the pressing need to install modern infrastructure in Soviet cities to support the economic and industrial growth that the regime promised and to meet the needs of an increasingly large urban population.

As a result, Soviet newspapers in Uzbekistan documented the construction of public transportation systems across the Soviet Union with a specific focus on the new Moscow metro. Tashkent newspapers celebrated the opening of each station, as they did for the Soviet capital's new river port, airport, bus depots, and train stations. Moscow had become the transportation hub of the Soviet Union in addition to serving as the heart of the socialist system. At the plenum of the Architects' Union in 1938, the Soviet capital was compared to London, Paris, and New York because all had subway systems. Attendees proposed constructing underground public transit in other large Soviet cities, particularly Kiev and Leningrad, to allow these cities to become true republic or regional centers, while special bus or trolleybus lines would modernize the traffic flow in other areas so as to "overtake" Europe and America in urban improvement.[79] For Tashkent, this trend would lead to the expansion of mechanized transportation (in this case, the tram) as an important feature in all subsequent urban renewal plans. Just like the Moscow metro, the Tashkent tram, then the trolleybus, and finally a metro system became symbols of the Uzbek capital's progress under socialism and a solution to the increasing population concentration in the Tashkent region. During the height of the industrialization campaign, as Andrew Jenks has shown, urban designers attempted to highlight modern machinery and Soviet technology in their designs.[80] Proposals to bring public transport to all sections of the Uzbek capital served as an important reminder of the "progressive nature" of the Soviet project particularly because the transportation system under tsarist rule focused on the Russian parts of the city. For these reasons, transportation lines in Tashkent were to be run through the Uzbek neighborhoods, ostensibly to connect them to the rest of the city and to provide Central Asian Tashkenters with a vehicle to take them on the ride toward socialist prosperity.

Pravda, Qizil O'zbekiston, Pravda Vostoka, and numerous other Soviet publications covered the tremendous changes that were occurring in Moscow and in cities across the Soviet Union. The transformation of Moscow also was featured in films (*Volga-Volga* and *Circus*), poetry, and the visual arts so that distant regions would become aware of the monumental changes that were occurring at the center of the Soviet Union and would thus get a preview of the future of socialism.[81] Soviet propaganda declared that Moscow was becoming more beautiful by the day. In a state where power was so centralized, the remaking of the Soviet capital clearly gave a glimpse of how Soviet planning would occur in the periphery, even if the final decision to reproduce the Moscow model in regional and republican centers had not yet been made public.

By 1937, Tashkent was officially viewed as a city with a bright future. Uzbeks theoretically had taken control of their own fortunes and were trying to remodel their capital, soon to be just as modern as any other Soviet city. This transformation of Tashkent was an important task for the Stalinist regime. Soviet administrators, like their predecessors, continued to view the traditional Asian city negatively, but they also noted that the Soviet transformation of the city was much more progressive than what had come before because it would alter the conditions of life for *all* residents of the city, not just the Russian elite. However, while there were similarities between imperial and early Soviet rule in Tashkent, a fundamental difference between the two regimes was evident in the extent to which they sought to transform Central Asian urban spaces.

Russian imperial planners sculpted a new European city in the Central Asian desert and hoped that this achievement would entice Muslim Central Asians to join the "modern world." Those who did not become convinced of European superiority could be left behind in the premodern conditions of Old Tashkent. After 1924, however, Soviet officials did not want to leave anything to chance and sought to take more active and coercive roles in the transformation of its citizens in Uzbekistan, as they were doing with the population throughout the Soviet Union. The Uzbeks were no longer just distant colonial subjects of the tsar but members of the Soviet state. Although some colonial methodologies remained, the official division between "colony" and "metropole" had been broken down. The Soviet regime, with its authoritarian aspiration for complete control over society, believed it was necessary to change *all* regions of the city, *all* areas of the Soviet Union, and *all* inhabitants of Soviet territory. The state found the "dual city" and segregated layout of imperial Tashkent to be unacceptable by the 1930s because it had the potential to help some Soviet citizens of Central Asia remain outside of Soviet society and state control, as many tried to do during the *hujum* campaigns of a few years before. By the end of the decade and after the initiation of the "socialist renovation" of Moscow, Party officials were determined to make fundamental changes to the cities in the Soviet periphery to tie these spaces and their inhabitants much more closely to the state and its ideology. They would soon declare that Tashkent needed to be remade in the image of the Soviet metropolis, just like the capitals of Ukraine, Kazakhstan, Georgia, or even the regional centers of Russia.

With the replication of the Moscow model across the Soviet Union, each republic soon received a showcase city to demonstrate how the Soviet project equalized traditional ethnic, gender, social, and class relationships. In this manner, Soviet officials were cognizant of the need to ensure that the former tsarist empire resembled a new type of state where no community was left untouched by Soviet modernity and ideology. In reproducing similar urban spaces across the Soviet Union, the state aimed to build uniform environments that could fashion a new and uniform Soviet culture. The goal of urban planning in Uzbekistan in the Stalinist period no longer was simply to awe local residents into believing in the superiority of the Soviet system, although altering physical spaces certainly remained an important component of the socialist urban renewal programs. In rebuilding socialist

Tashkent, the transformation of social norms, the sculpting of new citizens, and the enhancement of the state's ability to monitor and manage the residents of the city—both Uzbek and Russian speakers—became the primary concerns of the Soviet government. The creation of Soviet Tashkent was a part of an all-union state-building process, one that sought to pull every citizen and every city more closely to the Soviet center. In 1937, with the purges in full swing, Moscow decided that local officials could no longer be trusted to implement urban renewal in Central Asia and determined to tie Tashkent planning closer to the center as well. The leadership in Moscow sent direct representatives from Russia—many of whom were Central Asians who had been trained in new Stalinist institutions—to jump-start socialist urbanization programs across the Soviet Union. In 1937, the center took direct control of the campaign to make Soviet cities "socialist" and kept a tight rein on the Uzbek capital for years to come.

IMAGINING A "CULTURED" TASHKENT

On December 3, 1937, *Pravda Vostoka* profiled Mavjuda Abdurakhmanova, a young Stakhanovite, which was someone belonging to an elite category of Soviet worker who set records in fulfilling factory production quotas. An orphan, she was adopted by "progressive" Uzbek parents, who were determined to provide their new daughter with an education. This young Soviet girl would "never wear a *paranji* [veil], but would be equal with men and become literate," declared her father. After completing the fifth grade in 1934, Mavjuda enrolled in the training school of the Textile Kombinat, where she finished her education, and became a quilter, a popular profession for women according to worker biographies of the time. Mavjuda joined the Komsomol, quickly became a model employee, and served as a propaganda agitator and teacher of literacy. She later enjoyed helping other Uzbek women move from the confines of the home into the workplace and even received awards from the Central Committee of the Uzbek Communist Party.[1] Her journey to fame in Tashkent was described as a typical rise of the new Soviet person who grew into a skilled and socially active citizen under Stalinist rule. With people like Mavjuda, Tashkent was breaking away from its past.

Usman Yusupov, the newly appointed first secretary of the Uzbek Communist Party, echoed this sentiment that same year by comparing the successes of Soviet Uzbekistan to the oppression of its colonial predecessor. Presenting Soviet power as ending inequality and moving Soviet Uzbeks into a "happy life," Yusupov explained that the reforms of the revolutionary era enabled Uzbekistan to build an industrial base of its own, with the Tashkent Textile Kombinat being its most important achievement. According to Yusupov, "Uzbekistan had become the beacon that showed the way to freedom and happiness to all workers of the Colonial East, who still languished under colonial rule." The Party official remarked that the Uzbek people successfully severed the chains of colonial oppression and, with the help of the Russian people and under the leadership of the Communist Party, were creating a cultured urban environment in the Central Asian desert.[2] Tashkent, Yusupov concluded, was becoming a model city of the socialist future.

During that same year of 1937, at the height of the purges and one of the bloodiest periods in Soviet history, the Soviet Union embarked on a project of building planned, orderly, beautiful urban spaces to inspire its population with the promises of socialism. These new cities—Tashkent among them—were to showcase Soviet innovation and technology, and their reinvention would involve diverting rivers, erecting tall buildings, and transforming urban ghettos into beautiful city parks, all to show that the revolution had transformed the Russian Empire into the Soviet Union and that this new state strove to move beyond its "backward" past so criticized by Europeans. So, while the secret police physically removed ideologically undesirable citizens from Soviet society, construction workers tore up undesirable narrow city streets to install wide avenues, allowing light to penetrate formerly dark inner regions of cities and clean air to reach the working class that lived and labored in these spaces.[3] The urbanization project launched by the Soviet Union in 1937 was unprecedented in scope and in its elaborate vision for new Soviet cities, towns, and even villages. No part of the Soviet Union and no citizen of the country, regardless of ethnic background, would remain untouched by this massive urban renewal campaign. In short, while the NKVD rounded up scores of undesirable citizens and sent them to their deaths, the Party led others on a happy march toward the future—to urban modernity and communism.

What did this project mean for Central Asia and Central Asians? In the Uzbek SSR, the newly installed post-purge leadership, on cue from Moscow, decided that the Uzbek capital needed to speed up its transformation and make a definitive break with its cultural and architectural past. The revolution had officially liberated the region from colonialism, but the city and its residents—still struggling with the *hujum* campaign—had not yet met the idealized image of a socialist urban center.[4] The subsequent reconstruction plan for the Uzbek capital sought to create a European-style cityscape utterly unlike the Central Asian town.[5] This city would help sculpt new Soviet Central Asian citizens, who would reflect the highest ideals of Soviet ideology as productive, cultured laborers who were almost European in outlook but still possessed a local aura. Socialist Tashkent was to be a unified urban space in which every ethnic group enjoyed equal rights and opportunities but also possessed equal responsibilities to the state itself.

To realize this project, the Tashkent Gorispolkom, the executive committee of the city soviet, signed a contract in April 1937 with Mosoblproekt, the Moscow Oblast Planning Organization, to develop a general plan for the reconstruction of Tashkent. This agreement was part of the all-union project of building planned cities across the Soviet space. While local planners in Tashkent had tried to transform the city into a "modern" socialist space in the first two decades of Soviet rule, Moscow-based officials deemed these efforts inadequate and took over city planning in the Uzbek capital, as they did elsewhere in the Soviet Union. These Soviet urban experts aimed to provide local construction organizations with the technical assistance necessary to sculpt the city into an ideal Soviet environment—one that reflected the future of socialism, awed competing international powers, and instilled socialist culture in Central Asia. In this manner, the Soviet Union embarked on a large-scale enlightenment project to bring "modernity" and "order" to what Soviet planners (and their imperial predecessors) perceived as chaotic spaces, this time with Moscow holding a tighter rein than it ever had before.

To be completed by December 1938, the Mosoblproekt proposal sought to transform Tashkent through "rationally planned growth."[6] Tashkent, the largest city of Central Asia, was to contain one-half of the urban population of the republic and approximately 10 percent of the entire population of the Uzbek SSR.[7] However, creating a Soviet city was not only about moving the population into urban spaces. Tashkent also needed public parks and squares where the city's multiethnic communities could come together for cultural events, military parades, and other public demonstrations of Soviet rule. These interactions were envisioned as having transformative powers, almost as if traditional Uzbeks would enter one end of a parade square but emerge on the other side as strong Soviet citizens. The premier Soviet city in Asia likewise required model industrial factories with associated modern apartment buildings to transform local city residents into socially productive factory laborers. Soviet officials believed that if Tashkenters lived in modern conditions and worked in industrial institutions, city residents eventually would become modern Soviet people. Creating Soviet cities in the late 1930s was not only about erecting new buildings but, more importantly, was a means of transforming the region's residents into model Soviet citizens.

Creating an Uzbek Working Class

In the first twenty years after the revolution, Central Asia and Tashkent in particular witnessed a tremendous increase in population. By 1939, Tashkent's population had doubled from its 1924 figure, to approximately 600,000 residents.[8] Migration to the region showed few signs of slowing, with reportedly 188,168 people moving into the Uzbek SSR in 1938 and 1939 alone.[9] The majority of these migrants, including textile workers, irrigation specialists, medical doctors, engineers, and construction workers, came from Russia.[10] Many volunteered to come to the region and help build socialism, but others, after completing technical training or higher education, were sent to transform Central Asians. A few came seeking opportunity and advancement, while Soviet Koreans, the first set of ethnic deportees, were transferred in horrific conditions from their distant border area of the Soviet Union to the rural areas of Tashkent oblast. The consequences were devastating for large numbers of Soviet Koreans, who had been identified by the state as an untrustworthy border population that would collaborate with the enemy during a war between the Soviet Union and Japan. Thousands of Koreans died in squalid railway boxcars along the way or upon arrival in the outskirts of the Uzbek capital. When they arrived, local officials had made few preparations for them. Dumped in the unfamiliar Central Asian desert without local language skills, the new Korean population of Uzbekistan was left to fend for itself.[11] However, whether migration to the Tashkent region was voluntary or forced, it led to a diversification of ethnic groups, with peoples from all parts of the Soviet Union represented in the Uzbek capital region.[12] The Uzbek capital was becoming much more multiethnic in the 1930s, with numerous new Soviet minority groups moving into the region and bringing a new level of diversity to the traditionally dual Russian/Uzbek city.

Many of the migrants to Central Asia complained of harsh living conditions and difficulties in adjusting to their new environment. Those from the north had particular difficulty adjusting to the hot desert climate and the exotic nature of the city. A group of textile spinners from Moscow oblast, for example, voiced bitter dissatisfaction upon their arrival. The workers allegedly came to the city thinking they would build socialism and train the new Uzbek working class in textile production. They viewed themselves as the Russian "elder siblings" who hoped to show the path of revolutionary prosperity to the native Uzbeks. Back at home, they almost certainly were not the most skilled workers, but they nevertheless expected to be in positions of privilege in the upper echelons of Tashkent society because textile production was the leading industry in the region. They certainly did not anticipate being housed in the Old City among Uzbeks rather than in the modern urban spaces of the Russian sections of the city. They expressed dislike of their lives among Asian peoples about whom they knew little, and they frequently complained about the unclean and uncultured conditions of the Uzbek parts of city. One migrant worker, Pulatov, protested being housed in an Uzbek *kibitka* (mud hovel), where he and his family lived without windows, doors, or sinks. To his dismay, he had to fetch water from the nearby irrigation ditch and live just like his Uzbek neighbors in what he described as an unhealthy environment. Pulatov concluded his complaint by noting that Russian women and children could not withstand such harsh surroundings and needed to be moved immediately from these conditions. Only single men without families, he believed, could be expected to live in such squalor.[13] However, since the majority of workers at the Textile Kombinat were women, advocating that only men live in this section of the city was tantamount to demanding that no Russian workers live there. In making his complaint, Pulatov identified Uzbeks as completely different and inferior to Russians, who allegedly were accustomed to higher standards of living. Even though he and others came to help "train" the Uzbeks, Pulatov and others like him wanted little to do with their new Uzbek neighbors and preferred to live a segregated lifestyle, as did the generation of Russian migrants before him. So, despite the ethnic diversification that was occurring in the Uzbek capital in the 1930s, Tashkent, traditionally a "dual city" with separate Russian and Uzbek sections, remained as such in the early Soviet era because city residents—Uzbeks and Russian—did not necessarily want to live together.

Furthermore, most migrant workers had to be resourceful to improve their difficult living conditions. Liudmila Frolova, a textile worker at the Tashkent Textile Kombinat, lived on the street for months because the Kombinat lacked enough housing to settle the new cadre of workers it hoped to attract. Tashkent, like cities across the Soviet Union, had a severe housing crisis, and those who had recently arrived from the countryside or from a different republic were at the greatest disadvantage. Yet it was the Russians of Tashkent who complained the loudest about housing shortages and poor living conditions because they—not the Uzbeks of the city—lacked local community and family structures that could provide them with assistance that the state often could not. In an ironic footnote, many of these Soviet-era Slavic migrants lived in worse physical conditions than the Uzbek neighbors whose lives they had intended to "improve"; the Soviet system could not meet the needs of the increasing number of new residents in the city, while longtime residents remained in traditional homes and neighborhoods where their families had lived for generations. Water pumps, public baths, and other essentials of life might not have been "modern" in these traditionally Uzbek areas, but at least they existed, which was not necessarily true in the new Soviet sections of the city. Thus, the standard of living for many Uzbek families in the Old City was in some ways superior, a notion that Party officials and urban planners had difficulty acknowledging.

Fears over the rise of homelessness, especially of young children who spent their days hawking cigarettes or alcohol in the city's bazaars, also reinforced Tashkent's pre-revolutionary reputation as the crime capital of Central Asia.[14] Fitzroy MacLean, a Moscow-based British diplomat, stated that residents of Uzbekistan were obsessed with rising crime rates in the republic's capital in 1937–1938. Upon his arrival at the train station in the Uzbek capital, other travelers told him not to fall asleep outdoors in Tashkent because "anything might happen to you."[15] While Liudmila Frolova, the textile worker, was living on the streets, all of her belongings were stolen. Tashkent was not an ideal socialist city, with harmonious relations between ethnic and social groups, as depicted in Soviet propaganda of the time. However, the region's bazaars and rising crime rates became useful tools for Party propagandists to illustrate the supposed backwardness of traditional society. While collective farm markets proliferated across the Soviet Union and served as an important food source, in Tashkent, they represented both the chaos of capitalism and the primitiveness of the Central Asian past. In the mindset of many local Russian officials, the Central Asian bazaar was worse than the more developed capitalist department store or the small private shop that Soviet trade institutions replaced in Russia, Ukraine, and elsewhere.

Newspaper reports described the Central Asian market as a filthy place where prices were unregulated and extremely high. Sellers often were "criminals" who cheated both the state and their customers. In the Uzbek SSR, where the majority of Russians lived in the cities and Uzbeks were rural collective farmers, class, racial, and ethnic antagonisms converged in the Central Asian marketplace. The bazaar was not bad just because it was a remnant of the capitalist past. The Slavic residents—mostly new arrivals and factory workers—depended on the bazaar to a greater extent than did their Central Asian counterparts, who often had courtyard gardens and extended families near the city who could help secure food. Ideologues, city officials, and some residents viewed the market negatively because it remained a symbol of capitalism and of lingering Uzbek power in a region where Central Asians had long controlled the food supply and where they allegedly still made life in the socialist state more difficult.[16]

The Purges and the Reinvigoration of Tashkent Planning

The general dissatisfaction of the public with living standards, food short-ages, and poor working conditions continued to simmer throughout the late 1930s. However, city officials in 1937 found easy scapegoats for these ur-ban problems in Tashkent, as they did elsewhere, by identifying disloyal government figures and criminals who allegedly sabotaged the steady ur-banization of Tashkent and kept the city from becoming the "forepost" of the Soviet East. Enemies of the Soviet state and specifically the Uzbek people were identified as promoting ethnic animosities throughout Central Asia and fostering rapidly declining standards of living and food shortages. Party officials accused "wreckers" of corruption and halting the provision of basic services to the people of Tashkent with the goal of fomenting dis-content among the population. The Stalinist purges hit the Uzbek Com-munist Party particularly hard in 1938, with 70.8 percent of Party officials in district Party committees removed and a drastic decrease in ethnic Uz-bek membership in the Communist Party.[17] The share of Uzbeks who were Party members or candidates fell from 58.1 percent in 1936 to 47 percent by 1939.[18] Overall Party membership in Uzbekistan declined drastically in the mid-1930s, from 81,612 members in 1933 to a low of 28,458 in 1936 and 29,934 in 1937. Membership rose to 35,087 in 1939 but had not yet returned to 1933 levels before World War II.[19] During the purges in Uzbekistan, the most prominent people to fall were Fayzullah Khojaev, chair of the Uzbek Sovnarkom (Council of the People's Commissars), and Akmal Ikramov, first secretary of the Uzbek Communist Party, who were relieved of their duties in June and September 1937, respectively. Found guilty as enemies of the people along with Bukharin and Yagoda and other "Old Bolsheviks" at an infamous show trial, Stalin had them executed in 1938.[20]

Khojaev and Ikramov's collaborators in Tashkent were accused of de-stroying the economy of and the food supply chain into Tashkent, as well as slowing down the "beautification" of the city.[21] The lack of road maintenance (or even construction) left gaping holes in the streets, while the tram system had been neither repaired nor expanded, thereby impeding travel within the city center and between the center and the outskirts.[22] The newspaper *Pravda Vostoka* identified Yulchi Igamberdy, secretary of the Tashkent Oblast Yangi-Yol district committee, as especially dangerous, accusing him of organizing a band of eleven men who "ignited" ethnic conflict between recent settlers in Tashkent oblast and local residents.[23] Tashkent was said to be encircled by "wreckers," most of whom were identified as Uzbeks who actively fostered animosity in the city, in the countryside, and between the city and rural areas. At the height of the purges, the Tashkent region was described as being at war with Uzbek "bourgeois nationalists" and the enemy elements that surrounded the city, destroyed its transportation network, and controlled the region's food supply.[24] The purge of these men symbolized the end to the lingering pre-Stalinist power base of Uzbek Party leaders—many of whom were raised in the pre-Soviet Jadid tradition. Equally important, it brought about a new leadership in Tashkent that was much more closely tied to Moscow and the Stalin revolution, not to any potential local Communist Party power broker.

Pravda Vostoka and *Qizil O'zbekiston*, the Uzbek-language daily newspaper, were silent about the change in leadership in 1937. Usman Yusupov simply appeared as the first secretary of the Communist Party of Uzbekistan in October 1937. New leaders were immediately presented as loyal, well-trained communists who would lead Tashkent toward true socialist construction without the delays and inconveniences that their predecessors supposedly caused. Yusupov, a loyal follower of Stalin, was a typical product of the Stalinist political system. Born in 1900 in the Fergana Valley, he joined the Communist Party in 1926 while working at a cotton-processing factory. He quickly became a secretary in the Tashkent Party organization in 1927 and then received a promotion to the position of third secretary of the Uzbek Communist Party in 1929. Lacking formal education until 1934, he moved to Moscow to study Marxism-Leninism, only to return to Tashkent in late 1936.[25] Abduzhabar Abdurakhmanov, the new chair of the Uzbek Sovnarkom, followed a similar path to Russia before returning to the highest levels of the Uzbek Communist Party. A Tashkenter, he entered the party as a twenty-one-year-old factory worker in 1928. From 1935 to 1938, he studied at the Ivanov Industrial Institute and then returned to Uzbekistan to take up his new post.[26]

These men epitomized the new Soviet Uzbek citizen, who "decisively" struggled against enemies of the past. They were not tied to the pre-revolutionary political or cultural reform struggles and therefore depended on Moscow for their rise to positions of power. They also were more closely identified with the center and its ideal of creating a modern Tashkent, with specific Russian notions of modernity receiving greater emphasis. Mostly from humble backgrounds, the members of this new generation of Party leaders were products of the Soviet education system in the 1930s, with its values of Soviet/European *kul'turnost'*.[27] In effect, the purges and the rise of these new men told Soviet citizens that socialism had not caused Tashkent's infrastructure problems. Former Party leaders, closely tied to Tashkent's feudal, capitalistic, or religious past, had allegedly caused the harsh living and working conditions in the city.

After ousting republic-level leaders in Uzbekistan, the Stalinist system then took aim at officials on the city and district level. Local architects Stepan Polupanov, F. I. Dolgov, and A. I. Pavlov were singled out for failing to develop socialist Uzbek national architecture and for causing the deterioration of living standards for Uzbeks in the city.[28] The designers of the previous two plans for the reconstruction of Tashkent came under attack in 1938. Alexander Sil'chenkov, who had proposed creating a large urban park on the site of the Old City in the 1929 reconstruction plan, was accused of wasting "hundreds of thousands of rubles" in an unrealistic urban plan that called for the eviction of "tens of thousands" of workers from their homes in the Old City.[29] N. N. Semenov, who wrote the plan for 1933–1937, was criticized for his vision of Tashkent. His plan called for creating a utopian "Narkomat Prospekt," a street containing only government buildings, and for placing the headquarters of administrative organizations and republic-level ministries of Uzbekistan along Navoi Street, the central artery that was expanded in the 1929 plan to connect Tashkent's Red Square with the Old City. According to Semenov's critics, this plan was enormously expensive and called for the demolition of existing housing in a city already experiencing a terrible housing shortage.[30]

At a conference of the Uzbek Architects' Union in 1937, Aleksandr Kuznetsov, who would soon head the Mosoblproekt design team to develop the new Tashkent city plan, highlighted the fact that previous planners had all aimed to tear down the Old City, which not only compounded housing shortages but also destroyed the traditional neighborhoods and local customs. This approach, he claimed, was not the purpose of socialist urbanization, which aimed instead to transform the region and its traditions for the benefit of its local inhabitants, not to bring destruction to them. He argued that the failure to consider the needs or desires of the population had impeded all previous efforts to transform the city into a modern urban space and had the potential to turn residents against urban development programs from which they did not see any near-term benefits. Consequently, Kuznetsov and others declared that local residents must be included in the planning and design process, which would give them a greater stake in urban reconstruction and in Soviet life in general.

The criticisms leveled against these previous planners prompted Polupanov, who had survived the purges relatively intact, to propose renovations to his existing buildings in Tashkent. As described earlier, Polupanov, a constructivist architect from Kharkov, designed the Tashkent Government House on the Uzbek capital's Red Square in the early 1930s. To the modernist design of the original building he had already added columns, a double tribunal for holiday demonstrations, and a granite pedestal for its Lenin statue. These changes had been undertaken to make the building seem "monumental," and in many ways they mirrored the architectural forms that had been sanctioned during the socialist reconstruction of Moscow. Experimentation in urban design in the late 1930s was no longer a component of city planning, as it had been earlier in the decade. However, with the well-publicized reconstruction of Moscow in the mid-1930s and the publicly declared need to take local norms into consideration, in 1940 Polupanov revised the Government House yet again by transforming the interior of the building into a celebrated work of Soviet Uzbek national architecture. Writing in the journal *Arkhitektura SSSR,* Polupanov stated that architects in Uzbekistan needed to study traditional examples of Uzbek ornamentation and incorporate them into the mainstream of Soviet architecture.

In applying this technique to the Government House, Polupanov decreed that, with its stress on neoclassicism, the basic form of the redesigned building was "socialist" but that its decorations sprang from the "progressive" Uzbek past, an indication that Islamic decorative details had no place in this new architecture. In achieving this merger of socialist (universal) and Uzbek (particularistic) architecture, Polupanov focused on the transformation of the interior of the building, not on the exterior, as he had done a few years earlier. He added a second-floor balcony with pillars underneath and placed additional columns throughout the room to recall the neoclassical designs of Moscow. To make the room "Uzbek," he decorated the walls, ceilings, and columns with rosettes, signifying the importance of agriculture to Uzbekistan. Detailed carvings of cotton bolls, cotton stems, and cotton leaves covered the walls.[31] Thus, despite decrees to promote industrialization in the Uzbek region, the symbols adorning the new Soviet administrative offices in the republic remained tied firmly to agriculture.

With the cotton designs, Polupanov came up with a clear "recipe" for Uzbek national architecture. Polupanov, under severe criticism for his constructivist past, converted the Government House into a model of Soviet Uzbek architecture. He followed this achievement with the Uzbek pavilion, "a juxtaposition of delicate regional patterns and massive classical elements," built for the Moscow All-Union Agricultural Exhibition.[32] With these designs, Polupanov created a standardized format for Uzbek national architecture that lasted for years. Suddenly, architects from across the Soviet Union could easily design buildings for Uzbekistan even if they had never set foot in Central Asia. Ethnic Uzbeks remained rare in design bureaus and even at architecture training institutes at this time, so Soviet Uzbek architecture of the late 1930s was based on what central planners in (or from) Russia viewed as the Uzbek past. Although the revolution purportedly had "liberated" Uzbeks from colonial rule, Russians continued to develop the image of the new Uzbek capital just as they had in the tsarist period. And, it was largely Russian academics—anthropologists, sociologists, and historians—who helped determine what constituted Uzbek cultural characteristics. Even as they employed anticolonial rhetoric, Soviet planners in fact designed cityscapes similar to those that French and British designers had conceived for the urban areas of Egypt, India, and Algeria.[33] They also replicated some colonial methodologies across the Soviet landscape in the ways they went about designing these revolutionary urban spaces. The difference, however, is that it was not just Uzbek cities that were undergoing this process; diverse parts of Russia, too, were being transformed along the same ideological lines.

The Mosoblproekt Proposal

In developing an urban design for Central Asia, delegates to the Uzbek Architects' Union congress in 1938 declared that Tashkent lacked buildings of historical significance. Unlike Samarkand or Bukhara, with their long and established roles as major Silk Road cities and distinguished structures such as Samarkand's Registan, Tashkent was considered a city of mud-brick buildings with little character or importance. This declaration provided planners with a free hand in transforming the city. According to the resolution of the congress, the Architects' Union collectively agreed that Tashkent lagged behind most Soviet cities in its level of "modern development." They described Tashkent as a "backward" place that did not resemble a capital city at all but looked more like the typical Uzbek *kishlak,* or rural village. Formerly a provincial town with sections that were directly from the "Middle Ages," Tashkent had mud-and-straw structures in its Old City that would need to be removed immediately if the Uzbek capital was going to become a city of monumental architecture and industrialized construction.[34] Construction plans focused on the Old City, and these plans could, if implemented correctly, transform the lives of the city's residents not just by providing a new environment but also by making model socialist men and women of the city's diverse population.

The agreement between the Tashkent Gorispolkom and Mosoblproekt set the budget for developing the reconstruction plan at just under 1.2 million rubles. A needs analysis for the city, the development of a new plan, and the approval process were to be completed by December 1938.[35] Like other Soviet cities, Tashkent required "planned" growth; therefore, the project included a proposed breakdown by social origin and profession of future migrants to Tashkent. The target was for 52 percent of Tashkenters to be involved in industry and transportation, 9 percent were to be employees of political and economic institutions, 19 percent were to work in cultural or scientific professions, 9 percent were to be involved in construction, and 11 percent would be working in other professions.[36] With these population caps, Tashkent would no longer suffer from unforeseen population increases resulting from the migration of unskilled groups or peasants fleeing rural poverty. Planners tried to manage Tashkent's population to create a pool of residents that represented the most modern and advanced professions of the twentieth century. Professions such as garbage collectors, custodians, or plumbers—important jobs in a modern city—were not listed because they did not fit the image of an educated and elite urban population, while vague professions, such as "scientific workers" or "cultural figures," were prominent among the future population estimates. These guidelines had more than symbolic significance because they were geared to provide city officials with the ability to manage and monitor the urban population. With such detailed specifications for Tashkent's future residents, refashioning urban spaces not only concerned architecture and physical places but also gave officials the ability to decide who should live in the city, what they would do in the city, and where they would reside in the Uzbek capital.

The Mosoblproekt project also created industrial zoning regulations, with machine building and metallurgical operations to be located in northern Tashkent. The traditionally Uzbek section of the city was earmarked as an area for the production of agricultural equipment. Steam-engine repair facilities were to be located near the railroad, while the Tashkent Textile Kombinat anchored the textile-producing area to the southwest.[37] Tashkent needed to have certain types of factories, those that would mark its entrance into the modern age of the twentieth century. Interestingly, the production of agricultural equipment was placed in the traditionally Uzbek area of the city, silently reinforcing the image of Uzbeks as being occupied primarily with agriculture, while Russians labored in metallurgy, textile production, transportation, and heavy industry in the European sections of the city.[38] These traditional associations between ethnic groups and primary activities in the public imagination continued despite efforts to expand Uzbek participation in industrial labor. The state declared the liberation of the Uzbek people and the creation of an Uzbek working class but advanced policies that reinforced the opposite impression. Despite the declared goal of creating an anticolonial, modern, and multiethnic city, urban planners' perhaps subconscious pigeonholing of Uzbek society placed immediate barriers to the realization of this goal of social unity.

In addition, Mosoblproekt decreed that the development of Navoi Street, the major thoroughfare that ran from the administrative center into the Old City, would constitute the first phase of the reconstruction project. The Gorispolkom wanted quick construction of four-story apartment buildings on this street in order to house those who worked in the important industries and organizations of Tashkent.[39] In reviewing a detailed three-year plan for the street's growth, G. Berlichev of the Uzbek Architects' Union proposed the construction of a mixture of housing and administrative buildings for both republic- and union-level institutions.[40] To become the Uzbek equivalent of Moscow's Gorky Street, the Soviet version of New York's Fifth Avenue or Paris's Champs-Elysées, Tashkent's main avenue needed high-caliber occupants in impressive buildings to contrast with its existing modest architecture. However, Berlichev did not see his proposal as similar to the condemned "Narkomat Prospekt" because it combined a mixture of residential and administrative buildings, ostensibly to allow Uzbeks to live among some of the most prestigious government institutions of the city. He also argued that the reconstruction of Navoi became the first attempt to break down the *byt'* (way of life) of the Uzbek residents and entice them into the Soviet city.[41]

Unfortunately, except for the plan to demolish traditional Uzbek houses, it was never determined how this transformation of the Uzbek way of life would occur, especially since Uzbeks were not highly represented among employees in the institutions that planned to build on Navoi Street. Nonetheless, there was a general agreement that if one lived among "cultured" buildings one would automatically become "cultured." Soviet urban planners believed that transforming Tashkent into a modern European-Russian urban space itself would give sufficient incentive to Uzbeks to undergo personal conversions into modern citizens with Soviet rather than traditional (Islamic, feudal, or capitalistic) values.

However, although Tashkent was the center of Soviet Central Asia, its residents, especially Uzbeks, were not necessarily the focus of the socialist city. Mosoblproekt delegates rarely entertained Uzbeks' desires or complaints, despite Kuznetsov's specific instructions to do so. Planners from Moscow came to investigate the geology, geography, and economy of the region but not the need to house large Central Asian families, how Uzbeks used domestic space, or how Central Asians themselves constructed buildings. This failure to involve the city's population was not unique to Tashkent. The Russian residents of Moscow also had little say in how their city was being transformed. However, the difference was that the Mosoblproekt planners were designing for a city and culture with which they were not necessarily familiar, while Muscovites could more easily fit into the new vision for Soviet Moscow. The need to adapt Soviet construction to local norms in fact was not considered because the new Tashkent supposedly would transcend regional peculiarities rather than be controlled by them. Soviet planners had strong faith that transforming physical spaces would lead to the transformation of society. Therefore, urban designers neither desired nor recognized the need to study local cultural traditions.

Transforming Housing

Recognizing the low standard of living in the city, the Mosoblproekt plan also addressed the housing crisis by calling for large-scale apartment construction that would combine industrialized methods, local supplies, and Uzbek decorative motifs.[42] Although they made some alterations because of differences in climate and geography, Moscow-based planners generally used standard housing designs from other regions of the Soviet Union in construction along the main arteries of Tashkent, particularly along Navoi Street, which would serve as a main parade route from the Old City to Red Square and the main administrative districts of Tashkent. These new apartment buildings were largely three- or four-story neoclassical structures similar in appearance to those going up along Moscow's Gorky Street, the Soviet capital's main thoroughfare. Despite complaints that multistory buildings were unsuitable for the hot Central Asian climate and the city's location in an earthquake zone, Mosoblproekt declared that Tashkent was to be a city of four-story apartment buildings and noted that multistory buildings were needed to curb the city's sprawling growth. Kuznetsov and others argued that with the current population growth and the rising number of single-family homes, Tashkent threatened to cover an enormous geographic area unless decisive action was taken immediately.[43] Tall buildings would allow the city to install basic municipal services (transportation, water, electricity) more easily and cost effectively because planners could concentrate these resources in a small geographic area and not attempt to spread them across a dispersed urban space. Without overtly admitting the difficulty of outfitting a growing city during rapid industrialization in the 1930s, Mosoblproekt indicated that "enemy infiltration" was perhaps not the sole reason for Tashkent's cramped and filthy environment. Tashkent was simply expanding outward and doing so too quickly.

The Gorispolkom resolved that Tashkent was to be a compact urban center, not a spread-out "urban village" of chaotically arranged mud-brick homes. Tall buildings would make the city look like a European urban space and provide Tashkenters with easy access to Soviet institutions of cultural enlightenment. For example, planners decreed that an enormous city of one-story homes would make it impossible to build a "cultured" urban space in Central Asia because residents would have to travel twenty kilometers to the closest drama theater, an essential component of this new Soviet culture.[44] By building multistory apartment structures in the Uzbek capital, Soviet planners hoped to "modernize" the Uzbeks, although they could never quite explain why such buildings were "modern." However, the move toward increasing height clearly was a response to the fear that Soviet cities, particularly Central Asian ones, were less advanced than their Western European counterparts and, in some ways, had become even less modern in the twentieth century. Marxist-Leninist theory was based on a teleological course of history whereby societies went through successive stages of development before arriving at socialism and eventually communism. Urban life was considered more advanced than rural life, and the future establishment of communism was tied to urbanism.[45] Time and effort could not be wasted in the campaign to transform Central Asians into modern urbanites.

Four-story apartment buildings—tall structures for the region at the time—likewise were important because most modern twentieth-century urban areas had multistory buildings. After all, Moscow had tall structures and, as an Architects' Union resolution decreed, Tashkent needed to follow the Moscow model.[46] In a report to the Gorispolkom, Kuznetsov anticipated that Soviet planning would enable 78 percent of city residents to live in multistory apartment buildings by 1953, while 22 percent of Tashkenters would remain in two-story apartment buildings or single-family homes. In this manner, urban planning would facilitate a "fundamental break" with the housing practices of the past and a transformation in how Tashkenters lived their lives, with the Uzbek extended family diminishing to more of a Soviet nuclear one.[47] In addition, with the construction of taller buildings, new schools, and hospitals along the main streets of the Old Town, the Uzbek and Russian sections of the city soon would be similar in appearance, thereby signifying the unification of a bifurcated Eurasian city into a single Soviet urban space. In promoting tall apartment buildings, the Tashkent reconstruction plan attempted to banish the mud-brick home that imperial and Soviet administrators, ethnographers, and even tourists had denigrated since Russian soldiers entered the city in 1865.

In Soviet Tashkent, there also would be no distinction between Russians and Uzbeks in the type of housing they received or in the location of their housing unit. All residents of the "unified" Soviet capital of Uzbekistan were to live in similar spaces without distinction.[48] This ideal of apartment units housing small families underscored the basic Marxist-Leninist notion that history had led humans from feudalism to capitalism and then to socialism, before finally reaching communism. Just as Russians were described as more advanced than Uzbeks in this progression through history, Russian-style apartments for small nuclear families were seen as more advanced than Central Asian mud-brick homes. As the vanguard of the revolutionary state, the Russian people and the Communist Party officially provided assistance to the "lesser-developed" peoples of the Soviet Union to achieve communism. Urbanization was a central part of this Soviet transformation project, one no less important than industrialization or collectivization.

However, a shortage of construction materials severely hampered the building of "modern" homes, whether they were individual structures or apartment buildings. The Architects' Union complained that Uzbekistan depended on Russia for steel, cement, wood, trucks, and other supplies, causing the Uzbek branch of Gosplan and the Tashkent Gorispolkom to propose developing a construction material trust to serve the city.[49] In the meantime, materials for "mass" construction were also in short supply, while the scarcity of paper even interrupted the design of individual buildings. Tashkent officials attempted to create a new modern image for the city but lacked the basic infrastructure needed for implementing this plan. Such a large urbanization project required massive investment in the region's transportation and construction industries, which was still years away.

In 1940, Mitkhat Bulatov, the newly appointed Tashkent city architect at the Gorispolkom, was criticized for not "forcing" the construction of tall buildings on the city's main streets. Interestingly, Bulatov was a Tatar, not an Uzbek or a Russian, indicating that the Soviet regime followed the imperial Russian practice of installing Tatar bureaucrats as intermediaries between the state and the local Central Asian population. In Soviet Tashkent, it was a Tatar, an ethnic group traditionally more Russianized and secular than most Uzbeks, who helped to control and refashion Uzbek cities and society, as had his predecessors in the imperial bureaucracy.[50] Furthermore, Bulatov, like Yusupov, was a man of the "class of 1938," who rose up through Soviet educational institutions—in Bulatov's case, the Leningrad Civil Engineering Institute—and came to power after the purges.[51] Nonetheless, despite Bulatov's Soviet background and prominence, a local architect accused him of not monitoring the "eviction" process along Tashkent's reconstructed streets, noting that Uzbek residents were indeed moved from the vicinity of Navoi Street but often to plots on which they built new one-story mud-brick homes.[52]

Barely a year after the general plan had become the official "law" of urban development in Tashkent and Bulatov was put in charge of its implementation, this displeased architect called for its revision because no one followed the plan. The tremendous need to house a growing population and to find shelter for evicted residents clearly compounded the difficulties of transforming the Old City. Frantic appeals by Bulatov and the Gorispolkom to planning agencies, commissariats, and factories to adhere strictly to the plan went unmet, and these institutions built housing and factories wherever it was in their interest to do so. Sometimes they built unsanctioned production spaces right in the city center, where schools or parks had been planned. At other times, they just gave plots of land away for workers to build their own houses. Soviet construction bureaus clearly could not handle all of the tasks associated with the urban renewal. The 1937–1939 "General Plan for the Reconstruction of Tashkent" created a non-Soviet urban space with squalid shantytowns, polluting textile plants, and winding narrow pathways within the borders of the city as an unintended by-product of the effort to create a model socialist city environment with its classical-style buildings, wide avenues, and beautiful parks. As a result, although they had a plan for socialist reconstruction and the city was supposedly becoming "more Soviet," the lives of Tashkent citizens did not necessarily get any better.

Forging a "Cultured City"

Party officials commonly expressed frustration at the difficulties of making Tashkent into a "cultured" city.[53] Despite citywide hygiene education and propaganda campaigns in factories, neighborhoods, and schools, many people remained unable to wash their clothes or clean their living spaces with fresh water. Most residents had access only to contaminated irrigation ditches, and pollution increased as urban growth intensified.[54] The Gorispolkom also proved powerless to remove urban waste (human, industrial, and animal) from the city center.[55] With its filthy workers' barracks, mounds of rotting garbage, and continued reliance on animal-drawn transport, Tashkent was far from an ideal urban space.[56] The rates of preventable and infectious diseases reached high levels, with malaria, tuberculosis, dysentery, and diphtheria as major causes of death in the city.[57] The Tashkent state sanitation inspector singled out food-processing plants, especially meat-packing facilities, where unhygienic practices and factory waste caused serious illness in the city.[58] If planners believed that a model Navoi Street would positively transform the "way of life" of Uzbek residents, would living in urban squalor have the opposite effect?

Planners wanted to make Tashkent into a "cultured" city as part of the Soviet effort to transform workers or peasants into the new Soviet man and woman, who would be strong, hardworking, athletic citizens with good manners. Cultured Tashkenters were its Stakhanovite workers, exemplar students or healthy soldiers who were willing to destroy the enemies of the Soviet Union but also enjoyed evenings of opera and theater. On the other hand, uncultured citizens faced criticism for possessing no desire to improve and educate themselves, thereby remaining outside of Soviet society. Russian urban planners particularly identified Uzbeks for failing to live up to this "cultured" ideal. Russian delegates to the Architects' Union congress in Tashkent in April 1937 attacked the traditional Uzbek teahouse for playing too large a role in the Central Asian lifestyle, occasionally even comparing teahouses to brothels. Rude habits and bad manners, such as spitting, were equated with traditional "Uzbek" behaviors, such as eating with one's hands and relaxing on the floor. All three purportedly thrived in the teahouse environment.[59] Official discourse commonly described old-style teahouses as filled with stuffy air and smoky fumes; visitors "lounged" away their time and employees engaged in illegal trade.[60] Delegates argued that Uzbeks would no longer accept such conditions if they became familiar with the more "healthy" environment of the Tashkent workers' clubs, which the city's Russian-speaking population purportedly visited. Such criticism of native cultures recalls imperial Russian visions of the region and Western European attitudes toward local customs in the colonial world, indicating that negative Soviet interpretations of Asian areas were part of a pan-European perception of Asians and others.[61] It reflected Soviet ideology's place in the history of European thought and tradition.

However, Soviet architects and agitators believed that they could overcome this problem of segregated areas for relaxation if they incorporated nonreligious Uzbek decorations into the clubs, thereby fusing the Soviet workers' club with traditional community institutions to create "red teahouses."[62] These institutions were attached to factories and seen as ideal places to adapt Uzbek traditions to the Soviet era.[63] The red teahouse at the Kaganovich factory was built as a "proper" place for Uzbeks to relax. It was clean, contained newspapers, and showed films, which reportedly were popular among the workers and residents of the adjacent *mahalla*, or Uzbek neighborhood. A red teahouse in Tashkent's Oktiabr district was described as an example of proper Soviet "culture," with musical instruments, clean rugs, and a "red corner," where Soviet literature was available. However, despite their existence and Party activists' celebration of Uzbeks frequenting such places, officials expressed frustration that Central Asians wanted only to drink tea and relax there but not participate in programs that would help them better understand Soviet ideology. Naturally, members of Tashkent's various ethnic groups at times wanted rest without agitation, but Uzbeks came under particular attack for spending too much time in leisure at teahouses, while Russian workers were seen as more disciplined and efficient. Officials clearly were dissatisfied with Uzbeks who were just entering into the new Soviet institutions of Tashkent. Instead, they wanted the full participation of all in the cultural life of these Soviet Uzbek spaces, which would speed up the transformation of Central Asians into Soviet people.

Furthermore, changing Uzbek habits did not simply involve the Russification of Uzbek culture, although that certainly was a part of it. Soviet officials had hallowed images of the ideal Soviet citizen, and all groups—ethnic and social—were supposed to strive to achieve this ideal at least to some extent. "Being Uzbek" was not necessarily the problem in itself. The dilemma was that certain Uzbek cultural traits were defined as backward and were seen as impediments to the modernization of Soviet Central Asian society. Newly arrived urban workers from the Russian countryside, many of them former peasants, also were "backward" and needed to repudiate provincial cultural norms—such as not bathing or remaining under the influence of religion—which Soviet agitators, health workers, and educators identified as uncultured. All provincial traits needed to be excised from the Tashkent urban working class, regardless of whether they were backward Russian, Uzbek, or other customs. In this process, however, Uzbek citizens of the Soviet Union needed to become less particularly Asian in their habits because these Asian markers of uniqueness signified their supposed lack of development and identified them as provincial. If Uzbek residents of Tashkent moved out of their traditional homes, changed their manner of dress, and began to enjoy theater and other forms of high urban culture—just like the Russian workers eventually would—Uzbeks too could advance along the course of history to a higher level of cultural development. Consequently, "modernizing" the Uzbeks was part of a general campaign in the Soviet

Union to refashion humans to meet the idealized view of the citizen of a socialist state and to help all inhabitants of the Soviet Union move closer to realizing communism. Urban Russian workers were at the top of the hierarchy of Soviet society and were closest to this image of "cultured" Soviet citizens, while Russian peasants and "backward" Central Asians occupied inferior positions. This Soviet hierarchical structure dictated that newly arrived workers needed to be less peasantlike, that Siberian peoples needed to be less provincial or "stagnant," and that Uzbeks needed to be less "particular" in order to meet the ideal image of the Soviet citizen. The Soviet state ran an all-encompassing campaign to modernize every area of and each person within the Soviet Union.[64] Creating a model Tashkent was just one part of this project.

A Unified "Park" City

One of the long-standing Soviet goals in Tashkent was the unification of the Uzbek and Russian sections of the city. Planners argued that unification would occur if the reconstruction project erased the physical differences between the two communities. Massive construction that incorporated industrial methods would replace Old Tashkent, an agglomeration of one-story homes. Streets needed widening and lengthening, and, where possible, sections of the Old City were to be connected directly by tram to the major factories of Tashkent.[65] Even if industry had yet to be built in the Old City, Mosoblproekt wanted Uzbek residents to be more closely tied to the technologically advanced areas of Tashkent through main avenues and public transportation systems that gave residents direct access to the modernity that was nearby.

The Architects' Union continued to criticize Western European colonial systems for not adapting and improving conditions for the indigenous residents of colonial cities.[66] For its part, the Party leadership in Moscow wanted all Tashkenters to be touched by the reconstruction project and desired maximum participation of Tashkent's Uzbek residents in the rebuilding process. After all, the Soviet state was creating the new Soviet city for their benefit. However, since officials believed that many Tashkenters did not understand this altruistic aspect of the reconstruction effort, Mosoblproekt proposed that Tashkent follow the example of Moscow, Leningrad, and Kiev, which, "according to the conditions of the reconstruction, possessed the right to evict residents from main streets that were under renovation without providing them with new apartments or paying compensation except for the loss of their personal [and immovable] property."[67] Rebuilding the central areas of the Old City was a top priority, and nothing would be allowed to impede this effort, especially those residents who did not want to live in this refashioned Soviet capital of Uzbekistan. Even so, since the project would focus on Navoi and a few other main streets and would not provide housing or compensation for evicted residents, one could argue that the much-criticized Western European colonial construction was, in fact, exactly the same approach that Soviet planners took. In creating the Stalinist city, they built a new urban space that did not touch everyone in a positive way.

Given Tashkent's location in the desert, the expansion of irrigation canals and the establishment of gardens took on enormous importance. Studying and subsequently altering the city's "micro-climate" became an essential component of the reconstruction plan. This effort showed that the Stalinist state cared for its citizens' health by reducing the impact of summer heat and, more importantly, that it had the power to alter the forces of nature. The general plan for reconstruction of the city called for the expansion of city parkland to make Tashkent one of the "greenest" cities in the entire world.[68] Tashkent's squares and parks would serve as multiethnic meeting points and public areas for demonstrations of Soviet power. Flowing fountains of water were essential for showcasing Soviet technology's irrigation projects as well as for providing an oasis of coolness in the Central Asian heat. Parkland served distinct propaganda purposes in promoting interethnic ties and showcasing Soviet achievement in controlling the desert.

Bulatov early on had criticized Mosoblproekt's program for its lack of a large "Soviet-style park." He thought that Red Square, the symbolic center of power, needed to dominate the city. However, during public holidays, its small size limited the number of military units that could march, while the Government House, a three-story building, was not large enough to serve as the administrative center of the Uzbek SSR.[69] Bulatov also disapproved of Mosoblproekt's failure to incorporate enough greenery and water into the central administrative area of the city.[70] Water needed to flow from fountains, canals, and pools to reflect the beauty of the newly reconstructed city. Describing water as a "mirror" that could both isolate Red Square from the urban bustle and convey its importance as the center of the city, Bulatov called on Mosoblproekt to rework its (largely unchanged) vision of this area.[71] He argued that Red Square did not dominate the city but was dominated by it.[72]

Bulatov's solution to the problem of parkland was to design Komsomol Lake in the newly established Stalin Park of Culture. This well-ordered European-style park, complete with artificial lake (fed by a canal), created a common recreation area for all nationalities of Tashkent. Importantly, the park bordered the traditional Central Asian Besh Agach region on one side and swept toward the Ankhor Canal and the newer Russian part of the city on the other. The complex replaced a dusty, dry, and "haphazardly" constructed settlement of mud houses, shops, and bazaars. As such, the new complex was celebrated in the Soviet Uzbek press as an important stepping stone toward the transformation of Tashkent into a unified, rational, and industrial city, worthy of its status as a republican capital of the Soviet Union. However, once again, the Soviet planners reacted to the practice of building park spaces in the colonial cities of Africa and Asia. As Anthony King has noted, parks and recreation areas in colonial cities were geared to separate populations and to create a barrier between the European sections of the colonial city and the supposed filth of the native quarters. These areas set the ancient apart from the modern. They were designed to awe indigenous residents (and the colonizers) into recognizing the achievement of European societies.[73] In Tashkent, however, officials made a specific effort to note that Komsomol Park was not a division between the two sections of the city but a place where the two communities could come together. Colonial cities divided the urban population into a strict hierarchy, but Soviet planners claimed that socialist cities in Asia, purported to be the epitome of anticolonialism, would unite the region's diverse people into one urban population. In Tashkent's Komsomol Park, sports and recreation facilities were intended to improve the physical health of all Tashkenters, while cultural institutions would help mold their minds. In addition to the lake, with its swimming areas, boats, and bridges, the park included a seventeen-hundred-meter railroad for children. Its trains, except for their small size, were replicas of modern Soviet steam engines and cars; older children served as the railway's conductors, demonstrating that they too could participate in socially useful labor and train for future careers. As Soviet technology transported children around the perimeter of the park, their parents could stroll along tree-shaded paths, climb artificial hills, or watch films in outdoor cinemas.[74] Officially, Komsomol Lake represented great Soviet technological achievement and its potential to reorder nature. It created a desegregated urban area for the rest and relaxation of the multiethnic Tashkent population, all in the name of showing care for the mental and physical health of the Soviet citizen.

In spite of the mantra for industrial construction, Komsomol members used shovels and their hands to create a water park in the center of Tashkent.[75] The Uzbek press celebrated the achievement of these enthusiastic "hero builders," who removed rocks, dug canals, and constructed a lake in the middle of the desert. Using Soviet hydrotechnology and the initiative of its individual members, the Komsomol implemented the first large-scale and most visible aspect of Tashkent's reconstruction plan in record time.[76] Soviet publications and Party officials described these Komsomol members as having been transformed by their work. Altering the urban space purportedly led to personal transformations, but having residents participate in the city's rebirth was viewed as a faster track toward such conversions. Planners believed that residents would, by directly participating in the construction of "modern Tashkent," raise their consciousness and begin to understand the importance of the city's renovation.[77] Elite city planners guided the residents in renovating their city and showed Tashkenters how such modern spaces would affect their lives. The underlying belief was that the more Tashkenters understood about the goals of the city's renovation, the more involved in it they would become. And, the more active they became in transforming the city, the faster their personal transformations would take place.

Final Observations on the Mosoblproekt Proposal

The final reconstruction plan was published in *Arkhitektura SSSR* in 1939.[78] Newspapers and journals subsequently published detailed reconstruction plans for specific years and regions so that residents could understand that fundamental changes were occurring, even if those changes had net yet come to their specific neighborhood. Continuous propaganda on Tashkent's reconstruction plans served to involve the population in the rebuilding of the city and the changing way of life (*byt'*) of the Uzbek capital. Newspaper articles highlighted the abject poverty, the lack of health-care institutions, and the differences between the Old and New Cities before the revolution to provide reasons for the city's continuing problems and to publicize the enormous difficulties that the city allegedly was overcoming.[79] If one only read the newspaper and never stepped outside, one might have thought that Mosoblproekt had already created the socialist city.

The 1939 plan set general rules for reconstruction, called for the establishment of parks and theaters, and declared that the city should provide basic urban services, but it did not include any details on how to implement these changes. The initial phase of the reconstruction was to be completed within five to seven years, but Mosoblproekt did not provide a detailed roadmap of how to proceed in the first few years of socialist reconstruction.[80] The lack of a clear implementation program for the Mosoblproekt proposal and a shortage of qualified architects, engineers, and builders (especially Uzbeks) impeded the realization of the plan. The delayed arrival of material and construction workers from other regions of the Soviet Union also complicated the urban renewal project.[81] The Uzbek people were getting their "own" capital city to showcase their equality in the Stalin era, but it was designed and built by people from outside of Central Asia using labor, equipment, and technology that was imported from Russia. Despite its much-celebrated liberation from imperial Russian colonialism, the capital of Uzbekistan still greatly depended on the metropole for its continued development and modernization.

The Architects' Union also criticized Bulatov for being preoccupied with other tasks. In addition to overseeing the reconstruction of Tashkent, he was involved in the Sovietization of Samarkand and Bukhara, the building of the new Tashkent oblast city of Chirchik, and the construction of the Great Fergana Canal.[82] Indeed, Bulatov had too much work to do to supervise the details of what was being built in each individual region. The centralized structure of the reconstruction plan, in which a single architect and a single bureau of the Gorispolkom were together responsible for the plan's implementation, complicated the realization of the project. Moreover, the fact that Kuznetsov and the Mosoblproekt planning team lived and worked in Moscow made the enactment of the plan more challenging. Kuznetsov appeared in the city occasionally to promote the project before the Gorkom, Gorispolkom, Central Committee, or Architects' Union. Union members particularly resented his absence in Tashkent because Kuznetsov called on them not to "plan for paper" but to be actively involved in the construction of their designs.[83] Kuznetsov's construction site was the entire city of Tashkent, but he too created a plan on paper and then moved back to Moscow to work on other projects. The centralized system of urban planning in the Soviet Union, in which central design agencies planned cities in regions with which they had limited experience, complicated the reconstruction process. Local architects, who had good knowledge of the region and of the difficulties of creating an urban environment in the city, had reduced roles in the development process. Instead, they struggled to understand the guidelines of the general plan and to figure out how they could alter existing buildings to conform to it.[84]

Construction also was impeded by the heavy population concentration of this region, which consisted mostly of Uzbeks; all of the current residents had to be moved before new streets could be built. In addition, the majority of Tashkent's prominent organizations categorically refused to move into the reconstructed Old City, saying that building there was either too difficult or that they did not want to lose their "ties" to the rest of the city.[85] The Old Town did not possess the "comforts" or "culture" of the New City, and the heads of Tashkent's prominent organizations, staffed largely by

Russians, preferred not to work or live in the formerly Muslim section of the city. The language of their complaints implied a fear of being "exiled" to a distant province, not simply across the city. The reconstruction plan, ostensibly created to eliminate personal interests in urban development, could not overcome the collective desires of individual industries and organizations. When called to act, few organizations were willing to make the move across the Ankhor Canal, the traditional division between the Old and the New City. Despite appeals to break down the division between the Uzbek and Russian sections, ethnic segregation persisted. Tashkent planners wanted to unify the city, but residents preferred separate lives, at least at the start of the city's reconstruction effort. However, if Uzbeks were being pushed out of this area during the reconstruction process and Russians did not want to move into a formerly Uzbek area, for whom was this Stalinist city being built? That question was on the minds of many residents but was not publicly voiced for most of the next twenty years.

Finally, Mosoblproekt and the Architects' Union proposed building an outdoor museum devoted to Tashkent's reconstruction; its purpose would be to publicize the goals of the project and make institutions and others understand how they were supposed to participate in the urban renewal effort. Although newspapers covered the fundamental changes that occurred in Tashkent, planners believed that visitors should see actual models of projected streets, factories, and parks. If people understood that the Old City would possess all the comforts of Soviet life, no one would hesitate to move there. Exhibitions on the new Uzbek capital were to be shown throughout the city, but planners were unsure what exactly could be contained in this propaganda. Kuznetsov feared that the city's security would be jeopardized if too much information were disseminated. The need for open information to involve and inform the population collided with the Soviet desire for secrecy. Planners wanted to share the plan with residents but were uncertain of what they should tell them; it was a problem that undermined the overall goal of actively involving city residents in the transformation of urban space and society.

Others believed that preserving Old City structures in an outdoor exhibition would help ideologues explain how the Stalinist city elevated its residents' way of life. As the Uzbek quarter was being rebuilt, certain areas would not be destroyed but instead moved to a central location where an "Old Town model" would be reconstructed.[86] Old Tashkent was to become a museum exhibition, with Soviet officials deciding which aspects of traditional Central Asian life would be put on display. Future generations of Tashkenters then could compare the Old City, with its lack of modern conveniences, to the ideal city of the Stalinist era. The exhibit would explain the status of women, the poor education system, and the lack of health-care institutions in pre-revolutionary Uzbekistan so that visitors could understand how socialist reconstruction improved the city. The museum would allow Tashkent to be totally transformed into a twentieth-century urban space but would still provide residents with a foil against which they could compare the achievements of the Soviet era. Tashkent needed to be modern, but many argued that its new look would be much more impressive if parts of "pre-modern" Tashkent were preserved for comparison. However, the Gorispolkom, represented by Bulatov, opposed the "open-air" museum idea, stating that Tashkent, as a model city, needed to become a fully contemporary urban space in order to transform its residents into new Soviet men and women. If this transformation were to succeed, residents did not need reminders of the past in their everyday environment. If Tashkenters wanted to see how Uzbeks lived before the revolution, they could simply go to Bukhara, argued Bulatov.[87] Tashkent's physical space would need to convey its complete modernity in order to refashion Soviet life in Central Asia. Bulatov clearly had faith in the ability of idealized urban areas to transform society. This tension between the desire to preserve parts of the Old Town and the wish to do away with traditional Central Asian life in the capital of the Uzbek SSR continued throughout the Soviet era.

In the end, the debate over the museum was moot. If one wanted to see the conditions and way of life of Old Tashkent, one could just walk beyond the main thoroughfares, which themselves did not yet resemble model socialist avenues. Tashkent was supposed to follow Moscow's example as the "laboratory for urban planning" for Central Asia, but the experiment was faltering. Despite criticism that Bulatov, the Gorispolkom, and the Architects' Union had failed to implement the general plan, they had neither the time, nor the money, nor the power to force factories and individual organizations to follow Mosoblproekt's guidelines—until World War II transformed Tashkent in an unforeseen way. The Nazi invasion of the Soviet Union temporarily ended the socialist reconstruction of the Uzbek capital. The onslaught on Tashkent did not come from the German army but from Soviet evacuees and refugees who "invaded" Tashkent from Moscow, Leningrad, Kiev, and Minsk. The general reconstruction plan did not foresee the need to cope with this tremendous influx of refugees or the evacuation of the defense industry to the Uzbek capital. The only solution for these new problems was simple: put the general reconstruction plan back on the shelf and start again from scratch.

4   ◈   WAR AND EVACUATION

World War II brought about a demographic and social catastrophe for all peoples of the Soviet Union, whether they were located near the front lines or on the home front a great distance from actual combat. After a disastrous start, the Soviet Union ultimately won the war, but its economy, land, and people were devastated. When Hitler's armies invaded on June 22, 1941, they swiftly overcame front-line defenses and marched toward the interior of the country. Soviet cities fell in rapid succession: Riga and Minsk in late June, Smolensk in July, and Kiev in September. German and Finnish troops encircled Leningrad in late summer and early autumn, beginning a nine-hundred-day blockade of the city on September 26 and causing years of mass starvation, disease, and death in the second-largest city of the Soviet Union.[1] The Soviet capital itself was threatened in October 1941. The orderly socialist state, with its planned towns, planned growth, and planned military defenses, embarked on a five-year period of disarray that included tremendous military and civilian population losses—an estimated 26.6 million deaths during the war.[2]

The entire Soviet economy was mobilized for the war effort. On June 22, 1941, an emergency labor draft went into effect.[3] Starting in December 1941, defense industry employees were considered to be "mobilized" for the duration of the war.[4] Shirking one's labor obligations, even for a few hours, was a criminal offense across the Soviet Union. Factory work, agriculture, education, medical care, and a plethora of other fields were militarized to a previously unknown extent. As the situation on the front deteriorated in the fall of 1941, Soviet workers dismantled defense factories and put them on eastbound trains headed to such distant cities as Kuibyshev, Chkalov, Stalingrad, Alma-Ata, Novosibirsk, Tomsk, and Tashkent.[5] Intellectuals, artists, families of high-level Party officials, and other members of the Soviet elite departed front-line cities for the relative safety of the home front. In late 1941 and early 1942, Tashkent saw the arrival of prominent literary, theater, and academic figures, including Anna Akhmatova, Nadezhda Mandel'stam, Kornei Chukovskii, Aleksei Tolstoi, and Solomon Mikhoels, as well as industrial workers from airplane, bomb, and tank factories. More than 157,803 people moved to the Uzbek capital in 1941 alone, causing enormous strain on the city's urban infrastructure.[6] Wartime Tashkent suddenly possessed both a "cultured" citizenry and the skilled working class that it previously lacked, but the region tried in vain to absorb this increased population and more diversified economy. Its prewar urban plan for rational growth quickly went by the wayside as the city struggled to respond to its new wartime role as a vital industrial center with tens of thousands of refugees trying to survive in a hungry, disease-ridden, and overcrowded city. In short, the war fundamentally changed the course of Tashkent's urban development, and Soviet "rational" planning played almost no part in this transformation.

Preparing Tashkent for Invasion

Memoirs and historical accounts of Tashkent at war evoke hardship and discomfort.[7] Native Tashkenters and those new to the city recall difficult—at times atrocious—living conditions, with people crowded into dirty and damp apartments, mud structures, schools, factory buildings, and stables. Weakened by an inadequate supply of food, the population lived under the constant threat of disease and death. Even so, the fate of Tashkenters was much better than that of the residents in the European cities of the Soviet Union, who were subjected to brutal occupation, ethnic cleansing, mass starvation, forced labor in Nazi camps, executions, and constant bombardment.[8] Furthermore, in the Uzbek capital, thousands of kilometers from the battlefield, the war had little direct impact on the city in 1941. At an Uzbek

Central Committee meeting in October 1941, Butov, a Party secretary in Uzbekistan, expressed worry that the distant conflict had not yet changed the attitudes of the city's residents. He remarked that few "signs" of war existed in Tashkent and that officials needed to better rally the populace for the war effort: "walk through Tashkent and you can see that there are few war posters, and slogans are almost nonexistent with the exception of a few [on] individual windows."[9] Other Party leaders concurred that "the war in Tashkent is not being felt much" and that residents failed to understand that the Soviet Union was in a "life or death" situation.[10] According to Party documents, Tashkenters complained about petty issues, such as late trams and a poor supply of bread, while their compatriots in Ukraine and Russia experienced the horror of the front lines. Party officials clearly worried that Tashkenters, particularly those with few personal ties to regions under direct threat—in other words the city's Central Asian population—simply viewed the war as a distant problem with little impact on their daily lives. Soviet officials initially identified Central Asians as a weak link in the Soviet home front's defenses. In a time of peril for the Soviet project, would Tashkent's Uzbeks fight for the Soviet Union? This question was on the minds of local officials who embarked on an all-out campaign to tie the war directly to the residents of Uzbekistan in any way that they could.

However, Party officials frequently found themselves in the difficult position of explaining the poor progress of the war to a population that had little first-hand knowledge of the conflict. At the same time, local leaders were cautious about spreading alarm among the population over the disastrous Soviet response to the invasion. One Tashkenter's complaints illustrated this dilemma that faced Soviet propaganda officials in Central Asia and caused concern in the summer of 1941. This city resident noted that the Informburo had announced the need for a twelve-hour workday but doubted that it would ever announce the actual number of German soldiers killed or wounded. Another man's question caused concern for Party propagandists when he asked why, if the war was going according to plan, the Red Army just gave away "city after city" to the Nazis.[11] Tashkenters, unsure of the information that the state provided, were left to the mercy of rumors, including panicked reports of an imminent attack on Uzbekistan to transform it into a British colony. Tashkent was in an information vacuum, with no one knowing what actually was happening to the Soviet Union.[12] The Soviet obsession with secrecy, compounded by the war situation, clashed with the importance of telling the population what was occurring in the distant border regions and of building up popular support for the war. Because German bombs were not falling inside Tashkent's city limits, Party officials believed that local residents did not have the same understanding of the threat as did Kievans, Muscovites, Leningraders, or Odessans, but they also failed to provide the basic information many residents wanted and even needed to know.[13]

Nonetheless, despite these difficulties, the Uzbek Central Committee reported to Moscow on June 30, 1941, that outpourings of support for the Red Army were under way in Uzbekistan, especially in Tashkent and Samarkand oblasts. In the first week of the war, Tashkent oblast alone had 932 volunteers for the Red Army.[14] By July 2, the city of Tashkent had received 3,000 applications from local residents, including women, to join the army, while almost 1,500 people studied urban defense in the initial days of the conflict. Tashkent women also created sanitation brigades and organized study circles and inspection teams to ensure personal hygiene and urban cleanliness in wartime.[15] With men going to the front, women were expected to take on greater responsibilities to guarantee that the city of Tashkent continued to function. Likewise, women in Samarkand demanded that factories begin training courses to enable them to replace their husbands and brothers on the factory floor. By August 1941, more than 11,000 Samarkand women—Uzbeks and Tajiks included—had reportedly completed courses in metalworking, lathe operation, and tractor driving, all previously male-dominated professions.[16] This movement of women into productive labor was seen as an early victory for a Central Asia at war. In this regard, Uzbekistan was not much different from regions that were closer to the front lines. Popular outpourings of support for the state occurred throughout the Soviet Union, with thousands of citizens, regardless of age, ethnicity, race, or gender, volunteering for service on the front or the home front.[17]

And so, despite complaints of Party officials that Central Asians had failed to respond to the invasion, many residents—Uzbek and Russian, male and female—expressed their loyalty and patriotism to the state through public actions and displays of support for the Red Army. They rallied around the Soviet state and offered themselves or their children to fight and shed blood in the defense of socialism.[18] Alarmingly for local officials, however, was the fact that the "heroic support" in response to the war came mostly from two oblasts—Samarkand and Tashkent. Fergana and Andijan looked particularly troublesome to the Party and the NKVD, as did other provincial areas. Residents of these regions reportedly had not answered the call to arms in numbers as high as propagandists believed they should have, indicating that feelings of allegiance to the Soviet state were less strong outside the two largest—and most "Soviet"—cities of the republic.

Officials also expressed concern that the invasion brought out anti-

Soviet elements in these distant regions of the Uzbek SSR, with *kulaks*, German sympathizers, spies, counterrevolutionaries, Basmachis, and White Guardists suddenly appearing again with the ultimate goal of defeating the Red Army from the rear. The state began to look for enemies in its midst and, with its intense focus on uncovering such ideologically incorrect sentiments, it could undoubtedly find instances of anti-Soviet hostility when it actively sought it out. As a result, indications that people—especially those outside the two main cities of the republic—would not fight for the Soviet state appear to have proliferated between June and September 1941, according to Party reports.[19] And yet, by "uncovering" the presence of enemies in Central Asia, propagandists also underscored the ideological belief that the Soviet Union faced danger from all sides and that the Uzbek SSR's distance from Germany would not necessarily save Tashkent from the hostilities. By raising the threat level in the region, officials were not only expressing doubt about the "Sovietness" of some residents of Uzbekistan but also trying to firm up the patriotism of others.

Furthermore, although Party communiqués described Tashkent as responding "better" than other Uzbek regions, its show of loyalty still was not strong enough for many Soviet officials. There were reports of residents gossiping about the strength of the German army and the weakness of the Soviet military. Soviet officials expressed concern about "defeatist" attitudes among the urban population. Two Russian hydroelectric station engineers from Tashkent, for example, were caught stating in July 1941 that Germany would win the war because the "German army is strong—it consists of one nation, of pureblood Germans, but the Red Army is weaker because it is multinational."[20] These engineers believed that lacking any common bonds beyond socialism, the numerous ethno-national groups of the Soviet Union could not come together to fight the enemy. The two men were subsequently arrested for their comment, but their nationality indicates that Uzbeks were not the only ones whose loyalty may have been in doubt. The much-touted "unification" of the Uzbek capital, a dual Russian/Uzbek city, into a harmonious urban space clearly had not yet occurred. Forging a "Soviet city," for both Uzbeks and Russians, took more effort than merely rearranging geographic space.

NKVD and city officials actively looked for and reported on numerous cases of "defeatism" and avoidance of Red Army mobilization among Tashkent residents, usually focusing on Uzbeks.[21] In fairness, this tendency to shirk military service was not an ethnically Uzbek phenomenon; it even engulfed Moscow, where many Russians avoided the draft or hid their connections to the Party in the early days of the war.[22] But, in Tashkent, Party reports highlighted Uzbeks for avoiding the military draft, indicating that there was particular concern that Central Asians did not understand the need to defend the Soviet Union's distant borders and that Uzbeks could be a weak link in the Soviet Union's defense.[23] Officials thus began to speak of the importance of explaining that Red Army service was mandatory for all male Soviet citizens, regardless of ethnic background and the increasing war propaganda among Uzbek residents of the city. Officials also turned their attention to Uzbek women, urging them to enter the factory, not necessarily because of Soviet ideology but to help protect the lives of their men, who were destined for the front. In the past, Soviet ideology struggled against traditional Central Asian culture and the extended Uzbek family structure. Now, it aimed to use that family structure and the sense of responsibility to one's relatives to pull local women out of the home and into Soviet wartime activity.

This constant monitoring of the Tashkent population certainly enabled officials to express concern that harsh critics of the regime lived in their midst. Still, the fact that the state actively looked for expressions of defeatism or anti-Soviet sentiments once again contributed to the perception that Tashkenters had not yet realized the peril of the conflict and likely contributed to this sense that Uzbeks were yet not trusted citizens of the Soviet Union. A group of Uzbek men, for example, faced criticism for volunteering for the Red Army after they explained their decision to do so by claiming they were "starving" in Tashkent and had nothing to lose since Party officials would let the city starve to ensure the survival of Slavic regions of the Soviet state.[24] German forces were far from the city, but Party leaders worried that such statements—even when Uzbeks made the correct decisions for the wrong ideological reasons—indicated city residents' failure to comprehend the Nazi threat properly. The state then redoubled its efforts to build support for the war effort with a specific focus on tying a European war to a distant Asian population.

In the early days of the war in Tashkent, central Party officials built war propaganda on images of Russian nationalism and Russian historical figures—particularly the great military victories of Alexander Nevsky and Mikhail Kutuzov, who had defeated two previous invaders of Russia—the Teutonic Knights and Napoleon, respectively.[25] In many ways, these early propaganda campaigns mirrored the urban planning projects of the 1930s in that both were run by officials from the center and made little effort to adapt the basic program to the non-Russian regions. Still, like many of the urban planners, wartime propagandists in Tashkent quickly found themselves in a difficult bind because the centralized propaganda did not meet the needs of the local culture. Tashkent propagandists feared that Central Asians would not relate to such images and might not fight for Russia alone. In closed Party meetings, Uzbek officials questioned the effectiveness of using Russian nationalism to inspire martial feelings in a multiethnic population, especially when many of its ethnic groups did not always get along.[26] Moreover, for a population that lacked first-hand knowledge of the conflict, local Party officials argued that propaganda needed to reinforce the importance of Russia's survival to Central Asia and not just repeat the same motifs that were used in Soviet war speeches elsewhere.

Wartime propaganda in Tashkent soon began to underscore the idea that Uzbeks, as free and equal citizens of the Soviet Union, had the same responsibilities to the Soviet state as other nationalities and that fighting the Nazi threat thousands of miles from Tashkent was necessary to defend the new-found independence of the Uzbek people and their capital city. Newspaper articles also focused on the brutality Nazi forces would inflict on Central Asians if they successfully captured Moscow and sent their forces into Uzbekistan. The Soviet capital was seen as the last defense of Tashkent. If Moscow fell, it would be only a short time before the Nazi armies swept through Central Asia. Public speeches by Party leaders presented the Slavic core of the Soviet Union as the barrier that protected the Uzbek people from Nazi barbarity. Uzbeks learned that the "Russian home is your home, the Belorussian home is the Uzbek home. Your street begins in Belorussia and your *mahalla* begins in Ukraine."[27] The German path to Tashkent, Samarkand, and Bukhara traversed Minsk, Kiev, and Moscow, and Uzbek participation in the battles for these cities was essential to keep German "paws" out of Central Asia's historic cities and abundant cotton fields.[28] In defending Russian cities, Uzbeks learned they would be protecting their own homeland, history, and culture.

To underscore the threat against the Uzbek people, newspapers chronicled the horrific actions of "fascist cannibals," who murdered and tortured Soviet children, raped girls in front of their families, and buried or burned wounded soldiers alive. A published "Letter of the Uzbek people to Uzbek soldiers" reminded all Central Asians that "Hitlerite bandits long to defile the honor of our wives and daughters" and that it was imperative to "chop off the bloody paw of the monster that also is reaching toward Uzbekistan."[29] Efforts to promote fear of a ferocious and dehumanized enemy remained prominent throughout the war and gradually focused more on Uzbek themes.[30] In propaganda geared to Uzbekistan, writers made it clear that the enemy would not be satisfied solely with capturing Russian land or raping Ukrainian women. In building up a threat to Uzbek women, Soviet ideologists again tried to tie traditional notions of gender and the Uzbek family, which they had attempted to undermine only a few short years before, to the Soviet Union as a whole. Soviet patriotism, pride in Soviet Uzbek achievement, and the real fear of what Nazi rule would inflict on the Uzbek people were merged together to urge Uzbeks to fight for the Soviet Union.

Soviet war propagandists also attempted to localize the war through the use of specific Central Asian historical motifs, which was very similar to their use of Russian historical examples of expelling invaders from the Soviet Union at large. In discussing the need to create Uzbek national army units (which, in turn, supposedly provided an important propaganda tool), delegates to a Tashkent Obkom meeting in 1941 spoke of the need to use historical models of Uzbek military heroism, especially Timur Malik, an "Uzbek warrior" who defended Central Asians against the Mongol invasion for eleven years.[31] As the war dragged on, Uzbek authors, cinematographers, and dramatists produced works on the historical defense of Central Asia against "Arab or Mongol conquerors," on the life of the Central Asian poet Navoi, and on the successful campaigns against the Basmachis, all in an effort to combine Soviet and pre-Soviet motifs.[32] Propaganda speeches also popularized the architectural past of Uzbekistan. Soviet publications began to celebrate the "centuries-old" traditions of Central Asian construction and architecture, despite the recent history of the Tashkent reconstruction plan, which attempted to banish such structures from within the city limits.[33] Propaganda still declared Amir Timur (Tamerlane) or the emirs of Bukhara to be the historical oppressors of the Uzbek people, but it began to acknowledge the importance of safeguarding the historic cities and architectural monuments that these men had created. The new propaganda glorified and defended Central Asian cities' pre-Soviet traits, a remarkable change from the prewar era.

Attacks from the Air

Local leaders also sought to increase awareness of the Nazi threat in Tashkent by publicizing the dangers of air attacks and spies who had infiltrated the "deep home front" of the Soviet Union. On the purely functional level, air raid drills and civilian defense training increased security in the city and made each resident aware of his or her responsibilities in the defense of Tashkent. In addition to preparing residents for an attack, defense preparedness training had important propaganda purposes in raising public acknowledgment of the Nazi danger to the Soviet state. These drills emphasized that Tashkent easily could become a front-line city in the new conditions of twentieth-century air warfare. In the fall of 1942, with the front's eastward approach into the Caucasus and the Kuban, Soviet officials announced that Tashkent's distance from the battlefield no longer guaranteed its safety and that both the state and the citizens had responsibilities to protect the city and its infrastructure and economic resources from attack.[34] Tashkent's canals, transportation arteries, and factories—particularly those built under Soviet power—were described as particularly likely targets of German air forces or terrorist acts.[35] The technological achievements of Soviet Tashkent—like the historic monuments of the region—were coveted by the enemy and thus in danger. By merging the modern urban spaces of Tashkent with the traditional ones of Central Asia, officials hoped that city residents would respond to the threat.

Civil defense training programs initially were geared to males born in 1923 and 1924 and provided future soldiers with basic military skills. These courses trained Tashkenters with real machine guns, tanks, or grenades to simulate war conditions and create a heightened alert in the region.[36] The general assumption was that if residents understood and experienced real-life military training, they would be better prepared for military service and appreciate what their relatives did (or were about to do) on the battlefield, making the danger of war more personal. Propagandists constantly paraded the heroism of Uzbek soldiers on the front lines, believing that if residents of Uzbekistan knew of the sacrifices that Central Asians had already made, they too would support the war effort more actively and work that much harder on the factory floor or collective farm field.[37] These defense training courses and propaganda on Uzbek Red Army heroes sought to inspire residents to preserve scarce resources, increase military production, and make other sacrifices, just as soldiers did on daily basis at the front lines.

As time went on, though, city leaders moved to actively involve more women in these programs in an effort to pull them out of their homes and put them to work in productive wartime activities. They again tied these messages to a sense of family and community obligation to help support Uzbek fighters on the front lines. Uzbek newspapers frequently chronicled the exploits of Uzbek fighters to highlight the fact that Uzbek lives were in danger. In 1943, *Qizil O'zbekiston* profiled Rahima Olimova, a Komsomol member from Bukhara who was trained as a nurse in Uzbekistan and went off to the Ukrainian front to provide medical care to Soviet soldiers. The article describes the human suffering and sacrifice that she saw in war and the extraordinary actions she, an Uzbek woman, took to care for wounded military men. If Rahima Olimova could take care of the wounded on the front, the women of Tashkent, it was hoped, would follow her example and enter into productive labor at one of the numerous military hospitals in the region. This plea was tied to traditional notions of female labor in the hope that Uzbek women would adapt their role as caretakers of their own families to caretakers of the extended Soviet family, thereby entering modern Soviet institutions during the war. Soviet war propaganda was multileveled and complex, stating that if one was not inspired to fight for the Soviet system or against a threat to Central Asia or Russia, one certainly could become motivated to support a brother, father, or son whose life was in danger on the battlefield.

With its able-bodied men at the front, the Soviet state also expected women to make up for the loss of male employees in all sectors of the economy. However, in Uzbekistan, this campaign to involve women in the war effort was complicated by traditional Uzbek cultural, religious, and family traditions and by the difficulty of communicating across language and cultural barriers. Workers from the Tashkent Textile Kombinat played an important role in setting the example for women of the city to become trained factory workers, participate in socially productive labor, and exceed production quotas.[38] Muhabbat Nasyrova, a female Stakhanovite from the Textile Kombinat, spoke at a meeting of six thousand workers on the *kombinat* grounds in early July 1941, declaring that "we, women and girls of Uzbekistan, will defend our Motherland with all measures and, if it demands, take arms into our hands. Sacredly we will fulfill the order of Comrade Stalin to work selflessly to overfulfill the . . . plan and to give all our power to help the valiant Red Army to destroy the fascist bandits."[39] Elderly housewives and young girls were called to participate in the war effort through the sewing and collection of warm clothing, blankets, and other supplies that soldiers (and soldiers' families, especially refugees or evacuees in Tashkent) needed.[40] Prominent women made pleas to their Uzbek sisters to care for wounded soldiers and orphaned refugees in addition to, not in place of, entering the industrial labor force.[41]

Despite claims that thousands of women had answered the call to work in the factories, private Party communiqués show that many Uzbek women preferred to take part in the war effort through traditionally gender-specific tasks, such as caring for orphaned children, knitting articles of clothing, and gathering supplies for the troops. The Tashkent Obkom reported on October 20, 1941, that the percentage of new female Uzbek factory workers remained low. At the Tashselmash factory, only 10 out of 1,353 female workers hired since the start of the war were Uzbek.[42] Three years later, a Central Committee report noted that the percentage of Uzbeks in heavy industry had increased, but their share was still too small in the defense industry, where only 10 percent of the workers were of ethnic Uzbek background.[43] High levels of labor turnover in Tashkent complicated recruitment efforts. In 1943, 21,037 new workers joined the defense industry of Tashkent, but 22,649 defense workers (almost one-half the total number of defense workers) left factories that year alone—a statistic blamed on both supposedly irresponsible Uzbeks with poor labor discipline and irresponsible factory directors who did not improve worker living conditions or help Central Asian workers rise above entry-level positions.[44] Calls to defend the "equality of Soviet women" and Uzbek female "liberation" by becoming defense workers or tractor drivers were not always effective because most Uzbeks were simply used as unskilled laborers, while those of other ethnic groups—usually Russians, Ukrainians, or Jews—climbed the ranks of the factory hierarchy.[45] Every Soviet citizen had a role in the war, but that role often was determined by location, age, gender, or ethnicity.

Furthermore, not all Central Asian women wanted this wartime liberation or were comfortable with the new roles that the state demanded of them.[46] Many entered productive work temporarily out of urgent financial or familial necessity. They stopped working when they got the medicine or food their family needed or they switched factories in search of better conditions or access to scarce wartime commodities, such as flour, clothing, and soap. But, for some, entering into productive labor remained a dangerous act. In the Tashkent satellite city of Yangi-Yol, a husband attempted to stab his wife after she tried to attend a tractor-driving course, and another tried to murder his wife when she refused to drop out of a similar training program.[47] Central Asian women remained in a precarious position—they attracted criticism and potential punishment from the state for not participating fully in essential wartime labor obligations. Some suffered psychological distress if they did not "do something" while their male relatives fought and died on the front. However, they could face even harsher retribution from family members if they complied with the state and entered into socially productive labor outside the home against the wishes of their husbands, fathers, or fathers-in-law.[48] Wartime Uzbek women were caught between a polity that no longer just demanded but now urgently needed their active participation in society and a conservative culture that strove to preserve traditional roles. Unlike the situation in the 1930s, however, it was not just Soviet ideology that was breaking down traditional cultural barriers but also wartime exigencies, economic desperation, and external threats that state officials and Central Asian families both recognized.

Despite being in this bifurcated role, many prominent female Uzbek Stakhanovites and Komsomol workers remained public figures and served as models of sacrifice and devotion to the war effort. They proudly showed their loyalty through long hours of factory work, training new Soviet workers, learning nursing skills, and even traveling to the front to meet with Uzbek soldiers. Muhabbat Nasyrova, the Stakhanovite worker from the Textile Kombinat, participated in one of the official Uzbek delegations that traveled to meet with soldiers on the battlefield, brought them presents, and demonstrated the unity between those on the front and their fellow citizens who labored diligently at home in Central Asia. Nasyrova, R. Hamidova, a Kirov district Komsomol secretary from Tashkent, and B. Mirbabaeva, the first female Uzbek locomotive driver—all symbolic positions that illustrated the achievement of the women's liberation movement in the Soviet Union—journeyed with a group of male Stakhanovites and Party leaders to the western front in December 1941. In addition to delivering food and warm clothes, Nasyrova spoke to both male and female soldiers and described how the entire Soviet people had been united together behind the Red Army to defeat the Nazi threat. She and others in the delegation witnessed the horrors that the German army inflicted on the Soviet people—rape, torture, murder, and the physical destruction of Soviet cities, and recounted this first-hand experience in print.[49] An underlying goal of these trips was to show that if Nasyrova and other women could handle the dangers in the front-line areas, as soldiers did on a daily basis, then the home-front population, particularly nonworking Uzbek women, could certainly contribute to the war effort in less dramatic ways. In doing so, they were not simply defending modern "Soviet" society but also helping to preserve their own city and community.

Yuldash Akhunbabaev, chair of the Uzbek Sovnarkom, underscored the importance of Uzbek participation in the war effort, which included Uzbek workers who "fought" in the factories of Tashkent so that Uzbek soldiers on the front would be better armed than the enemy.[50] All efforts, especially in the early years of the war, were made to tie Uzbekistan closely to the battlefield. In return, newspapers published "thank-you letters" from soldiers on the front who wanted to express gratitude to the workers in Uzbekistan for their hard work. The message was clear—to win the war, the state had to be completely mobilized and unified. For the Uzbek capital, this meant that Tashkenters fought on the front, visited the front, and worked for the front. Lectures, newspaper articles, and posters constantly reminded workers that the war was not a distant conflict and that Uzbeks had intrinsic interests in what occurred on the battlefield.

A "Letter of the Uzbek people to Uzbek soldiers," published in *Pravda, Pravda Vostoka,* and *Qizil O'zbekiston* in the second year of the war, summed up most of the propaganda motifs that existed in wartime Uzbekistan. It reminded Uzbek soldiers and the residents of Uzbekistan of the horrors that the German army continually inflicted on Soviet citizens in Russia, Ukraine, and the Caucasus region. It informed Tashkenters of the mass rape and murder that would occur if Nazi forces were able to approach the city, and it reminded Uzbeks of the industrial and agricultural achievements that the Third Reich hoped to steal from them. The war against fascism was not simply a matter of the life and death of the Soviet Union but also of the very existence of Uzbekistan and the Uzbek people. The letter stated that the German army was

attempting to transform our Motherland into a slave market, to sell the Uzbeks like animals. They are trying to re-establish the power of khans and emirs and do all so that in place of water, the blood and tears of innocent orphans will flow through the great canals that we built with our hands. They want to erase Samarkand, the place where the Great Uzbek poet Navoi and the Uzbek scientist Ulug Beg worked, from the face of the earth; they want to lay waste to Fergana, where Mukhimi composed his inspirational poetry; and to set fire to Bukhara, on the walls of which the great Uzbek hero, Tarabi, struggled for freedom against the Mongol invaders. . . . Hitler intends to destroy our literature, our art, our songs, and our national culture.[51]

Propaganda attempted to persuade Uzbeks that the struggle against the Nazis was not just a war in the defense of socialism. It was a war to protect humanity from the horrific crimes of a dehumanized invader; it was a conflict with an enemy that, if left unchecked, was determined to cleanse Uzbekistan of its people, cities, history, and culture. Central Asia's past, and its bright present and future under socialism and alongside Russia, came together in this effort to mobilize the population. Soviet agitators and propagandists urgently attempted to particularize the war for Central Asians. Informing them of the heroism of their "ethnic brothers" in battle and reminding them of the ferocious German opponent, who wanted to extinguish the "bright" lives of all Soviet peoples—particularly Uzbeks—and ravage all Soviet cities, were the primary means of highlighting the war's direct importance to the people of the Central Asian home front.

The War Arrives in Tashkent

By the winter of 1941–1942, propaganda was no longer the principal way that distant Central Asians were experiencing war. With the evacuation crisis, declining food resources, and rising disease rates, the war suddenly arrived at Tashkent's doorstep, even if German tanks never got anywhere near the Uzbek capital. One of the main reasons for the victory of the Soviet Union over Nazi Germany was the ability of Soviet industry to produce tanks, guns, planes, and ammunition in greater numbers than its German counterpart could. This was a remarkable fact considering that the vast majority of defense-related enterprises originally were located in the more industrialized areas of the European Soviet Union, where the harshest battles of the war took place. Although the human costs of the evacuation were tremendous, with large numbers of Soviet citizens left behind or dying of infectious diseases, one of the early success stories of the Soviet war effort was the rapid transportation of industrial enterprises from regions near the front lines to the Urals, Central Asia, and Siberia. By moving entire industrial facilities and parts of their workforces from the European front lines to the rear, the Soviet Union was able not only to sustain but also eventually to increase production levels for defense materiel and, in the process, build a base of heavy industry in the distant, mostly agricultural areas of the Soviet east. In the western regions of the Soviet Union, the war brought devastation, while in Siberia and Central Asia, the conflict brought opportunities for unprecedented industrial growth.

After the Nazi invasion and the disastrous Soviet response, the Central Committee and Sovnarkom quickly recognized the need to move valuable industrial assets away from the advancing German army. On June 24, 1941, they set up the Evacuation Council to prioritize and direct the evacuation of industrial enterprises, skilled labor, and prominent citizens of the Soviet Union. Initially chaired by Lazar Kaganovich (until July 16, 1941, when he was replaced by N. M. Shvernik), the Evacuation Council consisted of eighty to eighty-five representatives from the Central Committee, Sovnarkom, Gosplan, and republic-level Sovnarkoms. The State Defense Committee (GKO), established on June 30, 1941, with Stalin and his principal lieutenants Molotov, Malenkov, Beria, and Voroshilov as members, oversaw the work of the Evacuation Council.[52] Together, the council and the GKO coordinated the evacuation of more than fifteen hundred factories from front-line cities to the eastern regions of the Soviet Union in 1941.[53] In August 1941, Tashkent acquired its first evacuated factory, Leningrad's Vulkan agricultural machine production plant, which had resumed production in the Uzbek capital by the end of October.[54] The main rush of evacuated industry into the Uzbek SSR occurred in two phases—autumn 1941 to spring 1942 and again in the late summer and fall of 1942.[55] Local officials from the Tashkent Gorispolkom and Gosplan UzSSR had the task of developing plans for receiving factories and their workers, identifying sites for reestablishing industries, allocating cars, trucks, and horses to transport industrial equipment from the train depot, coordinating a plan for housing and feeding evacuated workers, and identifying potential local labor pools.

The loss of large numbers of qualified local administrators and skilled male workers to the Red Army complicated the implementation of the evacuation. The Evacuation Council took overall responsibility for deciding which factories to transport, the number of railway cars needed, and where the factory would be relocated. Then, it turned the evacuation over to the Sovnarkom that had control over each enterprise and to the republic-level Sovnarkoms or central committees from which and to which the evacuated institution was transferred. The responsibility for implementing the evacuation was parceled out to a variety of local and union-level institutions (Commissariats of Trade, of Health, and of various industries).[56] However, many district Party leaders, new to their jobs, were unfamiliar with their responsibilities, which grew and changed as decrees and decisions were passed down from various agencies. The multiplicity of organizations involved on the central, republic, region, and city levels, combined with the rapidity of the German advances, meant that the state was unable to develop a large-scale union-wide evacuation plan. Consequently, despite the fact that GKO decisions took precedence over all others, the evacuation proceeded in an unpredictable manner.

Most of the research and cultural institutions evacuated to Uzbekistan were resettled in the capital, the city with the most modern infrastructure and the best-educated population in the republic. Similarly, the Uzbek capital received the vast majority of evacuated heavy industries—machine building, aviation, and train car construction—that were needed for defense work. Secondary cities of the Uzbek SSR, such as Namangan or Margilan, received the majority of light industry, such as food processing and textiles, indicating that the capital was and would remain the most economically advanced city during this period of intense industrialization.[57]

However, since decisions on where to place individual factories were frequently changed, local officials often were unable to identify locations and to prepare sites in advance for the reestablishment of evacuated enterprises. There were severe communication problems between the central state officials directing the evacuation and those in the regions into which evacuees and equipment were sent. Tashkent officials repeatedly complained throughout 1941 and early 1942 of the unexpected arrival of equipment from factories that they did not expect and often wondered what had happened to institutions that were destined for Tashkent but never arrived.[58] The prewar notion of rational urban planning quickly became difficult to implement as officials in Uzbekistan reacted to the continuously changing circumstances of war.

In November 1941, Gosplan UzSSR asked the Evacuation Council for detailed information on each evacuated institution destined for Uzbekistan so that it, republic-level commissariats, and the Gorispolkom could prepare for these new institutions.[59] This information ideally would allow factory directors and district officials to identify the number of square meters of production or storage space that could be used for evacuated enterprises, whether local structures could handle the demands of heavy industry, which potential sites contained heating, electricity, or water, and how close the facilities were to tram stops and the railroad. Gosplan attempted to develop a rational city plan for implementing the evacuation of industry into Tashkent—an action that occurred only five months into the war, after factories already had begun to arrive.[60] However, Gosplan relied on sporadic information and lacked time to prepare for the new arrivals. Planning for Tashkent's wartime industrialization quickly became impossible. Instead, Party officials, architects, and engineers had to show personal initiative in their response to the often unexpected arrival of important military factories, cultural institutions, and prominent citizens.[61]

The primary goal of the evacuation was to preserve the defense industry and the economic resources of the Soviet state; scant attention was paid to the safety or survival of people. This fact is underscored in the history of Moscow Aviation Factory no. 84, an airplane production facility. Its director explained in December 1941 that he could evacuate only 50 percent of his factory's employees from Moscow in mid-October, when the outlook for the Soviet capital looked particularly bleak. Of these evacuees, 5 percent never arrived in Tashkent and were presumably lost along the way either by being left behind at train stops or dying in transit. Nonetheless, his was considered a somewhat "successful" evacuation because much of the equipment needed to produce planes had made it to Tashkent and not fallen into Nazi hands. However, the failure to take enough skilled industrial workers soon complicated the resumption of production in Tashkent. The evacuation "saved" this factory from physical devastation, but it then had less than half the trained workforce necessary to produce the planes the Soviet Union so desperately needed.[62]

The need to evacuate plants near the front in great haste also meant that the disassembling of factories and the loading of equipment onto trains occurred in a disorganized manner. The hurried evacuation caused valuable machines to arrive in Tashkent broken or with missing parts. Other times, critical components were put onto the wrong train cars and did not arrive in Tashkent because they were lost, delayed, or diverted to another city along the way. These problems also impeded the reconstruction efforts and the commencement of military production in Central Asia. Aviation Factory no. 84 never received one hundred train cars of equipment despite its evacuation experience having been considered relatively good.[63] The Vulkan factory, the first one from Leningrad, arrived on August 22, 1941, but it also lacked the essential equipment needed to restart its mechanical workshop. Three months later, its director still had no idea of the whereabouts of its machinery.[64] The evacuation was as much about guaranteeing that equipment did not fall into German hands as it was about making sure it arrived in working order on the distant home front. The evacuation solved an immediate need, but the way in which it was carried out had long-term consequences that Tashkent, a city with few resources of its own and a spotty urban infrastructure, had to resolve.

In addition, although the Evacuation Council preserved vital industrial resources by transporting them out of harm's way in the first six months of the war, the history of uneven Soviet industrialization in the 1930s complicated the ability of the Soviet state to restart production in Uzbekistan, a cotton-growing region with limited, mostly light, industry. A factory director from Kharkov complained that his new Tashkent production area was 30 percent smaller than the Kharkov facility and that the local adobe brick buildings could not withstand the heat of industrial production. He demanded construction of new buildings with "modern technology," a request that Tashkent officials had difficulty meeting.[65] Problems with inadequate fuel and water supplies and the lack of semifinished industrial products remained vexing issues for Uzbekistan, which, in the past, either did not need such resources or could import them from other regions of the Soviet Union, most of which were suddenly under Nazi occupation or were the sites of brutal fighting. Since the 1920s, Tashkent had been a secondary player in the Soviet industrialization project, with the Uzbek's SSR focus having been on agriculture, textiles, and agricultural machinery. This unequal prewar distribution of economic and industrial resources across the Soviet Union, combined with transportation difficulties and the wartime losses of the sources of raw materials (especially coal and oil from Ukraine and the Caucasus), complicated the evacuation, industrial development, and urban growth of the wartime city.

Factories that did not bring their own road vehicles to the Uzbek capital also faced great problems because the existing transportation facilities of the city were inadequate to deal with the tremendous need to move equipment, goods, supplies, and people throughout the region. The Elektrostanok factory from Kharkov had six of its seven factory vehicles requisitioned by the Red Army even before it left Ukraine. The seventh, evacuated to Tashkent, did not work and could not be fixed because of a wartime shortage of rubber. The factory instead turned to "local animal-drawn" transportation that "absolutely did not meet even the minimal needs of the factory at the present moment." Elektrostanok requested four new "gas-powered" vehicles to use within the city and fifty thousand rubles so that it could purchase eight horses, plus harnesses and carts, to supply such things as food for the cafeteria and fuel to operate the plant equipment. Other transportation problems included overcrowded and inefficient public trams that forced workers to make multiple connections and walk great distances between home and work. The evacuation of industry and the enormous influx of people had stretched Tashkent's transportation structure beyond its limits. Animal transit returned as an important source of intra-city transportation, even in the "modern" sections of Tashkent. Donkeys, camels, and horses delivered raw materials and workers to one end of Tashkent's new factories so that tanks, engines, and planes could roll out the other.[66] Wartime Tashkent was a place where high Soviet technology merged with the city's low-tech urban infrastructure. This combination symbolized the fundamental dilemma of Tashkent after the revolution—a symbolic city that had entered Soviet modernity but remained stuck in the pre-Soviet traditional past.

Hierarchies of Evacuation

The evacuation process also revealed hierarchies of the Soviet social and economic system. As noted earlier, the movement of factories from the front lines was geared to preserve the economic potential and industrial might of the Soviet state, not to save the local population from German occupation. But, when evacuating people, the Soviet government focused on elite groups—industrial workers, defense workers, Party officials, and intellectuals; the peasantry, unskilled laborers, the sick, and the elderly were abandoned. If they did escape, they usually fled on their own. The swift movement of the Nazi armies also mandated that factories load their equipment and most important workers first, leaving thousands of loyal Soviet citizens behind to face the Nazi onslaught as the essential machinery of Soviet industry moved toward Tashkent.

Similarly, once in Tashkent, intellectuals and the highly trained—those capable of working in heavy or defense industries—received priority in acquiring official housing in the city. Many women and children were sent off to distant rural regions to work on collective farms. In this sense, one's position in the state and the skills one offered to the state largely determined whether one would be left to face the Nazis in the European areas of the Soviet Union or evacuated safely. Once evacuated, however, one's status also determined whether one was allowed to remain in the urban environment of the Uzbek capital or be banished outside the city limits.[67] In this light, it was not surprising that the children of Party and administrative officials, evacuated from the front without their parents, had the best chance of being placed in orphanages in the Uzbek capital. The offspring of industrial workers were given less priority in relocation assignments, although they had better chances of being placed in a city than did the few sons and daughters of peasants who had somehow made it safely to Tashkent.[68] The supposedly classless Soviet society exhibited strong notions of class whereby the position of one's parents in the Soviet hierarchy often determined where a child would spend the war.

Similarly, Tashkent institutions not deemed essential to the war effort were closed down, moved to other cities, or transformed to serve different purposes. Despite the need to educate a local workforce and increase wartime propaganda campaigns, institutions of public enlightenment—schools, libraries, teahouses, theaters, and movie halls—suffered almost immediately, as their buildings were converted into factories, military hospitals, or housing for the city's burgeoning population. The need for industrial production space frequently clashed with the desire to create an educated, healthy, and "civilized" workforce in Uzbekistan, but the more immediate problem of reconstructing factories won out over the long-term need for well-rounded citizens. Moscow Aviation Factory no. 84 was especially privileged after its evacuation to the Uzbek capital, where it remains to this day. Upon arrival, it acquired the housing and production space of many pre-existing Tashkent institutions. For example, it took over the Technical School of Light Industry facilities in order to house evacuated workers. It then located its production facilities in a civil aviation repair workshop and printing plant. The reconfiguration of these institutions to defense production indicates that high-technology military needs took precedence over civilian ones, like education, transportation, information distribution, and publishing.[69] Furthermore, with much of their machinery still missing, evacuated factories easily expropriated the training equipment, tools, and supplies from technical schools, food processing plants, and other institutions of light industry. Again, these expropriations solved immediate problems but had serious consequences for the health and well-being of Tashkenters.

The aviation factory director noted that many workers were housed in schools, which meant that students were displaced from the education system that provided basic skills—literacy and knowledge of Russian and math—needed for factory production and long-term success in Soviet society. Schools also served as a social safety net for urban children whose parents would be more productive on the factory floor if they were assured that their children were cared for in school and thus were resuming a relatively normal child's life during the horror of war. The director stated that "schools are needed both for the population of the city and for our staff. Many children, who were torn away from their homes, have not studied already for three months. Workers bring up the issue that we must educate our children. We consider it incorrect to take over schools to use as dormitories."[70] The lack of a safe place to put children also complicated efforts to bring Uzbek women into the factory. The recent *hujum* campaign had led some women to take the radical step of working outside the home, but without a safe school environment for their children, many women would be even more reluctant to take outside employment. Uzbek Central Committee reports and decrees from 1943 note that more Uzbeks were needed in the wartime factory workforce and that providing them and their children with a social safety net, basic education, and technical skills was essential to making them part of productive society in the 1940s.[71] Both female evacuees and Uzbek mothers agreed that the city needed more schools and childcare institutions if they were to become and remain productive wartime factory workers.

Nevertheless, educational institutions virtually vanished from the Tashkent urban landscape, a problem for a polity that needed more trained Uzbeks to take on industrial roles. Schools were being transformed not only for industrial use but also to house more important institutions of higher education. General education schools were the first to be evicted, largely because they were less crucial for the immediate war effort than were research institutions that could provide important defense work or factory training schools that instilled production knowledge for the defense industry. Elementary schools, technical training institutes, or "palaces of culture" were also transformed into military hospitals or polyclinics that treated wounded soldiers, disabled veterans, and ill evacuees.[72] Health care was pitted against education and cultural work, and, once again, the most pressing needs for the short term—returning soldiers to the front lines or workers to the factory—took precedence over educating future workers, even those who were about to enter into socially productive factory labor during the war years. Such an immediate emphasis on military production occurred across the Soviet Union and, in fact, in most other countries during the war. However, in Uzbekistan, despite the fact that "enlightening Tashkenters," expanding literacy, and teaching Russian constituted important parts of the prewar effort to create a "cultured" Soviet city in formerly "backward" Central Asia, local cultural institutions—the official markers of Soviet progress and Uzbek achievement—suffered disproportionally. Tashkent's educational institutions, theaters, and research institutes, which had been responsible for creating this "culture" in the prewar era, all lost positions of prominence in the city in the wartime crunch for space. Long-term planning was not on the minds of wartime officials, even if the immediate decisions administrators made created additional problems that needed to be addressed in the near future.

Other Tashkent facilities were disbanded outright during the evacuation, their functions often replaced by more prestigious institutions that arrived in the city from Russia or Ukraine in the fall and winter of 1941–1942. The Moscow Textile Institute took over the training school at the Tashkent Textile Institute as well as thirty rooms in the Textile Kombinat housing complex in order to house its faculty.[73] Privileged Muscovite academics had preference over local workers, teachers, and students in housing. Similarly, the Tashkent Conservatory lost its concert and training facilities to the Leningrad Conservatory.[74] The arrival of the Leningrad Conservatory began a sort of "musical chairs" scenario in the city because the celebrated Khiva movie theater of the 1930s no longer served its primary cultural/propaganda function when it was transformed into a concert hall for the Uzbek State Philharmonic, presumably pushed out of the old conservatory building upon the arrival of the Leningrad musicologists.[75] Large public film screenings—necessary forms of wartime propaganda—were then held in outdoor parks, a suitable venue in summer but less than ideal in the winter months. The pressing needs of the war again took precedence over the ultimate goals of transforming urban space, local society, and city residents.

Local higher education institutions suffered as well. The prestigious Tashkent Institute of Agriculture and Mechanized Irrigation, an important research center for Uzbekistan's agricultural economy, lost its building in October 1941 to the Moscow Academy for Metallic Machinery named after Stalin. The students of the Tashkent institute were sent out of the Uzbek capital to work on collective farms.[76] Residents of the Tashkent Pedagogical Institute dormitory were evicted so that evacuated members of the Union of Soviet Writers, prominent Moscow workers, and professors from the Frunze Military Academy could move in.[77] Tashkent also received numerous other evacuated educational and research institutions, including the Pulkovskaia Astronomical Observatory from Leningrad, the Leningrad Ethnography Institute, the Moscow Architectural Institute, the Seismology

Institute, the Odessa Institute of Engineers of Water Transport, the Moscow Theater of the Revolution, the Kiev Industrial Institute, the Kharkov Operetta Theater, and the Odessa Pharmaceutical Institute.[78] Again, these European institutions pushed local facilities out of the city or "merged" with them, which usually meant gaining the upper hand in any joint operations.[79] Likewise, the Soviet intelligentsia of Tashkent—formerly the leading sector of Central Asian Soviet society—suddenly found itself playing supporting roles in wartime society, while people like Anna Akhmatova, Aleksei Tolstoi, and Kornei Chukovskii—all evacuees to Tashkent—recreated literary salons and continued their intellectual work.[80] Tashkent's former cultural elite were provincial players in their own city or were themselves sent out to the Uzbek provinces to resume their work. Suddenly, the upper echelon of Tashkent's cultural prewar Soviet society was no longer viewed as important enough to live in the Uzbek capital itself.

As is clearly evident, the wartime transformation of Tashkent built up the city's industrial, economic, and cultural base and brought thousands of talented Soviet citizens to the region. In many ways, this evacuation of industry and important Soviet institutions succeeded in preserving these assets from destruction by the Nazis. However, the economic costs were tremendous. The wartime industrialization of the Uzbek capital expanded the region's potential and diversified its economy while simultaneously devastating its prewar urban infrastructure to the detriment of the city's permanent residents. In fact, between 1941 and 1945, the stress on creating heavy industry in Tashkent at the expense of light industry and local cultural institutions caused enormous hardship. The Soviet Union needed defense factories and talented scientists on the home front for the war effort, but the Soviet citizens of Central Asia also needed education for their children and light industry to provide them with clothing, pharmaceuticals, housing, and food if they were to survive the war and be productive workers. In this sense, the hierarchies of the evacuation, with certain industries, institutions, and peoples deemed more important than others, helped to guarantee the survival of the Soviet system but led to tremendous inequality, suffering, and even death in the "safety" of the Soviet home front.

Furthermore, there also appears to have been a hierarchy in the destination cities in which evacuees desired to be resettled. Cities in Siberia, with their more Russian environments, were the most sought-after locations at the start of the war. Some institutions did not wish to be evacuated to Tashkent in the summer of 1941, believing it to be a distant, foreign, and "uncivilized" city. However, as the confusion of the evacuation increased and the need to escape cities on the front lines became a pressing reality, evacuees became less particular about where they or their institution would be resettled. In a letter on June 30, 1941, to Aleksei Kosygin, deputy chair of the Council of People's Commissars, the head of the Academy of Sciences proposed that its Leningrad branch be moved to a large city with a pre-existing infrastructure of research institutes and laboratories that would enable its members to restart their work with minimal delays. The Academy of Sciences proposed Kazan, Saratov, Sverdlovsk, Tomsk, or Novosibirsk as the most preferable resettlement sites; there was no mention of any city in Central Asia. However, by July 24, 1941, with the front quickly moving toward Leningrad, the academy added Tashkent, Samarkand, and Alma-Ata as possible evacuation sites if the previous five were unfeasible. The president of the Belorussian Academy of Sciences also proposed that its surviving members, who no longer had institutional affiliations after the fall of Minsk, be sent to Kazan or Saratov as members of a Belorussian Academy of Sciences in these cities. On July 31, 1941, however, these academics "settled" for Tashkent, where they would "work in local institutes of higher education and in scientific institutions."[81]

Nonetheless, when faced with the choice of Tashkent, Osh (Kyrgyz SSR), or Leninabad (Tajik SSR), most of the Slavic and Jewish evacuees preferred the Uzbek capital, one of the more "European" cities in Central Asia. Many evacuees, concerned about cultural differences or survival in smaller Central Asian towns, requested permission to move to Tashkent, where they believed food and clean water were more plentiful or where they hoped to gain employment in fields in which they had been trained. The loss of the right to live in Tashkent remained a terrifying prospect for many Uzbek residents as well. People with criminal records or convictions for counterrevolutionary crimes, those who did not participate in socially productive labor, or those related to people with criminal records lost Tashkent registration during the war, as did the families of legal Tashkent residents who had been sent to another Uzbek city for long-term employment.[82] Uzbeks suddenly found themselves in danger of losing the right to live in their own capital city and of being sent to distant villages and towns, many of which lacked the community structures so necessary for survival during a time of war.

Likewise, a group of Moscow State University professors protested vehemently against being transferred from Tashkent to Ashgabat at the height of the evacuation. Evidently, two hundred professors and their families arrived in Tashkent, while five hundred of their colleagues and students arrived in Ashgabat, the capital of the Turkmen SSR, a clear indication of the confusion that had split this group in two. The professors clearly preferred

Tashkent because it already had an infrastructure that would enable the professors to work in their professions; they did not want to join their colleagues in the Turkmen SSR. Meanwhile, in Ashgabat, the university had an incompletely constructed building with no water pipes or electricity, making laboratory work impossible. In fact, the situation with working, living, and food conditions was so poor in Ashgabat that the academics "rebelled" and demanded re-evacuation in early May 1942.[83] Clearly, Uzbekistan was not at the bottom of the Soviet hierarchy because there was always someplace worse.

In fact, Tashkent was one of the preferred places in the region to spend the war. Among Central Asian cities, Alma-Ata, the capital of the Kazakh SSR, appears to have been the only other city in the region for which evacuees expressed a clear preference. Evacuees wanted a "modern" city with a European-style infrastructure and residents who spoke Russian at some basic level. These war migrants preferred Tashkent and Alma-Ata because they thought they could at least have a semblance of the life that they had enjoyed before the war. When given a choice, most evacuees preferred an urban environment over a rural area—largely because the majority of the Slavic and Jewish refugees were urban workers. If Tashkent was not a possibility for Uzbekistan's new residents, other major cities of the republic, most often Samarkand or the satellite cities of Tashkent oblast, were desired.

When evacuation to these locations was not possible, refugees seem to have preferred living in agricultural regions near the Uzbek capital and thus with proximity to the more Soviet urban environment that they understood. Almost no one desired to live in the distant rural regions of Central Asia. Many of those who lived in rural Bukhara, Kashkadarya, or Namangan oblasts often expressed a fervent desire for re-evacuation toward the front lines or even traveled unsanctioned in search of better or more familiar living or working conditions in or near the capital.[84] This desire for "modern" or "cultured" areas led to a constant movement of people throughout Central Asia. The living conditions in other parts of Central Asia, particularly in remote villages where evacuees received little assistance from collective farms, were deemed so poor that refugees continued to arrive in the Uzbek capital, no longer fleeing the Nazis but escaping the inhospitable environment of the remote Central Asian desert.[85] The Tashkent metropolitan area became a revolving door for wartime residents of Central Asia who were seeking survival. Many Party officials had long criticized Tashkent for not being "Soviet" enough, but, in comparison with some other urban areas in the region, the Uzbek capital was the "most Soviet" and by far one of the most preferable cities in Central Asia in which to spend the war. Wartime

Tashkent had finally become a "socialist" city. It was the magnet of opportunity and survival for the increasingly large population of Soviet citizens in wartime Central Asia, but the reality of life in the city was dismal.

Urban Planning

The evacuation and the desire to live in the Uzbek capital caused a tremendous population increase, with city officials unable to control the numbers of people living in or transiting the city, despite numerous efforts to put a population cap in place. In June 1942, the city's population was estimated at between 700,000 and 750,000 people, up from approximately 600,000 residents before the war.[86] By 1944, Yusupov stated that the city's population was approaching a million residents.[87] A migration of this magnitude strained the existing infrastructure of the city, and the prewar "Plan for the Reconstruction of Tashkent" could not keep up with the new Tashkent. In the 1930s, Mitkhat Bulatov, Aleksandr Kuznetsov, Stepan Polupanov, and others had planned a Central Asian socialist city of the future with ornate buildings, modern sewers, multistory apartments, and gardenlike parks. However, the war deprived them of the time and resources to implement their redevelopment projects. Once the conflict started, they no longer enjoyed the luxury of rational planning because hundreds of thousands of desperate and hungry Soviet citizens began streaming into the city. By the fall of 1941 and with winter approaching, Tashkent needed immediate solutions and had no use for idealistic paper proposals.

In 1942, the Sovnarkom created the Committee of Architectural Affairs under which it placed the prestigious Academy of Architecture, the main academic research institution for urban planning in the Soviet Union. During the war, the academy was evacuated from Moscow to Chimkent, Kazakhstan, a city near Tashkent. As will be discussed in later chapters, the period of their evacuation gave many prominent Soviet architects first-hand experience with the climatic, geographic, and supply issues of constructing cities in Central Asia, something that Aleksandr Kuznetsov and members of the original Mosoblproekt planning brigade lacked when they developed the 1937–1939 plan. The presence of the academy in Central Asia also provided local architects with contacts and opportunities for collaboration with some of the most experienced Soviet designers so that, as Kiev, Minsk, and Stalingrad were leveled by bombs, Tashkent ironically underwent unprecedented development.[88] The war also provided local Tashkent architects and planners with important practical expertise and offered them new opportunities to demonstrate local initiative now that the Gorispolkom could no longer rely on distant urban planners for help.

In March 1942, the Uzbek Sovnarkom organized its own "architectural construction committee" to approve construction projects for evacuated industries, to develop proposals for war-related "corrections" to the prewar reconstruction plans, and to provide an organizational framework for the planning and construction of all housing, hospital, and public buildings. The republic-level committee consisted of representatives of the Uzbek Sovnarkom, professors from the Moscow Architectural and the Central Asian Industrial Institutes, and members of the Academy of Architecture, indicating that while the committee was an "Uzbek" organization, Muscovites still controlled urban planning in the periphery.[89] The main difference was that Muscovites now lived in this periphery. However, the organization of this committee occurred late, after the majority of evacuated institutions had already arrived and been reestablished. Therefore, the committee had great difficulty in overseeing or regulating the reestablishment of these industries on the home front and in helping urban planners develop city projects proactively. Instead of anticipating the needs of Tashkent's wartime industrialization, planners used their own initiative and reacted to unforeseen problems. Yet these Tashkent planners—whether old or new to the city—should not be faulted for their failure to anticipate these tremendous changes because no one expected such a disastrous Soviet response to the Nazi invasion. The Soviet state as a whole lacked adequate plans for defending the union during the war, largely because of the belief that the Red Army would win a swift war on enemy territory. This lack of military preparation was a dereliction of duty that caused the deaths of millions on and near the front lines. However, the idea that a war in Europe would bring devastation to Tashkent was unfathomable when the original reconstruction plans were proposed in 1937. Preparing for such an event was just beyond the scope of prewar imagination.

One of the main tasks of the Committee of Architectural Affairs in Uzbekistan was to stabilize the evacuation-era urban growth. On March 24, 1942, Mitkhat Bulatov, the Tashkent city architect, appeared before the Committee of Architectural Affairs in Uzbekistan to answer questions on the extent to which the evacuation was hampering the Tashkent reconstruction project, a pressing concern of the committee. Members complained that Bulatov failed to coordinate the evacuation with the fundamental principles of the prewar "General Plan," the most important component of which was the elimination of the dual nature of the city, with its strict division of the Uzbek and Russian sections along the Ankhor Canal. Bulatov responded that coordinating the evacuation with the reconstruction plan had been accomplished successfully in the first few months of the evacuation, before the large-scale arrival of industry into the city. He implied that the capital had successfully absorbed the initial trickle of refugees and evacuated institutions, but, when migrants began flooding the city, the Gorispolkom could not abide by the dictates of the reconstruction project and transform the city's economy for war at the same time.[90] The job had simply become too overwhelming, and the city lacked the infrastructure and human resources to handle such a titanic task.

The city architect subsequently admitted that serious violations of the reconstruction plan had occurred, with factories being placed in parks, along the Salar Canal, and in the Tashkent art museum, a former department store, and a former prison.[91] These facilities were never far away from areas that were zoned for industry and were in regions that were geared for growth, but perhaps not for the industries that they received. Tashkent was becoming more industrial, an important marker of successful Soviet urban planning, but, as noted earlier, its own cultural institutions and "green areas" were sorely neglected and often destroyed, a problem for a polity that still aimed to inculcate new social norms among Central Asians and still needed such places for conducting wartime propaganda campaigns.

Furthermore, while state officials praised this industrial development, the new factories were located in heavily populated areas, thereby endangering public health.[92] In a few short months, Tashkent had become a "modern" city, with all the important symbols of Soviet heavy industry—chemical factories, electro-cable production, and airplane manufacture. Wartime industrial growth was viewed as a positive development, but the distribution of this industry was lopsided, with too much of it in the already built-up regions that had the basic infrastructure to support it. Other areas, namely the traditionally Central Asian sections of the city, were left out of this war-related industrialization and the infrastructure improvements it would have brought.[93] The belief that rapid industrialization would eliminate the ethnic division and create a unified Tashkent was not being realized during this time of intense urban growth.

In fact, instead of serving as the "iron law" of urban development, as originally envisioned, the reconstruction plan was adapted to suit the needs of the evacuation. The city population was constantly in flux, and the plan clearly needed to be changed to reflect this unforeseen growth. However, the Tashkent Gorispolkom and the Sovnarkom approved changes to industrial zoning regulations after the fact to reflect the reality of newly concentrated industrial centers in the city. The immediate needs of industry once again took precedence over rational urban planning. Industrial institutions, particularly evacuated ones, successfully ignored, overlooked, or got around state regulations. After admitting that water pollution levels recently had increased because evacuated factories were dumping waste into the city's canal irrigation (*aryk*) system, Bulatov noted that the Gorispolkom had difficulty solving this problem because it lacked information on how much toxic waste was being pumped into the city's canals. The city government ordered all factories to report the amount and nature of the pollutants that they expelled but received responses from only two institutions.[94] Although officially in charge of controlling urban growth, the city government and the city architect did not even have the power to force commissariats or military industrial factories to answer their inquiries. The Central Asian model city had finally gained an industrial base that was not simply symbolic, but this real industry hampered Tashkent's ability to develop into the idealized symbol of socialism in Asia. Soviet bureaucracy, which was disorganized and inefficient before the war, could not keep up with the chaos of the evacuation crisis.

Furthermore, a major problem for urban development during the evacuation was the complexity of industrial construction in wartime. In the prewar period, implementation of the "General Plan for the Reconstruction of Tashkent" was slow because the project depended on heavy-duty construction materials that had to be imported from the western regions of the Soviet Union. However, once these regions fell to the Nazis, Central Asia lost its source of supply for these materials altogether and had to streamline all construction efforts. In World War II, Soviet construction needed to be quick, simple, and efficient. The Uzbek Sovnarkom issued a decree in 1942 that all "construction of new housing needed to go along the lines of maximal simplicity (including dirt dugouts and semi-dirt buildings)."[95] Wartime urban planners of the "industrializing" Uzbek capital now needed to use nonindustrial methods and locally produced materials to speed up construction. Simplicity of design—not monumental structures with elaborate decorations—became the mantra of wartime city planning.

Adobe bricks, criticized two years earlier as unsuitable for a modern Soviet city, were now used to build the defense factories that were needed to save the Soviet Union from the Nazis. In fact, another Sovnarkom decree prohibited construction with building materials that had to be imported from other regions of the Soviet Union because transportation or construction delays would impede the shift of the economy toward military production.[96] This move away from industrial construction methods and materials toward the use of locally produced supplies fostered a reinterpretation of traditional building methods. City planners ceased denigrating traditional Uzbek homes; traditional Central Asian–style buildings suddenly were described as models for wartime construction because they were better suited to the climate and used local resources. After years of attempting to foster "progressive" European construction techniques, planners began to speak of the importance of learning traditional Central Asian construction methods—adobe brick-making, layouts designed for maximum ventilation and natural light, and mud-and-straw roofs—and of introducing into Soviet-style construction the local architectural forms that had existed in the region "for centuries."[97] Just as Soviet propaganda celebrated traditional Central Asian culture and history during the war and tried to use traditional notions of family and community obligation to pull Uzbek women into the factory, indigenous urban planning techniques were promoted as widely as necessary for the survival of the city and to meet the pressing need to build factory space and housing.

Some of Moscow's most prominent engineers and architects, along with their evacuated institutes, spent the duration of the war in Central Asia, and many developed building designs for the Uzbek capital while in the region. They recognized that they too lacked the local expertise needed to transform a Central Asian city at war and likewise spoke of the need to learn construction techniques from local Uzbek artisans, a reversal of the traditional hierarchy in the transmission of Soviet expertise. At a meeting of the Architects' Union in December 1942, one delegate demanded the incorporation of a wide variety of local construction methods into Soviet building technology to get around the supply shortage. Suddenly, the formerly "stagnant" and "particular" customs of Central Asia became useful again. The delegate stated that, "before the war[,] interest in local masters for the most part concerned the study of their architectural and artistic creativity. If, before the war, masters were used as artists or [artistic] designers, now interest appears from another angle—interest in national construction technology. . . . [Local] masters now are used on the construction of housing, which are being placed in the oblasts of the republic, [local] masters direct large construction projects. Local masters are invited to the construction of the metallurgical Kombinat, of baths and on other construction projects."[98] He reminded his colleagues that "local masters" often were acquainted with both Soviet and traditional construction methods and, with proper support and guidance, could easily fuse the two traditions. On the other hand, Russian or Ukrainian-trained "Soviet" architects relied too much on modern industrial methods that were no longer suitable for Tashkent. In a time of war, Soviet ideology merged with local traditions at multiple levels in an effort to shore up the Soviet Union's strength and its ability to defeat the Nazis.

In 1942, *Arkhitektura SSSR* published plans for new "evacuated industrial villages" to be reproduced across Central Asia using basic construction equipment and supplies—dirt bricks, mud for the roofs, and less use of wood. The author of the published piece, V. N. Semenov, reminded planners that the traditional orientation to the south and the extensive use of greenery, particularly pyramid-shaped poplar trees, were essential for offering some protection from the extreme temperatures in the region. He proposed that wartime buildings for evacuated industries and housing be square or rectangular structures with "simple roofs without any decorations or additions."[99] These designs would make construction easier, especially considering the wartime shortage of trained construction engineers and workers.

Semenov also proposed placing irrigation canals away from buildings so that water would not seep from the canals into building foundations; lining the irrigation system was not a priority during the war. He argued that irrigation should be established using traditional methods rather than large-scale Soviet endeavors.[100] He even suggested using the traditional Central Asian water reservoir, the *hauz,* as decoration and taking advantage of its natural cooling capability. Soviet fountains, sewage systems, and water pipes supposedly had replaced the traditional *hauz,* the square water collection pool that Soviet and Russian colonial administrators had once described as a breeding ground for disease. After 1941, however, Soviet officials could see the *hauz* as a convenient way to collect water for urban residents since Soviet technology could not do the job effectively. Soviet officials reinterpreted their prewar views of traditional Central Asian urban planning, and some even proposed that only traditional solutions, not modern Soviet counterparts, were suitable in Central Asia's unique geography and climate. Two architects, G. Zakharov and Z. Charnysheva, even argued in *Arkhitektura SSSR* that the "Old Towns" of Central Asia, with their winding streets, inner courtyards, lack of windows along the street, and *aryk* drainage canals, all examples of "Eastern exoticism" to Europeans, actually suited local conditions, particularly during the Soviet-German confrontation, when the state could not invest money in urban infrastructures. As such, wartime urban planners argued a novel idea—that Soviet architects actually could learn from the architectural past of Central Asia and that local construction methods could help Soviet planners better respond to wartime exigencies.[101] For the moment, Uzbek architects were better able to create Soviet cities than were their Russian and Ukrainian colleagues.

Envisioning Victory

The Soviet state was founded on the need for a constant mobilization of the population and a continuous militarization of society. During the war, the Soviet Union was thus theoretically in its natural state. However, a close examination of urbanism on the Central Asian home front reveals a fundamental weakness of the Soviet system, namely, its inefficient bureaucracy, which had difficulty responding to wartime conditions. During the war, the state hoped to maintain tight control over its population, the movement of evacuees and equipment, the resettlement of institutions, and the development of home-front cities, but this task proved impossible. Individual resourcefulness—not guidance from the state—kept the system functioning and facilitated survival on the Central Asian home front. A prominent example of this trend concerned the wartime reinterpretation of Central Asian architecture and construction traditions, which enabled the wartime state to provide the population with a few basic services. Although Tashkent experienced tremendous hardship and deprivation, the city survived and even supported the war effort. This success was largely because of an unexpected flexibility within the Soviet polity and the adaptability of its residents, city planners, and factory officials, who were able to respond to years of continual crises and hardship.

By 1944, with the war finally proceeding in the Soviet Union's favor, Gosplan UzSSR turned its attention away from guaranteeing the city's (and the union's) immediate survival and toward planning for the future. It proposed the construction of fifty new multistory apartment complexes to help house some of the urban residents who lived in harsh wartime conditions. Internal transportation—road improvements, the paving of streets, and the arrival of new tram cars—plus the installation of sewage systems and the construction of hotels all grew in public importance. After "solving" the initial problems of developing an infrastructure to support the evacuated industries, Tashkent went on a building spree to solve the immediate issues of daily life—water, energy, and schools.[102] However, city administrators still urged the conservation of energy, the improvement of irrigation construction, and greater economy regarding heating fuel.

Having witnessed the problems of supplying an industrialized urban center in the middle of the Central Asian desert, administrators also proposed searching for new sources of raw materials for the rapidly growing city.[103] As a result, a large metallurgy complex was established at Begovat, a small town to which Soviet deportees and Japanese prisoners of war were sent, to provide the defense industry with iron and steel to make planes and tanks. A coal-producing project was put in place at Angren, near Tashkent, to supply the newly industrializing Uzbek SSR with new sources of energy and heat. In addition, water reservoirs and hydroelectric stations were created along Central Asian rivers and canals to provide Tashkent, Samarkand, and other areas with electricity and water to allow for maximum production in their new factories.[104]

These newly established facilities remained in the region after the war, as did the Chkalov airplane production facility (formerly Aviation Factory no. 84), a parachute factory, the expanded Tashkent Textile Kombinat, and a few other industrial enterprises. However, most wartime cultural institutions, with the exception of the Uzbek Academy of Sciences (created with the help of evacuees during the war), quickly returned to their cities of origin. Elite Soviet workers and intellectuals also departed Central Asia in the later years of the war, while average refugees and non-elite laborers were left behind, often in poorly constructed wartime barracks or mud structures.[105] Tashkent became an industrial and cultured city in the war, but many of the notable evacuated institutions and enterprises quickly left the Uzbek capital after the Red Army liberated cities in the European parts of the Soviet Union. This Central Asian city had been transformed into a wartime center for Soviet industry and intellectual life, but it was only a temporary change. As the Nazi threat decreased, the European cities of the Soviet Union took back this prominent role.

Still, despite the hardship and confusion of the war, city planners never forgot about the importance of building a model city in Soviet Central Asia. In 1942, the Sovnarkom ordered the resumption of construction on the Tashkent Opera and Ballet Theater (the Navoi Theater), originally designed in 1934 by Aleksei Shchusev but put on hold with the outbreak of war; large-scale construction in the city, however, resumed only with the end of the conflict and the arrival of Japanese prisoner-of-war labor in the region.[106] The year that was the turning point in the war, 1943, saw the construction of the Mukhimi (Tashsoviet) Theater, an 850-seat facility for Uzbek comedy and drama. The decision to build the theater came on June 30, 1943; one month and ten days later, the construction site had been prepared and workers assembled. In less than six months, construction was completed by replacing "deficit" construction supplies (wood and steel) with locally produced bricks.[107] In spite of the pressing need for housing and health-care institutions, the building of public structures once again took precedence over the construction of living space. Throughout the war and evacuation crisis, not all proposals were simply reactions to military imperatives. As the city began to recover from the confusion of the evacuation, officials urged the resumption of rational urban planning for the postwar era. At the first opportunity, Yusupov, Bulatov, and Sodik Khusainov, the Gorispolkom chairman, revived the idea of building a beautiful and communist Tashkent of the future, with large and elaborate public structures, even though they could not yet meet the demands of the wartime present.

The Ankhor Canal, spring 2000. Photograph by the author

Chilanzar construction site, late 1950s or early 1960s. Courtesy Russian State Archive of Film and Photodocuments, Krasnogorsk, Russia

Plaster model of the proposed Tashkent Administrative Center. From T. F. Kadyrova, *Arkhitektura sovetskogo Uzbekistana*

Tashkent *tramvai,* crossing Ankhor Canal in central Tashkent, circa 1940s.
Courtesy Russian State Archive of Film and Photodocuments, Krasnogorsk, Russia

Street scene outside Tashkent's Pedagogical Institute. Courtesy Russian Collection,
Russian State Archive of Film and Photodocuments, Krasnogorsk, Russia

Above, Navoi Monument, in front of Dom Sovetov along Navoi Street, mid-twentieth century. Courtesy Russian State Archive of Film and Photodocuments, Krasnogorsk, Russia

Left, Close-up of Navoi Street housing construction from mid-1930s. From T. F. Kadyrova, *Arkhitektura sovetskogo Uzbekistana*

Newly constructed "*khrushcheby*" (standardized Khruschev-era buildings) and
movie theater, near Chilanzar. Note the lack of greenery in the new planned
environment. Courtesy Russian State Archive of Film and Photodocuments,
Krasnogorsk, Russia

Navoi Street housing and retail construction with newly strung electric lines, mid-
twentieth century. Courtesy Russian State Archive of Film and Photodocuments,
Krasnogorsk, Russia

Prefabricated housing construction in Tashkent, late 1950s or early 1960s. Note the lack of balconies on this multilevel housing. Courtesy Russian State Archive of Film and Photodocuments, Krasnogorsk, Russia

Uzbek-Soviet architecture in central Tashkent, featuring lancet arches as well as light-colored stucco to deflect sunlight. Courtesy Russian State Archive of Film and Photodocuments, Krasnogorsk, Russia

New Khrushchev-era housing, park, and bus stop. Courtesy Russian State Archive of Film and Photodocuments, Krasnogorsk, Russia

The new, postwar Tashkent urban environment, with increased options for transportation. Courtesy Russian State Archive of Film and Photodocuments, Krasnogorsk, Russia

Old Tashkent, circa 1930s, with people wearing traditional Uzbek clothing.
Courtesy Russian State Archive of Film and Photodocuments, Krasnogorsk, Russia

The ideal Soviet Tashkent. Courtesy Russian State Archive of Film and Photodocuments, Krasnogorsk, Russia

Old Tashkent *mahalla* with electric utility lines, circa 1950s. Courtesy Russian State Archive of Film and Photodocuments, Krasnogorsk, Russia

A street in Old Tashkent. Note how the narrow roadway and trees provide shade for pedestrians, something many Soviet buildings did not do. Courtesy Russian State Archive of Film and Photodocuments, Krasnogorsk, Russia

Post-Soviet façade remodeling of Brezhnev-era construction, 2002. Photograph by the author

Students arriving at Tashkent's Pedagogical Institute, built in 1938. Courtesy Russian State Archive of Film and Photodocuments, Krasnogorsk, Russia

Construction site in Tashkent's New City area. Courtesy Russian State Archive of Film and Photodocuments, Krasnogorsk, Russia

Tashkent transportation via tram. Courtesy Russian State Archive of Film and Photodocuments, Krasnogorsk, Russia

Navoi Street intersection where Uzbek-Soviet architecture can be seen. Courtesy
Russian State Archive of Film and Photodocuments, Krasnogorsk, Russia

Central Tashkent transportation via automobile. Courtesy Russian State Archive
of Film and Photodocuments, Krasnogorsk, Russia

The newly constructed Vatan/Rodina theater, 1930s. Courtesy Russian State Archive of Film and Photodocuments, Krasnogorsk, Russia

Administrative building, central Tashkent, mid-twentieth century. Courtesy Russian State Archive of Film and Photodocuments, Krasnogorsk, Russia

CENTRAL ASIAN LIVES AT WAR

One of the starved travelers from our train, who stole a boiled beetroot
from a stall, barely saved his life by running faster than the half dozen
Uzbeks who pursued him with their knives drawn. There is no doubt
in my mind that they would have killed him if he had not managed to
lose himself in the innards of our train. The angry Uzbeks kept walking
around the train for a long time waiting for him to emerge. It now seems
unreal that anybody would kill a man for stealing a boiled beetroot, but
at that time we thought the Uzbeks' reaction normal and even justified.

—Aleksander Topolski, 1999

The mechanics of the Soviet state's response to the war, from the efforts to
mobilize the Tashkent population to the creation of a wartime industrial
center in the Uzbek capital, are only one aspect of the wartime situation
that unfolded in Soviet Central Asia. For a fuller understanding of what
transpired, one must also investigate how the residents of the city—Uzbeks,
long-term Russian Tashkenters, and the recent arrivals who had escaped
the brutality of the front lines—experienced the war years. While Tashkent
certainly provided refuge from the battlefield horrors of the Nazi-Soviet
conflagration, survival in the Uzbek capital was by no means guaranteed.
Fear, outrage, patriotism, and despair were all emotions that surfaced on
the Central Asian home front. Initially, however, the Nazi invasion and reports of the fall of Soviet cities in rapid succession caused panic to spread
throughout the region. Rumors of the impending arrival of German forces
in Central Asia, exaggerated accounts of up to 5 million people dead in the
battle of Kiev, and the evacuation of thousands of wounded soldiers to the

Uzbek capital fueled speculation that the Soviet experiment was nearing a disastrous conclusion.[1] Defeatist attitudes, such as the comments of a Tashkent shoe factory worker who claimed that the Soviet Union had "100 Red Army men standing behind one machine gun," occasionally gave way to outright anti-Soviet statements that, at best, showed little attachment to the Soviet system or, at worst, cheered on the enemy.[2] One Textile Kombinat worker, Shkaev, refused to help the war effort, stating that he would not work "for swine [*svolochi*] and would not work" for the duration of the war.[3] A Russian construction worker believed that "Hitler would make red meat out of the Red Army," while an Uzbek Tashkenter, who was mobilized into the army, stated that he "would go fight for the *kulaks*" instead.[4] These statements create a complicated picture of the mood of Soviet Tashkent at war. While Soviet officials expressed concern that Tashkent residents were detached from the war effort at the start, comments like these by both Russians and Uzbeks indicate that parts of the multiethnic Tashkent population were overtly hostile to Soviet rule.

During the war, there was a constant tension between the confidence of state propaganda and a sense of insecurity within Soviet society. Officially, the Soviet people were unified for victory over the Nazi threat, but many residents of the home front were unsure of the outcome of the war and thus prepared for all contingencies. The attempts of Party and state officials to forge a unified community in the wartime socialist city clashed with the reality of life in Uzbekistan, a place where hunger, poverty, and disease ravaged the population. These hardships on the home front were exacerbated by the evacuation crisis, which opened up deep ethno-national divisions among the region's diverse population. Various ethnic groups from across the Soviet Union suddenly had to live together, and they immediately viewed each other as competitors for the region's scarce resources, particularly food, medicine, clothing, and shelter. These shortages increased the sense of instability and vulnerability among the wartime population of Uzbekistan. Few people felt comfortable or at home in Tashkent, a city that was out of harm's way and to which countless Soviet citizens fled. Instead, many found Central Asia's reported safety to be illusory, causing residents—Uzbek, Russian, Jewish, Korean, Polish, and countless other groups—to rely only on themselves, not on the state, the city, or their neighbors, for survival. The recollections of the city's wartime residents demonstrate that the gulf between the public image of a Soviet people united for victory and the struggles of home-front life—characterized by desperation, starvation, and disease—grew tremendously large, with devastating consequences for many city residents.

Images of the "Other" in Tashkent

As noted earlier, the poor military defense of Soviet territory led to a rise in anti-Soviet sentiment among some sectors of the population. Many Tashkent residents, unclear of the future of their region as Soviet territory, anticipated a regime change in which Soviet power pulled out due to either a collapse of the government in Moscow or the capitulation of Central Asia to the Nazis. In the initial months of war, publicized pronouncements on the loyalty and heroism of Soviet citizens on the battlefield conflicted with rumors of tremendous defeats on the front lines. Some residents of Tashkent began to prepare for a future that might not include Soviet rule. At first, the Russians of Central Asia expressed immediate concern about their future in the region if Soviet power dissolved. As Natalia Gromova has noted, the Russians of Tashkent panicked in 1941 as Nazi troops moved toward Moscow and rumors persisted of a joint British-American attack from India that would transform Uzbekistan from a Soviet republic into an Anglo-American colony. She paraphrased the sentiment of the time: "What would happen then? How would Uzbeks relate to the avalanche of refugees from Russia? The mood was somber."[5] Tashkent and the entire Central Asian region had, in the past, been a refuge from World War I and the Russian civil war. Suddenly, however, with the enormity of the Soviet military catastrophe, the region's "safety" from German bombs was negated by the potential for angry reactions of Central Asians against Soviet/Russian rule if the socialist system collapsed. In the minds of local residents, the Soviet Union was under attack from the West (Germany) but also was threatened from within, namely from non-Russians who were not yet completely "civilized" Soviet citizens.

Aleksander Wat, a Polish intellectual and former deportee, has chronicled his travels through the region.[6] He notes that Europeans feared that Uzbeks were "preparing for an uprising. The Russians, the Jews, the fugitives, the refugees—everybody was expecting a bloodbath."[7] Party communiqués reported that Europeans were getting ready to flee from the region should the Soviet system collapse. One local Russian evidently stated that "Russians were sending their wives and children to Russia because all the Uzbeks will slit [pererezhut] Russian throats" during a time of war.[8] In fact, as Leningrad's workforce packed up their factories for evacuation to the safety of Tashkent, some Russians in Central Asia ironically began to send their families to what they believed was the safety of European Russia because they feared that angry Uzbek mobs might take revenge on them. The fear of wild and uncivilized Eastern peoples whom Soviet power had not yet "tamed" returned, recalling years of negative perceptions of Muslims and Asians in the Russian mindset.[9] Moreover, many Russian, Jewish, and other migrants to the region escaped death at the hands of the Nazis but felt threatened by their new Asian environment. These Russian residents of Tashkent dehumanized their Uzbek neighbors, creating (or recreating) an image of Central Asians as primitive or barbaric.[10] Their critiques and ethnic slurs focused on the sharpness and size of Uzbek knives and on the Uzbeks' willingness to use them against migrants. In fact, in a time of purported Soviet unity against the Nazis, many of these critiques were remarkably similar to the memoir literature of the pre-revolutionary period in which European travelers portrayed Central Asian emirs and khans as brutal barbarians because of their treatment of locals and foreigners alike. Furthermore, this wartime language recalls that used in the anti-German propaganda that was published in Soviet newspapers of the time, indicating that residents both internalized and at times inverted state language to solidify pre-existing ethnic prejudices.

However, it was not just the Russians who helped raise the level of fear and turmoil in the region. Uzbeks at times uttered equally harsh statements against the Russians. An Uzbek Komsomol member—supposedly a model Soviet worker—told a Russian colleague that "if Hitler or Germany goes and takes Russia, then we will crush all of you here and we will speak to you very differently."[11] In some cases, Uzbeks used almost the same language as Russians in describing how Central Asians would threaten Russians once Soviet power dissolved. Hotheads in both groups came to a general agreement that the future of the region would not be pleasant if the Nazis (or British) got anywhere close to Central Asia or if the Soviet system collapsed from within. One man, called Dadabaev, told his Russian co-workers that "soon, we will slice you all up."[12] In Tashkent, an officially decreed "unified" city, people saw the war as an opportunity for change, and many began to envision a city where Soviet power was no longer present, even if the details of the post-Soviet city remained indefinite and fluid.[13] Even so, for many Tashkenters, that imagined future was as frightening as the Nazi hordes sweeping through the steppe toward the Central Asian home front.

Not all ethnic insults concerned Russians or Uzbeks, however. In many, these two dominant ethnic groups came to agreement in their dislike of a more recent arrival: the scores of Jews who arrived in the region after fleeing Hitler's forces. One man, Kulakov, after hearing rumors of the deportation of Jews from Germany and occupied Europe, stated that "they got what they deserved."[14] Dorit Bader Whiteman notes that Uzbeks insulted Jews who stood in bread lines and occasionally even stole their food or pushed them out of line. Misha Raitzin, a child evacuee from Ukraine, wrote that the Russian and Uzbek children in his mixed Tashkent neighborhood used to call him a "kike" (*zhid*) and beat him up simply for being a Jew.[15] Furthermore, Party reports cite residents' complaints that "Tashkent had become filled with Jews."[16] Residents at times expressed anger at the recent arrivals, particularly as their own relatives went off to the front, underscoring a common Soviet wartime and postwar prejudice that Soviet Jews shirked their front-line military responsibilities to work in the institutions of the home front.

While Jews in Tashkent might have encountered ethnic slurs, anti-Semitic attacks were much harsher in the rural regions surrounding the city. Local collective farmers allegedly raped Jewish evacuees, who did not have any adult male relatives to protect them. One collective farm administrator stated, "It's time to kick out all the Jews," while others refused to accept Jews as workers, even though there were labor shortages.[17] Some collective farmers complained that Jewish evacuees—many of them urbanites—lacked skills and were of little help in the Uzbek countryside. According to local collective farmers, the Jewish evacuees offered them almost nothing of use but soaked up scarce resources. Some collective farm directors defied Soviet government decrees outright and refused to provide medical care, housing, or food to the evacuees who were placed in their midst, presumably so that evacuees would move to a different location. Such situations led to a large out-migration of evacuees from the countryside into towns and factories, where Jews and others believed they would have more control over their futures. This type of treatment led to the mass movement of hungry, ill, and desperate war migrants across the region and exacerbated the problem of overcrowding in Tashkent, Samarkand, and other major urban centers in Central Asia, where the majority of war refugees converged.

Although anti-Semitism existed in the Tashkent region before the war, the increase in attacks against Jews likely was a wartime phenomenon that was directed primarily at Ashkenazi Jews, those who arrived by the thousands in 1941 and 1942 from the European areas of the Soviet Union. No large numbers of verbal or physical assaults against Bukharan Jews, who often spoke Uzbek and Tajik, were well acquainted with the local lifestyle, and had a traditional place within Central Asian society, were noted in Party documents. Furthermore, although Misha Raitzin describes being bullied because of his Jewish background, he notes that practicing Muslims in Tashkent often were friendly and helpful to practicing Jews. In fact, his parents got along well with their Uzbek neighbors because, he believes, they kept kosher and his mother always covered her hair. These actions underscored for many local Uzbeks that the Raitzins were a traditional family rather than a modern Soviet one.[18] Evidence suggests that Jews were not attacked simply because they were Jewish. While their ethnic and religious origins certainly played a role in their persecution, many Jewish evacuees possibly were singled out for being outsiders whom Central Asians identified closely with the Soviet system that had brought so much upheaval and suffering to the region. With the war and evacuation, the harsh reality of Soviet life in Tashkent simply got worse. Still, many Uzbeks tolerated those local Jews who clearly did not represent the Soviet state but who suffered, like many Central Asians, from the state's antireligious ideology and its continual attempts to transform traditional cultures.

Wartime Images of Tashkent

Central Asian residents clearly did not care for the masses of refugees that invaded their cities and villages. As discussed above, many Uzbeks demonstrated tremendous hostility toward refugees because they arrived unexpectedly in their communities and caused shortages of food, housing, and medicine. In return, the migrant Jews, Russians, and other Slavs frequently had negative impressions of the indigenous Central Asians, often colored by orientalist views of Eastern peoples. War memoirs and many archival reports provide a sense of the animosity felt toward Uzbeks because of their alleged wealth and the abundance of food they had at their disposal, although Party communiqués indicate that most Uzbeks remained as hungry as their non-Uzbek neighbors during the war years.[19] Animosity toward Central Asians increased because many Slavic city residents and new migrants to the city believed that the indigenous population controlled the sources of food and took advantage of the war situation to sell goods at the bazaar at high prices.[20] While traveling to Tashkent, the writer Nadezhda Mandel'stam was temporarily placed in a Kazakh collective farm where, she believed, local peasants were "well fed" and lived well but did not share their riches with outsiders.[21] Urban residents, especially evacuees, had a difficult time acquiring the basic necessities of life because they often lacked extended family and community structures in the region that could help them find additional food supplies. Tashkent once again was seen as a European city, surrounded by a sea of Central Asians, with the Central Asian population in control of the city's lifeline. This dependence of urbanites on another ethnic group was clearly resented by many, particularly during this time of deprivation.

Europeans also were wary of Tashkent as a city, seeing it as a completely foreign environment compared to the Soviet towns they knew. Memoir descriptions of the Uzbek capital depict a city of a different time and culture or, as Kornei Chukovskii wrote, a different "planet."[22] Wartime visitors overlooked its similarities to other Soviet cities and saw it only as a distant place of desert exile, with exotic trees, animals, and people. Like visitors before the revolution, Europeans who arrived during the war remarked on the drab and enclosed atmosphere of the Central Asian home. Speaking of rural Uzbekistan, Wat noted that the "natives lived a life apart. Their clay homesteads were surrounded by walls, like those in Morocco— they reminded me of the films about Morocco I'd seen. The homes had interior courtyards completely hidden from sight. The married women wore veils made of horsehair."[23] Other memoirs mention the strange lifestyle, the camels on the streets, women in *paranjis*, and the *arba* or donkey cart, the "vehicle of Central Asia which has changed little over the millennia," as if animal-drawn carts were not present in Russia, or elsewhere.[24] For many, Tashkent, the "city of bread," had become a distant place of confusion, misery, and decay, not the city of plenty they had anticipated. Although airplanes and trains made possible relatively rapid travel between Tashkent and Russia, wartime residents still spoke of Tashkent as a faraway place of exile and a city with few redeeming qualities. The region was cut off from the central parts of the Soviet Union that were being devastated by the war. Memoirs and archival reports present the migrant-filled Uzbek capital as a lonely place in a desolate desert in a country that was threatened by real and potential enemies. These sentiments of despair were similar to those expressed by nineteenth-century memoirists and travel writers in Russian Turkestan, although the urgency of despair was certainly increased in the wartime environment and by the knowledge that the Central Asian home front had become one of the few remaining lifelines for the entire Soviet Union.

Despite these grim reminders of suffering, some residents attempted to make the best of their wartime lives. Many attempted to adapt the city to their needs by creating tiny communities of high culture—little Moscows or Leningrads—in the Central Asian desert. With so many prominent literary, artistic, and theatrical figures in the city, wartime residents could enjoy a rather vibrant cultural life for a Soviet city during World War II. The home of the poet Anna Akhmatova, which was located in a region of the city that had many prominent evacuated writers and intellectuals, became a veritable literary salon.[25] Some memoirs recall vibrant discussions at restaurants, concerts performed by musicians evacuated from Moscow, and comedy and drama performances by some of the Soviet Union's most famous actors. Soviet writer Aleksei Tolstoi even compared the Uzbek capital to one of the great cities of exile, noting that "Tashkent was the Istanbul for the poor."[26] For Tolstoi and other prominent figures in the arts, Tashkent, like the metropolis in Turkey, was a place where European intellectuals could escape the harsh reality of war, live in relative comfort, and even continue their cultural pursuits. Such important Soviet evacuees migrated thousands of kilometers from the center of European Russia during World War II and created parallels between their lives and those of prominent non-Soviet intellectuals in forced exile. Still, their lives were vastly different from those of average wartime refugees, industrial workers, or local Uzbek residents, who lacked the time, the energy, or the resources to visit restaurants and cultural events. These less fortunate residents of Tashkent simply were too busy with the more mundane tasks of survival.

Evacuating Humans

Many intellectuals and Party members traveled to Tashkent in relatively comfortable conditions, but the evacuation process for the majority of Tashkent's new arrivals was harsh. Most wartime evacuees came to the region in crowded trains that lacked heat, had sporadic supplies of food or water, and little space for personal belongings.[27] Deportees, whether they were Koreans, Poles, Japanese POWs, Soviet Germans, or Crimean Tatars who were exiled to the region during the war, complained of atrocious transportation conditions in squalid boxcars or cattle cars without heat, water, or toilets.[28] Death rates among these groups were extraordinarily high. Many evacuees—and even more deportees—were lost along the way, either as casualties of German bombs, victims of disease and hunger, or simply by becoming separated from family members while in transit. Aleksander Topolski, a Polish citizen and deportee who, after the GULAG freed him, traveled across Central Asia to join the Polish Anders Army at Yangi-Yol (Tashkent oblast), wrote that Central Asian train cars epitomized "human misery on the move—grey-faced men, women and children sitting on benches or on the floor between benches. Any space not occupied by people was filled with bundles, bags, and suitcases. There was a pervading stench of cheap tobacco, unwashed human bodies, excrement, and the vomit of wailing babies."[29] The lack of toilets, bathing facilities, and clean water along the way led to unsanitary conditions and illness. While the evacuation initially saved enormous numbers of people, the subsequent spread of infectious diseases across Central Asia devastated migrants and Central Asians alike. Dysentery, malaria, cholera, tuberculosis, and typhus rates skyrocketed in the early 1940s because there were not enough drugs or doctors to help treat the sick.[30] In an ironic twist of fate, it was the migration of Soviet Europeans into the Tashkent region, not the long-criticized unsanitary conditions of local Uzbek culture, that led to mass outbreaks of disease in wartime Uzbekistan.

When evacuees arrived in the city, they were met by a flurry of bureaucrats who attempted in vain to bring order to the overcrowded Tashkent train station. Workers of the Tashkent *evakopunkt* checked travel documents of evacuees to ascertain who had traveled to Tashkent on an official basis. Official evacuees were those whose transportation to the Uzbek capital had been sanctioned by the Soviet state through their place of employment, usually a factory or cultural/educational institution that had been evacuated from the front. Those without official travel documents for Tashkent (refugees and people destined for other Central Asian cities) and those who could not work were sent out of the city as soon as possible, as were many members of deported ethnic groups, who were often sent to isolated areas of Tashkent oblast to fend for themselves. To ease the population explosion in Tashkent, officials also decreed in December 1941 that seriously ill evacuees and their families be removed from trains before they arrived in Tashkent to avoid becoming burdens on an already strained city infrastructure and to prevent further outbreaks of disease among city residents, particularly among workers at Tashkent's new military industrial factories. Similarly, single women and disabled soldiers who lacked family ties in Tashkent were to be sent elsewhere in the Uzbek SSR because officials feared that their presence in the capital might entice their relatives to make their own journeys to the city.[31]

The Tashkent *evakopunkt,* like others across the Soviet home front, had varied functions. It conducted the registration of all evacuees—officially within three days of arrival—and provided them with food, medical care, and a place to stay either permanently or temporarily. In theory, *evakopunkt* doctors examined evacuees to identify those with infectious diseases, isolate the ill, and provide others with vaccines and preventive care. The entire *evakopunkt* was zoned off from the surrounding area of the city, and NKVD officers guarded it to prevent potentially infectious arrivals from mixing with the permanent population. The *evakopunkt* reception area was located on the main grounds of the Tashkent railroad station and could serve up to two thousand people at a time.[32] Despite efforts to bring organization to the evacuation in Tashkent, the multiplicity of agencies involved in the receiving, registering, and settling of the evacuees led to chaos. Trains would arrive, dumping passengers off even when there was no room left at the *evakopunkt* to receive them. Those who arrived in the evening often found the *evakopunkt* closed, with no working canteen, no bread available, and occasionally no *kipiatok* (hot water that had been boiled to make it potable), the only beverage available to travelers. *Evakopunkt* officials complained that they often lacked information on the number of trains arriving, the time of arrival, the number of people entering the city, or the number of passengers who needed transport beyond Tashkent. This confusion led to situations in which the *evakopunkt* temporarily lacked the staff to process large numbers of unexpected travelers or the means to send transit passengers to their final destination. Hungry migrants camped out at the railroad station for extended periods of time not knowing when, how, or to what place they would eventually move.[33] One refugee wrote of his fellow migrants that "hundreds, perhaps thousands of people lay on the sidewalk and street in front of the train station. Some rested against little bundles, but for many, their only pillow was their fist. I caught sight of open sores oozing on swollen legs. Lice crawled over their bodies and clung to their hair. I had never seen such filth. The stench from sweat and waste was sickening. I listened to the sporadic outbursts of hacking coughs and to the deeper, rattling sounds of the very ill, who lay, almost prostrate[,] on the ground."[34] Many evacuees, disoriented and sick after their arduous trip to Central Asia and having seen fellow travelers get mugged in daylight at the Tashkent railway station, became wary of letting go of their belongings, travel documents, or food even for a few seconds during registration or medical checks. Others—the ill or weak—lay on the ground, waiting for medical help, registration, instructions on how they could receive employment or housing, or information on where they would be sent. With continually arriving trains, *evakopunkt,* militia, and NKVD officials could not process passengers fast enough. Even if they could, the city did not have shelter for such large numbers of evacuees, particularly in the rush period between December 1941 and March 1942. The Soviet polity had once aimed for absolute control over the lives, movements, and even thoughts of its citizens. In wartime, reaching this goal was no longer even remotely possible.

To ensure that refugees/evacuees washed themselves and to decrease the threat of infectious diseases, the Tashkent Gorispolkom turned over to the *evakopunkt* the *banyas* (Russian bathhouses) located near the railroad station.[35] However, these facilities were overcrowded and lacked soap, towels, and a stable water supply, making it difficult for travelers to clean themselves. Theft also was a major problem at these facilities, and it forced evacuees to guard their belongings because leaving them under the supervision of attendants did not guarantee their safety. The head of the Bukhara *evakopunkt* traveled to Tashkent and used one of the municipal *banya*s near the railroad station. He witnessed the way that attendants returned laundered clothing to bathers: the attendants simply threw the packets of clean clothes into a corner, thus forcing naked patrons to scuffle with one another to regain their belongings.[36] As archival documents and memoir accounts attest, losing one's shirt, pants, underwear, or shoes was a major problem because clothing was in short supply and often irreplaceable.[37] The battle to preserve one's belongings while bathing became as important for survival as the bath itself. Chaos reigned in the institutions that were supposed to supply basic necessities to and guarantee the health of the new residents of Tashkent.

Individual factories in Tashkent—pre-existing facilities and evacuated plants—were expected to take part in the registration process by assisting the Gorispolkom in finding space in the city to house recent arrivals and by transporting them to their new homes. After all, the new arrivals would be their workers who had been evacuated or other evacuees soon to join them on the production floor. Considering the shortage of industrial labor in the region, Tashkent factories had incentives to help out the "unorganized" migrants, the healthiest and most skilled of whom they quickly recruited as workers. Even so, finding them housing remained difficult. This predicament resulted in lengthy delays in settling and employing evacuees and in continual complaints by evacuees and native Tashkenters who suddenly found themselves either living in ever more crowded buildings or banished from the city limits altogether.[38] In ten years, Soviet housing plans went from Stepan Polupanov's model housing commune to model four-story apartments and then to official instructions to convert into housing various structures that had never been imagined for use as human shelter, including bathrooms, underground dugouts, stables, storage sheds, outdoor tents, schools, and clubs.[39]

While some Tashkenters were evicted from the city and others lived in overcrowded buildings, officials and residents alike complained about the endless numbers of migrants who managed to work their way into Tashkent by bribing militia or *evakopunkt* officials for Tashkent registration or by having factory administrators, often personal acquaintances, put them on factory staff lists even if they lacked appropriate skills. Officially, access to Tashkent was strictly controlled, but as Maria Belkina has remarked, those with money, jewelry, or other valuables could settle in the city after bribing local officials.[40] It became clear that wealth or privilege gave certain evacuees power to maneuver their way through the evacuation and to survive the war years. In fact, the procurator (chief prosecutor) of the Uzbek SSR criticized those who had large sums of cash or expensive jewelry or used *blat* (personal connections) because doing so gave evacuees as a group a bad reputation among the local population.[41] In a classless society, markers of class and ethnic privilege determined where one spent the war—under German occupation, in endangered cities, in the relative safety of home-front urban centers, or in the distant Central Asian countryside.

Workers' Lives in Central Asia

Throughout the war years, newspaper articles publicized the need to keep Tashkent clean—both to lower disease rates and to create a "cultured" environment. Even in wartime, the Soviet state did not completely cease its effort to create model citizens and ideal urban spaces, at least in its rhetoric. However, the pressing dilemma of controlling infections eventually took precedence over "civilizing" campaigns in propaganda for urban cleanliness. To create "clean" and "cultured" wartime spaces, city officials mandated that construction workers speed up housing construction and urban beautification projects, install sewers and water pipes, and enclose or build linings for the city's filthy drainage canals.[42] In 1942, a physician from the Tashkent Textile Kombinat health service spoke of the need to conduct an anti-cholera campaign among workers of the textile factory, with the mandatory vaccination of all employees and their families in the factory's housing areas. Nonetheless, the *kombinat*'s workers noted that the campaign for cleanliness in the factory largely failed. With all employees involved in production, the wartime workshop lacked cleaning staff to conduct disinfection work, resulting in a dangerously dirty working environment. The lack of glass on windows, a shortage of shoes for workers, and the arrival of winter caused a flu epidemic at the factory.[43] The inability to take simple precautions increased illness rates and contributed to high rates of factory turnover—and employee death—during the war.

Party officials in Tashkent recognized that inferior health standards, food shortages, and the poor living conditions of urban residents—native Tashkenters, Russian residents, and recently arrived evacuees alike—all contributed to falling industrial output. In 1942, the Central Committee and Sovnarkom ordered the construction of the Northern Tashkent Canal in order to expand the area of arable agricultural land in the region, which, it was hoped, would eventually help to satisfy the needs of the city population and to provide food for those on the front lines.[44] Factories created gardens to provide additional produce for workers, while most of the open land in the city was converted to vegetable plots, although the urban residents, many of them new to the Central Asian climate, were not always adept at keeping plants and animals alive.[45] Petty and violent crime increased in the wartime city as residents pilfered food and supplies from their workplaces and from each other. One memoirist recalls an evening when thieves came into his home, slaughtered his goat, and took the carcass, leaving behind only the bloody remains and depriving the family of a vital food source.[46] V. S. Turman, an evacuated Textile Kombinat employee, was murdered by colleagues at a factory storage room. Her assailants stabbed her eighteen times before stealing the cloth and leather that she was guarding. Evacuees spoke of Turman as an honest Soviet worker who had been saved from Hitler's bombs in Kiev, only to be killed by "bandit hands" on the home front; they demanded harsh punishment for her murderers.[47] Daily life in Tashkent's industrial workplaces became increasingly unruly and dangerous as employees competed for scarce food and other resources they could use to trade on the black market. Bartering, whether of family heirlooms or stolen goods, was so prevalent that most people had sold all their possessions by the end of the war. To survive, many Tashkenters were forced to commit theft.

Fighting crime, preventing disease, and monitoring the conditions of housing were seen as necessary to show "concern" for the workers in their homes. *Fabkom* officials declared that meeting these needs was an essential factor in stabilizing the workforce. Desertion rates continued to rise throughout the war, especially among Uzbeks, indicating that even in the later years of the war, the military conflict had not yet created a stable urban workforce with a large indigenous Central Asian representation. In 1944, for example, some Tashkent factories experienced extremely high turnover rates—almost 100 percent—among Uzbek employees.[48] An Uzbek Central Committee report identified four main reasons for this high turnover rate among native Central Asians. The first was the lack of "care" for Uzbek workers, likened to the failure to provide for the needs of all workers in the city. Second, training programs were poorly organized and not conducted in Uzbek, thereby preventing many labor recruits from fully understanding their jobs. Third, the majority of Tashkent's newly recruited Uzbek workers came from the countryside, where their families remained, and where many believed food was slightly more plentiful; the village thus drew many of these workers to return. Finally, the Central Committee report noted that officials in Namangan and other cities simply rounded up people at bazaars or train stations and sent them to the capital to work. These "railroad-" and "bazaar-" recruited workers were not the most reliable Soviet citizens, often had infectious diseases, and did not necessarily want to move to the Uzbek capital.[49] They deserted the factory in large numbers and attempted to return home. Fighting desertion under these circumstances remained an enormous challenge, even when deserters were put on trial.[50]

However, one should not think that the problem of keeping Uzbeks at work in factory production indicates that they were not tied to the Soviet state or did not have feelings of allegiance to the socialist polity. For evidence to the contrary, one need only look at how many Uzbeks became infused with Soviet propaganda and notions of Soviet patriotism during the war years, as was evident in their treatment of ethno-national groups that the Soviet state identified as wartime internal enemies. By the middle of the conflict, many Uzbeks expressed resentment toward Tashkent's small ethnic German population as well as outright hostility toward the Crimean Tatar deportees, who arrived in the Tashkent region in 1944. Uzbeks, whose patriotism had been doubted at numerous times by the state and who were considered harder to keep in factory jobs, certainly showed their loyalty to the state in their harsh treatment of these outsiders, whom they considered to be actively anti-Soviet and the cause of their years of wartime suffering.

In the spring of 1944, with the Nazi armies finally in retreat and the Soviet Union recovering lands that had been under occupation, Soviet leaders and security officials—Stalin and NKVD chief Beria foremost among them—identified ethnic groups that they considered to have been disloyal to the Soviet cause during Nazi occupation. The Crimean Tatar population of the Black Sea region—along with a variety of other ethnic groups, such as the Chechens, Meshketian Turks, Volga Germans, and Ingush—was identified as having collaborated with the Nazi occupiers, although there is no overwhelming evidence that their cooperation with the Germans was much more extensive than that of other Soviet groups.[51] Nonetheless, having been identified as internal Soviet enemies, the Crimean Tatars were deported en masse to the distant home front, with Uzbekistan and Tashkent oblast in particular receiving the bulk of them.[52] Upon the arrival of deportees, Uzbeks did not welcome any who had reportedly assisted the Nazis. In most cases, having heard three years of war propaganda that demonized fascists and having made enormous wartime sacrifices of their own, with Uzbek family members dying on the front in great numbers, local Uzbeks treated the Crimean Tatars as true enemies of the state. Some Tashkent oblast villagers stoned the deportees—even children—upon their arrival in the Tashkent region.[53] Other Uzbeks expressed anger that they, loyal Soviet citizens, suddenly had to live alongside internal Soviet enemies, and they questioned why Uzbekistan became the "dumping ground" for such traitors. One Uzbek man complained that the Crimean Tatars should not have been "sent to a good place like Uzbekistan, they at least should have been sent to a place in Siberia for their crime against the Motherland," a clear indication that he identified with the Soviet project and the larger Soviet state.[54] Others reacted violently toward the forced migrants, even murdering the deportees in punishment for the destruction they supposedly had brought to the Soviet people.[55] These actions are telling because Uzbeks had little contact with Crimean Tatars (who were also Muslims) before 1944, yet they conveyed a sense of Soviet identity, solidified by the war, and took reprisals against outsiders who had allegedly allied themselves with the Germans during the Nazi-Soviet conflict. Uzbeks might not always have acted as Party leaders had hoped and might have been more difficult to entice and keep in factory production, but these residents certainly demonstrated their allegiance to the Soviet Union in their mistreatment of the region's new Crimean Tatar population.

Uzbek collective farmers outside the city punished these deportees both for their alleged collaboration as well as for their presence in Uzbekistan. One Uzbek village brigade leader was arrested for beating up a young Crimean Tatar boy whose special settler parents allowed the child to come to the cotton field. The brigade leader threw the young boy into an irrigation canal after the attack, and documents suggest that the child might not have survived. Another brigade leader attacked and killed a female Crimean Tatar special settler in March 1945.[56] Local residents of Uzbekistan expressed both anger at the deportees and fear over what the deportations meant to them. Rumors proliferated across the Uzbek countryside that the Crimean Tatars had hidden German spies in their midst and planned to poison the food and water supplies of the region.[57] Some local residents even feared that the deportation of the Tatars was only a start and that Uzbeks and Russians soon would be forcibly removed from certain parts of Uzbekistan.[58] Once again, mixed messages from the state regarding Crimean Tatar deportations helped to spread wild rumors around the Uzbek SSR as residents tried to understand why the state had sent to live among them people whom they were told had contributed to their years of wartime deprivation and had helped the Nazis kill their sons and brothers on the front lines. In the war years, Soviet identity clearly gained ground among the Uzbeks, who lashed out much more harshly against these deportees than they had against previous migrants, such as the prewar Korean deportees, to whom many Uzbeks were simply indifferent.

Extreme Hardship

Despite attempts to curb high desertion rates, contain infectious diseases, and lessen the strain of hunger, city officials made little headway in addressing residents' concerns, although Party organs carefully documented Tashkenters' complaints and the declining living standards in the Uzbek capital. Gorispolkom files from the Tashkent City Archive in fact contain excerpts of intercepted letters and telegrams from city residents to their relatives in the Red Army. These letters chronicle the harsh conditions of life for average Tashkenters—both Uzbek and Russian—who lacked the privileges and connections that some of the more prominent evacuees and local Party members possessed. Just as in other cities across the Soviet Union, the Tashkent Gorispolkom attempted to investigate and ameliorate the truly desperate cases of hardship in the city, especially because the state expended so much time and effort in propagandizing the fact that the families of Soviet soldiers were treated well on the distant home front. Even so, the families of active duty military personnel clearly felt neglected and angry over their fate. Many blamed the state and frequently lashed out at local bureaucrats and factory administrators who took little interest in their lives on the home front while their husbands, fathers, brothers, and sons shed their blood for the Soviet state. Tashkent families of all ethnic groups wanted and expected more for their sacrifices, but the city rarely delivered or did so only after it was too late. In this sense, looking at Tashkent provides an important case study of how residents of home-front cities interacted with local, state, and Party institutions during the war.

In March 1943, E. A. Chentsova, a teacher, wrote to her husband that his family was "freezing and starving" in Tashkent. She lacked food for the children and had sold all of the household belongings except for one bicycle. Malnourished and suffering from sclerosis, she could barely take care of her two children, her only reason for living. She complained that she did not receive enough help from the school, local officials, or the *voenkomat*, the military district office that conducted the draft and performed military functions at the local level. The director of the school

even told me, "What more help do you want? Do we really not give you much help? We give [your family] three meals, we brought heating fuel, I also added two boxes of matches and an electric lamp." The Commissar began to yell at me, saying that I should not talk to my boss that way. I started to cry and told him that I will not come to him for anything, even if that means we die from starvation. . . . The director turns out to be an asshole and tries to make my life horrible at every step.[59]

When residents on the home front could not get local officials to respond with the help that they thought they deserved, they often turned to the military. They pressured *voenkomat* officials in the Uzbek capital to provide financial assistance and relief from the wartime tax burden for soldier families. However, citizens without documentation that their relatives served in the military had no proof of army service and, therefore, experienced difficulty in getting exemptions or aid. Uzbek Tashkenters also understood that military service provided important benefits from the state and lobbied the city for assistance. Tashkenters of all nationalities contacted their relatives in the army to have them use whatever military connections they had to improve the conditions of life on the home front.[60]

G. I. Dergachev, for example, asked his brother on the front to enlist the assistance of his commander in relieving the "family of a Red Army soldier" from military taxes. The Dergachev family was in a horrible financial situation and survived mainly from of the sale of their mother's blood. He wrote, "Mom has become so bad and weak and we tell her she must stop giving blood, but she says that if she stops, we will all get weak."[61] Lacking help from the state or from the military, many women across the Soviet home front, like Dergachev's mother, were forced to endanger their lives in a desperate attempt to keep their children alive. A. M. Vergun similarly wrote to her husband on the front, saying that she had sold almost everything at the market, thus leaving their son home alone "in tears and hunger," and that the only thing she had left to sell was her blood, which would get her an eight-hundred-gram bread ration card.[62] These are letters of desperation. The families writing them mention little about the ideology of the war or about the heroism of their relatives in the Soviet military, as contemporary propaganda articles described. Instead, these residents were unbearably anxious about their ability to survive the war, even though they were experiencing no direct physical danger from the enemy. The Uzbek capital was far from the front, considered a "safe city," and did not experience the same level of starvation and destruction as did Leningrad, Minsk, or Stalingrad, but survival on the Soviet home front was by no means guaranteed. Tashkenters of all ethnic groups suffered tremendously and feared for the future of their families, especially for their children.

Another woman wrote to a relative on the front that her family found themselves in "nightmarish" conditions in the Uzbek capital. They received a telegram telling them to "move immediately," and their belongings were quickly thrown out on the street, although it is unclear why they were evicted from their home: "We haven't had a word from you. We are stuck in the most nightmarish conditions in a basement on cement and without anything. . . . [I] only need to wait until the spring, yes it's true that we will receive [relief] in the spring, but in the spring they will lay me out in a grave."[63] More fortunate evacuees lived above ground in apartments, but as N. V. Puchkova of the Tashkent satellite town of Chirchik noted, apartment conditions also were far from ideal with chunks of concrete falling off of her building onto the street. She complained that while some residents had been given land for individual gardens, she received nothing: "In general, I have not seen such heartless treatment of families of military service men anywhere."[64] She does not ask for direct help from the city, military, or her relative. She simply complains about her life and criticizes the callous nature of the Soviet system for its mistreatment of soldiers' families.[65]

Others complained that *blat* (connections) was the key to survival and that, without it, they would see no improvement in their lives. Puchkova most likely falls into this category with her anger over being overlooked for a garden plot. Officially, having a family member in the army provided one with better access to state aid, but having money and knowing the right people offered better guarantees for attaining a slightly higher standard of living. L. M. Bogomolskaia wrote to her brother that "I can't get settled anywhere, there are no possibilities, everywhere you need *blat,* but I have none of it, and I am not one of those types of peoples. You, of course, know me best. . . . One needs a lot of money and I have nothing, as you yourself know."[66] Another Russian woman complained that she was evicted from her home but was uncertain of what rights she had because the documents she was given by the landlord were in Uzbek, without a Russian translation. She felt discriminated against and was particularly angry that, despite her son's service in war, the landlord could simply throw her belongings on the street. Many of Tashkent's Russians (both permanent residents and evacuees), officially the leading national group in Soviet society, felt like second-rate citizens in wartime Uzbekistan, even if they had privileges that other groups did not—such as access to closed cafeterias or polyclinics that served the workers of individual factories or cultural institutions.[67] Nonetheless, this Russian woman, not knowing what recourse she could take, complained that she had little faith in the law in Uzbekistan because "everything here is done for money."[68] This woman, however, lashed out at the Uzbek nature of the city and Uzbek greed as the cause of her suffering. In the wartime socialist city, money—the marker of the capitalist system of the past—remained the key to survival, but once again, the complaints of Russians took on ethnic undertones.

The lives of some were clearly confounded by ethnic prejudice, as the discussion of Uzbeks' anger at the Tatar deportees has shown. Their harsh reaction clearly was an indication of anger against an "enemy" group being dumped into their midst. Tashkent's own ethnic German population suffered as well, even though they were so far from the front lines that they could not have provided active assistance to the Nazis. Some ethnic Germans were banished from the city itself, while others were dismissed from their jobs in Tashkent factories, a frightening prospect since employment was the prime means of securing food and housing. One ethnic German woman, a native of Tashkent, suspected that her nationality was the reason for losing her job, despite the fact that she believed herself to be a loyal Soviet citizen, one whose son and two brothers had died while serving in the Red Army on the front.[69] Even people with German-sounding last names were exiled from the Uzbek capital with little regard for their status as "loyal" workers in the Soviet Union or proof of real connections with Germany. One woman protested her expulsion in a letter to the Tashkent Gorispolkom on February 5, 1942. She claimed that both she and her husband were Russians, did not know how they came to have a German surname, and did not identify with Germany in any way. Nonetheless, she was expelled from the city; similarly, another Russian woman, married to a Soviet German, protested her expulsion, stating that "my tragedy, the tragedy of my life is that I am a Russian, Soviet woman, kicked out of my native hearth [ochagi], from the city where I spent my youth[,] for being a German."[70] Her marriage, perfectly legitimate before the war, brought devastation upon her a decade later and caused her to be banished from her native Tashkent to the countryside, where her survival, she believed, would be much more difficult. The war further solidified ethnic categories, with the identification and punishment of nationalities that had been declared internal or external enemies. With city residents in such a fight for survival, the slightest whiff of disloyalty—even if imagined—could have devastating consequences, with not only the state but also fellow residents regarding such people as enemies.

However, ethnicity was not always an issue as people struggled to maintain a meager existence. One woman, Teplitskaia, angrily complained to her husband about the difficulties his children endured in Uzbekistan. She identified specific local leaders as being dishonest and condemned much of the Soviet system as inefficient, corrupt, and indifferent to the needs of most normal families, particularly those with relatives on the front lines. However, the local official was not an Uzbek or a German but a man called Migurenko. The official responsible for assisting families of Red Army soldiers, he provided Teplitskaia with no assistance, while allegedly using his position to enrich himself. She wrote that "he knows how to set himself up. He is very sly. I once turned to him with a request that when he gives out store coupons, that he would keep us in mind for at least one pair of shoes" for her children. However, Migurenko responded that he could not provide her with assistance because his own children went barefoot. Teplitskaia did not believe him, stating, "Just think, his kids are clothed and the wives of *frontoviki* [front-line soldiers] and their children complain and receive nothing, or they help them only on paper and write a lot about it in the newspaper. I think that such a system could only exist here, I cannot even imagine that they relate everywhere as [they do] here. One answer [that they give] is that there are so many of you and that we can't provide for all of you and, therefore, it is better to give nothing to everyone."[71] People with privileges carefully guarded their advantages, whether these amounted to better access to food, better paying jobs, or improved housing conditions. Offering payoffs to officials or using one's position to provide favors became essential means of improving one's life in the Uzbek capital, which was also the case across the Soviet landscape during the war and for most of the Soviet era. Personal connections and money were essential to surviving the war. Teplitskaia's comments are insightful because they indicate that ethnically Uzbek officials were not the only ones who mistreated evacuees or family members of Red Army soldiers, as has so often been implied in Russian memoirs or letters. Ukrainians, Russians, Jews, and others, like Migurenko, also were complicit in this "lack of care" shown to fellow European migrants in Central Asia. Soviet bureaucrats of European background were not necessarily any better than ethnically Uzbek officials in their treatment of war refugees.

Young Tashkenters, people with virtually no clout in the Soviet system, occasionally wrote heart-rending letters, asking relatives on the front for help and guidance on how to survive the war. Tashkent children grew up quickly and often took on adult responsibilities, frequently showing a remarkable understanding of how to function effectively in the Soviet world. One girl wrote, "Mommy cannot work because she is in poor health. Grandma helped us, but she died on January 24, 1943. Now, we are left just the three of us: Mommy, little Liuda, and me. We live very badly. We sold all we had. Now we have nothing left to sell and are in an inescapable situation. We can't wait for help because Daddy already died on the front."[72] In fact, when a mother died, older children often took on parental roles in helping their younger siblings or elderly grandparents survive. Children quickly had to learn how to maneuver through the tremendously complicated Soviet bureaucracy. Another girl, for example, asked her father to send money immediately to help save her mother's life, informing him that the mother would die unless he sent money to purchase animal fat.[73] Considering that the statements from these personal letters were recorded by censors and delivered to the Tashkent Gorispolkom for investigation, it is doubtful that the letters ever made it to the front. If they did, however, there was no guarantee that money sent from father-soldiers on the front would ever reach their families, as is evident in the complaints of servicemen who attempted to wire money home.[74]

As mentioned previously, many Tashkenters asked their relatives in the army to intercede on their behalf to improve their standard of living. Even so, having a relative's military commander on the front write to Tashkent did not ensure that action would be taken. Many soldiers' families shuffled between city assistance agencies in futile quests for help. A woman wrote to her son that his request from the battlefield to the Tashkent Gorispolkom led neither to an investigation of their standard of living nor to amelioration of their poverty. The Gorispolkom informed the woman that the son's request had been forwarded to the district soviet from which aid would come. However, financial assistance never arrived, and the mother again asked her son to enlist the help of his commander to force the Gorispolkom, which had already once "refused to provide material assistance to your mother," to help the family.[75] Giving an indication of how bad conditions were in Tashkent, a woman—likely an Uzbek—came down with pellagra, an illness caused by a vitamin deficiency. Although she had a prescription, she was unable to get it filled: "You have a prescription form, go to the *voenkomat,* it will give it to you. The *voenkomat* commissar said that the women's committee was responsible, but the women's committee said that I could receive it only if I were a girl under age 13 and that they are not able to give it to adults. 'Go to the *voentorg* [trade supply organization or store for military families]. In the *voentorg,* they said that they . . . had no [medicine], they give it only to commanding officers and that they had no nutritionally valuable food."[76]

As a relative of a soldier, she had access to a social welfare system that served military families. However, since almost every family had some connection to the military, assistance was far from guaranteed. There were simply too many military families in Tashkent that needed help. Similarly, a sixty-eight-year-old Uzbek complained to his son that the family received no assistance from local authorities. He noted that he had been refused help by the district soviet officials, who informed him that his daughter should be responsible for supporting the family. However, the daughter was ill, and the father maneuvered the maze of Tashkent organizations—district soviet, district *voenkomat,* oblast *voenkomat,* and back to the district soviet. This sick and elderly man traveled the city in a futile search for help that he, the father of an Uzbek Red Army soldier, deserved from the Soviet state, or so he stated.[77] He expressed patriotism in his Sovietness and honor in the work that his son was doing on the front but lashed out at the state itself for its ineptitude. Soviet bureaucracy, hopelessly inefficient and frustrating to those who had to deal with it in peacetime, had devastating consequences during the war. The poorly functioning bureaucracy stopped functioning in many respects.

Uzbek Tashkenters frequently turned to family members for assistance when nothing came from the state. However, this approach did not always work because some families were too large or too poor and therefore did not have enough to spread around. One Uzbek woman, identified as Ibragimova, wrote to her husband that "their three children suffered without heating fuel. And that your relatives, nobody, pays absolutely any attention to our situation."[78] Uzbeks noted that many forms of assistance—familial and state—broke down during the war, leaving residents on their own.[79] Another Uzbek woman despondently wrote to her brother on the front lines that every day she "waits for her death" in wartime Tashkent.[80] Her expectations of perishing in Central Asia were no different than those of migrants from other republics of the Soviet Union and indicated that Uzbeks were not in a significantly better material situation than were evacuees, as many Russian-speaking residents of wartime Tashkent implied.

However, there were successes when Tashkenters received help in the city either officially or through personal relationships. Anna Aleksandrova wrote to her husband that she could purchase only three kilos of corn flour with her salary of three hundred rubles. Upon investigation, the Kuibyshev district *voenkomat* determined that her complaints were true, that the family did not have enough to eat, and that she and her two small children needed food, which the district *voenkomat* and her husband's former employer, Uzbekvino, provided.[81] At times, Uzbeks were criticized for their indifference to refugees, but there were numerous reports of assistance across ethnic lines, particularly with regard to orphaned children, who either found permanent homes through adoption by Central Asian families or provision of temporary shelter for the duration of the war. Shaakhmed Shamakhmudov and his wife, Bakhri Akhmedova, took care of fourteen orphaned children, supposedly answering the state's call to provide assistance in caring for those who had lost their parents to German bombs.[82] Not everyone was indifferent to the plight of refugees, particularly children. The state, recognizing its inability to provide assistance, actively asked locals to help; it did so by commissioning propaganda works by Uzbek and Russian authors, such as Gafur Gulom, who wrote a poem titled "You Are Not an

Orphan!" and Kornei Chukovskii, who wrote about the plight of refugee children in Central Asia in the 1942 work "Uzbekistan and Children."[83] At a meeting of Tashkent women in 1941, prominent Tashkent residents called on all women of Uzbekistan to take the burden of caring for children off the state so that it could concentrate on "destroying the rabid fascist dogs."[84] Many compassionate Uzbek families listened to these pleas, looked at the desperation around them, and took charitable action, thereby saving the lives of countless war orphans.

Nonetheless, ignoring the needs of others remained a problem. A shocking example of death caused by the indifference of local officials in the model Soviet city of Central Asia concerned the family of Anatoly Golubev. He was mobilized into the Red Army in May 1942, although for some reason he was assigned to a defense factory in Samarkand. He left a family—a wife and three children—behind in the Uzbek capital. During his absence, his wife came down with pellagra, an illness that was common in wartime Tashkent and in the GULAGS, an indication that the standard of living in a major Soviet city had decreased in the war to the level of the infamous forced labor camps. The disease caused seizures, psychological disorders, diarrhea, and exhaustion. Golubev's four-year-old daughter and eight-month-old son died of the illness, but because the mother was bedridden, no one moved the body of the young boy or informed officials of his death. Presumably having been made aware of the death by the smell of a decaying body, the chair of the district *ispolkom*, A. A. Popova, and a neighbor eventually investigated the apartment. They found an "impoverished and starving family." They also learned that a doctor had once visited the family and prescribed medicine, but, like the Uzbek woman with pellagra, the prescription could not be filled. No additional treatment or check-ups were conducted. It was clear that the officials had warning of the family's dire situation; there were records of doctors, city officials, and neighbors all visiting the home. Popova even declared on October 5, 1942, that the district *ispolkom* would provide immediate medical and financial assistance, but the Golubevs still received nothing. On October 18, 1942, the sick mother died, leaving her thirteen-year-old daughter to dispose of the body. The girl was unable to do so and the body lay in the bed for five days, eventually decaying and even beginning to collapse in on itself. Informed of the death of his wife and children, Golubev returned from Samarkand on October 22. Despite an abominable stench in the apartment, he could arrange the removal of the body and burial only with great difficulty on October 23, five days after his wife's death. Both he and his surviving daughter testified that, by the end, maggots had eaten off the dead woman's face.[85]

The procurator of Tashkent oblast and the military procurator for the Central Asian Military District (SAVO) blamed the housing committee and militia for not assisting in the removal of the body. After all, there was "no way that they could not have known about [this situation], but took no action." They also informed Vassilii Emtsov, the Tashkent Gorkom chairman, that the starvation and death of this family showed that district committees failed to pay attention to the needs of relatives of men who had been mobilized into the army or defense industry. However, there is no indication that criminal charges were filed against the doctor, district *ispolkom* chair, neighbor, housing committee members, or militia, all of whom could have but chose not to intervene either before or after the deaths.[86] Tashkent's bureaucracy and the callousness of Soviet officials caused these horrifying deaths and, most likely, traumatized the surviving child. This family's destruction was not a Nazi atrocity but one the Soviets produced on their own. Soviet citizens on the "distant home front" of Tashkent may have been spared German bombs, bullets, and ethnic cleansing, but they were not safe from the Soviet system itself.

During the Nazi-Soviet conflict, Tashkent was a city of migrants. Russians, Ukrainians, Jews, Uzbeks, and others traveled to the city in search of refuge, food, and a better life. Soviet historians have chronicled cases of home-front heroism among residents who toiled in factories and collective farms to supply the Soviet military with ammunition and food. Many Uzbeks and Russian inhabitants of the republic also opened their arms and homes to desperate refugees and evacuees. These stories are true and have been amply retold in Soviet and post-independence Uzbek historiography.[87] Still, wartime experiences on the home front also demonstrate that migrants looked at Tashkent as a distant, frightening, and dangerous place. Local residents and migrants alike initially were unsure of the outcome of the Nazi-Soviet conflict and expressed concern over a future that they believed would be different no matter which side won the conflict. This uncertainty and the shortage of basic necessities brought about a spike in ethnic tensions between Central Asia's indigenous and migrant populations. Although there were examples of Soviet-style "friendship of the peoples," the war did not necessarily bring the Soviet people together and frequently deepened internal divisions in society. However, the war also provided Uzbeks with intimate knowledge of other Soviet groups—some of it positive and some of it negative. These interactions with other members of Soviet society solidified local identities and helped Central Asians form sharper opinions of the Soviet system, at times voicing anger at the state and other times expressing pride in their "Sovietness." Many residents—Uzbek, Russian, and others—tried to use their Sovietness to get what they needed in a city where food, shelter, medicine, and fuel were all in short supply.

In a contradictory way, Tashkent was not just a city of atrocious living conditions, material want, and ethnic hatred. Tashkent was also a city where elite Russian intellectuals created their own cultural world and were able to escape the shock of the war as privileged refugees. Still, few seemed happy in the Uzbek capital, and everyone spoke of their personal or familial hardships. Feelings of desperation varied from person to person, mostly depending on the circumstances through which one came to live in Tashkent. Prominent cultural evacuees and Soviet officials traveled to the model Soviet city in Central Asia by crowded passenger trains, and many of them returned a few years later in American-designed Douglas airplanes. Polish deportees walked from prison camps toward the Soviet-Persian border in a desperate attempt to leave the Soviet state. Prisoners of war and deportees were placed in cattle cars and then abandoned in the Tashkent region and other parts of Central Asia, with massive loss of life. Indigenous Central Asians often were rounded up at markets and transportation centers across the region and, with little say in the matter, sent to work in Tashkent factories.

Once in the city, these groups struggled for survival, often against each other. For the intellectual evacuees, it was a psychological battle to survive the war and return home to Moscow, Leningrad, or Kiev. This desire gave them reasons for living. Others engaged in a physical battle for survival. For the Golubev family, Tashkent meant a futile struggle against disease and starvation; their horrendous deaths were just one of the shocking cases of suffering in this large, multiethnic Soviet city. However, many were luckier or perhaps more astute at maneuvering through the chaos, selling what they could, bribing officials, stealing from others, or using whatever status they had in the system to get ahead. Everyone sold their belongings on the Tashkent black market, so much so that by the end of the war there was not much of a market for used goods.[88] In the end, wartime Tashkent was a city of many lives. At times, these individual experiences converged. Other times, Tashkenters lived entirely different existences in a city with tremendous economic, ethnic, and social divisions.

Even so, the social fabric of the state did not break, although it frayed tremendously in the Uzbek capital under the pressure of war, disease, starvation, and urban squalor. The Soviet system was built on an ideology of total mobilization. Every aspect and member of that society needed to participate in the Soviet project. The Soviet Union was well suited to an era of total war, when the conflict with Germany deeply affected distant areas of the Soviet Union, as these descriptions of wartime Tashkent indicate. Although many fled the front lines, Soviet citizens could never truly escape the consequences of war, even in cities where life was comparatively normal. To survive, they were forced to interact with that society and solve the problems of urban life that the Soviet government could not manage. In turn, although it was slow and clumsy in its response to the constant changes of the war, the Soviet system was able to instill a sense of purpose among a desperate population, often with promises of an easier life after the war. These declarations of a happy Soviet future gave Tashkenters of all stripes, like the inhabitants of other cities, incentives to push on toward victory. Yet, with these promises, the state likely sowed the seeds of future dissatisfaction among many residents who, through personal and familial sacrifice, had begun to identify more closely with the socialist system during the war years and believed that life would improve when the horror of the conflict was over. The shock of the Nazi invasion and the pain that it caused in every sector of Soviet society kept the city functioning during a time of enormous confusion. After the war, however, governing and transforming this Soviet city would remain difficult, particularly when the Nazi threat was no longer a part of daily life and the constant struggle to survive eased a bit. With these changes, the population soon would start to make more frequent demands of the state that had promised them a better future.

THE POSTWAR SOVIET CITY, 1945–1953

The evacuation of defense and heavy industry transformed Tashkent into an industrial powerhouse with official markers of Soviet achievement—metallurgy, aircraft manufacturing, ammunitions production, and coal mining. During the war, Tashkent manufactured bombs but did not suffer from them. By the end of the conflict, the population bordered on close to a million, although the city soon lost some of its most qualified workers and intellectuals when many factories, cultural institutions, and evacuees returned home. Despite the Soviet ideological belief in the inevitability of war, the 1937–1939 reconstruction plan did not anticipate the chaotic wartime industrialization of this once distant capital of a largely agrarian Soviet republic. Tashkent's "New Industrial Face," the subject of many celebratory articles in *Pravda Vostoka* and *Qizil O'zbekiston,* had finally appeared, but the reality of life in 1945 was far from the Soviet ideal and the region was in shambles.[1]

In the early 1940s, most Central Asian cities expanded their urban infrastructure—public transportation, sewer systems, and electricity supplies—in the wartime effort to meet the tremendous increase in population, but these projects largely remained in varying states of disrepair. In Tashkent, tram tracks were now broken and underground pipes remained partially installed or severed, spilling waste and water into the streets and canals of the city. Unsanitary conditions, overcrowding, and industrial pollution caused disease rates to rise. Demobilized soldiers from Central Asia complained about the state of their home cities upon return: "We understand that less attention was spent on the urban economy during these years because of the war, but we mandate that everything be done to preserve what was completed before the war."[2] Recognizing Tashkent's dismal postwar conditions, the union Sovnarkom published a decree on March 6, 1946, entitled "On the means for improving the urban economy of Tashkent." It called for improvements in the standard of living and a transformation of the economy to meet peacetime needs.[3] The decree was similar to those published for other cities of the Soviet Union and did not list any concrete measures to change conditions in the city. The mere fact that a decree was promulgated was meant to demonstrate that the state cared about Tashkent, although it lacked the resources or will to do much about the complaints of Tashkenters.

The population increase during the war and the need to reestablish hastily evacuated industries in the city created distortions to its urban development project. During the war, the completion of the model avenue of Navoi Street had been put on hold, with half-completed building sites standing idle for years. Meanwhile, the city's residents continued to live in cramped and unsanitary housing—dark underground basements, unheated worker barracks, stairwells or hallways of administrative buildings, and mud hovels.[4] Although the Gorispolkom officially promoted the construction of apartment buildings for citizens in need of shelter, the state put a higher priority on monumental structures, worthy of an international power, as the means to show its "care" for the people. After the horror and hardship of war, the public areas of the Soviet city architecturally and rhetorically needed to evoke the bright future of a victorious state that had defeated fascism and was prepared to take the revolution around the globe. However, the needs of Tashkenters once again were secondary to other priorities and internal ideological battles as the Party sought to tighten its hold on postwar Soviet society in Central Asia.

Uzbek Traditions Revisited

On July 21, 1945, *Pravda Vostoka* published an exposé on the postwar condition of the Tashkent Central Telegraph building on Navoi Street. Although

the building's foundation was laid in 1935, construction was still not finished ten years later. The outside shell, radio receiver room, and main floor
evidently had been completed before the conflict, but the structure had a
variety of uses during the war. It served as a dormitory, a training school for
accountants, and temporary facilities for numerous evacuated educational
institutions. Each occupant adapted the building to suit its own needs,
tearing down walls, ripping up floor boards, and removing valuable supplies and equipment to use for other purposes. The ventilation system that
cooled the radio receiver was broken, making the Central Telegraph office
incapable of sending a simple Telex message.[5] This official description of
wartime destruction in Tashkent conveyed the impression that the building's residents, many of them temporary Tashkenters, looted the facility
before moving on to other sections of the city or back to European parts of
the Soviet Union after combat ended. Ironically, while the Red Army pil-
laged Germany, Soviet citizens and institutions were depicted as doing the
same to the semi-occupied and unfinished buildings in Tashkent. It was not
postwar anger or retribution that caused such destruction but the desperate
need to survive in the poor urban conditions of postwar Central Asia.

Part of the problem was that Mitkhat Bulatov, the city planner, had difficulty advancing "rational" urban planning in a time of immense wartime
urbanization. During the war, industrial zoning laws were neglected as
the Uzbek capital was forced to house its evacuated heavy industries anywhere it could, including in residential areas, parks, schools, and institutes
of higher education. Bulatov came under harsh criticism by the Gorkom
for failing to direct the Mosoblproekt program, a largely unfair critique
considering the tempo of the evacuation process and the strain of having
more than 2 million refugees pass through Tashkent. Clearly, Bulatov and
the Gorispolkom lacked the power to oppose the State Defense Committee
(GKO), union-level ministries, military factories, the Uzbek Central Committee, Sovnarkom, and other organizations that spurred most of the region's wartime development. In war, he and other planners responded to
but could not direct the city's unprecedented growth.

Furthermore, while propagandists celebrated the might of the Soviet
people in Uzbekistan during the war and their "heroism" in building a
base of heavy industry, it had become clear that this achievement was not
widespread throughout the region. "Socialist Tashkent" was supposed to be
a unified city where the division between the traditionally Uzbek and the
Russian sections had been erased, but the Old City had yet to receive a large
influx of heavy industry, a sign of modernity according to Soviet ideology.
During the war, this region of Tashkent lacked a pre-existing infrastructure

that could facilitate the establishment of evacuated factories and the transformation of existing facilities to military needs.[6]

Professor B. A. Korshunov, an architect who in 1946 served on a special commission to study the effects of the war on Tashkent's reconstruction plan, noted that the city unexpectedly grew toward the east and north, primarily Russian areas, with the establishment of military factories, including the Chkalov airplane production plant and the Pod'emnik machine parts facility.[7] Metallurgical operations were developed in northern Tashkent, an area that also served as a residential region, with mass construction of individual homes in violation of the city's zoning regulations. However, the Old City barely felt the impact of the evacuation of industry. The residents of the "unified" Uzbek capital in many respects struggled together against the Nazi threat but still experienced physical divisions and occupational separation as they went about their daily lives in the early postwar years. This segregation was underscored in a speech delivered in 1948 by Mukhamedov, a *raikom* secretary from the Old City's Oktiabr district who declared that the "day was not far off, when our city, Tashkent, and the workers of our region will hear the factory bell—the symbol of the working class in our country."[8] Industrial factories, allegedly the dream of Soviet citizens, were still absent from this Uzbek section of Tashkent.

The war intervened in the urban planning process in a variety of unforeseen ways. The evacuation brought prominent members of the Academy of Architecture from Moscow to Central Asia. While based primarily in Chimkent, Kazakhstan, across the border from Tashkent oblast, a branch of the academy was established in Tashkent. The presence of the Academy of Architecture in Central Asia allowed prominent Soviet architects and planners to gain actual living experience in the region. During their years of evacuation, these Moscow-based officials gained new understanding of the topography, climatic conditions, and general cultural traditions of Central Asia and Central Asians.[9] In the early postwar liberalization of intellectual thought, they tried to use this knowledge to find solutions to the chaotic nature of Tashkent city planning.

The results of these architects' experiences in the region could be seen in early postwar plans and academic publications. In June 1945, one architect defended his candidate's dissertation by arguing that the Health Commissariat of the Soviet Union neglected the needs of Central Asians when it designed hospitals and polyclinics. Citing his experiences of evacuation in Central Asia, he stated that Soviet health officials and engineers should study the climatic influences and how they related to health care and disease.[10] He noted that hospitals in Morocco, Italy, California, Australia, and other areas with warm climates were built specifically to decrease summer heat and protect patient rooms from the sun, sand, and wind. However, Tashkent hospital buildings typically had been designed in Moscow and did not reflect the needs of Tashkent, where the average temperature was 27.5 degrees Celsius.[11] He proposed that Soviet planners, if they were to safeguard public health, needed to look at Western examples for planning Central Asian medical facilities, a proposal that would not have been possible before the war. He also claimed that studying the traditional architecture of Central Asian homes would provide insights into how modern buildings could better regulate heat and dust and ultimately improve the comfort and well-being of patients.[12] These new interpretations of traditional architecture indicated a turning point, when planners finally abandoned previous Soviet and imperial Russian views of Central Asia as an unhygienic area that needed complete transformation.

In 1946, a commission of architects and engineers began to investigate the suitability of the prewar Kuznetsov proposal for postwar Tashkent. Many commission members questioned the need for tall buildings in Central Asia because the climate, which evacuees had described as unbearable, and the threat of earthquakes contradicted such construction. Perhaps single-story structures, the traditional Uzbek living accommodation, were more appropriate for the region, some argued. Furthermore, there were renewed calls to investigate the conventional use of trees and plants in the city and new views of the traditional *hauz* or water collection pools that dominated historic Central Asian urban centers. The native Central Asian sections of Tashkent suddenly were not as dry, dusty, and "naked" as commonly presented in prewar literature. In her academic history of Uzbek architecture, Veronika Voronina noted that the customary center of Uzbek urban life was actually a "blooming" garden, not the desert wasteland that prewar propagandists disparaged. These gardens were located beyond the streets and in the inner courtyards of the city's mosques and madrasas.[13] The Old City of Tashkent lacked European-style public gardens, but it was not as desolate as formerly described. Voronina called for extensive study of the traditional use of the *hauz* and the possibility that the grapevines in and around the centers of Uzbek life (the bazaar, mosque, and teahouse) might be adapted for use in Soviet urban planning.

She wrote that these features of long-established Uzbek culture should be incorporated into parks to create "green oases" that were not simply "European" in design, like Komsomol Park of 1939, but a mixture of modern Soviet styles and Uzbek traditions. These proposed parks could serve as the unifying points of the city, places where Russian and Central Asian customs would merge, eventually bringing about a unity among the city's residents. Perhaps the European-Russian-Soviet enlightenment project did not need to change everything in the city. Cleaning of the *hauz,* long denigrated by Russian and Soviet officials as a breeding point for infectious disease, could be done efficiently with Soviet science. In the prewar era, the transformation of urban space meant the destruction of existing settlements, but in the postwar period, it frequently called for the adaptation of existing structures.

Professor Korshunov concurred that courtyards off the streets actually contained the gardens that Soviet planners originally found lacking. These courtyards were the center of the Uzbek home, the *hovle:* "As a rule, the Old Town has no planting along the streets[:] there[,] streets are narrow and bending; there are passageways toward the homes along dusty roads [which] are in search of shade. But on the other hand, inside the quarters of the Old City and inside individual plots that are behind the blind walls are wonderful gardens with fruit and nut trees [and] grapevines, all of which are dependent on artificial water supplies."[14] These traditional features controlled the "micro-climate" as effectively as did Soviet parkland, an admission that reflected both a more relaxed view toward local culture during the war and an acknowledgment that studying established methods of Central Asian planting could give Soviet agronomists an idea of what types of trees might grow well. The prewar planting campaigns to make the city's streets and parks beautiful largely failed, with plants dying in record numbers due to neglect, a lack of water, or poor choice of plant species. Local varieties, especially those bearing fruit, more accurately reflected what plants could thrive in the harsh desert climate and Tashkent's need for readily available supplementary foods. In fact, individual fruit and vegetable gardens kept the wartime city alive, while many public gardens perished. Local customs, individual initiative, and native plants had kept the city blooming when Soviet technology and food distribution systems could not.[15]

Furthermore, as previously mentioned, the Uzbek *mahalla* consisted of traditional homes that ideologists believed impeded the active participation of Uzbeks in Soviet society. Often housing extended families, Uzbek homes were largely private structures with limited access to the street.[16] Just as Russian colonial planners did not acknowledge the existence of gardens within the Uzbek *hovle,* the happenings inside the Uzbek home had been a mystery to Soviet, particularly Russian, administrators. Destroying the physical home of Central Asian residents was seen as an important mechanism for gaining more detailed knowledge of Uzbek residents, which would help the state transform them into model citizens. However, the evacuation years gave a new perspective on conventional Central Asian living arrangements, causing urban planners to reevaluate the need for the destruction of the Old City. Some critics no longer viewed the *mahalla* as centered on the exclusivity of the family unit in which women and children were exploited by male relatives behind the exterior walls of the *hovle*. In fact, Bulatov and others began to argue that the *mahallas* actually were based on a communal understanding of a neighborhood in which each household relied on the help and assistance of their neighbors, as many families did during the war.[17] In other words, the single gate of the *hovle* that opened toward the street was no more closed to its neighbors than the Russian apartment door. The individual Uzbek home was different but not necessarily alien to the Soviet city.

Bulatov explained that this *mahalla* spirit need not be destroyed but could be transformed into an early version of the Soviet "micro-district," where communities would live in a compact area that could supply residents with all their needs: schools, bathhouses, stores, teahouses, workers' clubs, and other facilities. By adapting the *mahalla* to the socialist city, the Soviet state could achieve one of its long-standing goals of transforming the Uzbek into a model Soviet citizen. "Soviet *mahallas*" could facilitate enlightenment campaigns, break the influence of private trade with the introduction of modern Soviet stores, and make Uzbeks and Uzbekistan more hygienic with Russian-style bathhouses and "modern" sanitation. Once again, adaptation of the Central Asian community to Soviet life, not destruction, was a common theme of early postwar planning. It was viewed as a much more effective approach than the complete depopulation and subsequent transformation of the city's long-established Uzbek neighborhoods.

A. D. Karpov, a member of the commission, also noted that creating a large industrial center in Central Asia was much more difficult than previously envisioned. He argued that industrialization demanded a tremendous increase in population, which, for economic and transportation reasons, called for compact housing areas. However, he expressed concern that forcing Tashkent residents into multistory apartment blocks would negatively affect their health and destroy native traditions, a clear sign of a more liberal attitude toward Uzbek customs brought about by the war. Karpov stated that compact living areas were in "sharp conflict with the climatic conditions and hygienic needs of Tashkent. The reconstruction of Tashkent demands the construction of large apartment blocks, [which in turn] calls for the tremendous removal, actually, in truth, almost the complete destruction of the existing Asian region of the city; [the reconstruction] is in conflict with the existing way of life of the population and the traditions which have existed for centuries."[18] He believed that the original plans to build main thoroughfares through the Old City destroyed the national character of Tashkent. In fact, he even accused Kuznetsov of proposing a design for the Uzbek capital that had little relationship to the region but instead recalled Soviet cities of the north. In this manner, Tashkent would not be "national in form and socialist in content" but would simply be a large urban center without any individual character. Interestingly enough, Karpov, a Russian, fought to preserve the Uzbek way of life.

Karpov did not refute the need for four-story apartment buildings but noted that they should be in specific regions, while the remainder of the city could consist of numerous small-scale settlements of one-story structures that would be connected to industrial areas through a system of direct roadways.[19] He also proposed that the Old City already was a functioning "micro-district" that needed only to be tied more closely to the city through transportation lines. The majority of existing settlements could be preserved by breaking them down into smaller administrative units instead of having one large amorphous "Old Town." Since the Uzbek quarter had frequently been portrayed as a barren and disease-ridden area that was both foreign and threatening to pre-revolutionary Russian and post-1917 Soviet culture, breaking down the region into component parts also would have positive effects on state efforts to monitor and control the residents inside.[20] Such an action would make reinforcing Soviet values easier. In his arguments, Karpov implied that "Sovietizing" the Old City in stages with a sculptor's knife would be easier than transforming the area all at once with a bulldozer.

These initial postwar proposals for Tashkent came close to offering an alternative vision for the model Soviet Central Asian city. Unlike the period before the war, in 1946 the reviewers of the commission's initial work indicated that all Soviet cities did not necessarily need compact areas with tall buildings and wide, straight avenues. Although no one dared say so explicitly, perhaps the Moscow model did not work in Central Asia. The Old City's winding streets were no longer seen as a negative since they made sense in a desert climate and were preferred by the majority of the city's residents. Narrow streets with frequent curves offered shade from the sun and shelter from dust storms that broad, Soviet-style avenues could not, especially if all the trees planted along them subsequently died in the dry heat. Ironically, preserving the city's narrow streets quite possibly could have shown the "care" of the state for the people better than the Soviet attempt to change the "micro-climate," which had not yet shown any results. In general, these proposals reflect the fact that the war years gave Soviet citizens much more personal and intellectual freedom to explore alternative solutions and that the Soviet polity itself depended on such individual resourcefulness for its survival during the war.

These views also underscored the Tashkent reality in a time of tremendous economic difficulty. The Uzbek capital was an enormously large city of small buildings. Many residents already lived in conditions that Party officials deemed unsuitable for human habitation. Accommodating the existing housing structure was both a cheaper and an easier way to deal with the housing situation than continually destroying existing shelters to build new apartment complexes. Especially because money was earmarked for rebuilding the areas of the Soviet Union that had been devastated by the German occupation and retreat, Tashkent had neither the funds for a major housing initiative nor the local infrastructure for large-scale construction. For a very short time, reality trumped ideology in devising a city plan for the Soviet Uzbek capital. The transformation or destruction of the Old City was not a priority in the immediate postwar era because Tashkent had many more pressing problems to solve.

The Los Angeles of Central Asia

In Moscow, one architect, S. Motolianskii, looked to the United States, the Soviet Union's wartime ally, as a model for Central Asian urban planning. Reflecting the intellectual thaw during the war, he described Los Angeles as the American "analogue" to Tashkent. Motolianskii noted that Los Angeles, although a bit larger in population, had a similar climate and geography, with seismic activity being of particular concern for both cities. Southern California also grew tremendously during World War II due to its defense industries and its being a hub for food supply distribution. He observed that Los Angeles, with a population of more than 1.2 million in 1930, was a city of one-story private homes on individual plots with gardens and that a compact urban center was not necessary in this major city.[21] Although Motolianskii was not so daring as to propose that Tashkent follow the model of Los Angeles, he used the California analogy to highlight why the existing proposals were difficult to implement.[22]

Other members of the commission proposed the decentralization of Tashkent, which, due to its hot climate and neighboring mountain ranges, could not become an industrial area without tremendous negative health effects from air pollution, a notion that also recalled the situation in Southern California. The commission argued that Tashkent had already witnessed increases in respiratory illnesses (especially among children) during the rapid industrialization of the war years. Air pollution, compounded by

tremendously hot summers, decreased worker productivity and living standards.[23] Tashkent, in other words, had a smog problem. One-story buildings were presented as the most efficient way to improve the health and
industrial productivity of Tashkent's residents, with taller buildings being
suitable for the region only if planners followed the "American" model of
incorporating "air cooling" systems to reduce heat and provide cleaner air.[24]
The commission went out on a limb against the traditional urban model for
Soviet city construction.

Still, the commission also noted some positive aspects of the Soviet city,
based on the Moscow model. Korshunov, who proposed reorienting the Old
City into a series of Uzbek *mahalla* micro-districts, noted the importance
of maintaining Tashkent's radial street structure. He argued that Tashkent's
circular street plan in the Russian section of the city recalled Moscow and
Paris, two prominent European capitals, but that Tashkent's radial grid was
simply too large.[25] Tashkent, with an ideal population of a million, did not
need to replicate two of the most important European cities but should recall them on a smaller scale. Korshunov also noted the need for public urban parks. Tashkent also did not need a park like that of Versailles, but he
believed that a maximum number of trees should be planted in order to
make Tashkent resemble "an island of greenery" for passengers who were
approaching Tashkent from the air.[26] One notes the intense concern over
the public image of the city, even from the sky, which was not the usual
form of travel to the Uzbek capital in 1946. Just as Soviet planners struggled
to create beautiful parks around urban railroad stations, the image of the
area from above in the most modern form of transportation was equally
important. Kuznetsov wanted to build a Potemkin village along the main
thoroughfares of the city; Korshunov proposed establishing one from the
air. The tension between the reality, a sprawling desert city, and the ideal, a
lush and "green" metropolis, persisted.[27]

On September 13, 1946, the commission discussed its findings before the
Committee of Architectural Affairs of the Council of Ministers of the Soviet
Union in Moscow. Arkady Mordvinov, who chaired the meeting, declared
that the Mosoblproekt plan of 1937–1939 indeed ignored the local conditions
of Tashkent and was unrealistic.[28] Mordvinov singled out the proposed
Tashkent Hotel, designed by Bulatov and L. G. Karash, for being too high
even though it had been planned for the city center, near Red Square and
the site of the pre-revolutionary Voskresenskii Market.[29] Bulatov, the man
in charge of reconstructing the entire city, was guilty of designing a building that was too tall for the comfort of hotel guests. The fear that this hotel
might tower over the neighboring three-story Government House and the

entire administrative complex on Red Square may also have provoked this rebuke because the symbolic heart of Soviet rule in Central Asia could not be overshadowed by neighboring structures. The administrative center, long decried as a failure of Soviet design with its constructivist buildings, needed to take precedence in urban planning. Mordvinov believed the city administrative center should be built with modern materials, have tall structures, and incorporate ample parkland and water. By late 1946, the Committee of Architectural Affairs decreed that the city administrative region and parade ground took precedence in Tashkent's postwar urban renewal project, causing Bulatov's hotel to remain unfinished for more than ten years.[30]

The city architect accepted Mordvinov's critique, agreeing that the hotel was too tall. Bulatov acknowledged the criticism and added that Tashkent needed to incorporate more water into the city center complex. Doing so, he believed, would not be a problem since water supposedly was "everywhere" in Central Asia and Soviet hydrotechnology simply needed to access it. In these discussions, planners ironically described water as a natural component of the Uzbek environment instead of an artificial addition to the city. Incorporating the Neva River into Leningrad's reconstruction or the Black Sea into Sevastopol's rebuilding effort made perfect sense, but Tashkent's planners were attempting to incorporate a natural resource that, in fact, did not exist.[31] Nevertheless, the myth of the Soviet state as provider of water to the Central Asian desert was central to the Tashkent landscape, even if water itself was not. The massive use and misuse of water became essential components of Tashkent city planning for years to come. Water became a major means of showcasing the power and technical achievements of the Soviet Union, even as water diversion led to devastating long-term environmental consequences.

However, these men were Moscow-based architects. They criticized Kuznetsov's plan for failing to take into account Tashkent's social and climate conditions, but many of them also had little experience in Uzbekistan or any other part of Central Asia. Vladimir Semenov admitted that he did "not know the city since he was only there for one day," but he still decided that a proposed eighteen-meter tower was "uncharacteristic" for the Uzbek capital that he had not really seen. Such construction, he argued, was too much of an "American thing."[32] Despite Motolianskii's Los Angeles analogy of earlier in the year, by late 1946, the cold war had dawned and American architecture was no longer a viable comparison. With Moscow tightening its grip on Tashkent's city planning, the Soviet capital once again became the primary "school" for urban planning. The intellectual relaxation of the war era ended, as did most positive views of the traditional Central Asian city. Uzbek sections of Tashkent once again required complete "transformation" to give Central Asians their own micro-version of Moscow. Old Town Tashkent again became an exotic and backward place in the minds of most Soviet planners and bureaucrats (both Uzbek and Russian) who oversaw the city's reconstruction into a Soviet urban space. Despite calls for unity and friendship among Soviet peoples, prominent Moscow officials again looked down upon Tashkent and local architects' ability to design a socialist city. The hierarchy of Soviet cities was once again evident, alongside the hierarchy of Soviet ethno-national groups. Tashkent, the capital of the Uzbek people, was denigrated by prominent officials in the metropole, just as Muscovites considered Uzbeks to be the "little" brothers in the happy ranks of the Soviet family. These Muscovites once again sought to design paper proposals that had little correlation to the reality on the ground in Tashkent.

Kuznetsov's Response

Kuznetsov defended his prewar plan for Tashkent in 1948, noting that economic difficulties were being used as an excuse for the failure to reconstruct the Old City. He argued that as the victor in World War II, the state needed its cities to reflect the Soviet Union's new global status. Thus, it could not leave the Uzbek settlement alone and build a modern Soviet city next door. Doing so, he noted, would be reminiscent of French colonialism, which ignored the needs of the native inhabitants while the colonists built themselves a modern urban space. This approach allegedly was "foreign" to the Soviet project that, in theory and rhetoric, reacted against Western colonialism and provided the Uzbeks with their own national republic. The drive for decolonization in Asia and Africa suddenly gave Tashkent's socialist urban renewal project added importance. In one of his last speeches concerning Tashkent, Kuznetsov brought ideology and world politics back into the fold. As the Soviet Union and the United States competed for influence in Asia and the Middle East, Kuznetsov implied that his plan showed that Uzbeks flourished in the Soviet Union with their own modern capital city.[33] Colonial peoples, stuck in premodern urban spaces under Western rule, did not. Despite decrees to the contrary, Soviet planners certainly engaged in the international discussion and study of empire, usually declaring that they were determined to complete Tashkent's transformation into a postcolonial socialist urban space.

Nonetheless, Kuznetsov again advocated that Tashkent's native quarter be "completely rebuilt according to the European model."[34] Re-creating Tashkent in the image of modern Moscow was the only solution to the colonial dilemma at a time when colonial empires were collapsing throughout

Asia. Such urban reconstruction efforts supposedly reinforced the notion that Uzbeks were not oppressed subjects of Moscow but equal citizens of the Soviet state. When Tashkent was successfully remade in the image of Moscow, there would be no difference between the Russian and Uzbek standard of living. For this reason, the reconstruction of the Old City became a "political task," which, Kuznetsov admitted, was much more difficult than he had originally thought, suggesting that even the twenty-year time period for which his proposal had been designed was, in fact, not long enough for a Central Asian city.[35] Was he quietly admitting that Uzbeks were not quite ready for "modern Soviet life"? He spoke of the need to "force" the construction of industry in the traditionally Central Asian sections, especially industry that did not need a direct connection to the railroad, which was on the other side of town. He proposed the establishment of a printing press, sewing factory, and a metal-working factory. Although advocating for industrialization in the Old City, Kuznetsov clearly had not changed his opinion of the type of industry Uzbekistan needed. Tashkenters allegedly had proven themselves capable of building heavy industry and fighting in the Red Army during the war, but the Old City was still left out of Kuznetsov's calculus for establishing such factories in the region. Although Tashkent was to show the achievement of the Uzbek people under Soviet power, the Slavic residents clearly remained the leading ethnic group in the city. The Russian side of Tashkent, with its new airplane factory, charged forward toward communism while the Uzbek Old City, with its sewing factories, dutifully followed behind.

Kuznetsov also criticized the fact that little investment had gone into the reconstruction plan. Without monetary expenditures, a Soviet city in Central Asia could not be built successfully. He wrote that "to try to do such work in small doses, as is taking place now, will never be able to solve the problem. We need solid funds, which will give the possibility to widen the practical and scientific work on the plan for the city."[36] According to Kuznetsov, Tashkent's problem was not the fault of his plan. The problem lay in the way in which it was implemented. In other words, Bulatov was the culprit. Even after the war, Kuznetsov felt that the plan was adequate but that the way in which it had been enacted distorted the outcome. He accepted criticism that the reconstruction had not yet provided its expected results and admitted his responsibility for being overly optimistic about the amount of time it would take to build "New Tashkent." Surprisingly, however, he did not blame the war. The defense of the 1937–1939 plan was Kuznetsov's last gasp in Tashkent city planning. Although he continued to plan other cities, there are no archival records in either Moscow or Tashkent to indicate Kuznetsov's further involvement in actively creating the ideal Uzbek capital. After the war, the Academy of Architecture, the Ministry of Urban Construction, and Tashgorproekt, the Tashkent City Planning Organization, became the primary shapers of city. Planning moved from the center to the periphery, even if final approval still rested in Moscow. Interestingly, despite harsh criticism of him throughout the 1940s, Bulatov continued to play a prominent role in the city's redevelopment, serving both as the city architect and as the head of Tashgorproekt into the 1960s.

The Uzbek and Turkmen Earthquakes of the 1940s

On November 3, 1946, an earthquake struck eastern Uzbekistan, destroying thousands of houses, administrative buildings, and medical facilities throughout the region. Namangan, Fergana, Andijan, and Tashkent oblasts were particularly hard hit, but minor damage occurred in the Uzbek capital itself, where the most visible signs of destruction were the partial collapse of a maternity ward and the toppling of the city water tower.[37] Although no figures on human fatalities could be found in archives or published sources, large numbers of livestock were killed in rural areas, indicating that humans likely fell victim to this disaster as well.[38] The physical damage to the region's infrastructure was severe. The Ministry of Enlightenment noted that 119 schools and 6 kindergartens needed to be rebuilt, while 390 schools across the republic needed major repairs.[39] The ministry also closed 11 institutes, some in Tashkent and in Tashkent oblast, due to structural damage. In addition to the thousands of individual homes whose roofs collapsed and walls cracked, approximately 1,500 apartment buildings in the main cities of the region were listed as destroyed or severely damaged.[40] Soviet technology could not withstand the power of nature despite its effort to reorder the physical landscape of Central Asia.

In January 1947, the Council of Ministers of the Soviet Union issued a decree "on the liquidation of the consequences of the earthquake in the Uzbek SSR" in which the Uzbek Council of Ministers was to take all necessary measures to assist the regions that were adversely affected. The reconstruction of schools and medical facilities, including interim temporary structures, received the highest priority. The Soviet government earmarked 27 million rubles to help rebuild these areas. Three thousand construction and transportation workers were mobilized for six months to work on reconstruction, and a total of 2 million rubles was allocated for individual residents to repair or rebuild their homes.[41] Although the Committee on Architecture had just declared that, in Tashkent, the construction of individual one-story houses should be limited, the government (union, republic, and city) continued to promote individual construction and the reestablishment of private housing as the easiest means to meet pressing needs. Furthermore, the scope of the damage in these four oblasts caused urban planners to discuss the minimum strength requirements needed for Central Asian buildings. Tashkent officially could withstand an earthquake of similar magnitude, but construction was shoddy, with structures falling apart only a few years after completion. Tashkent's engineers urged increased attention to earthquake preparedness to ensure the safety of the city's structures and the inhabitants within them.

However, on October 6, 1948, these engineers were again rattled by another more devastating earthquake, measuring 7.3 on the Richter scale, in Ashgabat, the capital of neighboring Turkmenistan. The destruction in Turkmenistan shocked Tashkent's urban planners, and Soviet officials did not admit the extent of the human loss in the city until the *glasnost'* era, when, in 1988, they released the horrific death toll of 110,000 victims out of a population of 132,000 residents.[42] Although rescue teams arrived to "liquidate the consequences" of the earthquake, there were few survivors to help. Instead, "liquidating the consequences" meant digging mass graves and studying the reasons for the large-scale collapse of buildings, especially those constructed in the Soviet era.

According to a 1949 report on the Turkmen earthquake by D. Kuz'menko, the senior inspector for the Main State Architecture and Construction Control Bureau (Glavgosarkhstroikontrol'), the majority of the buildings that were destroyed had been built either before 1939 or after 1943. Between 1940 and 1943, by instruction of the Commissariat of Construction, Ashgabat buildings were built to withstand an earthquake of 8 on the Richter scale; however, the commissariat reduced the city's seismic protection zone during the war to 7, largely due to the tremendous need to build housing and industrial structures quickly during the wartime evacuation.[43] The end result was almost complete destruction in the city.[44] Thousands died due to the cutting of corners, shoddy workmanship, poor planning, and quick construction.

The Uzbek Architects' Union also sent a team to Turkmenistan, headed by P. P. Moskatsov, to study why buildings collapsed so easily. Moskatsov opened his report with the shocking admission that "Death rejoiced" in the massive devastation of Ashgabat.[45] Echoing the findings of the Glavgosarkhstroikontrol', Moskatov remarked that Tashkent's structures were similar to those in Ashgabat and that buildings from every period of Tashkent's recent history—the construction of the imperial "New City" at the turn of the century, the traditional *hovle,* the rushed buildings of the evacuation era, and

"Soviet" architectural achievements—were vulnerable to collapse if Tashkent experienced a similar earthquake. Locally made adobe-style bricks, a common material in Tashkent's buildings, were cited as contributing to the majority of human losses. Due to the lack of industrial construction materials, such hand-made bricks were used not only in single-story individual homes but also in "modern" Soviet-style multilevel buildings.[46] The annihilation of Ashgabat by the forces of nature was a clear warning to Tashkent and Moskatov that they needed to conduct more research into Tashkent's ability to withstand such an earthquake. Like the Uzbek capital, Ashgabat had survived the war without damage, but after the earthquake it was in no better shape than Minsk, Stalingrad, or Sevastopol.

The Tashkent City Center

Concerns over seismic activity in the Tashkent region and the potential for vertical ground movement during a tremor were discussed throughout the 1940s and 1950s.[47] While insisting that all buildings could withstand the forces of nature, specific concern focused on the strength of the city administrative center. Although the Gorispolkom decided that "solving" the housing crisis was the priority for the postwar effort, Tashkent urban planners still concentrated most of their attention on designing monumental structures in the heart of the Uzbek capital. Building a compact and beautiful public space was a quicker and easier way to impress and "show the state's care for" its citizens than building apartments or schools for the population.

As a result, a competition was held in 1946 to design a new administrative center for the Uzbek SSR to replace the Government House, originally planned as a constructivist building in the late 1920s with a design by Stepan Polupanov. The Academy of Architecture rejected the majority of the proposals for the new government complex allegedly because they expressed excessive national characteristics. One project included a rather interesting plan by the Tashkent architects V. E. Arkhangelskii and A. A. Sidorov, who proposed a series of cupolas surmounting the government buildings, a design recalling the impressive architecture of Samarkand, the Uzbek SSR's second-largest city.[48] Sidorov and Arkhangelskii were criticized for their use of cupolas and pointed arches which, according to general agreement at an Uzbek Architects' Union meeting in February 1948, evoked a style of Central Asian monumentalism of the Middle Ages, not the more progressive influences of Soviet Uzbekistan. Instead, the authors of the project were informed that they should have taken their examples from ancient Greece and Rome, which were certainly not part of Central Asia's heritage.[49]

The most promising project, by Abdullah Babakhanov, V. Volchek, and Polupanov, was estimated to cost up to 70 million rubles.[50] This proposal envisioned reconstructing the city center around Tashkent's Red Square, which would be surrounded on all four sides by the symbols of Soviet power and achievement: the Supreme Soviet, the Council of Ministers, the Central Committee and the Academy of Sciences of Uzbekistan, and the Palace of Cotton Workers, although the last two institutions were later dropped from the project. The Uzbek Supreme Soviet building would be placed on the site of the existing Government House and become the tallest structure in the city, with a sixty-meter spire at its center. The building was designed so that it could be seen from all sections of the city. The spire, reminiscent of those on the seven sister skyscrapers in Moscow, would serve as an orientation point that could focus the population's attention toward the center of Soviet power in Uzbekistan.[51] Moscow again emerged as the planning model for Tashkent designs.

In this proposal, Tashkent's Lenin Monument, built in 1936, would be moved to the front of the Supreme Soviet building, while the "Uzbek national character" of the complex was to be found in its lancet porticos (arches surrounding a covered walkway that encircled the building), an internal courtyard with water pools (*hauz*), and a rear exit that opened toward the Ankhor Canal.[52] The city's "natural" landscape—an artificial canal—was tied to the architectural center of Uzbekistan. The remaining structures on Red Square largely reflected the period's tendency toward neoclassicism: columned structures with internal courtyards, which evoked ancient Greece. The ensemble of administrative buildings was tied together by making generous use of Tashkent's limited water resources for a canal-fed pool of water in the complex's center, complete with fountains (situated to make the streams of water frame the spire of the Supreme Soviet) and a system of small-scale canals that would surround the complex.[53] Water, not traditionally in large supply in the region, was presented as the fundamental component of "Uzbek national architecture." It was perceived as essential to the so-called economic and cultural flowering of the republic under socialism. Water also constituted proof of the progress of the Uzbek people under Soviet rule, which enabled them to develop the region into a mechanized agricultural and industrial republic. Such extensive use of water was meant to impress Tashkenters and foreign visitors from equally parched colonial areas and convince them of the ability of socialism to promote modernization.

Members of the Academy of Architecture submitted their opinions on the proposed government center. Aleksei Shchusev, the designer of Lenin's

Tomb, noted that the grouping of buildings around the square suited Uzbek national peculiarities rather well because the arrangement transformed Red Square into an "internal' courtyard surrounded by the most important administrative structures in the republic.[54] This design recalled the traditional Uzbek house, the *hovle*, with its partly enclosed inner square. It also heeded Korshunov's call to adapt the traditional internal gardens of the Central Asian madrasa to suit the new Soviet environment. Nevertheless, in light of the campaign against cosmopolitanism that spread throughout Soviet art and culture at this time, Shchusev was obliged to criticize the proposal. He accused Babakhanov, Volchek, and Polupanov of "formalist" tendencies because the complex did not correctly depict "Soviet democracy." The interior of the meeting hall of the Supreme Soviet did not reflect Soviet notions of equality because it was decorated in an exaggerated and pompous style. Shchusev noted that the complex looked more like the palace of an Eastern despot than the center of a socialist city.[55]

Similar accusations were made by other members of the review committee. Semenov noted the importance of the reconstruction of Tashkent, stating that Tashkent was a unique city that was both Russian and Uzbek and that the administrative center needed to fuse the national characteristics of both peoples. This fusion was to symbolize the merger of the Soviet Union's ethno-national groups into a common Soviet people and the creation of a stable and unified multiethnic society in Central Asia. However, the plan allegedly failed to depict sufficient Russian characteristics because the tall spire on the top of the Supreme Soviet building was reminiscent of Central Asian minarets. Spires, suitable for Moscow's skyscrapers, evidently provoked negative reactions when proposed for Tashkent, indicating that the Moscow model perhaps was not universally adaptable and could be interpreted differently when applied to a non-Russian republic. Such structures were often deemed too "Islamic" or "archaic" for Central Asia, and Tashkent architects unexpectedly received criticism for their inability to create an administrative complex that united Soviet architecture with the "progressive" traditions of the Uzbek past.[56] For Semenov, Tashkent's city center was too Uzbek, even if all of its designers were not.

A. Aliyev, an Uzbek and future minister of communal economy for the republic, disagreed, noting the political importance of Tashkent's city center in Soviet international affairs. He argued that, given Uzbekistan's location, architects must take special care in reconstructing the Uzbek capital to reflect its Asian roots. For Aliyev, the proposed administrative center was too Russian. It represented neither Uzbeks' status as a "liberated" colonial people nor the potential role that Soviet Uzbekistan and Tashkent in particular could play in the Soviet-American struggle for influence in Asia. He stated,

> We must have it so that people who come to [visit] us [in Tashkent] see that we are not nakedly copying European architecture, but that here exists its own national expressions. Therefore, our architects . . . must search for new forms with consideration of architecture of the past and former traditions of the Uzbek people. . . . The council of architecture is meeting here and we ask you to criticize us, but at the same time help us, and show us the true path so that our Government House could become a masterpiece of general culture and of the culture of the Soviet people with elements of our past culture.[57]

According to Aliyev and his allies on the commission, Tashkent had to simultaneously look modern and possess elements of the Uzbek national character.[58] However, commission members could not quite identify what "proper Uzbek national characteristics" were, although they knew what they were not—namely, grand structures with lancet arches, narrow windows, or tall towers. Tashkent's administrative architecture was not supposed to look too "Eastern." It was supposed to be grand enough to impress, with some accommodation to Asian "peculiarities," but still give the impression that important business was being performed inside.[59] Developing Soviet-Uzbek architecture was left to individuals, who then struggled to come up with ideologically acceptable designs based on ambiguous instructions.

Two committee members, Shchusev and Iakov Kornfeld, expressed concern over the strength of the building, suggesting that the architects had not designed it to withstand an earthquake.[60] The building, Shchusev remarked, needed to be made of reinforced concrete and to possess a much more solid foundation because the Supreme Soviet was not an ordinary Tashkent building. It was unacceptable for it to crumble from seismic movement, like so many other structures; it needed to last for centuries.[61] These comments are insightful because they underscored a vaguely voiced concern over monumental Uzbek architecture in ideological discourse. Tashkent, the center of new world power in Asia, competed with the image of a previous empire in the region. Samarkand, with the Registan, Gul-Emir, and other impressive architectural achievements of the Amir Timur (Tamerlane) era, stood in the backdrop of the new socialist city. Amir Timur's rule officially had been discredited by the Soviet regime, but his architecture still stood, albeit in varying states of decay. Architects were not supposed to copy the Registan, but they were supposed to build something that surpassed it in beauty, impressiveness, *and* longevity. Despite numerous earthquakes, the harsh Central Asian weather, and lack of modern construction technology, Amir Timur's city still stood. Building a lasting Soviet structure was of vital importance. A collapse of the Supreme Soviet building or the Lenin Monument would send the wrong message to Tashkenters and, in fact, the entire world. Soviet technology needed to control and reorder, not merely withstand, the power of nature.

The incorporation of water into the "ensemble" of the city center also caused controversy. The Academy of Sciences building was removed from the final proposal and replaced by a large decorative water reservoir that would serve as a mirror to reflect the image of the complex and also help cool down the entire area, an important consideration since the complex would hold large-scale public demonstrations of Soviet power. The proposal also called for a canal to surround the entire complex to isolate the area from the bustle of surrounding streets.[62] The symbolic administrative center of the Uzbek SSR was in the heart of the capital but removed from the mundane activities that occurred in the neighboring buildings and on the roads of the city.

However, not everyone agreed that this design effectively used the water supply in the city. Shchusev argued that such extensive use of water would be prohibitively expensive and that taking it directly from the not-so-clean Ankhor Canal was the only feasible solution.[63] P. A. Spyshkov, an engineer, similarly argued that industrial pollution, not money, was the primary problem with this proposal. He noted that the canals and *aryk*s from which the pools and fountains on Red Square would be filled ran through densely built areas, potentially creating an awkward situation in which toxic water would spout freely onto Tashkent's Red Square.[64] Dirty water and smelly air did not create an optimal environment for the center of Soviet life in Central Asia, and planners needed to rethink water usage to guarantee a pleasant and clean environment at the core of Soviet power. Little concern, however, was voiced for the polluted water that ran through the densely populated residential areas, but pollution in the symbolic heart of Soviet Central Asia could not be allowed. Others expressed worry that the lack of shade on the square would make public parades difficult. Such concerns were well founded because the administrative complex was the all-important site for orchestrated demonstrations of Soviet power. Collapsing from the heat or stench of the air under direct view of the new government center was not to be allowed in socialist Tashkent. Nonetheless, more concern was placed on the public orchestration of the parades than on the welfare of the Soviet citizens who were to participate in them.

In the end, the water issue contributed to the failure to implement this project. On April 30, 1948, at a citywide meeting of the Uzbek Architects' Union to discuss the problem of "formalism in architecture," the entire complex was severely criticized, partly due to its excessive use of water resources: "The monumentality of water on the square and in the parks that surround the buildings reached such wide development that the majority of Red Square has been taken over by a pool, while the entire complex of buildings is encircled by a band of water, which makes [the complex] appear like an island that is poorly connected to the city by narrow little bridges."[65] Although the Central Committee and Council of Ministers buildings were "dressed in classical clothes," Polupanov's desire to incorporate as much water as possible "unmasked" the true character of the buildings and uncovered his interest in "scientific fantasy," not progressive construction. The Supreme Soviet, Council of Ministers, and Central Committee buildings were supposed to exude an aura of importance and showcase the immense power of Soviet technology. In the eyes of many planners, however, Polupanov's design instead looked more like a water park than a government center. The project was canceled in 1949, and the much-criticized Government House again underwent renovation. Surprisingly, Polupanov was given the commission to remodel the building, his fourth attempt to get it right.[66]

Navoi Theater

While Tashkent leaders actively criticized most construction projects in the city, Architects' Union members singled out the Navoi Opera and Ballet Theater as a true success of Soviet Uzbek planning. V. E. Babievskii, a prominent Tashkent architect, described the recently completed theater at an April 1948 Architects' Union meeting as an effective "assimilation" of Uzbek national architecture within modern Soviet construction.[67] The building contained few "archaic" decorations that were present in most Tashkent structures. Instead, it possessed classical forms (front and side columns with rounded, not pointed, triumphal arches at the entryway; the base of each column was made of Uzbek marble). Inside, individual rooms were decorated with inlaid carvings, each representing one of the six major regions of Uzbekistan: Tashkent, Samarkand, Bukhara, Khiva, Fergana, and Termez. Most importantly, it was produced with high-quality local construction supplies, including yellow bricks that had been manufactured in Uzbekistan using industrial methods.[68] Aleksei Shchusev's original plan from 1934 called for a 200,000-square-meter theater with a seating capacity of twenty-five hundred, which, had the design not been reworked during the late 1930s and the war years, could easily have been labeled "gigantomania."[69] Ground was broken in 1940, but construction stopped until 1943. The final construction push occurred between 1945 and 1947, with Russian builders, Uzbek artisans, and Japanese prisoners of war working on the project.[70]

The sited selected for the theater was that of the former Voskresenskii Market. The choice was filled with significance: the theater would transform a "medieval" bazaar and social "cesspool" into a well-tended and comfortable city square, even though the market had actually been established by Russian colonists during the tsarist period.[71] The theater was placed on the far side of the square, eventually to be surrounded by trees, asphalt sidewalks, and a large decorative fountain. From the roof terrace, one could see the mountains at Chimgan in the distance, thereby creating a tie between the theater and the true natural landscape of the city.[72] The complex, which was located a few short blocks from the proposed city center, would serve as the anchor for an urban renewal project that would eventually be joined by Bulatov's Tashkent Hotel (in 1958) and TsUM, the Central Department Store (in 1964), to create a city block that would contain important markers of Tashkent's "cultured" status: a theater for classical European art forms, a Soviet style-shopping arcade, and a first-class hotel. Whether they visited the theater or not, Tashkenters were supposed to recognize that the building represented an achievement in Soviet Uzbek national architecture and served as an important site in the city's postwar cultural life. The placement of the Uzbek opera theater in the center of the city sought to show that modern Soviet culture dominated city life. Furthermore, the structure supposedly was built with the well-being of the population in mind. Its "yellow brick" façade reflected the sunlight, while the covered arcade at the entrance shaded visitors as they waited to enter the theater. In fact, the entire building was meant to express the "democratic" character of Tashkent. The theater was not only available to "millions" of Soviet citizens; it was "owned" by the people of Tashkent.[73] The Navoi Opera and Ballet Theater was yet another example of the emphasis on impressive public structures, not buildings for everyday use.

Although Babievskii and others celebrated the building as a successful unification of Uzbek and Soviet architecture, there was criticism that its exterior relied too much on traditional Uzbek motifs and did not express the "feelings of the victorious people [who emerged into] greatness from the war [and] the pathos of the Soviet people who did not stop their creative work even in the years of war." Four cupola-shaped spires crowned the top of the main portal, which one architect claimed resembled tiny minarets. In addition, the outer columns needed sculptures that could glorify modern

Soviet themes; instead, Shchusev left them bare.[74] Voronina concurred that the building's front façade could have been better organized to make the entryway more monumental. She also described the lack of sculpture at its entrance as a throwback to the "dead dogmas" of Islam.[75] Modern sculptures of the human form would have allowed the building to serve a culture/agitation purpose from both the outside and inside. The "ideal" Soviet Uzbek building was not so "ideal" after all.

Voronina also criticized the interior, stating that the right-angle shape of the stage was excessively simple for a building of such importance.[76] However, the plaster carvings in the foyer were seen as a true achievement in "modern" Uzbek arts. Such decoration replaced the ordinary painting with which Soviet theaters had been decorated in the past, thus showing the fusion of Uzbek traditions into the entryway of a modern public building. The internal decorations evidently improved when one entered the individual rooms, which each represented an oblast of the Uzbek SSR. Uzbek artisans traveled to the capital to create plaster wall carvings that would convey the cultural heritage of their home regions, transferring their skills in woodcarving to the more advanced construction material of plaster. The Tashkent Room, obviously the most important, was designed by Tashpulat Aslankulov, the acclaimed "National Artist of the Uzbek SSR," who received awards for successfully reworking carvings, reputedly indicative of Tashkent housing structures, into monumental art suitable for a palace. The Samarkand Room incorporated marble and plaster decorative carvings that reflected the monumentality and grandeur of Samarkand. The Bukharan Room was designed by Usta-Shirin Muradov, the "illustrious Bukharan master and honored academic." Meanwhile, the Khiva Room successfully transformed wooden miniature decorations, common to this eastern region of the republic, into a stone-and-plaster masterpiece that represented the "rich culture" of Khivan art forms.[77]

The descriptions of the Fergana and Termez rooms were presented in much humbler terms. The Fergana Room consisted of individual plaster panels that, together, produced a "picturesque" (*zhivopisnyi*) whole, while the Termez Room was the smallest; "its modest flat carvings wonderfully express the uniqueness and beauty of the decorative arts of the southern regions of Uzbekistan."[78] Interestingly, although all rooms were deemed beautiful, an *Arkhitektura i stroitel'svo* journal article used varying levels of praise for each room. Just as a there was a hierarchy of Soviet peoples in the Soviet Union as a whole, there likewise existed a hierarchy of oblasts within the Uzbek SSR, as reflected in the descriptions of each room in the Navoi Theater. Tashkent, the capital and center of industry and culture in Central

Asia, was the most important oblast, and its room received the most praise. Samarkand, the second most important city, possessed industry and a long history, so it was next after Tashkent, followed by Bukhara, Khiva, and Fergana. Unlucky Termez was at the bottom of the hierarchy, with its small room garnering the least amount of commentary in the article. In fact, Termez's position relative to Tashkent was similar to the Uzbek capital's relationship to Moscow. A distant borderland (with Afghanistan) and a place to which Tashkenters did not relish traveling, Termez was in a relationship of subservience to Tashkent just as Tashkent deferred to the Soviet capital. This status was clearly represented in the size of its room and the modesty of its ornamentation. Tashkent's room was "monumental," while Termez's was "humble."[79] Tashkent, the heart of Uzbekistan and the model urban area in Central Asia, was to be the inspiration for regional leaders who would shape their socialist cities in its image. Moscow led in the overall Soviet urban renewal process for republic and regional capitals, but Tashkent, as Moscow's surrogate, guided the urban reconstruction programs for Uzbekistan's other urban centers.

Since Tashkent was the model socialist city for Central Asia, this acclaim given to the theater meant that it became the most celebrated building in Soviet Uzbekistan. Although it lacked one of the most important features of Soviet architecture—sculpture—an adjustment could be made in the future. The theater became an important marker of post-revolutionary success. Shchusev won a Stalin Prize for this masterpiece of Uzbek national architecture, as did the Uzbek artists who designed the decorations for the individual oblast rooms. However, in analyzing who received the awards, one must recognize that Shchusev, the Russian architect who designed the building and oversaw its construction using Soviet technology, garnered the most praise, while his Uzbek counterparts were seen as craftsmen, skilled in handicrafts but not holding commanding positions as construction engineers or architects.[80] The Soviet pecking order, with Russian technical experts above Uzbek handicraft laborers, is apparent again in the history of this prize-winning building.

Moreover, Shchusev, like others before him, was celebrated for creating Uzbek national architecture even though he was not Uzbek.[81] In fact, he was adept at creating national architecture across the Soviet Union. It did not matter for which nation he created this architecture. In Russia, he designed the NKVD building on Dzerzhinsky Square, the Komsomol ringline metro station, and the Moscow Hotel right outside Red Square in the Soviet capital. In Leningrad, he was the architect of the Pulkovskaia Observatory, built in 1944. In the national republics of the Soviet Union, he designed the Kazakh SSR Academy of Sciences building and the Institute of Marx, Engels, and Lenin in Tbilisi, and he served as a consultant on the postwar design of the Kishinev railway station in Moldova.[82] With his experience in designing important buildings in Russia, he was uniquely qualified to adapt the Moscow model to suit the needs of national architecture. Throughout this era, Russian architects like Shchusev created designs that they believed national architecture should resemble.[83] In fact, Shchusev's buildings in Kazakhstan and Uzbekistan were remarkably similar, indicating that there was a centralized view of what could be considered "national" for Central Asia.

In addition, one also must note the lack of Uzbek voices in discussions over the reconstruction of Tashkent. Uzbeks were not widely heard in the discussions about city planning in the 1940s because Uzbeks did not play a primary role in this process at that time. Although Abdullah Babakhanov was the chair of the Uzbek Architects' Union, he was one of the few ethnically Uzbek architects working in Tashkent planning. The Architects' Union and the Central Asian Industrial Institute constantly lamented the lack of Uzbek cadres in the city's planning organizations and educational institutions for architects and engineers.[84] The Architects' Union continually decreed that they needed to be more active in training Central Asian cadres. However, they had difficulty finding and training qualified candidates, although a new group of architecture and engineering students entered institutes after demobilization. Army experience eventually would help put Uzbeks into positions of power within the planning process, but these veterans were still in school and would not rise to prominence in Tashkent planning organizations for another decade.

The Public Image of Tashkent

In 1952, the Tashkent Gorispolkom achieved another concrete success in transforming Tashkent into a Soviet city with the public unveiling of a Stalin statue on Revolution Square, the heart of pre-revolutionary Tashkent. With this new monument, urban planners created a second "city center" for Soviet Tashkent. N. Tomsky, a Stalin Prize–winning sculptor, designed the monument to the *vozhd'* (leader) for this park, located a few short blocks away from Red Square on the site of the original Kaufman monument of the pre-revolutionary era. Babakhanov designed the statue's pedestal with the help of another Tashkent figure, V. Volchek, symbolizing the joint effort by the city's Uzbek and Russian populations to build the most important monument in the city. Choosing the site was a careful and lengthy process, involving Boris Iofan and Ivan Fomin of the Union Academy of Architecture in Moscow, who found the "prettiest" site in the city for this statue, although Iofan admitted to having selected the site without ever visiting Tashkent.[85] The Kuranty, a recently completed clock tower that marked the victory of the Soviet Union over the Nazis, was located across the street from the park, thereby directly connecting the Soviet Union's triumph in war to the Soviet leader.[86]

This symbolic change in Revolution Square, formerly imperial Konstantinov/Kaufman Square, was important. In the tsarist period, the Kaufman statue in the square had been surrounded by important markers of tsarist society—banks, seminaries, and a gymnasium. Now, Revolution Square, with Stalin at its center, was the focus of a region that unified the Kuranty, Institutes of Higher Education, and Red Square, which was a short distance away. Kaufman, a military figure, was responsible for the transformation of Tashkent into a model colonial city. Despite the exploitation of colonialism, Soviet scholars had recently declared the capture of Tashkent by Russian forces in 1865 to have been a progressive step in the history of the city.[87] The *vozhd'*, also a military commander, was the initiator of Tashkent's second transformation and pushed Tashkent even further along the "path of development" than his predecessor had. Hence, he deserved this spot of honor in the city. In fact, the placement of the Stalin statue in Revolution Square perhaps was more important symbolically than the efforts to rebuild the city center in 1948 because Revolution Square was a circular park from which many of Tashkent's important avenues radiated outward. Stalin stood at the center of the city and marked Tashkent's urban heart, to which all attention purportedly focused. Suddenly, all roads in Tashkent began with or led to Stalin.

According to travel guides of the late 1940s and 1950s, Tashkent successfully had erased the border between the European and Asian sections of the city; problems still occurred, but Tashkent was on its way toward modernity. In official discourse, industrial growth was evenly distributed throughout the city, providing Uzbeks with opportunities that they lacked before the revolution.[88] The increasing importance of industrial production spurred population growth, the establishment of a modern energy supply system, and an improvement of public transportation. The book *Shahar Toshkent*, published in 1949, declared that the city had successfully updated its transport system with functioning buses, trams, and trolleys that traveled on properly paved streets.[89] In fact, Viktor Vitkovich, author of *Puteshestvie po Sovetskomu Uzbekistanu* (1951), wrote of Tashkent's particular smell—that of asphalt "swimming under the sun"—to prove that the city was not the dusty desert town of the past but a modern metropolis.[90]

A marker of the urban lifestyle, asphalt was a public indicator of the Soviet system's success in converting an agricultural society into an industrial and urban state. Tashkent was a new type of Asian city, a state-of-the-art urban area to which Soviet propagandists strove to direct the attention of leaders of the postcolonial and socialist worlds.[91] Similarly, a poem, "Navoi kuchasi," was published in honor of Navoi Street, the city's main modern thoroughfare, declaring it to be the "the True street / That will lead us / To Communism."[92] In official discourse, Tashkent's urban space had been transformed into a beautiful, efficient, and well-tended socialist environment. Tashkent had left its dark past, entered socialism, and was moving toward communism. Rebuilding Tashkent and creating Navoi Street was helping Tashkenters make this journey into the future. Clearly, modern cities were important parts of the ideological foundation of the future communist society.

Nonetheless, Tashkent planners still had difficulty re-engineering the city into an ideal urban space. Tashkent's lack of wartime destruction may actually have made the task more challenging. Total war brought devastation in the western parts of the Soviet Union but development in the eastern areas. Kiev and Minsk could be rebuilt from scratch, but Tashkent supposedly needed only to clean the industrial soot off of its buildings. However, its prewar city planning failures, the Government House, the telegraph building, and the traditional Old City all survived the war but were now joined by collapsing barracks, broken tram lines, and already decaying wartime factory and housing construction. Despite numerous efforts and ample discussion on how to fix these problems and create a "rational" environment, architects, engineers, and builders still could not realize the model Tashkent that they envisioned. In a strange way, the destroyed Kiev likely had an advantage. It could rise from the ashes of war as a city reborn, while Tashkent was left with all of its prewar infrastructure problems, including its "premodern" Central Asian section.

Urban planners knew what was wrong with postwar Tashkent but could not develop a proposal to fix it in the immediate postwar period. The wartime and early postwar liberalized attitudes toward the Uzbek home, and foreign architectural examples for desert cities quickly fell victim to the politics of the cold war. These efforts were followed by proposals to build a monumental city that recalled the classical age and foresaw a bright future for the Soviet Union, a particularly important propaganda goal of the regime in its effort to garner influence in Asia and Africa.[93] However, these plans were too expensive and remained unfeasible in an area that still lacked an infrastructure to supply the material needed for industrial construction projects. Individual planners likewise continually faltered in developing this new Soviet city. They knew "progressive Uzbek architecture" had been declared good but did not know how to merge local artistic and cultural traditions with Soviet norms in practice. The failure of an architect to propose a plan could bring criticism, but developing the wrong plan could be downright dangerous late in the Stalin era. As a result, the mantra of "showing care for the people" was solved neither by building mass housing that citizens wanted nor by creating the bright public structures in the city center that the state proposed. However, even if Tashkent did not look "Soviet" in bricks and mortar, it certainly did on the pages of *Pravda Vostoka* and *Qizil O'zbekiston*.[94]

7 CENTRAL ASIAN TASHKENT AND THE POSTWAR SOVIET STATE

In 1946, Hujum Abdullah-Khojaeva received for her tenth-grade graduation a gold medal and a bouquet of flowers from the director of her school, Ekaterina Ermolaeva.[1] *Pravda Vostoka* celebrated her achievement at Tashkent school no. 110 as a sign that postwar Uzbekistan allowed its girls—guided by Soviet ideology and with the help of the Russian people—to gain full education and political enlightenment. Hujum, who represented all Uzbek women, was depicted as moving from a dark past to a bright future in the city of Tashkent. Her favorite activities were important markers for success in Soviet society: attending school and getting her education, scientific experimentation, reading classical and modern literature, and visiting wounded soldiers in Tashkent hospitals. While she enjoyed reading about Russian history at the Tashkent Central Library, she grew increasingly attracted to its books on Central Asian literature and culture.[2] In her interests and activities, she was portrayed as both a Soviet and Central Asian girl. Walking home from her graduation party, "clean fresh air" blew through the new city landscape as Hujum imagined her future at Moscow State University, where she planned to become Soviet scientist. According to the local newspaper, her ultimate wish was to return from Moscow to the Uzbek capital to help spread knowledge among the Uzbek people.[3] The message again was clear: the dark oppression of the Uzbek past had been relegated to history, and opportunities were open to Uzbek citizens, particularly women, to succeed in postwar Tashkent.

Hujum was the ideal Soviet Uzbek citizen. A woman, she represented the achievement of the "surrogate proletariat," the oppressed female class that socialism sought to liberate in Central Asia.[4] Her publicly reported achievements and her bright future symbolized a new era for the postwar generation. Her counterpart, the new Uzbek man, was a well-trained worker or an intellectual/engineer, forged in war and now building a socialist society in Asia. Such individuals included Rismat Dadamatov, a demobilized soldier who returned to Tashkent to resume industrial labor at one of the city's new wartime factories, and Abdullah Babakhanov, the demobilized architect who designed buildings for Soviet Tashkent as chair of the Uzbek Architects' Union. Their new positions and their public images showed that Uzbekistan was not just an agrarian socialist republic but also possessed citizens with the technical skills that the state rated highly. Interestingly, however, the model Uzbek male was a skilled adult, while the ideal Uzbek female was still a child, indicating lingering gender hierarchies in official conceptions of indigenous residents of postwar Soviet Tashkent.

Still, Uzbek Tashkenters were in most ways of secondary importance among citizens in the republic's capital. Officially, they held the reins of power, and prominent Uzbeks certainly rose in the Soviet ranks. On the whole, however, Asians were still underrepresented in Tashkent industry, education, administration, and Soviet intellectual culture. The Uzbek people had been declared "liberated" from their past and now possessed their own workers' state. However, it was much easier to make declarations of political and economic programs than to implement them, as this study has shown. For central Party officials, there were still too few Uzbek workers in the city's socialist institutions, a problem for ideologists who aimed to involve every sector of society and each ethno-national group in the building of socialism. Despite declared intentions to increase Uzbek membership in the Communist Party and to improve living standards, the crash industrialization and urbanization projects largely neglected Uzbeks and left them outside of Tashkent's new urban spaces. Succeeding in the Soviet system of postwar Tashkent was hard for most residents, but Uzbek Tashkenters suffered from specific prejudices and difficulties that other ethnic groups did not have to endure. While these Tashkenters were gradually growing into their roles as Soviet citizens, many did not always fit neatly into the categories that Soviet ideology had created for them.

Uzbeks in Postwar Production

An early postwar Gosplan report to Usman Yusupov expressed concern that the lack of trained Uzbeks in the engineering and industrial fields in Tashkent remained a serious impediment to economic growth. While the report noted mass enrollments of Central Asians in the city's new institutes of higher education as far back as 1930, the majority of these specialized Uzbeks subsequently rose to high Party and government posts or were killed in the war, leaving Uzbekistan with a serious lack of skilled industrial engineers, technicians, and workers, especially as many wartime evacuees returned home after the fighting ended.[5] This report likewise noted that Uzbeks in leadership positions had "lost their taste for production and forgot their specialty," indicating that Tashkent—and Uzbekistan as a whole—lacked a cadre of native Central Asians with the technical skills needed in socialism.[6] The war prompted economic and industrial development in the region, but the sheer human losses inflicted on all peoples of the Soviet Union and the mass migrations of the war devastated Uzbekistan's skilled working class. The Uzbek SSR's most loyal Soviet workers perished in great numbers in the Red Army, and the skills of their quickly trained wartime replacements paled in comparison.

Training new Uzbek workers was not an easy task in the late 1940s. Tashkent was transformed into an industrial center, but, as previously mentioned, its schools, universities, and training institutes lost their facilities, equipment, and best teachers during the war. In the postwar years, the pressing need to keep production going meant that buildings were not returned to their original use. Postwar schools were both crowded and unevenly distributed throughout the city. The Technical School of Light Industry of Uzbekistan, for example, reestablished a "peacetime" academic schedule on November 15, 1945. However, this schedule proved difficult to implement because the school lacked a place in which to hold classes. A dormitory for Chkalov Tashkent Aviation Factory no. 84 (formerly Moscow Aviation Factory no. 84) still occupied the school's prewar building, forcing classes to be held in various rooms across the city. Poor public transportation and the geographic space between facilities made it almost impossible for students to attend classes on a regular basis. The school administrators made acquiring a permanent space a priority, yet an educational institution that trained workers for the local light industry could not compete for resources with those of an airplane factory, a component of the Soviet defense industry. Despite numerous requests to the Council of Ministers for the return or replacement of its property, the school neither received a new building nor compensation for the laboratory and training equipment that had been mobilized for the war effort. Sheer logistical difficulties complicated the Tashkent educational system's ability to teach young Uzbeks and help transform them into Soviet workers.

The lack of buildings and equipment hampered the work of the full spectrum of educational institutions, from factory training schools to the prestigious Central Asian Industrial Institute. Evacuated professors left the city after the war, draining the pool of instructors to train the next generation of Tashkent workers. In addition, training courses mostly were conducted in Russian.[7] Many Uzbeks, especially those mobilized into Tashkent factories from rural areas, could not understand the information and skills that they were expected to absorb; many simply left the factory, often not knowing how to perform their jobs at even a basic level. A food shortage also caused students (and teachers) to leave training programs in search of opportunities that might provide them with more nutrition or more culturally appropriate types of food.[8] Since many workers arrived at the factory on their first foray into a more Russian and Soviet world, they also did not want to eat foods either to which they had a cultural or religious aversion (e.g., pork) or with which they were unacquainted (e.g., potatoes or cabbage). These difficulties exacerbated the problem of recruiting new Uzbeks into industrial training schools and retaining them thereafter.

As a result, the numbers of highly qualified Uzbeks in factory production remained remarkably small, according to central Party documents. As of 1946, only forty-eight Uzbek engineers and nineteen technicians worked in all union-level factories in Uzbekistan. Even so, being an Uzbek and trained as an engineer did not necessarily mean that one was used as an engineer at these facilities. In fact, Uzbeks and Party leaders complained that factory administrators rarely employed Central Asians in their trained specialties.[9] Instead, the majority of Uzbek workers remained in low-ranking jobs, often performing hard manual labor whether or not they were qualified for more technical work. Party leaders noted the low numbers of trained Uzbek citizens in Tashkent factories and decreed the need to do better, but there also was little incentive for Uzbeks to improve their skills and subsequently remain in industrial labor if training conditions were inadequate and if one's expertise was not a factor in the distribution of jobs. These policies led to the de facto segregation of the Tashkent factory floor, a fact about which many Uzbek Tashkenters complained. The popular notion of Russians being elite industrial workers and Uzbeks remaining agricultural cotton pickers—or serving on factory cleaning crews—persisted in the postwar era. This gap between the public declarations of Uzbek prosperity and postcolonial industrial modernity in Tashkent and the reality of life for the local Uzbek workforce became increasingly evident, a problem for a polity that sought to highlight socialist equality and success during the postwar era of global decolonization.

Two years later, the figures were not much better. According to the Uzbek Statistical Administration, there were 198,222 industrial workers in the Uzbek workers' state in 1948. However, while Soviet propagandists celebrated this large number of workers in a largely rural Asian region, this working class included only 38,686 Uzbeks, less than 20 percent of the total number of workers, even though they constituted approximately 80 percent of the population. The head of the Uzbek statistical bureau expressed additional concern when the Central Asian industrial workforce was broken down by gender. Of these Uzbek workers, 29,919 were male (15 percent of the total number of industrial workers), while 8,767 were women (less than 1 percent of the total number of industrial workers).[10] Clearly, the "surrogate proletariat" in Central Asia was not represented in the leading class of the Uzbek workers' state. Central Asian representation was seen as especially needed in construction, irrigation, textile production, heavy industry, transportation, medicine, and education, a list that indicates Uzbeks were still missing from most sectors of the economy after the war, except that of agricultural labor.[11] Rather than guiding the Uzbek people, and Uzbek women in particular, toward communism, the Russian "elder brothers" had apparently become the primary workers of the Uzbek workers' state. This discrepancy between the Uzbek ideal of liberation and the enduring power hierarchies between ethnic groups complicated efforts to highlight the prosperity and the adaptability of the socialist system, a notion that was increasingly becoming an important part of Soviet foreign policy.

Declining Standards of Living

Although Tashkent and Uzbekistan did not suffer from the postwar famine to the same degree as the central regions of the country, its residents remained cold and hungry. Tashkent's factories, responsible for housing most of the city's workers, also failed to find suitable shelter for their own employees, many of whom continued to live in basements, hallways, bathrooms, or along city streets. Others were relegated to barracks or dormitories that were "unfit for humans," as a Tashkent Textile Kombinat *fabkom* official explained. One of the *kombinat*'s dormitories was particularly filthy, had no heat, and had water pooled on its floors. In winter, the water froze into a large sheet of ice inside the building.[12] Such difficult conditions impeded the recruitment of new workers. A goal of the Soviet project was to train and "enlighten" local Central Asians, but the absence of housing, bedding, furniture, or food clearly made the journey from "Asian darkness into Soviet light" much more difficult in Tashkent.

Some Tashkenters attempted to take matters into their own hands, although the lack of resources frustrated their ability to repair their apartments or build shelters of their own. A textile worker complained that he had worked at the factory for eleven years but still lived in a mud hut with a leaky roof and dirt floor. Managers repeatedly refused his requests for a proper apartment or for supplies with which he could repair his home.[13] Some others were even less fortunate. A young mother—presumably a war widow—lived along a canal with her small son. When she requested an apartment, she too was refused, forcing her to be an unofficial squatter in the factory building.[14] She was resourceful and "solved the problem on her own," but the solution was far from ideal for both her and the factory, which failed to evict her because there was no suitable alternative shelter.

Party officials cited failure to improve the living spaces of Uzbek students and workers as a prime reason for high Uzbek dropout rates in training programs and factories. Factory housing for Uzbeks was in particularly poor condition, often much worse than for their Russian counterparts. Furniture was lacking at Uzbek worker/student dorms, even though the introduction of European-style tables, chairs, and desks into the Central Asian lifestyle was one of the purported goals of Sovietization and the creation of "modern Uzbek culture."[15] The Pod'emnik factory in Tashkent housed its Uzbek workers all together in the dark basement of an unfinished building with bare floors, broken windows, and constant water leaks. This ninety-square-meter dorm room housed forty-two Uzbek trainees, who slept in filthy bunk beds so that everyone fit in the room.[16] All housing in Tashkent was tight, but Party officials noted particularly cramped and unsanitary environments for Uzbek workers, underscoring the prejudicial notion that the Uzbek workers were used to unhygienic living conditions and could stand them better than Russians could. However, instead of becoming transformed into model Soviet workers, these people, many of whom had been mobilized into the factory during the war, frequently just moved back home to escape urban squalor, an option that was not easily available to former evacuees and other migrant workers from regions outside of Central Asia. This greater ability to move gave Uzbeks more power over their own fates than other ethnic groups in the city but also caused state and Party officials in Tashkent to identify them as less reliably "Soviet."

Tashkent workers also voiced anger over the postwar food supply. During wartime, most recognized the need to sacrifice for the front, but the war was now over and food remained in short supply. Ration cards remained the key to survival for Tashkent residents—both Uzbek and Russian. Even so, rationing did not guarantee a steady supply of bread, let alone such luxuries as meat, potatoes, cooking fat, or milk. Residents—after sacrificing for the war with the hope of a better future—started to make demands on the state to improve the food situation. However, Soviet trade establishments in the city did not help alleviate the problem. Such institutions ostensibly were to liberate workers from the "corruption" and "filth" of the Central Asian bazaar but, according to resident complaints, cheated Tashkenters from their ration allotments and had little food to offer, forcing consumers to rely on the black market. Participation in illegal trade as a buyer or a seller remained the primary means of feeding one's family because citizens—Russians and Uzbeks—simply could not survive without it.

Workers, particularly war veterans, complained loudly about poor living standards in the Uzbek capital. One demobilized Uzbek complained that he expended too much effort securing food in Tashkent. Although he had received a bread ration of 6.4 kilograms per week, the state-run bakery gave him only 6 kilograms, causing him to be as wary of swindlers at official shops as he was at the traditional bazaar.[17] Another veteran complained that the quality of the food in postwar Tashkent was no better than what was given to soldiers at the front.[18] In a wartime army, poor food was understandable, but not at home in Tashkent, supposedly the "blooming garden" of Asia. This was not the victorious state that Tashkenters envisioned after the conflict was over. An Uzbek veteran and father assessed the food situation at the Textile Kombinat's pioneer camp, where the moral and physical health of children was supposed to be strengthened. This Stakhanovite worker complained that campers were provided with "overflowing glasses of sand" for lunch.[19] A parent could bear his own hunger but not that of his children. Women were especially angry over supply problems, probably because they dealt with the issue more often than men did. Furthermore, many Tashkent women no longer had husbands and thus had to become the primary breadwinners in the family. Female workers reiterated that they could not be expected to work well at the factory if they were hungry and, more importantly, if they constantly worried about the survival of their children. One mother guaranteed that workers would fulfill their production quotas if the factory provided their children with both clothing and shoes. Another grumbled that she lacked the time both to work and to find food in a hungry city, stating "we cannot go to the Bazaar. The working class demands help. Without fat, we can't go far, on one potato we can't go far; our hearts are upset when our children stay at home hungry."[20]

In their complaints, mothers also reminded the Soviet government that they had responded to its call to work in the factory during the war. They learned typically male professions and became Stakhanovites, but they were rewarded with nothing for their wartime sacrifices. Anger and popular discontent began to bubble up in Tashkent. The Soviet people did not just defeat fascism and help transform the Soviet Union into a global power only to have the next generation, for whom they fought the war, go hungry in one of the major—and least damaged—cities of the Soviet Union. Tashkent workers claimed that they deserved better food and assistance from Party workers and, in fact, even started to demand it, a trend that crossed ethnic lines in the city. One worker claimed, "When there was a war, it was difficult times and we dragged everything we could to the bazaar so that we could have something for our stomachs, but now we don't want to do that anymore."[21] These Tashkenters presented themselves as loyal Soviet citizens who had fulfilled their duty of defending socialism during the war and had been hopeful for a better future. Such comments were not anti-Soviet per se but should be viewed as part of an effort to bring the problems of everyday life to the attention of city and Party officials. In response, however, Party officials often worried about the loyalty of such people given the sheer difficulty they had in meeting popular demands. The war clearly increased popular expectations of what the Soviet state could and should do for its people. Making demands on the state and believing that the state owed them for their wartime sacrifices became a fundamental component of expressing one's postwar Soviet identity, with Tashkenters of all nationalities being no exception.

Some residents argued against poor postwar working conditions, such as a lack of heat in winter and stifling heat in summer. The failure to provide drinking water in factories—a major component of all previous urban plans—caused dehydration or high rates of infectious diseases and digestive problems for workers, who were forced to drink from dirty drainage canals that ran alongside industrial areas.[22] Citing this problem, one angry worker questioned the logic of the whole Tashkent reconstruction plan, which she felt did not show any "care" for the city's residents. She inverted Soviet propaganda that celebrated the post-revolutionary achievement of delivering water to the parched Central Asian landscape, stating that fountains of gushing water that decorated government buildings, sometimes even overflowing onto the street, did not quench the thirst of Soviet workers.[23] Voicing anger that Soviet power "solved" the century-long need of Central Asians for water only to waste it in excessive public displays, she and others questioned the value of Soviet Tashkent's urban plan and the notion of Soviet success and prosperity that residents had heard for years. In undermining Soviet propaganda, she was not necessarily voicing a sense of disloyalty to the state but expressing dissatisfaction that the state—now a major world power—continued to neglect the needs of its citizens in Central Asia and to squander resources that could and should have been put to better use.

Price hikes on rationed goods compounded Tashkenters' problems in 1946 and stirred anger and protests at factories across the city. Despite the state's efforts to control the population by transforming city spaces, price increases at factory cafeterias caused disturbances, with Central Asian workers identified as being more troublesome than their Russian counterparts. "Negative moods among the population" were found among Central Asian men in Tashkent whose families lived in nearby villages. These workers feared that, although they were urban workers, their families would not be eligible for urban rations because they were rural residents. In anger, these men threw down their ration cards and walked off the production line.[24] Such actions were considered extremely dangerous in the Uzbek capital, which was temporarily home to a considerable number of Central Asian (Uzbek, Kazakh, and Tajik) workers who had left their families in Tashkent oblast villages. A perennial problem of Tashkent factory directors was the recruitment and retention of their Central Asian industrial workers. When indigenous employees asserted their ethnicity and protested the price increases with their feet, the nationality imbalance of the Tashkent workforce widened even further. This problem caused even "Sovietized" Uzbeks, who had previously participated in socially productive labor, to remove themselves, most often temporarily, from direct participation in the new socialist society and leave the "modern" city of Tashkent, an option that, again, was not always available to Russian workers who had no other place to go. The status of Uzbeks as an ethno-national minority gave them additional power and options to manage their own fate in postwar Soviet society.

In late summer and early fall of 1947, rumors about the end of the ration system began to spread throughout Tashkent. Some residents expressed delight over the possible return to "normal" trade. Nevertheless, many could not quite figure out how bread would be distributed if rationing did not exist. Would bread be affordable after the end of rationing or would bread be available only through illegal channels? Some even demanded to know what preparations the Soviet state would make to ensure the security of the grain supply when rationing was abolished.[25] No one liked rationing, but many people could not fathom what life would bring without it. It had become a fundamental part of the Soviet experience as they lived it. This concern was especially prevalent in the more Russian sections of Tashkent, where Uzbek rural Party officials and collective farm chairmen were seen as benefiting from their proximity to sources of food. Uzbekistan's urban regions, with their large Slavic and Jewish populations, depended on the republic's rural areas, occupied mostly by Uzbeks, for survival. Some feared that the end of rationing would leave the lives of urban Russians in the hands of rural Uzbeks, a threatening prospect for Russians who still harbored negative images—and a lack of personal knowledge—of their rural Central Asian neighbors. The Russian working class might have been the leading sector of society that "guided" the Uzbeks toward communism, but rural Central Asians were still perceived as having power over the food chain, as they had at various times in the past. The reliance of the city dwellers on rural peasants of a different nationality took on ethnic undertones in postwar Tashkent, a situation that was a by-product of the sharp national and status differences between Russianized cities and Uzbek collective farms.

In addition, with shortages of consumer goods and housing space in the Uzbek capital, food and building supplies became important commodities. Those with access to them had the potential to become wealthy, at least in Soviet terms. The theft of supplies from factories, train station storage facilities, and stores was a prime means of acquiring goods for sale at illegal and inflated prices. Pilfering by railroad workers, who had special access to hard-to-find goods entering and leaving the city (the main transport hub for Central Asian trade), was a massive problem in the postwar era.[26] Restaurant and cafeteria workers also were involved in illegal smuggling rings and the black market. Furthermore, it was not only line workers in these facilities but also some of the premier administrators in Tashkent's food sector who were caught selling off valuable state food products for personal profit. The directors of the famous National Restaurant in Tashkent and the Confectionery Trust were arrested for organizing an illegal baking factory that sold up to twenty-five hundred *somsas*, or Uzbek meat pies, per day.[27] In all cases, officials in the Office of the Public Prosecutor saw the de facto privatization of state enterprises as a growing and troubling phenomenon in a socialist city, although they once again tended to focus more on Uzbek foods and Uzbek smuggling, while paying less attention to similar crimes committed by Russians.[28] The Soviet black market was certainly not a Central Asian phenomenon; it thrived all across the Soviet Union. Archival documents chronicle similar problems in Russia, but when security officials investigated the problem in Uzbekistan, they focused as much on the nationality of those committing the crime as on the crime itself. This tendency gives the impression that Uzbeks were more willing participants in anti-Soviet economic activity, while it also likely reveals biases among those who actively sought out and uncovered such crimes in Tashkent. Nonetheless, the situation underscores fissures in Tashkent's social fabric that caused concern for Party and city officials.

Furthermore, the city of Tashkent had 224 "red teahouses" in 1949, but Party propagandists viewed many of these facilities as places where economic and cultural "crimes of the past"—private trade, religious propagation, or prostitution—persisted rather than as model sites for cultural enlightenment. To combat this perceived problem, the Uzbek Council of Ministers ordered the closure of all nonofficial and de facto "privatized" state teahouses in 1949. Many operations responded by simply changing locations, but this decision clearly indicates that Party officials identified Tashkent's Uzbek cultural institutions, even its "Sovietized" ones, as less suited to modern urban life, more susceptible to corruption, and less entrenched in socialist culture.[29] In response to the Council of Ministers' order, the Tashkent Gorispolkom closed down the red teahouse at the Textile Kombinat, which *kombinat* workers had constructed on their own to provide a safe area where they could rest between shifts, attend lectures, and wait for transportation home. However, since it lacked official status, it suddenly ran afoul of state authority. It was quickly shuttered, much to the dismay of local residents, who reiterated that it was a true Soviet institution that served both the physical and cultural needs of workers and urban residents of the region. They demanded that the city revisit its decision and reopen the facility so that they could continue their cultural enlightenment work. After reviewing these complaints, the Gorispolkom eventually reconsidered its decision and declared the closure a mistake.[30] However, there is no archival indication that action was taken to remedy the situation. Although workers' taking initiative on the factory floor was valued highly, the state remained wary of institutions and individual citizen efforts that were not under its control, especially when they concerned cultural campaigns to involve Central Asians more actively in Soviet society.

Rising crime compounded the concern of Textile Kombinat workers over the closure of their teahouse. In a collective letter to Yusupov in 1953, Textile Kombinat workers described their factory compound as being located in one of the most dangerous spots in the city. The *kombinat* purportedly was one of the main Soviet "tourist sites" in Central Asia.[31] However, this celebrated factory was also located on the main artery into the city, and anyone traveling that thoroughfare would see numerous dirty stores and derelict buildings. Workers argued that the Textile Kombinat no longer "glistened" as the travel guides declared.[32] Instead, it was in a state of decay. Due to the factory's location at an entry point into Tashkent, visitors from other oblasts frequently parked their cars all around the facility to avoid militia and traffic inspectors in the city center. This transformation of the neighborhood into a large parking lot allegedly enticed criminal "parasites" to prey on both the cars and innocent workers who congregated there. One collective farm worker visiting Tashkent was stabbed to death while waiting outside the main gates.[33] Many night workers arrived four hours before their shift to avoid traversing the dark and dangerous city. However, when they arrived, they had to wait outside the plant entrance for their shift to start (since the red teahouse remained closed), leaving them at the mercy of thieves and violent criminals. Another worker was mugged at the entrance to the facility in September 1953. He fell to the ground, was stripped naked, and then was beaten to death with a steel rod.[34] Stories like these not only undermined the Textile Kombinat's image of being a model factory but once again hurt worker recruitment efforts as word of the "danger" of that part of Tashkent spread through the city and throughout the Uzbek SSR. Soviet officials tried desperately to get new workers, especially Uzbek women, into factory production, but if entering the work force meant getting mugged, raped, or killed in street violence around the Textile Kombinat, why would an Uzbek put herself at risk?

Crime, however, was not the sole problem negatively affecting the city's image and efforts to bring more Uzbek workers into factory production. Training Central Asians workers in Soviet society was not an easy task. The failure rate among students in the Uzbek education system was one of the highest in all of Central Asia, leading to high dropout rates, which further impeded attempts to attract and keep workers in Tashkent factories and also contributed to the rising crime rates. In 1946, 36 percent of Uzbek students were forced to repeat a grade, a figure that was double the rates in the Kyrgyz (17 percent) and Tajik (18 percent) SSRs.[35] Dropout rates for Uzbek girls were even higher, and girls left school earlier, especially in rural areas of the region. Tashkent oblast celebrated its success in increasing female participation in the fifth through seventh grades between 1947 and 1948. However, after careful analysis, education officials noted that the increase in the number of girls in their schools (twenty-two hundred more girls were enrolled) was the result of more Russian girls attending school, while the number of Uzbek females actually declined by thirty-one hundred.[36] Party officials viewed the situation of Uzbek girls not fulfilling the minimal requirements of the education system as a problem for the future of the Uzbek economy and the transformation of Uzbek girls into Soviet women. Party leaders explained that the "feudal nature of Uzbek culture" and the increased "influence" of Islam during the war years contributed to the low level of female participation in the education system, one of the main avenues through which the state sought to mold its diverse population into Soviet citizens.[37]

The Russian-language skills among Uzbek students in Tashkent also concerned Party leaders. Sodik Khusainov, chair of the Tashkent Gorispolkom, declared in 1948 that the situation of Russian-language teaching in the city was especially problematic because the "Russian language is the most important means to raise a child in the internationalist spirit and to guarantee a general cultural level."[38] "Culture" meant "Sovietized Russian culture," and the ideal Tashkent was based on a European urban model. Russification was a key to success in Soviet Central Asia; to become a more Soviet city, Tashkent had to become more modern, with straight avenues and residents who spoke the language of the modern socialist future with greater fluency. To this end, Russian language conversation courses were organized in the Uzbek capital for Central Asian students so that Uzbek children would be able to interact with their Russian counterparts in Russian. However, the sheer fact that such classes were needed indicates that interaction between youth of various ethnic groups was not yet prevalent.[39] Even children appeared unable to overcome linguistic and cultural barriers through the mutual language of play. Despite the effort to bring together the two main ethnic groups of Tashkent into one urban people, these observations underscore the fact that the failure to create a socially cohesive Tashkent went far beyond the difficulty of creating an architecturally unified urban space. Just as places of residence and work remained largely segregated, the education system, too, failed to promote a multiethnic space for learning.

The Russification of Tashkent's education system left Uzbek parents with few options. While libraries and schools were constructed across Tashkent oblast to help educate the Uzbek population, the majority of books in the libraries were in Russian, while most of the facilities were in such bad states of repair that either they or their contents were unusable.[40] If parents wanted their children to succeed in the new Uzbekistan, they had to make sure their children knew Russian by sending them to Russian-language schools. Such schools gave their children opportunities for future advancement but limited their contact with Central Asian culture. Since *sliianie,* or the merger of the numerous national groups into one Soviet people, was an eventual goal of the Soviet project, Russian-Soviet society viewed Uzbek parents who sent their children to Russian schools as progressive.[41] However, *sliianie* was made difficult by the fact that it was Uzbeks who were expected to surrender their traditions into a more European-based cultural and value system during Sovietization. Russian parents were not expected to send their children to Uzbek schools, and Slavic residents of Tashkent rarely made moves toward Uzbek culture, again underscoring discrepancies in ethnic power relations in the Soviet Union. Furthermore, to facilitate this transition toward greater use of Russian, Uzbek institutions were frequently underfunded as the city of Tashkent moved to renovate its urban infrastructure into a more modern "Soviet" space.

For Uzbeks with poor Russian-language skills, the main option was an Uzbek-language school. While some Uzbek schools were perfectly adequate in delivering basic education, they did not provide students with the skills needed to succeed in all levels of industry and education. Some Uzbek-language schoolteachers were poorly trained, possibly even illiterate, and had difficulty explaining technical concepts or Russian grammar—the keys to success in the Soviet education system. Uzbek-language higher education programs existed but were afterthoughts and frequently deemed inferior by students, educational administrators, and employers alike. Tashkent professors complained of having to work harder with Uzbeks, whom they described as unable to meet academic standards and unable to understand basic classroom instructions. It appears that educating Tashkent's Russians was easier, cheaper, and led to better results than educating the city's Uzbeks. Some of these difficulties arose from postwar infrastructure problems, such as the failure to reconvert school buildings back to civilian use.[42] The Gorkom noted that many children in Uzbek areas simply did not go to school because there were no educational facilities nearby. This trend complicated educational campaigns for Uzbek girls, whose parents at times forbade trips to distant schools under the belief that the city was either too dangerous or that their female children did not need an education. The fear of rising crime rates converged with traditional views of female education and labor, making it difficult for propagandists to implement postwar Soviet enlightenment campaigns. The state had grand designs for transforming Tashkent girls into Soviet Uzbek women but neglected the fundamental building blocks necessary to facilitate that transition. For example, even though only 33.5 percent of the city's Uzbek girls studied at Tashkent schools in 1948, the Uzbek capital was the leading region in the republic for the education of girls.[43] The consequences of this failure to invest heavily in Tashkent's Uzbek-language school system were continued high dropout rates, particularly for girls, and an increased stratification of society. Russians and fluent Russian-speaking Uzbeks were at the top of Tashkent's Soviet society. Uzbeks with minimal Russian-language skills were somewhere in the middle, while non-Russian speakers, particularly women, remained toward the bottom, often causing particular concern among Party leaders that Uzbeks were having difficulty fitting into the role of model Soviet citizen. This problem persisted until the 1960s, when Khrushchev's push for new housing and school construction finally saw some results in Tashkent and gave residents greater opportunities and personal stakes in the success of the Soviet project in Tashkent.[44] Idealized visions for a future Soviet Tashkent in the late 1940s clearly were not realized in the short term; urban landscape planners a decade later had more success in turning their vision into reality.

Women in Tashkent

Tashkent Party officials worried about the continued lack of women in industrial roles in the capital. With the war over and the return of men to factories, some women left productive labor. After the trauma of 1941–1945, Tashkenters of all ethnic groups wanted to revert to a simpler life, as Soviet citizens did across the Soviet Union. However, this possibility was open only to those women who had not been left widowed by the conflict or who had extended family structures that could help them and their children survive. The simple fact that the Uzbek residents were indigenous to the region and had these extended family or community structures, while the Russians were migrants to Tashkent, immediately gave Uzbek women more economic freedom not to work. Soviet officials cited traditional Uzbek culture as the reason for a larger number of nonworking women in the city, but it appears that demographics and economic realities also played an important role.

The entry of previously nonworking women into productive labor during the war was presented as a positive development that somehow needed to be reinforced in the postwar years. To continue their active participation in society, women were to be provided with education and material assistance to help them in their roles as both workers and mothers in the Soviet state. However, as already shown, even Russian women (and men) complained of the difficulty of combining these two roles in a society where women were expected to work but where food was difficult to acquire, crime rates were soaring, child- and health-care facilities were lacking, and kindergartens and schools were poorly run and unevenly distributed throughout the city. The transformation of the urban space could not keep up with these new gender roles, particularly because the construction of additional crèches proceeded at such a slow pace. A high birthrate in Central Asia compounded the issue. A report on maternal health noted that, for the Soviet Union as a whole, to keep 1,000 women in the work force the state needed to provide an average of 169.5 places in nursery schools and kindergartens for these women's children. In Uzbekistan, however, the corresponding number was 253.5 spots in child-care institutions.[45] Uzbek women had more children than their Russian counterparts, and, therefore, the state needed to provide them with more help to free them from domestic duties. In the difficult decision over whether a woman should care for her children at home or enter the workplace, many Uzbek Tashkenters chose to stay out of the factory for cultural and practical reasons, often depending on the extended family and courtyard gardens for economic survival. For many nonelite women in more northern parts of the Soviet Union, this option was not readily available. The geographic and climatic particulars of Tashkent provided female residents with choices that were not available to average people in other Soviet cities.

Harsh working conditions also were cited as reasons why workers left the factory. Protective clothing was not available, increasing the possibility of fatal or disabling accidents among employees, many of whom were widowed mothers or working women with disabled veteran husbands. In addition, at a *fabkom* meeting to discuss the grievances of female workers, many employees voiced anger over the lack of laundry and bathing facilities in the compound. With limited public bathhouses in the city and no private bathrooms in apartments or barracks, workers depended on the communal showers in the Textile Kombinat to keep themselves clean. Workers constantly bemoaned the condition of these facilities, which were unsanitary and had inadequate supplies of water and soap. Some urban planners called for improving public bathhouses to remedy the situation, but implementation of these pledges was relegated to the distant future. While most women could bear these inconveniences and delays, they refused to put up with the lack of gender-segregated bathing areas in the facility. Workers expressed outrage that, lacking showers of their own, men had begun to use the women's bathing facilities at the Textile Kombinat. The lack of two shower rooms was not a problem during the war, but, with the return of soldiers from the front, men and women were forced to share the showers. In 1949, female workers had had enough, complaining that bathing "together was never appropriate."[46] Such a lack of concern for the welfare and needs of women workers was cited as a reason for increasing employee resignations.

Russian female employees did not want to use unisex bathing facilities, but forcing Uzbeks to do so was inconceivable. Going from veiled seclusion to unisex showering in one generation was not what had been envisioned when the campaigns to involve Uzbek women in productive labor began or when women rushed into the factory during the war. Such instances certainly reinforced popular notions that Uzbek female participation in Soviet life would lead to a collapse of moral values in Uzbek society. At the Textile Kombinat in 1949, 67 percent of the 14,285 workers were women. Soviet ideologists celebrated this high number of women in production as a sign of the "liberation" of Central Asian women from the "feudal-*bey* patriarchal system" of the past. However, official descriptions fail to mention that a mere 1,149 of the workers were Uzbek; of this number, only 280 were women.[47] Furthermore, many of these Asian workers had been on the job for years but had not risen above entry-level positions. However, in the view of various Soviet propagandists, female Central Asian workers possessed surprisingly "poor work discipline" and increasingly chose to stop working once they got married. Some of Soviet Uzbekistan's most promising women followed this trend, such as Karima Olyanova, the former deputy minister of agriculture of the Uzbek SSR, Fatima Yuldashbaeva, former employee at the Central Committee of the Uzbek Communist Party, and Salimova, former secretary of the Central Committee of the Komsomol of the Uzbek SSR.[48] At the Textile Kombinat, the situation was not much different. Kaminova, a prominent Party member and weaver since 1940, married another Uzbek Party member and quit working in 1948. Did the Party member wife want to stop working or was it her Party member husband who told her to do so? Party officials did not know, but either answer would have been troubling to them. Another woman, Basygova, the Textile Kombinat's representative to the city soviet, quit working after her marriage to an Uzbek in 1949, as did Nasyrova, who had, as documents suggest, visited the front with one of the official wartime home-front delegations.[49] Party leaders at the factory were puzzled as to why some of the best workers, Party leaders, and Stakhanovites left, because they had been perceived to be the most loyal and skilled female employees. These women had "made it" in Soviet society but chose to turn their backs on their achievements and the opportunities that Soviet power had given them. These women also had been presented to the population as ideals of Soviet Uzbek womanhood only a few years before, and *fabkom* officials viewed the inability to keep them at the *kombinat* as a negative example for younger Uzbek workers—both male and female.[50]

Interestingly, Party reports rarely discuss how these families survived on one less salary, an issue that could have been used to warn women not to leave the factory. In addition, besides expressing shock and disbelief over the fact that women left the work force after the war, officials did little investigation as to why the women actually left. Party documents do not report that the women had been contacted, questioned, punished, or personally implored to come back to work. Once the women left, documents describe them as virtually out of the grasp of the Soviet state and back in the hands of oppressive fathers-in-law and husbands in the traditional Uzbek neighborhoods in the city. Besides public criticism of their actions and private discussion over the negative influence of these cases, there was little recorded on what efforts factory officials might have made to entice these women back into production.[51]

One of the causes for the loss of Uzbek female workers perhaps was a negative perception of single Russian women workers among Uzbeks. With the loss of most of a generation of men in the war, many Russian women were left with few choices if they wished to become mothers. The rise of single motherhood was a common pattern in postwar Soviet life, but in Uzbekistan, this phenomenon had a negative impact among Uzbek female workers, for whom having a child out of wedlock was considered much more shameful than it was among Russians. A collapse of sexual morality in Tashkent was described as a threat to Soviet progress and culture in the region. One Russian *kombinat* worker was accused of numerous sex scandals that reportedly demeaned the image of Soviet female laborers. Her neighbors in the Textile Kombinat housing compound denounced her to the *fabkom* chair in 1950. They described her as a "loose woman" who had been impregnated by two different men and then started sleeping with a third. She soon had to have "another" abortion.[52] This behavior was seen as disgraceful by her neighbors and fellow *kombinat* workers. A high abortion rate among Russian workers at the factory also was troubling for the health of employees and reputation of the entire *kombinat*.[53] Factory officials seemed particularly concerned about this issue because of the difficulty in recruiting and retaining Central Asian women. Party leaders likewise had to struggle against instances of factory supervisors raping or seducing young female employees and trainees.[54] If "becoming a Soviet worker" meant losing one's honor like some Russian women had, why would Uzbeks encourage their daughters to follow the example of Russians?

However, if Russian women had the option of becoming single mothers, what course of action was open to Uzbek women who wanted a family when there were few unmarried men around? A postwar report on the persistence of Uzbek cultural norms remarked that some female Party members in Uzbekistan "have retreated back into their family obligations and are walking away from participating in [the] social life of the country." The previously mentioned examples from the Textile Kombinat were illustrations of this problem. However, the report's author, Lomakin, expressed more concern over the growth of polygamy in Tashkent oblast, citing instances of female Uzbek Party leaders in the neighboring Parkent region who became second wives of Party and collective farm activists. While male Party leaders occasionally committed polygamy and "marriage violations," criticism and investigation of the men was less pronounced. Lomakin appeared to have been more troubled by the fact that prominent female communists, "liberated from the Uzbek past," also were complicit in breaking marriage laws. This trend indicated to Lomakin that the influence of "reactionary Islam" had increased during the war among people who already had been "transformed" into Soviet citizens.[55] The solution to this problem was unclear to most officials because many of these people still considered themselves to be active communists and did not see any contradiction between this behavior and their "Sovietness."

While Islam did enjoy a marked revival in the more religiously tolerant wartime climate, the postwar gender imbalance left women with few choices for marriage since Uzbek men were in short supply. This demographic issue was rarely addressed in either discussions of the rise in out-of-wedlock births among Russians or polygamy among Uzbeks. While polygamy was reported across Tashkent, the Parkent case was most shocking because six of the most prominent female Communist Party members in the region chose to become second wives.[56] Their actions could not be dismissed as a sign of continued victimization by an oppressive patriarchal system because the question of female agency could not be ignored. These women were not typical victims of "traditional" society but had been "liberated" from the constraints of conservative Uzbek culture to become active participants in building socialism. Then, they made an active choice to become a second wife. Such decisions, in fact, went against the teleological course of Marxist history as Soviet ideology interpreted it.[57] The fact that some Soviet women retreated to traditional lifestyles behind the closed gates and winding streets of the Uzbek city boggled the minds of officials, even though women elsewhere in the Soviet Union desired a similar domestic life after the horrors of war. However, women elsewhere did not have the same type of "Old City," with family gardens and food supplies, to which they could retreat. In Tashkent, this trend provided urban planners with increased incentive to speed up the transformation of urban space.

Lomakin also remained concerned about the continued presence of women in *paranjis* on the streets of the capital. In the Lenin district of

Tashkent, prominent Party officials, including the secretary of the Party organization at the Psychological Hospital, were criticized for "forcing" their female family members to wear *paranjis* when they stepped outside the home. The district Party committee was accused of failing "to fight dangerous cultural traditions of the past and to pay attention to the appearance of feudal-*bey* relations toward women." With such actions by prominent leaders in the region, there was little doubt expressed as to why so few Uzbek women became involved in industrial production, the ultimate marker of success in the postwar years.[58] In these cases, it was the men who were criticized for forcing their wives, daughters, or mothers to wear the *paranji*. The women again were seen as powerless victims who did whatever their men told them. Again, agency is not mentioned. They were never interviewed or allowed to explain why they wore the *paranji*.

The Soviet Uzbek poet Zulfiya's *Literaturnaia Gazeta* article in 1950 was indicative of this view. She opened her story by recalling the work of Habiba Yusupova, an Uzbek who taught literacy courses to thousands of Uzbek women. She depicts an elderly Yusupova driving along the reconstructed Navoi Street in her own car to teach literacy classes to the next generation of Uzbek women. With Yusupova's help, formerly "oppressed" Uzbek girls now were the "women of Soviet Uzbekistan, having become engineers, doctors, masters of factories, collective farms, and the arts."[59] She stated that the Stalin epoch had brought a spiritual revolution to the region, with an enormous cultural growth among Uzbeks, one of the many Soviet peoples of Central Asia. Zulfiya's Soviet Tashkent was a beautiful city, with wide streets and open spaces reminiscent of the famous painting, *New Moscow*, by Yuri Pimenov. However, the author noted that the liberation of women had not been completed. In *rural* regions of the republic, bright students were forced to leave the Soviet education system to marry old men and wear the *paranji*, while men had two and even three wives. But she makes clear distinctions between urban spaces, where the practice was less common, and agricultural regions, where it occurred more frequently.

However, even along Navoi Street, Soviet Tashkent's main thoroughfare, Zulfiya saw an Uzbek woman in a *paranji*. She stopped to speak to the young woman at the Navoi Monument, the symbol of Central Asian enlightened thought, and told her to lift her veil. After reluctantly doing so, the young woman admitted to being illiterate. Zulfiya spotted a theater advertisement for the opera *Gul'sara* at the new Navoi Opera and Ballet Theater, the symbol of Soviet Uzbek cultural achievement. *Gul'sara* is the story of an Uzbek woman who, at the age of twenty-five, takes off her *paranji*. "Her life was harder than yours," Zulfiya told the veiled woman. "There were *beys*, *ishany* [spiritual guides, long criticized by the Soviet regime], and basmachis, but she [Gul'sara] saw the *light* and escaped toward freedom."[60] While walking past the new construction in the city, she showed the veiled woman the enormous Soviet land excavators that construction workers used to transform the city. It appears that technology and urban life were supposed to convince her to tear off her head covering and join Soviet society. At the end of Navoi Street, the veiled woman disappeared into the maze of the Old City, but Zulfiya declared that they would meet again. She describes the unnamed Uzbek woman as a victim who must be helped through Soviet modernization and urbanization efforts. Although she lived in an urban area, this young woman is depicted as peasantlike, almost as if Tashkent's Old Town was no different from the agricultural regions outside the city. Zulfiya, in fact, never asks the woman why she dresses as she does but simply assumes that she lacked agency to control her fate and that she was still a part of the "irrationality" of her traditional culture. However, Zulfiya's message was clear: with the assistance of Uzbek intellectuals and through more frequent interaction with life in the reconstructed Soviet city, the young woman's future would be much brighter. The importance of urban planning and infrastructure development for transforming identities cannot be underestimated in the Soviet mindset of the time.

Zulfiya's article was important in that it highlighted postwar concerns over the lingering tendency of some women to wear the veil, particularly in the Old City and in the countryside. It also pointed to some troubling cases about which Soviet officials had to worry. For example, a young Soviet nurse and Party member, Karaviakova, married an Uzbek man and started to wear traditional Uzbek attire. Instead of assuming the role of the older "Russian sibling" and pulling her Central Asian husband along toward Soviet cultural ideals, this Russian woman shockingly started to wear the *paranji* and completely severed all ties with the Communist Party.[61] While the intermingling of national groups was viewed as a progressive step toward the creation of a common Soviet people, it was Uzbeks who were expected to take on Russian/Soviet customs, not the other way around. The overpowering influence and control of an "irrational" patriarchal family structure could not be used to explain her situation, as had been argued in other cases. This Russian woman had other choices but chose a more domestic lifestyle.

Similarly, the wedding of Turab Kamilov, the head of communications at Tashkent Telegraph, also shocked Party leaders. This thirty-two-year-old Communist Party member married a woman twelve years younger than he; they were entering into neither a polygamous nor an underage marriage.

The problem was that the bride appeared in a *paranji* at her state wedding ceremony at the regional ZAGS, the official state registration bureau for marriage ceremonies. Despite appeals by ZAGS employees that she take off the veil, Kamilov, the Communist Party member, would not permit her to appear with her face exposed. Ten other instances of brides in *paranjis* appearing for their wedding to Communist Party members were reported at this particular ZAGS bureau in 1948.[62] These were not poorly educated people or those from the periphery but people who worked at prominent institutions in Tashkent. When it came to registering marriages, many Tashkenters subverted the state bureau, the organ that was supposed to supplant religious ceremonies and traditional rituals of life. However, since ZAGS was the only organization that could perform legal marriages, its officials were forced to sanction the marriage of people who publicly wore signs of the traditional faith and values that the Soviet system, ZAGS in particular, fought to eradicate. These Uzbeks did not oppose or rebel outright against this institution of the Soviet control but instead used it for their own purposes, an indication that they were not outside of Soviet society but actively participated in it and adapted it to their needs, even if their adaptation was not ideologically sound.

Examining Uzbek Bodies

As this study shows, the Soviet state infiltrated Central Asian communities and ordered the destruction and subsequent reconstruction of traditional neighborhoods and buildings. However, Soviet officials were not satisfied with simply controlling urban spaces and outward signs of culture; they also actively monitored the intimate details of their citizens' lives and used new Soviet institutions—schools, ZAGS, hospitals, and communal apartments—as a means to monitor what citizens thought and how they behaved. With this intrusiveness regarding the lives of citizens, the state's concern over arranged marriage among Uzbeks grew in the postwar years, and the continued prevalence of underage marriages remained a blot on "modern" Soviet society in Uzbekistan. *Literaturnaia Gazeta* exposed the problem to readers across the Soviet Union in December 1953 by recounting the story of a twelve-year-old girl in a regional center of Tashkent oblast; the area's short distance from the Uzbek capital was underscored for readers.[63] This child enjoyed studying, but her father, the chairman of an agricultural soviet, arranged her marriage to an adult man. On her wedding night, "her childhood was stolen" by an "evil hand [that] took the right to knowledge, a happy childhood, and warm dreams from the future from this little girl." In indirect terms, the article suggests that such marriage arrangements were tantamount to parental and community condoning of child rape. More shocking, however, was that the Uzbek director of her school knew of her parents' plans but did not "sound the alarm" to save this Soviet girl. Building Soviet schools was part of an effort to create new Soviet citizens and protect children from ideologies of the past, but some teachers and Party leaders in these institutions turned a blind eye to such flagrant deviations from Soviet cultural norms.[64]

Some child marriages were hidden from the state by the fact that the religious ceremony, the *nikoh,* was performed first while the girl was still underage, making the marriage official according to Islamic law. Such couples would then wait to register the marriage under Soviet law until the bride was of legal age. Occasionally, this trick would get exposed, especially if the couple had a child before a state wedding had been arranged. In addition, Soviet doctors—another arm of the "modern" Soviet state in Tashkent— could facilitate underage marriage. Soviet physicians were regularly called to conduct physical examinations of young brides to confirm that they were of legal age before ZAGS officials would register an Uzbek wedding. However, doctor's certificates of maturity were easy to purchase from healthcare officials in Soviet hospitals. The Soviet state instituted invasive physical exams of young women, but the inefficient Soviet administration and bureaucratic corruption allowed families to maneuver through the Soviet legal and medical systems to adapt traditional customs to the new Soviet era. As a result, individuals technically did not ignore Soviet regulations or avoid the institutions of the Soviet state but used these institutions to adapt their culture to the new governing realities of Uzbekistan.[65] Uzbeks were thus not existing apart from Soviet life but were trying to use the system to their own advantage, just like thousands of other Soviet citizens were. However, the fact that Uzbek religious traditions were more easily identifiable than many Russian religions traditions made them more noticeable.

The campaigns to monitor the health and well-being of Tashkent women and girls were not solely about illness or backwardness. They concerned Soviet ideals of modernization in Tashkent and surrounding areas. In investigating women's bodies and decreeing that some brides were too young and some Soviet workers were too promiscuous, the state expressed its concern that its female citizens had not yet become model socialist women. While so much attention was focused on Uzbek women not meeting the ideals of socialist femininity, neither Russian nor Uzbek Tashkenters in fact easily fit the ideal of Soviet womanhood, in which women were to be highly trained technicians, culturally knowledgeable, willing to fight for and defend the socialist system, *and* loving mothers who gave birth to many children to make up for the wartime population loss. The problem was that Russian urban women were often industrial workers but did not meet the conservative image of the Soviet hero-mother. Uzbek women, in turn, fulfilled the maternal role but not the hero-worker model. The lives of the women of Uzbekistan exemplified the dilemma of modern womanhood and, more importantly, the failure of the Soviet state to deliver on basic promises and provide for the fundamental needs of its citizens.

Furthermore, Soviet officials were not only interested in monitoring the intimate details of women's bodies; they also examined boys to determine the prevalence of Islamic circumcision rites. Soviet officials noted a rise in circumcisions to "massive" proportions in Tashkent oblast in 1948; each circumcision was followed by an elaborate community celebration or *sunnat toi,* with the consumption of enormous quantities of food. While some officials focused on economic arguments—that local Uzbeks were squandering food and other resources during these celebrations, health-care workers stated that the procedure endangered the health of Central Asian children, an argument they also used against Jewish circumcision traditions.[66] Soviet officials argued that the procedure was medically unnecessary, unsanitary, and often performed by people of "dubious" character who lacked training, such as anyone who had experience with cutting.[67] This criticism recalls the arguments used against tsarist era healers and barbers who performed basic health-care functions for the indigenous population of imperial Tashkent, often with devastating consequences for public health. Both publicly and privately, the continued prevalence of circumcision proved the alleged "backward" and "reactionary" nature of Uzbek culture that ethnographers and medical professionals had deemed harmful to Soviet society.[68] Soviet doctors argued that the procedure was unnecessary and caused infection, while the Tashkent-based Muslim Spiritual Board of Central Asia and Kazakhstan, the official Soviet Islamic religious organization in the region, declared the practice unnecessary for Muslims.[69] Nevertheless, Islamic circumcision ceremonies survived the entire Soviet era, and Muslims, in fact, appear to have had more success than Jews in resisting state pressure to end this tradition.[70] In many ways, circumcision remains an important distinction between the indigenous and European populations of post-Soviet Uzbekistan.

The Communist Party frequently investigated its Tashkent members for having their sons circumcised.[71] When criticized, these Party members often claimed that the child's grandparents arranged the procedure and that they, the Communist Party members, had no control over it. However, whether the excuse was true or not, in deflecting blame onto grandparents, these "guilty" communists implied that they themselves could not lead their families away from traditional religious and cultural practices toward Soviet enlightenment. This explanation indicated to Party agitators that the "patriarchal" structure of Central Asian society continued to exert an influence in Soviet life. Communists were supposed to fight such "vestiges" of the past, not be controlled by them. They were supposed to bring Soviet values into their homes and communities, not to have one foot in each part—traditional and Soviet—of Uzbek society. This effort of Party members to incorporate religious traditions into their Soviet lives, even if it was only their private lives, was not an exclusive Central Asian phenomenon because Party members in Russia and Ukraine occasionally were criticized for having their children baptized in secret.[72] Furthermore, ethnographers noted that even the Soviet intellectual and political elites, who were the more Russified Uzbek elements of the population, were "guilty" of upholding these traditions, often simply sending their sons away to rural Central Asian towns so that the procedure and celebration would not be noticed by authorities in the modern capital.[73] Once again, Central Asians were able to take advantage of their indigenous status and the fact they could easily return to the Uzbek countryside for food, shelter, or to sustain some local traditions. In addition, since baptism did not leave a permanent mark and circumcision did, it was easier for Soviet officials to record and investigate this cultural and religious tradition than it was to monitor lingering Christian customs among the Slavic population, even though many Russians and Ukrainians in the European sections of the Soviet Union followed the same pattern of sending their children to rural relatives for baptism and other traditional rites. However, Soviet officials seemed much more emphatic in their efforts to monitor and curb traditional Central Asian practices. In fact, during medical exams at orphanages, hospitals, and youth camps in Uzbekistan, medical staff documented and reported cases of their young patients having been circumcised, a clear indication of intense Soviet concern over this issue.[74]

Furthermore, although Soviet physicians declared that the procedure was not medically necessary, some doctors occasionally performed circumcisions for Uzbek parents. Party leaders were especially concerned that this religious tradition was continuing, but they masked their concern under the guise of promoting personal hygiene.[75] In the late 1950s, Uzbek Party officials expressed concern over rising instances of "medical" circumcisions. In March 1957, the head of the Kazakh Committee for the Affairs of Religious Cults wrote to his Uzbek counterpart to complain about the relative ease with which people could arrange for the procedure in Soviet hospitals in Tashkent, which performed this "religious rite . . . as if it were sanctioned by the health-care agencies."[76] Kazakhs evidently heard rumors of the prevalence of the procedure in the Uzbek capital and requested similar services in their own republic. For Party leaders, these demands indicated a rising belief among Uzbeks and Kazakhs that if Soviet health-care workers performed the procedure, it was both safe and endorsed by the Soviet state. Tashkent's proximity to the Kazakh border also raised the possibility of Kazakh residents traveling from Chimkent and other regions to the Uzbek capital for the procedure at the city's new health-care facilities, important symbols of modern Soviet life in Central Asia. Once again, Uzbeks (and their Kazakh neighbors) used the new state institutions of Tashkent for their own purposes, namely the continuation of local cultural norms by folding them into modern Soviet practices. They accepted the validity of these new Soviet institutions and made them part of their lives, an indication of the gradual transformation of local cultural norms into the new Soviet reality. These Uzbek Tashkenters also showed they had a good understanding of how to maneuver through the socialist world in Central Asia, and they took advantage of the corruption and disorder that were endemic throughout the state bureaucracy. Tashkenters were gradually accepting of and functioning in the new Soviet reality but still tried to merge their own customs into that new reality, at the same time that Tashkent urban designers were trying to incorporate traditional Uzbek architectural motifs into the modern Soviet city. By the end of the Stalin era, both Party ideologists and the city's residents were trying to figure out ways to unite traditional cultures with Soviet norms. With time, they both would have success, even if neither side would have anticipated the end results.

The Soviet regime was not only interested in controlling the public spaces of Tashkent but also desired control over the private lives of Tashkenters. Soviet ideologists tried to reorder the housing structure of the city and transform the extended Uzbek family into nuclear family apartment dwellers. "Red teahouses" and workers' clubs were built to control the rest and relaxation time of Tashkent residents, transforming them into connoisseurs of high Soviet culture—opera, theater, and Soviet/Russian literature and classical music. Sports, particularly soccer, were geared to involve young Soviet citizens in activities outside the Uzbek home. These efforts were meant to mold the minds of these children and to get them to think and voice their thoughts through the prism of socialist ideology. Native traditions were deemed backward, and diverse Soviet nationalities, despite being able to decorate their lives with national symbols, were supposed to assimilate into a central Soviet culture, based on Soviet interpretations of modernity and high European cultural ideals. The infrastructure changes in Tashkent were part of the campaign to transform the private lives and minds of Soviet citizens.

The new "Soviet Uzbek" identity that was created for Tashkenters was associated with productive labor, officially on the factory floor or in an educational institution. Soviet Uzbeks were not supposed to possess any public markers of their religious or "feudal" past, namely attendance at mosques, having female family members who either were secluded at home or under veils, or marrying off children at early ages before they finished school. When Party officials looked for signs of traditionalism, they could clearly see evidence of continued Uzbek "backwardness," partly because they were tasked with uncovering signs of local peculiarity. These signs of traditional culture also were much easier to identify than in the Slavic republics, where the Soviet system originated. While Soviet officials were actively trying to uncover evidence of anti-Soviet behavior and agitators among Tashkent's indigenous population, they looked less often for indications of the overall acceptance of Soviet values, institutions, and ways of life, which were prevalent across the city in the ways in which people tried to adapt their personal reality to postwar Soviet life. Furthermore, as Uzbeks interacted more overtly in the public sphere of Soviet society after the war, many Central Asian residents of the Tashkent region began to incorporate some of these images of the modern Soviet citizen into their own lives, even if they privately continued some regional or local traditions. Meanwhile, Soviet security officials dwelled on the peculiarities—not the similarities—of Tashkent to the rest of the Soviet Union. In attempting to continue and adapt some customs, Uzbeks were not much different from other Soviet ethnic groups and used many of the same coping methods.

Postwar Uzbek citizens also began to act like their non–Central Asian counterparts in one critical way. They made demands on the Soviet state and started using state institutions and state-sponsored language for their own benefit. Uzbek veterans and Stakhanovites requested help in feeding and clothing their children, indicating a belief that their wartime service and sacrifice for socialism should be rewarded by the state itself. Others walked off the production line to protest Soviet policies that did not provide them or their extended families with the same benefits that others allegedly received in the hungry years after the war. Central Asian citizens, like their Russian counterparts, also began to ask central, local, and factory officials for assistance in securing housing, soap, clothing, and food, even leaving the factory and the city when their aspirations for promotion or material goods went unmet. With Soviet pressure to keep Central Asians in production, Uzbek workers' job actions gave them extra power to make requests of the state. In turn, the state needed such people because they served as positive role models for their neighbors across Uzbekistan, the entire region, and Asia at large.

Veiled brides at ZAGS, doctors' certificates for underage brides, and circumcision requests at Soviet hospitals also showed that Central Asians did not exclude themselves from Soviet society or resist all efforts to transform them. Instead, these phenomena indicate that Uzbeks were gradually learning how to function in and adapt to Soviet life, often trying to fuse their own culture with new Soviet norms. In addition, many people learned to use the language of the state themselves in making their demands or excusing their behavior. In a strange way, inventing national characteristics for Soviet Uzbekistan and decreeing what defined a "Soviet Uzbek" or "Soviet Uzbek architecture" was easy. City officials and planners quickly went about creating "Uzbek national decorations" on its apartment buildings, teahouses, and schools. But getting Uzbeks in and around Tashkent to accept the new identity, cultural forms, and life rituals was more challenging and only occurred with time. The public anger in the 1950s over the failure of the Soviet state to meet its promises was an important turning point in the population's acceptance of these Soviet identities. Outspoken Uzbeks showed that they were becoming active members of the socialist system and were beginning to have a voice in that system, even if the state did not always view them as meeting the ideal image of a Soviet citizen and even if they still attempted to preserve some local customs.

Soviet officials in turn made increased demands on their citizens. The state politicized family life, rewarding women who gave birth to numerous Soviet citizens in Soviet hospitals and who reared them in a Soviet environment. In the name of creating a cultured and refined society, the Soviet state denounced adultery and drunkenness and abolished polygamy and arranged child marriages. Still, the state was not content with managing the public actions of its citizens. Soviet ideology also desired control of intimate details of Soviet citizens' lives, including their bodies. The body of a Soviet citizen—male or female—was observed and recorded by medical professionals, as is common throughout the modern world. However, Soviet medical professionals and Party ideologists were not only interested in one's health but also attempted to figure out what one's individual choice over one's body or that of one's child meant for the Soviet state. Personal hygiene, pregnancy, abortion, circumcision, physical examinations of brides, and questions over personal modesty with the veil all came under the purview of the Soviet state, which, in the name of caring for and improving its citizens, attempted to control personal decisions, such as what medical procedures one underwent, where one worked, when one married, what one wore, and if one studied. The state not only sought to transform Soviet cities in Central Asia through invading the Uzbek sections and destroying them but also continued trying to invade the home and, ultimately, the minds and bodies of its citizens. And yet, time and again, it found itself lacking the very resources needed to achieve its ambitious goals. With the evident gap between claims and reality, the passage of time was becoming the primary tool of transformation.

REDESIGNING TASHKENT
AFTER STALIN

News of Stalin's death on March 5, 1953, arrived in Tashkent on the following morning in brief articles in *Qizil O'zbekiston* and *Pravda Vostoka*. These newspapers devoted the remainder of that day's issues to mundane stories of economic, industrial, and cultural affairs. However, Tashkent quickly went into mourning, with black and crimson cloth hanging from buildings and "spontaneous" memorial meetings taking place at factories and education institutions throughout the city. Mourners moved toward the city center, where a crowd of people encircled Revolution Square, where the Stalin monument stood. The number of visitors reportedly was so large that the crowd not only gathered around the statue of the Soviet leader but also formed a line that snaked through the urban center toward the Old City.[1] Mourning was a multiethnic endeavor centered at the heart of the Soviet city but spreading outward to include all sections of the Uzbek capital.

The death of Stalin and leadership changes in both Moscow and Tashkent did not alter the desire to reorder the Uzbek capital and make it a modern European/Russian-style city with a unified multiethnic community. Although there was less stress on monumental public architecture and more emphasis on large buildings for everyday purposes (hospitals, schools, and apartment complexes), beautiful city spaces and idealized gardenlike parks remained at the forefront of Soviet construction campaigns to present a positive image of the Soviet state at home and abroad. Tashkent, the center of Soviet rule in Asia, remained an important symbol of socialism and the promises that the Soviet system offered to its citizens. However, once state-sponsored coercion and control decreased during Khrushchev's de-Stalinization campaign, people became increasingly vocal in their dissatisfaction with persistently poor living standards, forcing Party officials to begin addressing popular frustration over quality-of-life issues in the Uzbek capital and surrounding areas.

As they had in the 1930s, Soviet leaders looked to the past to find scapegoats for the low living standards in Soviet cities and for rising disappointment with socialism among the population. In the mid-1950s, city politicians and planners identified the previous regime of Stalin and his supporters as the primary causes of the hard reality of life in Tashkent and other urban areas. Hence, although the architects and planners did not change, opinions on their past designs certainly changed, unleashing sharp criticism of Stalinist architecture for its "gigantic" and ornate construction, excessive costs, minimal local initiative, and delays in construction. Still, in developing new urban projects and declaring that they would solve the problems of the city, Tashkent planners from the mid-1950s to the late 1960s repeated many of the same trends, the most egregious example being their failure to engage the local population in the city's redevelopment plans. Under Khrushchev, state officials in Moscow still strove to bring their vision of an orderly socialist city to this distant and "chaotic" Asian space. As Soviet citizens in the Uzbek capital, Tashkenters still needed to fit into Khrushchev's reconstructed Soviet city. Clearly, the notion that a reconstructed Tashkent should help mold Central Asians into Soviet citizens did not change over the Stalin-Khrushchev divide. Similarly, inefficient construction, shoddy workmanship, and the belief that an elite few knew more about Tashkent than city residents themselves persisted under both leaders.

The Death of Stalin

The death of Stalin caused shockwaves to reverberate across the Soviet Union; Tashkent was no exception. Stalin had been the undisputed leader of the Soviet Union for more than twenty-five years and had led the country through tremendous upheaval—domestic and international. Despite the devastation of famine, industrialization, collectivization, the terror, and the war, many Soviet citizens could not imagine a future without him. Soviet officials exacerbated citizen grief by making special efforts to create a public show of mourning and to turn the funeral of the leader into a demonstration of Soviet power and resolve, paying particular attention to the use of reconstructed urban spaces in these orchestrations. On March 7, 1953, two days after Stalin's death and on cue from Moscow, Uzbek Party officials and press organs developed a unified program for presenting the death of Stalin to city residents, falling back on the pre-existing language of the cult of Lenin. Like Lenin, the *vozhd'* (leader) might have died, but he still lived on in the achievements of the Uzbek people, in the freedoms that he had granted them as full members of the Soviet family, and in the desire of the Soviet people to serve the Stalinist goal of creating communism. At a memorial meeting at the "Tashkent Textile Kombinat named after Stalin," A. Akhmadzhanov, a Textile Kombinat supervisor, spoke of Stalin as a great friend of Uzbekistan and its capital city. Arriving at the *kombinat* construction site in 1932 as a simple Uzbek laborer with no qualifications, Akhmadzhanov entered the Stalinist system that, he said, enabled him to fulfill his potential. He received training in Moscow, after which he returned to the Uzbek capital to help transform it into an industrial center and ultimately rose to a leadership position at the *kombinat.* Upon the death of the leader, he and other workers of Tashkent's premier factory did not stop production, despite their psychological trauma over the news.[2] Akhmadzhanov's words underscored the idea that although Stalin was dead, his Tashkent factories would continue the Stalinist task of producing fabric, metal, and machines. Stalin's Central Asian "children" had been raised and educated under Soviet power. Upon his death, they were now officially "adults" and would make their father proud. The Soviet leader had given them the tools to succeed in the transformation from pre-revolutionary oppression to full-scale socialism.

In official accounts of Tashkent's mourning and funeral service, women and Uzbek Tashkenters assumed leading roles. In fact, Russian male voices are not prominent at all in published reports. Whether they toiled in physical labor at a city factory or in desk jobs at one of Tashkent's institutes of higher education, Uzbek Tashkenters saw their views of Stalin take center stage in both Uzbek- and Russian-language accounts.[3] Zulfiya, the female Uzbek poet, highlighted the national coloring of public mourning by remarking on the large number of Uzbek women who made pilgrimages to the Stalin statue in the center of the city. Mothers with children, factory workers, and female academics came to place flowers at the pedestal of the "greatest of men," who was responsible for the liberation of Uzbek women.[4] Tashkent's city space was unified to mark the death of Stalin.

This Soviet unity was underscored by the fact that the Tashkent funeral service was timed to coincide with the actual ceremony in Moscow. Functioning in its role as the Soviet capital in Central Asia, Tashkent had a wake and memorial service similar to the services in Moscow, with Tashkent's Stalin monument serving in place of a corpse.[5] Columns of mourners—Party officials, military officers, factory workers, students, housewives, Stalin-laureate artists, academics, and children—filed into Tashkent's Revolution Square to pay their respects to the bronze image of Stalin.[6] The Moscow funeral ceremony was broadcast by radio throughout the city center to allow residents to follow every detail of the events in the Soviet capital, from the speeches on Moscow's Red Square to the interment of the body in Lenin's Tomb. Tashkent's diverse ethnic and professional groups, men as well as women, congregated together in grief to show that the Uzbek capital stood alongside Moscow and hundreds of other cities of the "multiethnic Soviet family" in remembering the *vozhd'*. This professed unity was an important component of the new leadership's efforts to firm up its power and transition the Soviet people into the new, but uncertain, post-Stalin reality, as William Taubman has noted.[7]

After Stalin's body was placed in the tomb in Moscow, cities across the Soviet Union honored the *vozhd'* with "industrial salutes." In Tashkent, all cars, trucks, and trains stopped so that factory bells, automobile horns, and steam engine whistles could ring out in "symphonic" unison in memory of the *vozhd'*.[8] This orchestra of industrial sounds symbolized the transition of the Soviet Union into an economic powerhouse, but this aspect of the ceremony also symbolized the Uzbek SSR's transformation from a colonial backwater whose primary form of transportation was the donkey or ass into an industrial center of the Soviet East, complete with cars, trucks, and a modern railway. By highlighting how Uzbekistan had changed under socialism in official discourse, the death of Stalin had local significance for this ethno-national group.

In Tashkent, unlike Moscow, where approximately one hundred mourners were trampled to death in a chaotic push to pay their respects to the Soviet leader, there were no reports of hysterical grieving, mass shoving, or people being crushed to death.[9] After all, there was no body to view in Tashkent, and the city center lacked the high concentration of buildings that the Soviet capital possessed. The fact that Tashkent's urban development had so far failed to provide the city with a high-density and compact center proved useful in this orchestration of Soviet power because it provided mourners with space to spread out. The marble-and-metal statue of the "God-like" Soviet leader also was less likely to evoke a frenzied emotional attachment among residents of the Uzbek capital than his actual corpse caused among Muscovites. Even so, archival documents indicate that the official version of Tashkent's farewell ceremonies as an Uzbek, or at least a multiethnic, affair was not completely accurate. Russian Tashkenters appeared to have been more moved than their Uzbek neighbors to express their condolences over the death of Stalin in letters to Party leaders, a fact that is conveyed through the paucity of Uzbek-language correspondence in the Tashkent central and city archives or by writers with Uzbek-sounding names. Individual or institutional letters from the Uzbek capital most frequently were signed by people with Slavic last names or by Uzbeks who chose to write in Russian, although these letters were usually written in poor Russian, possibly indicating that they were not orchestrated from above by Party or factory leaders but were true expressions of sentiment. Interestingly, this was not the case with letters that arrived from Andijan, Namangan, and other regions, the majority of which were in Uzbek.[10]

Most of this correspondence evoked pride in Soviet rule and faith in Stalin or the Stalinist project; letters often cited Soviet heroism in World War II, the liberation of women, or the general unity and friendship of the Soviet people. Declarations of the tremendous growth of the Uzbek culture or thanks to Stalin for his support of Central Asians were rare, a surprising notion considering the fact that local propaganda constantly played on this theme. Although the letters were mailed from Tashkent and were written by Uzbeks, the content of most of them indicates that they could have been written from almost any Soviet city, signifying that the authors of these condolence notes frequently identified themselves more with the Soviet system as opposed to favoring a regional Central Asian identity. Even if the city did not yet resemble its idealized urban plan, its residents were voicing their "Sovietness" in their expressions of grief. A. Babadzhanov, by name obviously not a Russian, followed this trend. Likely a young boy, he decorated his letter with airplane wings and red stars and even declared that Stalin's efforts to found a "powerful and undefeatable Soviet air force" would serve as an important memory and form of protection for all Soviet people.[11] Although he was a native Central Asian, Babadzhanov wrote in Russian on the general theme of Stalin's wisdom and Soviet military strength. For this member of the young generation, most likely steeped in socialist youth institutions—Soviet schools and the Pioneer or Komsomol organizations—Central Asia was not pivotal to his identity during this time of mourning. For Babadzhanov, the loss of the *vozhd'* was a Soviet, not necessarily an Uzbek, affair. By not evoking ethnic particularity in any form, Babadzhanov seems to trumpet his Soviet identity over his Central Asian one. For a considerable part of the population, Tashkent had become "Soviet," especially in the way it marked Stalin's death.[12]

Despite the lack of Uzbek national characteristics in these letters, the message coming from the people, both prominent leaders and average citizens, was clear. Although Stalin was dead, the Soviet people were determined to continue the construction of a communist society; letter writers occasionally expressed oaths of loyalty to the dead leader. Tashkent residents, whether they represented city institutions or were simply pensioners, students, or workers who wrote on their own, were keenly aware of the language needed in such correspondence. Although the state carefully organized the pomp and ceremony of the funeral, the fact that letters from across Uzbekistan were dated immediately after his death (during the period from March 6 to March 24, 1953) suggests that feelings of sorrow and support for the Soviet state were not simply orchestrations of elite Party members. Many Uzbeks were truly moved by the death of the only leader they had ever known. Consequently, they expressed their grief in an ideologically appropriate manner. These Soviet citizens, sometimes in Uzbek or in broken Russian, knew how to interact with state officials through the trope of the "letter to the *vozhd'*," even if the *vozhd'* was no longer alive.

While the preponderance of Russian-language letters from Tashkent itself could indicate that there was slightly less interest in Stalin's passing among Uzbek residents of the capital city, it also likely reflects the increasing prevalence of the Russian language in the most "Sovietized" city in Central Asia. Bilingualism was growing, even if knowledge of Russian grammar and prose style remained poor, as the letters from Central Asians in Tashkent archives clearly indicate. Uzbek Tashkenters were more exposed to the language than were Central Asians in other Uzbek provincial cities and towns, and they were more used to and comfortable with it than their ethnic counterparts in more remote parts of the country, even if Soviet officials still denigrated Tashkenters' ability to speak Russian, the common language of the socialist future. It also could be a sign of the reality of the government and cultural structures of Tashkent at the time, where decisions over what the state should record and what archivists should preserve still were made by Russian officials and academics, while the new cadre of bilingual Soviet Uzbek elite—soon to enter many of these government, Party, and cultural institutions in the late 1950s and 1960s—was just completing its rise through the postwar education system and preparing to assume positions of more responsibility. In provincial areas, where Russian-language skills were less prevalent, there clearly existed a greater need to preserve Uzbek-language letters because Russian-language speakers were few and far between. In Tashkent, there was an ample supply of correspondence from Central Asians who had a working literacy—even if extremely basic—in Russian. In this puzzle over Uzbek and Russian letters of Stalinist mourning, one sees a growing gap between the increasingly Soviet Uzbek center of Tashkent, with its greater use of the Russian language, and the more distant areas of Uzbekistan. Tashkent was clearly becoming more "Soviet," while the rest of the Uzbek SSR trailed behind.

Housing Shortages and Rising Anger

Despite publicly declared affection for Stalin and grief over his death, life quickly returned to normal for most Tashkenters. The city's housing problem—overcrowded apartments, dilapidated barracks, and numerous shantytowns—remained a serious blot on the region's image as a modern socialist space. A major urban center, Tashkent received its share of migrants, especially demobilized soldiers and agricultural specialists who came to work in the city's agricultural and irrigation institutes to increase the region's food and cotton production.[13] However, the Soviet state still lacked the infrastructure to house them or even to help them solve their housing problems on their own. Between 1953 and 1956, more than twenty-nine hundred veteran military officers settled in Tashkent, yet, as of August 1956, the city was still unable to house a significant number of these families.[14] Even Tashkent's privileged, those lucky enough to receive apartments or plots of land for individual homes, remained dissatisfied with their lot. On April 27, 1956, *Pravda Vostoka* published a letter describing the lives of residents of the postwar "Molotov 'individual housing' area," which accommodated members of Tashkent's cultural and industrial elite. This community consisted of a diverse group of Tashkenters—Uzbeks, Russians, Armenians, and others—all of whom had reached positions of status in Soviet society as building engineers, medical doctors, hydrotechnical specialists, agronomists, industrial workers, institute researchers, and professors at Central Asian State University.[15] As a multiethnic community of successful Soviet citizens, this region should have symbolized the achievement of creating an ethnically diverse and highly skilled populace all peacefully living side by side in a major Soviet city. Nonetheless, the residents were not so much united by their sense of achievement or cross-ethnic Soviet identity as by their common frustration with the city administration over problems with transportation, electricity, water supply, sanitation, and lighting. With these tremendous urban problems, the Soviet system was creating a unified urban community, but not for the desired reasons.

In this letter of April 27, 1956, residents expressed anger that they had to walk one and one-half kilometers across mud streets and dark pathways to the nearest trolleybus station. To illuminate their homes, they were forced to purchase kerosene lamps on the black market. Water was unavailable, forcing residents to travel one-half kilometer to a communal pump that was often broken. Bathhouses, stores, and any sort of enlightenment institution—theater, library, or teahouse—were nowhere near, despite Soviet efforts to instill new norms of public hygiene and culture among its citizens. Radio reception—a key component of mass education and propaganda— was impaired both by the lack of electricity and poor transmission from the Tashkent radio tower, which could not beam its signal to some of the newer and more remote parts of the city.[16] Tashkent was not just a dual Russian/ Uzbek urban area; it was also divided between the modern Soviet center and the rest of the city, which was replete with dirty shantytowns, distant suburban areas, poor transportation systems, and filthy water. Both versions of Tashkent were creations of twentieth-century Soviet rule. The construction of a socialist city in Central Asia had yet to create a well-supplied, comfortable, or orderly urban environment. This disconnect between the promises of socialist Tashkent and the reality city residents faced on a daily basis led to increased anger and resentment across the Uzbek capital, threatening to open up cracks in the much-lauded "Tashkent" model of socialism's universal adaptability beyond its European origins. With the threat of Stalinist repression gone, Soviet leaders in Central Asia soon would have to address these annoyances of daily life, which united broad sections of the population in frustration with the Soviet Union's failed promises, but this anger was not necessarily directed against the Soviet polity as a whole.

In fact, Tashkenters' lives often went from bad to much worse as builders tried to implement numerous reconstruction projects. Although the Old City lacked many "modern" conveniences (udobstva), it had a general physical and social infrastructure that had not yet been created in the newer regions of the city. The older region possessed Central Asian–style teahouses, bazaars, and local bathhouses (hammoms). Because urban planners had already plowed main arteries through the Old Town, public transportation was never too far away, unlike in the outlying regions of the city. Furthermore, local families had lived there for generations and frequently were related by marriage, thereby providing each other with a support network outside the confines of the Soviet state.[17] Why would one want to move to a distant region of the city where one would have to build everything anew, often without the community support structure?[18] Why would Uzbeks, whose families were usually considerably larger than those of Russians, want to move into small apartment units, originally designed in Russia for Russians and built in areas of Tashkent where urban services, transportation, and trees often did not arrive for years? Simply put, the traditionally Central Asian sections of the city, divided into individual neighborhoods or *mahallas*, suited the lifestyle of Uzbek residents, who were far less mobile than European inhabitants of the city. Soviet architects derided the condition of housing and of urban life in the Old City and destroyed these pre-existing communities but did not offer residents anything better. The infrastructure of the traditional Uzbek *mahallas* was not fully "modern," but at least it existed in some form. Soviet planners, despite their well-meaning intentions, could not guarantee the same in the new regions of Tashkent and often delivered conditions that turned out to be much worse.

In 1956, M. Guliamov, a Party secretary from the Frunze district of Tashkent, responded to the increasingly vocal discontent among city residents by explaining to his Gorkom colleagues that city Party and administrative leaders simply "dressed themselves up in promises" but continually failed to deliver an improved standard of living to local residents. He noted that the only medical services available in his region were the hospital and maternity ward of the Textile Kombinat and that pregnant women who did not work for the *kombinat* were not permitted to use the facility. It was a shocking revelation, considering the stress that public-health workers placed on giving birth in sanitary "Soviet" hospitals to ensure that Soviet children, particularly Uzbek children, would be healthy and productive members of society.[19] Although the Ministry of Health and the Council of Ministers of Uzbekistan promised, with much fanfare, to provide funds for the construction of new health-care facilities for the region in 1952, the money was never allocated and construction never began. Guliamov noted that "the population already does not believe us and considers us to be gasbags. This is how it turned out. A decision [about improving the standard of living] arises, and we immediately bring this decision to the attention of the workers and with that, everything stops. We don't do anything and the people justly state 'we do not believe you anymore.'"[20] City leaders recognized that the growing chasm between the public declarations of achievement in the Stalin era and the reality of life caused credibility problems for the Party and state. Guliamov proposed toning down the rhetorical promises and speeding up the delivery of services, an indication of the need to respond during the Khrushchev era of greater openness.

Guliamov further argued that the failure to construct working sanitation systems endangered public health. He estimated that more than 70 percent of the urban population drank contaminated water directly from the *aryk* system because only 25 to 30 percent of city residents had had their homes connected to the water supply pipes.[21] The secretary for the Oktiabr district Party committee noted that *aryk* water pollution was especially problematic for residents of the Old Town. Without a sewer system, the City Infectious Disease Hospital no. 1, a maternity hospital, and a tuberculosis facility simply discarded their human, medical, and hazardous waste into a central canal that served as the main source of drinking and washing water for thousands of Central Asian residents.[22] Such facilities were supposed to have been removed from the city center years before, but infectious waste continued to flow freely into the water supply of the city and surrounding oblast, disseminating disease rather than "quenching" the thirst of the Uzbek people, as hydrotechnology specialists had claimed. The failure to deal with these health-care institutions was another example of the empty promises that the Party and state had yet to fulfill and of the Soviet Union's false propaganda about bringing modern socialism to Asia, propaganda disseminated both at home and overseas in its public diplomacy outreach.

In addition to having biological waste in its drinking water supply, Tashkent remained a filthy city in other aspects as well. Guliamov stated in August 1956 that the city's "bacterial pollution" level was "ten times" the acceptable norms of Soviet environmental health standards, while air pollution was "nine times" the acceptable norms.[23] Trash rotted in city streets, apartment entryways, and city parks. The sanitary conditions in Tashkent were so bad that Alexander Zotov, a veteran and the head architect of Uz-Gosproekt, an urban planning organization, noted that at least 50 percent of Tashkent housing areas were unsuitable for human habitation. One area, Figelskii Street, won the dubious nickname of "New York" among Tashkenters because its sanitary conditions were so horrific that it recalled the purported filth of the capitalist metropolis in the United States, of which residents knew from anti-American propaganda.[24] Under no circumstances should the model Soviet city in Central Asia, home to a "liberated" Soviet minority group, have been comparable to any part of New York City, home to large numbers of African Americans who struggled at the time for basic civil rights and economic opportunity—things that socialism reportedly had provided to national minorities in the Soviet Union years before. These less-than-pristine regions of Tashkent, of course, were far removed from the main thoroughfares and squares of the city center, where urban city services worked more efficiently, especially when foreign delegations visited the city. However, Gorispolkom officials and Architects' Union members began to discuss such quality-of-life issues as by-products of large-scale architectural plans. Simple solutions, not elaborate public works, finally gained attention after the death of Stalin, when the state recognized the need to address a disgruntled populace.[25]

With de-Stalinization, Uzbek Party officials found easy scapegoats for urban overcrowding, dilapidated housing, and insufficient municipal services. Although the movement away from Stalinist practices began shortly after his death, Khrushchev waited until 1956 to initiate his full-scale campaign of de-Stalinization. In his "Secret Speech" before the Twentieth Party Congress, Khrushchev provided limited exposure to the crimes of the Stalin regime—the terror of 1937, the lack of preparedness for the Nazi invasion, the ethnic deportations of World War II, and postwar purges. According to Khrushchev, Stalin had allegedly destroyed democracy within the Party and used the resources of the state to buttress his own cult of personality, depriving the citizenry of needed resources to improve their lives.[26] Khrushchev's goal was to identify the crimes of the Soviet period with Stalin, not with the system itself, of which he was a leading product. Khrushchev-era city bureaucrats emphasized that the Stalin-era stress on monumental public structures—rather than on large-scale housing or school construction—was the reason for the failure of the Soviet state to meet the needs of its citizens.

However, since Stalin was dead and the problems continued for a few years after the change in leadership, Khrushchev planners suddenly turned their attention to the "little" Stalinists across the Soviet Union and made them scapegoats for continued poor living standards and low economic output. In Uzbekistan, Usman Yusupov, former first Party secretary of the Uzbek Central Committee and minister of cotton production of the Soviet Union (1950–1953), became the most prominent Uzbek Party figure to fall from power after the death of the *vozhd'* and in Khrushchev's effort to consolidate his own power base in the region. Blaming Stalin and his "closest" allies for the crimes of the 1930s and 1940s and for wasting scarce economic resources was an effective way for Khrushchev and his supporters on the local level to purge the Party leadership and solidify power in both the center and the regions.

De-Stalinization and De-Yusupovication

Yusupov was an extraordinarily powerful figure in the Uzbek SSR and subsequently in the Soviet Union as a whole; he rose to the top of the Soviet Uzbek political system during the purges of 1937, ending up in Moscow toward the end of the Stalinist period. He returned to Tashkent after the death of the *vozhd'* to serve as chair of the Council of Ministers of the Uzbek SSR, but, without his benefactor, his hold on power was in a declining spiral until 1955, when he was removed from that office and made director of a state farm, a clear sign of the remarkable change in his status as a result of de-Stalinization. At the plenum of the Central Committee of the Uzbek Communist Party held December 10–13, 1954—a meeting that quickly turned into a general condemnation of corruption and nepotism under Yusupov's leadership—Arif Alimov, secretary of the Tashkent Obkom, accused Yusupov of destroying the "collegiality" of the Uzbek Communist Party. With this criticism, Alimov opened the floodgates to accusations against Yusupov, all of which implied that he was a greedy and uneducated bureaucrat who preferred surrounding himself with illiterates and sycophants rather than with loyal Party officials.[27] His former subordinates described him as an Uzbek nationalist with both anti-Tajik and anti-Russian tendencies, a fierce criticism since these two ethnic groups were the largest minorities in the Uzbek SSR.[28] In fact, after Yusupov had been in leadership positions in the Soviet state for sixteen years, Party members suddenly discovered Yusupov's "nationalist tendencies," an accusation that Yusupov had used years before to discredit his own rivals.

Malik Abdurazakov, the Tashkent Gorkom secretary, argued that Yusupov was too slow in implementing reforms that could have increased the city's food supply. He angrily charged that the Council of Ministers under Yusupov had ordered the mobilization of city workers into Tashkent oblast collective farms to help prepare grapevines for subsequent shipment to Crimea. Tashkenters were hungry and understood the need to help regional farmers harvest fruits and vegetables in a time of crisis. Tashkenters also willingly helped rural citizens with the cotton harvests because ensuring a high cotton output was the duty of all residents of Uzbekistan. However, forcing Tashkenters to send food to a distant region of the Soviet Union when they themselves experienced food supply problems was too much to ask of them.[29] Earlier, Yusupov had been accused of Uzbek nationalism and giving preferences to Uzbeks over Tajiks and Slavs. Now, he was accused of the opposite, namely, providing food aid to distant Russians and Ukrainians at the expense of Central Asian workers. Yusupov suddenly could do nothing right.

The Gorkom secretary also accused Yusupov of building personal mansions—at a cost of more than 2 million rubles—in Tashkent and Yangi-Yol, his native town that was only a short distance from the Uzbek capital. Critics noted that if the money, construction supplies, and workers who built

Yusupov's homes had been used for apartment construction in Tashkent, the city could have "gotten out of the housing crisis." Furthermore, while city residents lived in cramped flats or dormitories with an average of 1.5 square meters of living space per person, Yusupov's Yangi-Yol complex was allegedly a 5-hectare compound with a 1,200-square-meter house and an "army of Uzbek [servants]."[30] The Khrushchev-era explanation for Tashkent overcrowding and urban squalor was clear: previous leaders had enriched themselves while forcing the Soviet people to live in substandard conditions.

In addition to the accusations about acquiring lavish personal property using scarce state resources, all to the detriment of Tashkent workers, Yusupov was accused of wasting money on unrealistic urban renewal plans for the Uzbek capital that were, in effect, monumental public tributes to his rule. Yusupov suddenly became one of the main causes for the state's failure to transform Tashkent's urban space in the 1940s and 1950s. Delegates accused him of wasting money during the war on the construction of the Mukhimi (Tashsovet) Theater in Tashkent.[31] The theater, which by the 1950s was in danger of collapse due to shoddy construction, was described as a waste of "millions" during a time of tremendous economic hardship for the city.[32] This critique contradicted previous views that had celebrated the beautification of the city and the state's concern for the cultural upbringing and enlightenment of Tashkenters during the war.

Furthermore, Uzbek Party officials used Yusupov's postwar desire to construct a public transportation system on artificial waterways in a desert city as ammunition against him. This plan had called for the use of boats on the city's canals to create "water trams" to move pedestrians off the street and ferry them along the larger artificial waterways of the city. By the 1950s, Yusupov's rivals had deemed the project an unrealistic plan to "turn Tashkent into a second Venice." Such a proposal certainly would have been a striking statement about Yusupov's leadership and the ability of Soviet science to refashion the natural landscape of the Soviet Union. It also indicated that the model of Tashkent was clearly a European one, with Yusupov trying to imitate one of the Western world's main cultural and tourist sites. But, as one senior Uzbek Communist Party member argued, such a transportation system would have been an unrealistic waste of money and, in fact, was a comical proposal to divert the government's attention from the real needs of Tashkenters. The delegate criticized the plan for showcasing the power of individual Party leaders and the "cults of personality" that proliferated at the central and local levels.[33]

Beautiful city centers remained important, but the message was clear:

Tashkent officials should not get carried away with designing public spaces at the expense of the general comfort of the population. This water transport project was a good example of such a proposal because it clearly would have diminished the quality of life of Tashkenters even more. The boats evidently would have used a sewage canal that urban planners hoped, against Yusupov's wishes, to enclose in "modern" pipes, thereby preventing an improvement in public health.[34] With these arguments, officials explained that the origins of the city's cramped and unsanitary environment were found in the excesses of the Stalin era, particularly in the monuments that were built to glorify the numerous cults of personality (Stalin's and Yusupov's) in Uzbekistan. In the post-Stalin/post-Yusupov era, on cue from Moscow, Tashkent city planners publicly refocused their projects to serve the people and meet their physical needs.[35] The future of Uzbek Soviet city planning was to concentrate on achievable goals, namely transportation, sanitation, housing, and schools—all symbols of Soviet achievement that would have transformative influences on the residents of the city. The leadership had changed, but the desire to mold Soviet citizens persisted across the Stalin-Khrushchev divide.

In the era of de-Stalinization, Stalinism clearly died a slow death. Even though the *vozhd'* was dead, his cult of personality criticized, and some of the crimes of the era exposed, Stalinist methods were used to rid Uzbekistan of those whom the new leaders deemed responsible. Yusupov and others were described as having no redeeming qualities whatsoever, which was very similar to the rhetoric used to purge the Uzbek and Tashkent Party organizations in the late 1930s.[36] Yusupov did not just squander scarce resources on his personal homes or on unrealistic public works projects; investigators also uncovered his "ties" to pre-revolutionary enemies of the Soviet system and traitors to the state during the war. Yusupov suddenly was not a loyal servant of the revolution but a secret traitor who had worked against Soviet rule—accusations that were used by Yusupov himself to send the previous generation of Uzbek Communist Party officials to their deaths in 1937–1938.[37] However, while there are clear similarities between de-Stalinization and the Stalinist purges, a fundamental difference between the two must be noted, namely, the fact that there was considerably less violence during Khrushchev's cleansing campaign. Although Yusupov's character was publicly destroyed, there was no state-sponsored bloodshed during his fall from power. Although disgraced, Yusupov lived out his career as the director of a state farm, eventually receiving a state pension in 1959.[38] His physical removal from Soviet society was no longer necessary, and Yusupov lived until his natural death in 1966.[39]

Developing Khrushchev-Era Uzbek Architecture

Khrushchev's efforts to discredit Stalin included a carefully managed campaign of liberalizing Soviet society. He allowed the publication of works that supported his policies of exposing the crimes of the previous leadership, particularly of Party members who might contest his power base. He did not liberalize all sectors of society, however.[40] In architecture, he provided room for local officials to refashion the way in which they built cities, moving away from the elaborate structures of the Stalin era to more cost-effective construction projects. In 1957, he initiated a program to increase housing construction to improve the low standard of living in Soviet cities. A new state decree, entitled "On Developing Housing Construction in the USSR," called for a union-wide project to build apartment buildings, reorganize the administrative structure of city construction, and decrease the complexity of building projects in Soviet cities.[41]

These construction programs still stressed the need to build model cities that could showcase the modernity and the uniqueness of socialism. However, architects now were critical of urban planning in the 1940s and early 1950s. At a general meeting of architects of Central Asia in Kazakhstan, N. Glinka, deputy head of the Turkmen Architects' Union, criticized recent Central Asian construction for possessing too many "Eastern styles" and creating cities that were reminiscent of those in Iran, Egypt, or Turkey. Soviet Central Asia, he argued, was different from these regions in that its heritage included both Asian and Russian classical styles as well as, most recently, Soviet industrialization.[42] On the other hand, V. A. Lavrov proposed that Uzbek architects look to the cultural heritage of other "Asian" peoples, specifically to those who were closely aligned to the Soviet system, for incorporation into the new architectural styles of the region. Tashkent, he argued, needed to be an Uzbek and Soviet city that represented the highest ideals of a modern Asian urban space: "Our urban planning practices serve as an example for People's Democracies, in particular, the actions of our Central Asian republics particularly interest our friends from Korea and China. This raises our responsibility even higher, demanding from us high-quality work, wide erudition, and understanding of [how to] creatively use all the richness of the past history of the East for the construction of a modern Central Asia."[43] In the Khrushchev era, Tashkent did not need multi-story apartment buildings with elaborate national decorations for its own sake. Each building and each decorative element was to have a purpose, namely, to create an urban space that could serve as a center of socialism for all of Asia. Through Khrushchev's Tashkent, the Soviet Union attempted to convey that it was not simply another European imperialist power. Instead, the Soviet Union should be seen as an Asian state that had ties to its Asian neighbors and offered an alternative to American or Western European domination. Elements of urban design that were excessively nationalistic, overtly elaborate, too "European," or too "Muslim" served the wrong purpose. The end result of this confusion over Uzbek Soviet architecture led Khrushchev-era planners to stress the need for contemporary and simple designs, indicating that Soviet architecture was moving full circle—back to the pre-Stalinist model of modernist construction and urban design.

In the late 1950s, architects once again debated the goal of Soviet urban planning. They underscored the point that good urban design would help create a communist society. As Semyon Tutuchenko, a secretary of the central Architects' Union, stated in 1958, "It is possible to build a city in such a way that it helps to create such a [communist] society, but it is also possible to build a city in such a way that it does not help create this society. Man creates the city, but the city forms the man."[44] Buildings, decorations, and other structures that neither promoted Soviet ideology nor fashioned an orderly socialist space were deemed unnecessary and to be inhibiting the advancement of socialism and the transformation of individuals into model Soviet citizens. The 1930s mantra of "cultured" physical environments as being capable of producing "refined" citizens witnessed a rebirth in the mid-1950s. A city that wasted resources could not effectively mold the city's residents, who, living under such conditions, would themselves become inefficient or lazy. The idea of building a new Soviet city as a means to create new Soviet citizens in Central Asia spanned the Stalin/post-Stalin divide.

Previous Tashkent urban renewal projects became prime examples of Soviet bureaucratic failures that inhibited the advancement of socialism in Central Asia. Architects were criticized for their past inability to develop inexpensive designs that conveyed both Uzbek cultural heritage and modern socialism. In the 1950s, the numerous renovation projects of the Government House came under criticism for excessive costs and little progress. The Supreme Soviet meeting hall in the complex was seen as simply "architecture for architecture's sake." Its large vestibule and multicolumned entrance cost 300,000 rubles to install, while the expensive second-floor balcony area was not accessible because no stairway was installed. The inside of the building might have looked "Uzbek," but this "Uzbekness" served no practical purpose, except for increasing costs and making the second-floor balcony useless.[45] The fact that so much time and effort had gone into "fixing" this building mandated that architects and builders get their designs right in the first place.[46] If Party leaders committed such mistakes, normal residents might follow their lead. A city with prominent examples of inefficiency and waste might instill these traits among its residents.

The city's Navoi Monument was in no better shape; its inscription plaque, telling visitors that the monument was dedicated to the Central Asian poet, fell off in the rain due to "poor engineering."[47] In fact, the monumental architecture of the 1940s and early 1950s had become a subject of scorn and mockery at Architects' Union meetings. Such structures were seen as misguided expressions of the cults of personality and gigantism of the previous regime. If Soviet monuments to the region's "enlightened" past could not last more than a few years, how permanent would Soviet ideology and values be in the mindsets of Tashkenters, particularly when the monumental architecture of Tamerlane remained standing as a symbol of the region's past glory?

Full Speed Ahead toward Communism

Despite the previous history of shortcomings in construction, Khrushchev-era workers started up their bulldozers and picked up their shovels to get to work on creating a modern, although less grand, Uzbek capital. New guidelines to speed up construction, reduce costs, and improve quality control were proposed. Excessive decorations were to be eliminated from buildings, and the use of standardized architecture plans was expanded. In 1956, the Ministry of Construction established a new building agency, Glavtashkent-stroi, to organize the prefabricated construction of housing and schools in the city. In order to facilitate the transition to industrialized large-scale building projects, the Uzbek minister of construction reorganized all stages of urban construction under this organization. One of the main problems in Tashkent's renovation efforts had been the lack of coordination between sanitation, transportation, and building agencies. Each bureau worked at different tempos, leading to situations in which newly paved streets or trolleybus lines were removed to put in sewer and water pipes. Installing plumbing systems after the fact further increased costs because it required tearing up sidewalks, entryways, and tramlines to create underground public services. Such an approach also made living in tall buildings challenging if, as some Tashkenters experienced, one had to descend four flights of stairs to use an outhouse because sewage systems had not yet been installed. It is no wonder that the "model" apartments were deemed inferior to the traditional one-story homes.[48]

To accelerate building projects, reinforced concrete slab and brick factories, wood processing facilities, and even a "housing production *kombinat*" that created prefabricated apartment units were established in the region.[49] Given the difficulties of building in the Old City, the placement of large prefabricated structures usually extended only to the outskirts of the city, a tendency that left the model city center with an "uncapital-like" (*nestolichnyi*) mixture of one-story structures and monumental Stalinist architecture, eventually surrounded by multistory Khrushchev-era apartment buildings.[50] However, the move toward tall prefabricated buildings caused concern for some engineers and geologists who questioned whether such construction methods were suitable in a region that was susceptible to devastating earthquakes, like the one that destroyed Ashgabat in 1948.

In spite of these concerns, engineers and construction specialists ignored warning signs and declared modern building technology to be safe for the region. While discussing the need to produce inexpensive mass housing in Uzbekistan in 1955, R. R. Abdurasulov, an engineer and architect, noted that Tashkent's building codes ensured that city buildings could withstand an earthquake of up to 8.0 in magnitude. However, since the city had not experienced a quake of such strength for at least eighty years, he proposed lowering the building codes to resist a 7.0-magnitude quake. That standard would reflect the strength of more typical earthquakes in the region, an argument that Usman Yusupov had initiated a year earlier.[51] In Abdurasulov's justifications, current building codes simply added to the costs of building and made the move toward mechanized and industrialized construction more difficult: "The protection of the people in an earthquake is a serious matter, but . . . over-insurance is not necessary, especially when it calls for greater expenditures of state funds, increasing the use of cement and steel, and lengthening the period of completion." These strict building codes allegedly decreased construction worker productivity and added to the cost of construction by approximately 20 percent.[52] No one discussed the fact that the shift to inexpensive construction exacerbated the tendency to cut corners and use substandard supplies. Buildings might have been designed to survive an earthquake, but were they built to withstand one? Planners did not address this question.

Furthermore, although residents, city officials, and architects complained of unstable structures and building foundations, little was done to renovate or retrofit such structures. The need to increase construction productivity and decrease costs, combined with the fact that Tashkent buildings were rarely built to standards, put the city's population into homes, schools, and hospitals that might not be able to withstand a Central Asian earthquake, about which both historians and scientists expressed concern.[53] To show that the state "cared" for the people of Tashkent, urban planners increased apartment construction in the city but lowered safety standards.

Ironically, this decision to show the Party's "concern" for its Central Asian residents put them into buildings that could not guarantee their safety, despite claims to the contrary. The need for quick fixes trumped all concern for quality, longevity, and comfort in the apartments that were going up across Tashkent, as they did throughout the Soviet Union itself and even the Soviet bloc countries.

Chilanzar, the Model City District

One chief task of the Tashkent Housing Construction Kombinat, completed in 1959, was the creation of the new Chilanzar district of the city. The plan for the *kombinat* was to produce "100,000 square meters of housing per year," and Chilanzar became the model test site for the region's industrially produced apartment units. Originally designed as part of the revised reconstruction plan of 1954, Chilanzar provided inexpensive and simple housing structures that could be assembled quickly on building sites in Tashkent.[54] If successful, smaller "Chilanzars" would be reproduced across Central Asia, transforming disorderly desert towns into virtually identical Soviet settlements, which would make them easier to build, maintain, and monitor. The groundbreaking for the Chilanzar district was organized by Glavtashkentstroi, which, according to Mitkhat Bulatov, still the city architect, succeeded in concentrating construction in specific regions of Tashkent. Of the 188 housing projects under its auspices in 1957, 81 were in the Chilanzar area. This concentration of building sites and their administrative organization under Glavtashkentstroi reduced construction costs and improved control over various agencies that were responsible for creating the new Tashkent housing region.[55] With the Chilanzar housing project, Tashkent was finally doing something right, or so city architects declared.

Chilanzar was the typical Soviet micro-district in which housing, schools, clubs, and stores were to be located centrally, in one area. Although the height of its buildings did not originally exceed four stories, Chilanzar was considered a Khrushchev success story in official discourse. As Tashkent's equivalent to Moscow's Yugo-zapadnaia district, Chilanzar was described in newspaper articles as a formerly remote area of the city that lacked any sort of ties to the center of Tashkent, except via animal-drawn carts. With Chilanzar's modernization, a section of the "liberated" Uzbek capital had finally come to look just like a region of Moscow and Tashkent could become the idealized modern city of the East.[56] With the addition of the Chilanzar district, Bulatov, remarkably having survived both Stalinism and de-Stalinization, had a new weapon in his battle against the mud-brick home and the traditional winding street that Soviet administrators (and their imperial predecessors) had long criticized as dirty, irrational, and uncontrollable.

Chilanzar, Tashkent's version of the rectangular Soviet apartment block, aimed to transform the city for the benefit of its residents, astonish its foreign visitors, and solidify the power of the state over city residents, who all would live in identical and easy-to-monitor rectangular boxes. Chilanzar, like similar districts that were built across the Soviet Union, was a fundamental tool of social control: Tashkenters would move out of private, individual housing spaces and into the more communal environment of an apartment complex. State officials—housing committee members, militia officers, and *dezhurnyi* (often elderly men or women who stood guard at building entries)—closely scrutinized the actions of Soviet citizens in their homes, monitoring when they arrived home, with whom they associated, and what activities they enjoyed. These large-scale housing complexes thus had important social and political ramifications beyond their symbolic value as modern multistory structures. They essentially were tools to complete the transformation of extended Uzbek families into smaller nuclear units with Soviet attitudes toward labor, culture, religion, and gender.

However, despite favorable press coverage, Chilanzar suffered from serious problems. V. A. Malmre, an Estonian architect who traveled to Tashkent, noted that the placement of Chilanzar was not ideal. It was on the edge of an already "modern" area. He noted that it provided the city with needed housing units but should have been placed closer to the city center. Although it was cheaper and easier to build on the edge of the city than in the Old City, Malmre argued, Chilanzar did not solve the problem of the pre-revolutionary Old Town's persistent presence only a short distance from Red Square.[57] If Chilanzar was supposed to be the weapon against the Old City and its traditions, why did the city fail to use it effectively by placing this district on the outskirts of the city? Tashkent's "outer" cityscape was changing, but its inner core remained the same.

Leonid Volynskii, a Russian traveler to Uzbekistan in 1961, described the Chilanzar residential district in an even harsher tone in the journal *Novyi mir*.[58] Although Chilanzar's design on paper and in plaster models looked beautiful, with green parks, refreshing pools, and play areas for children, the reality paled in comparison, according to Volynskii. In place of paved pathways and green spaces for the relaxation of the region's proposed 200,000 residents, garbage, automobile parts, and construction debris constituted the scene Volynskii describes. The most striking feature of the area was its complete "nakedness" in a city that Soviet power supposedly had transformed into a "flourishing garden." Without trees, cafes, or green spaces, residents had little refuge from the heat, noise, and dirt of the Uzbek capital. This reality was, in fact, in direct contrast to the Chilanzar area from fifteen years before, when war evacuees used the region for growing fruits and vegetables.[59] Urban planners tore up gardens and replaced them with concrete in the name of building socialism. The situation was so troubling for Volynskii that he could not imagine the future of Chilanzar after one-quarter of the population of Tashkent had moved to the area, as planners envisioned.[60]

Chilanzar residents also remained unhappy with their new homes. To decrease costs, stairways and entryways were reduced to a minimal size, a problem that made moving furniture into apartments a challenge.[61] Furthermore, the problem of moving furniture was not only an inconvenience but possibly also an ideological issue in Central Asia. For years, Party leaders and propagandists had stressed the importance of getting Uzbek households to use Western-style furniture, considering it to be a sign of Soviet Uzbek modernity and culture as opposed to the traditional customs of sitting, eating, sleeping, and socializing on the floor. The narrow stairways of the Soviet housing block had much larger implications in Central Asia than they did in Russia, for which these housing complexes had originally been designed, once again underscoring the difficulty planners faced in their one-size-fits-all approach toward urban planning.

Chilanzar residents subsequently solved the furniture problem with the help of construction cranes, which lifted their belongings into the air and through apartment windows. Still, they continued to complain that the poor design of apartments did not give them space to hang wet laundry, store cots or winter clothing, or find a place to hold potatoes, rice, and other food products, except on their apartment terraces. Outdoor balconies had been added to the buildings to provide residents with an area to escape the heat of the reinforced steel–and–concrete buildings, which trapped the hot desert air. However, with their terraces transformed into storage sheds and with no community green spaces, shaded cafes, or teahouses, Chilanzar residents had no place to escape the brutal Tashkent summer.[62] Despite years of debating the need to change the region's micro-climate, designers again forgot about the Tashkent climate, a problem that dated back to Kuznetsov's Mosoblproekt proposal of 1937–1939. Post-Stalinist architecture was supposed to address these quality-of-life issues but did not, despite—or perhaps because of—the pressing need to "solve" the housing issue quickly.

Chilanzar also was poorly built. Its prefabricated design ensured maximum output of housing space but did not consider the quality or look of the building.[63] Plumbing, central heating, and electricity remained problematic in the region, even though the Khrushchev-era establishment of Glavtash-kentstroi was supposed to have solved this problem. The subsequent bureaucratic battles that Tashkenters faced to get these services installed required enormous time and expense, a fact that archival documents confirm.[64] Disgusted by Chilanzar and other recent construction attempts in the Uzbek capital, Volynskii proposed that the best way to look at the complex was through the wrong end of binoculars so as to avoid seeing its basic flaws—the cracks, exposed pipes, peeling paint, couches hoisted into the sky, and balconies that sagged under the weight of residents' belongings.[65] Chilanzar was not "inexpensive" industrial construction; it was just cheap.

Tashkenters clearly were afterthoughts to these designs. Residents were supposed to fit unquestionably into the rectangular boxes that the state made for them, even though they could have told the designers how to make these buildings more comfortable and desirable. Once again, cities were not supposed to suit the customs of their inhabitants; inhabitants were supposed to transform their customs to suit the new Soviet city. Unfortunately for Soviet planners, the desires and individual needs of Soviet citizens—particularly non-Russian ones—could not be determined through quantifiable calculations made by Gosplan bureaucrats. The result was that Chilanzar did not become the prime choice of housing for those who were evicted from the center or suffered in cramped communal flats or worker barracks. With Chilanzar, the rapidly expanding city of individual homes simply gained a new type of structure, the tall building, to add to its suburban outskirts.

Uzbek National "Peculiarities" and Soviet Housing Construction

Despite the increase in the construction of prefabricated housing, the expansion of individual home construction in the Uzbek capital also continued at a rapid pace. In a brochure he wrote for the Uzbek Architects' Union, Bulatov claimed that the lack of discipline among urban planners in Uzbekistan caused cities to grow into enormous territories.[66] City administrators, republic-level Party officials, and architects were so focused on creating an impressive urban center around Navoi Street, the Red, Revolution, and Navoi Theater squares, and Komsomol Park that no one took control of individual housing construction from either a design or a zoning perspective. Despite the fact that Khrushchev planners were instructed to solve quality-of-life issues, much of their attention remained on the city center, leaving residents with no choice but to take matters into their own hands. Given that Soviet Tashkent was supposed to be a monumental city with multistory buildings, planners ignored the issue of individual home construction; the actual environment of the city should have led planners to realize that individual home construction would continue apace because that type of structure suited the climate, addressed the housing crunch and the difficulty of supplying the city with building supplies, and met the desires of the population. The end result of this neglect by urban planners was that Uzbekistan had become the republic with the largest percentage of individually constructed homes in the Soviet Union, with Tashkent as the city with the largest percentage of private houses in the entire Soviet Union.[67] Tashkent in 1958 was a "Soviet" city in which 86 percent of its buildings had only one story, 8.5 percent had two stories, and only 5.5 percent were three- or four-story structures.[68] This development was in direct conflict with all previous Soviet-era urban plans for the city. Moscow's surrogate capital in Central Asian had become a large urban *kishlak,* or Uzbek village.

The problem of the proliferation of private homes in Tashkent was not news to Party officials or members of the Architects' Union either in Moscow or Tashkent. Konstantin Simonov, the Soviet journalist and writer, lived part-time in the Old City of Tashkent from 1957 to 1960. Simonov resided in a recently built individual home in the region that, according to the reconstruction plan, had been zoned for high-rise buildings but had yet to see many tall structures. Even the Soviet elite lived in single-family homes, an indication that this form of housing remained popular among all sectors of the multiethnic urban population and that breaking the rules on individual housing was not just an ethnic Uzbek phenomenon. However, among the newly constructed Soviet buildings and private houses stood scattered traditional Uzbek mud-brick homes, including that of Simonov's next-door neighbor, an elderly Uzbek who was "born on that street and was not particularly inclined to move from it." For two years, this neighbor successfully battled against TashTram, the public transportation system that attempted to evict him in order to build a tramline through the area. His property had a two-hundred-meter walled courtyard that extended out toward the street and, according to Simonov, ended at the spot where the newly laid pavement began. This mud wall prevented the city from installing a sidewalk. TashTram eventually ran out of patience with him and redirected the tramline around his home.[69] Thus, the modern Soviet transportation system, meant to displace the winding maze of Old City streets, curved like the rest of the Uzbek quarter because this native Tashkenter obstinately refused to move. Since an evicted resident had the legal right to choose another plot of land for his home, this Uzbek spent two years declining all proposed alternative sites, claiming they were unsuitable. He clearly understood Soviet laws, accepted them, and used them for his own benefit, but this strategy only delayed the inevitable. According to Simonov, he finally chose a new building site after rejecting five previous plots. He even began construction on a new home, but he stretched this process out as long as possible. From conversations with his Uzbek neighbor, Simonov inferred that the man still was "in no hurry to move."[70] He had neither a positive (reward) nor negative (punishment) incentive in the Khrushchev era. Simonov, sympathetic toward the plight of his Uzbek neighbor, seemed amused at the man's resourcefulness in preserving his way of life and in forcing city agencies to accommodate his wishes. Although he tried to buck the system, this Uzbek man did so in a decidedly Soviet fashion, using whatever power and privilege he had in that system to his own advantage.

Nonetheless, the problem was not only that Uzbeks did not want to move into apartments. Some Uzbek residents felt that they were unwelcome in the new Soviet buildings. Ethnic animosities persisted in the region, often over the issue of the destruction of the Old Town. The post-Stalin era saw an increase in resentment among Uzbek residents of the city who felt that they were being pushed out of their native town by Russian immigrants and Soviet architects who wanted to destroy their homes and cover their yards with pavement. In the eyes of some Uzbeks, the "modernization" of Tashkent was transforming the Uzbek capital into a city for Russians. As early as 1950, an Uzbek Tashkenter recognized this trend as discriminatory against native Central Asians. In a letter to the Party, he complained that the traditional *mahallas* of the city were being destroyed and replaced by wide avenues with tall apartment buildings. He argued that he was not opposed to Tashkent's new look and actually liked the "cultured" apartment buildings. For him, the problem was not that Uzbeks did not want modern Soviet apartments, as Party officials suggested, but that Uzbeks were never given such apartments.[71] The official line was to "push" native Central Asians into block housing in the effort to "civilize" them, but this man's statements underscored a fundamental problem in urban renewal in Central Asia whereby the declared goals of the urban plan ran afoul of the hierarchical system of Soviet nationalities policies, with ethnic Russians and industrial workers at the upper levels. Once again, an Uzbek evoked the language of the state—the equality of ethnic minorities—to show that he understood Soviet ideology and what it was supposed to bring him in order to get what he wanted out of the state. In doing so, he showed he had acquired a stake in the system itself.

Designing for Uzbeks

Semyon Tutuchenko, secretary of the central Architects' Union, warned in 1958 that Tashkent was able to fulfill only one part of the plan for urban construction—that of individual homes, despite the authorities' lack of attention to this housing sector. He noted that, in 1957, the state built 79,000 square meters of housing in Tashkent, but city residents themselves built a combined 106,000 square meters of housing on their own, with little outside support.[72] He cited Uzbeks as being responsible for the expansion of private construction and noted that one-half of the indigenous population remained in traditional homes in the Old City, although evidence clearly suggests that Russians and other ethnic groups also preferred detached houses with courtyards in the hot desert climate of Tashkent.[73] Nonetheless, the efforts to curb independent housing construction were no more successful than in previous decades.

Tutuchenko described a recent visit that he and Bulatov had made to the Old City, where they met with residents whose homes had been designated for demolition. He inquired as to whether residents were excited about moving to modern Soviet-style apartment buildings. One Uzbek-speaking man, after Bulatov assured him he would not be arrested if he spoke the truth, responded that he had absolutely no desire to move to a Soviet apartment and did not want Tutuchenko's help in speeding up the process. Although surprised, Tutuchenko eventually decided that the man was not "stupid" or "uncultured" for not desiring a "magnificent" apartment. The problem was that architects spent too little time inside Uzbek homes, where they could study the needs of Uzbek families and the Uzbek "way of life" (byt'). Tutuchenko described how he explored the man's house, noting that the man's wife disappeared when the two strangers appeared. He remarked that Uzbeks were still different from the Russians for whom these apartments originally had been designed. He also noticed a special alcove where korpuchas (cushions) were stored. Korpuchas were essential components of an Uzbek home and were used in place of European-style chairs for relaxing and as beds for sleeping. When not in use, they were stored in this alcove. However, Soviet apartments, even when they made accommodations for the heat and sun, did not include a space for korpuchas and generally failed to accommodate other Uzbek cultural norms.[74]

In the end, Tutuchenko tied the problem of individual home construction to the failure of planners to consider Uzbek sensitivities in planning apartments. If the Architects' Union really wanted to curb the expansion of individual home construction, they needed to stop trying to transform

Uzbeks into "refined" apartment dwellers and begin transforming apartments to suit Uzbek needs. Uzbek apartment buildings, despite how many cotton decorations had been painted on the walls, were simply Soviet boxes that did not fit with the way of life of this national republic. Tutuchenko realized that an "apartment [that did not consider *byt*'] could kill just [as effectively] as a knife."[75] In the Khrushchev era, one began to hear the argument that Uzbeks could be made into apartment dwellers, but only if planners made concessions to Central Asian cultural needs in planning buildings. Still, the need to "transform" Tashkent's Uzbek residents remained unchanged across the Stalin/Khrushchev divide. Even so, it is important to note a turning point in Tutuchenko's comments. While Soviet planners did not necessarily "give up" on using space to transform people, they no longer were as adamant on destroying the traditions of Central Asian Tashkent and appeared more willing to accommodate local cultural peculiarities, particularly as Uzbeks in turn began to show a greater willingness to accept some of the new Soviet trends. The ideal of creating "civilized" Soviet citizens with an appreciation for a modern or European lifestyle continued, but planners no longer viewed the traditions of Tashkent's Uzbek residents as irredeemably "backward." In fact, Uzbek customs became almost "quaint," causing Soviet officials to discuss the need to accommodate some of these traits. This new interpretation of Uzbek *byt*' indicated a significant change from the Stalinist past, when repression—not time and a partial accommodation by the state—was the primary tool of creating Soviet Uzbeks.

Leonid Volynskii's aforementioned *Novyi mir* article concurred with Tutuchenko's closed Party statements, indicating that Soviet society had become more open to discussing the issue of cultural destruction in just a few short years. Volynskii's views of Chilanzar have already been presented, but his article delves more deeply into the problems of Tashkent. Volynskii also wrote that the massive expansion of the city during the Soviet period had severed the Uzbek capital from its history. Tashkent was not Samarkand, a city where local history and a Central Asian feel had been preserved with the restoration of traditional buildings in addition to the construction of modern ones. However, Tashkent "renovation" projects simply led to the destruction of the old, followed by construction of new Soviet structures that simply aped the architectural styles of the past. According to Volynskii, these new Soviet buildings were just "Uzbek in form" and lacked any true historical or cultural connection to the region.[76] Volynskii inferred that Soviet Tashkent was an artificial city without a past; equally troubling, he was not optimistic about its socialist present or future.

Volynskii also questioned whether Soviet-era construction had made the city more comfortable for its residents, a goal that propaganda had loudly declared to domestic and foreign audiences, even if architects were divided on the issue. Volynskii realized that the temperature in summer was four or five degrees cooler in traditional mud-brick homes than elsewhere in Tashkent. In winter, these thick adobe bricks protected residents from the cold and wind. Soviet engineers had expended great effort to create "modern" technology that would transform the climate of the region but had failed to look at traditional forms of architecture as a viable solution to the large temperature fluctuations of Central Asia.[77] Planners had gone about building the Uzbek Soviet city all wrong. Instead of simply copying the "outer" look of such buildings, planners should have used the "inner content" of the structures—local ventilation systems, wall-thickness norms, and shading features—to make Soviet architecture more suitable to Uzbekistan.[78] This realization also indicated a fundamental change in Soviet policy toward local traditions. Regional building practices that diverged from the Soviet norm no longer were seen as simply irrational but were to be studied for possible incorporation into modern construction. Soviet cities no longer needed to be built exactly alike to create uniform citizens because each Soviet urban space was slightly different, from the Arctic Sea to the Afghan border. This admission was certainly a reflection of the more open environment in the Soviet Union of the 1960s and beyond.

New Proposals for Fixing the "Ideal City"

At the Congress of Uzbek Intellectuals in 1962, Sharaf Rashidov, first secretary of the Uzbek Communist Party, acknowledged that Tashkent construction organizations had failed to fulfill their urban renewal plans. He opined that not only was construction behind schedule but also the quality of completed buildings was not up to par. Rashidov similarly recognized that Uzbek Communist Party agitators had not yet fully elevated Uzbeks into "people of the communist society" and that remnants of Uzbekistan's "feudal" past remained a stumbling block for creating communism in Central Asia.[79] With descriptions such as these, it is clear that Tashkent was not the ideal city that propagandists made it out to be.

Similarly, K. M. Murtazaev, first secretary of the Tashkent Gorkom, noted that city Party officials still had a considerable amount of work to do before Tashkent would be transformed into a communist city. Agitators needed to work against the continued presence of "capitalism" in Tashkent's economic structure; speculation and black market transactions remained a serious concern. Murtazaev also acknowledged that the city was unable to meet its construction norms and admitted that a psychology of private property survived in the Tashkent mindset, perhaps referring both to the persistent desire of residents for individual houses and the continuing reliance of the city's consumers on goods provided by speculators.[80] However, he argued that Tashkent was far from the disaster that some made it out to be. He assured his audience that Tashkent had become a leading city of the Soviet Union and that its titular ethnic group was a happy and loyal member of the Soviet family of nations.[81]

Nevertheless, Soviet officials began private investigations into what had gone wrong in Tashkent. Archival documents support the argument that Tashkent's transformation into a Soviet urban space was less successful than that of other Soviet metropolitan areas. Party reports described the urban reconstruction project in Tashkent as particularly problematic. Officials in Moscow and Tashkent addressed a variety of questions. Why did Tashkent lag behind other Soviet cities in educational standards, medical care, housing norms, and industrial output? Why did Tashkent remain, as Bulatov put it, one of the most "stagnant" cities of the Soviet Union?[82] Why was the health of Tashkenters so poor, with more than ten thousand residents falling ill from typhoid in 1959, a rate twelve times higher than the general Soviet average?[83]

The general conclusion in these reports for why Tashkent remained one of the most "backward" cities of the Soviet Union was that it had one of the longest journeys to make in the shift from a "feudal-colonial" past to a communist future. Despite protests to the contrary, both public and behind-the-scenes discussions implied that European cities of the Soviet Union were more suited to socialism than Asian ones because the former already were "modern" before they became "Soviet." The ability of Marxism-Leninism to help societies speed through capitalism was more difficult than originally envisioned. As a 1964 study of the city's problems stated, Tashkent also was not Magnitogorsk, the model industrial city that was built from scratch under the Soviet system.[84] Tashkent had to contend with a complicated urban structure—physical and cultural—that continued to make the Sovietization of the city difficult. Even the neighboring Tajik capital of Dushanbe (Stalinabad) had an easier time because it was transformed from a small village settlement into a capital city and, therefore, lacked the historical baggage of being a large city with residents of long standing and an enormous maze of winding streets. The foundation beneath Soviet Tashkent was older, more Asian, and much more difficult to stabilize, causing architects, construction workers, and agitators to face a "titanic job" in their efforts to create a new Tashkent.[85] Building a Soviet city from scratch was less challenging than transforming a pre-existing city, especially a large Central Asian one.

Bulatov concluded that Tashkent's role as the most "modern" city in the region also contributed to a problem of uncontrolled growth because it was simply easier to put additional factories into the Tashkent region than it was to establish new industrial areas in other parts of Central Asia. After all, Tashkent had an existing infrastructure for factory production that other regional centers lacked, even if that infrastructure did not compare with the major industrial areas of Russia or Ukraine. Bulatov explained that prior to the 1960s, the bulk of all industrial investment in Uzbekistan went to Russified Tashkent and to the new Soviet industrialized urban centers outside the city. Tashkent, the largest and most urbanized area in Central Asia, grew because it was simply easier to place investment and migrants in the Uzbek capital region, a trend that compounded the city's problems.[86] By 1964, Tashkent contained 1.2 million urban residents within its limits, suburban zones, and satellite areas. This enormous size compounded the problems of bringing transportation systems, water, electricity, and other services to this industrial area. To curb this growth and save Tashkent from its own success, urban planners decreed that Tashkent needed strict population limits and encouraged industrial growth in and migration to the western regions of the republic—Urgench, Nukus, and Bukhara.[87]

Economic reality and public exposés against the Tashkent model in the 1960s also caused a reevaluation of some of the fundamental assumptions that urban planners had held for many years. Soviet power purportedly had transformed Tashkent into a "green oasis" of flowering gardens, luscious fruit, and bountiful fields of cotton. However, Bulatov, responsible in the past for expanding the use of water in public parks, finally admitted that water was a scarce commodity. Although he had declared in 1948 that natural springs were "everywhere," he acknowledged in 1962 that underground water actually accounted for only 10 percent of the water supply.[88] The rest came from diverted water sources and artificial reservoirs. He noted that diversion projects increased the water supply, enabling Tashkent oblast to irrigate new fields and increase industrial investment. However, the need to showcase Soviet hydrotechnology through the creation of artificial lakes and public fountains compounded the water-supply problem, as did "modern technology," presumably, the indoor plumbing for the city's new apartment buildings. Tashkent was having a serious problem supplying itself and the surrounding agricultural regions with water.

Consequently, Bulatov now acknowledged that certain parts of the "flowering garden" would have to be sacrificed to reality because it used up too many resources and the Khrushchev-era stress on economizing demanded water-use reform. Bulatov admitted that hydrotechnological and urban planning innovations, while successful in bringing water to the region, ultimately had failed to solve the "centuries-old thirst" of the Central Asian region. On the contrary, it made the Uzbek SSR thirstier as more people moved to the city and industries used more water. With the "virgin lands" campaign and the expansion of the cotton monoculture soaking up ever more regional resources, Bulatov admitted that drought-resistant plant varieties should be planted in city parks to allow water to be diverted to the cotton fields. Despite calls for improving the quality of life in the city, cotton, not food for city residents or trees to shade them from the sun, remained the priority of regional planners in the 1960s and beyond.[89]

However, other problems, such as the construction of the sewer system, finally gained attention as planners looked more realistically at the needs of Tashkent and its residents. To the surprise of many Tashkenters, the installation of sewage, water, and gas pipes finally began in the mid-1960s. These unexpected achievements in urban planning enabled the Gorispolkom to have outdoor water pumps removed and gas tanks for cooking taken off the streets; the city also started to clean up the debris in and around its canals.[90] Housing, hospital, and school construction also increased. Putting the city in order and ensuring that Tashkent's public forms of modern Soviet life took root and functioned, even if on a rudimentary basis, were impressive achievements.[91] Complaints over poor conditions persisted, but the state finally tried to improve the standard of living of Tashkenters through tangible means and not simply by impressing them with the ornate theaters, fountains of cascading water, and large sports stadiums—although these structures certainly remained important parts of urban planning in the decades to come.[92] The state finally seemed interested in showing practical "care" for its citizens through direct action rather than simply making paper proposals and public declarations of success. The new Tashkent city plan, developed between 1960 and 1964 and approved in 1966, pushed for a more even-handed approach to urban growth throughout the Tashkent region, including the redevelopment of sections of the city and of outlying areas.[93] City officials were no longer seeking improvements for just the city centers but were trying to make the entire Tashkent metropolitan region more livable.

In the process, architects began to address citizen concerns and needs in the design phase of urban reconstruction. In 1965, planners proposed an "experimental" micro-district for the Oktiabr district of the Old City. The complex, named Mahalla after the Uzbek word for a local neighborhood, finally allowed for the adaptive use of "progressive" traditions of Uzbek communities in Soviet housing construction. Underscoring the importance of outdoor personal space to Uzbek residents accustomed to living outdoors for six to eight months of the year, the experimental region was proposed to have a mixed-use residential area of gardens, apartment towers, apartment blocks, and townhouses. Instead of evicting residents piecemeal and pushing them to distant areas where they possessed no community ties, the Mahalla project envisioned moving entire neighborhoods as a group because the "native population is not inclined to migrate and carefully cultivates its ties to their neighbors and relations, created over the course of generations."[94] Tashkent's previous reconstruction efforts had failed because planners and builders did not consider the social interactions of friends, neighbors, and family members in the Old Town. Tashkent planners now recognized that the urban communities that had existed for years could serve as the fundamental building blocks of a functional socialist urban space and that Uzbek residents might be enticed into transforming themselves into Soviet apartment dwellers if entire neighborhoods were moved together.[95] Soviet planners at last saw the importance of safeguarding urban relationships. Creating a Soviet city no longer concerned just bricks, mortar, and utopian designs. People, formerly ignored, gained recognition as important components of the urban environment.

The new Mahalla district would contain a mixture of tall and small buildings that purportedly would meet the particular needs of larger Uzbek families, a problem for which the Chilanzar district had been faulted. The proposal was ambitious and called for placing small families in sixteen- and nine-story apartment towers with elevators and air-conditioning to help battle the Tashkent summer. The smallest families would be placed in the tallest buildings, while medium-sized families would receive housing in four- to nine-story buildings with balconies or verandas to provide relief from the heat. Many of the four-story buildings for larger families would be divided into bi-level apartments that gave each unit its own "outdoor" space. Apartment units on the first and second floors would each have an outdoor courtyard, while third- or fourth-floor apartments would be given access to nature through rooftop gardens.[96] The ideal "apartment" for Tashkent's largest families (residents with three or more children of preschool age) was a bi-level apartment in a two-story building, each with a small outdoor area.[97] These units for large families were to resemble Western-style townhouses.

The goal of the Mahalla project was to consolidate the geographic space of the former Old City residential area and increase the concentration of people without necessarily destroying the ability of residents to continue their indoor/outdoor lifestyles. In 1965, Tashkent city officials finally proposed a plan for the transformation of the Old City that did not mean the total destruction of the traditional Tashkent way of life. This effort sought to merge Soviet apartment construction technology with the local residents' desire to live among neighbors of long standing and closer to the outdoors, so that they could experience the cooling effect of nature, as they had for centuries. Adapting to local or national cultures no longer simply meant decorating walls and doorways with images of cotton, although that practice continued and even intensified. However, the concept for the Mahalla micro-district came too late. It, along with the new city plan, was still in the design stage in 1966 when the city was shaken from below by an earthquake. This event proved that Soviet technology, despite its claims, still could not control the power of nature. The earthquake's destruction created the blank slate that urban planners had wanted for years and gave them free rein to build a new Soviet city. Unfortunately for city residents, the Mahalla micro-district project was still on the drawing board and appeared too complicated to realize after the earthquake created an immediate need for constructing new housing complexes on a mass scale across the Tashkent cityscape.

THE TASHKENT MODEL

The young city raised from the ruins
Erected with love by the whole country
The city became a monument to friendship
In it there are sons from all over.
Like Moscow, Tashkent is a tall beam of light,
A kind guard of the best ideals
Moscow, the capital, has an ambassador
In the East—our city.

—From "Moscow's Ambassador in the East," by Khamid Guliam

Throughout the Soviet era, Party leaders made special effort to present Tashkent as an important international center. It was a "model" Asian city and an example of how socialism could be adapted beyond its original European roots to assist "less developed" or even "backward" societies in advancing out of poverty and colonialism. City officials, academics, and Party propagandists endeavored to demonstrate that non-Europeans in the Soviet Union, under the Communist Party's leadership, could improve themselves and create modern, "civilized," industrial societies. The achievements of the Uzbek people, often considered one of the more "stagnant" nationalities by Soviet officials, were presented to visitors and Soviet citizens alike as proof of the adaptability of socialism to Asia, the Middle East, and other parts of the colonial and postcolonial world. Central Asia's public successes—its modern urban centers, large industrial factories, and newly created national art forms (opera and ballet)—supposedly demonstrated that a colonized people could move from oppression to the bright era of socialism

234

without ever having to experience the hardship of Western-style capitalism. The "Tashkent model" was the Soviet adaptation of the Marxist creed about the course of history that allowed certain societies to speed through the capitalist stage of development and arrive safely in socialism.

Despite many "cracks" in the Tashkent ideal, Soviet propaganda persistently celebrated the physical renovation of the Uzbek capital city into a twentieth-century urban space as proof of the equality of national minorities under socialism. The reconstructed Tashkent—a "fully modern" city—and its residents became diplomatic tools that Soviet officials used to help spread socialism throughout the colonial and postcolonial space during the height of the cold war. In the Khrushchev and Brezhnev eras, the Uzbek capital became a prime meeting place for Soviet-sponsored international conferences, cultural festivals, and sporting events that brought delegates from the Middle East, Asia, and elsewhere across the developing world, all regions that allegedly lacked contemporary urban spaces at a time of intense ideological competition between the United States and the Soviet Union. Soviet officials declared these regions to be at approximately the same stage of economic and cultural development as pre-revolutionary Uzbekistan. They subsequently celebrated the equality of Soviet national minorities, the "freedom" from reactionary Islam, the renovation of the Uzbek capital city into a twentieth-century urban space, and the "help" given to the city by other Soviet republics both during foreigners' visits to Tashkent as well as on Tashkenters' official overseas trips, mostly to the Middle East and Asia. This Tashkent model of socialist decolonization reached its zenith in the mid-1960s, only to come crashing down during the destruction of the earthquake in 1966. Soviet technological achievement and urban planning efforts had aimed to reorder the physical landscape of Central Asia, but Soviet ideology could not withstand such a powerful force of nature, despite its continual claims to the contrary.

A Model City for the Cold War

In the late 1950s and early 1960s, cold war Tashkent became a tourist magnet for Asians, Africans, and Latin Americans who traveled to the region on cultural and government exchanges. High-level visitors marveled at the beauty and achievement of Tashkent, or at least the impressive parts of the city—its tree-lined main streets, the Navoi Theater, water diversion projects, and model factories—that state officials arranged for them to see. Tashkent's newspapers ran full-page cover stories on each visiting delegation, whose members were treated to the best that the city could offer.[1] Soviet hosts presented Tashkent's wide avenues, European-style theaters, modern industrial enterprises, and newly built housing compounds as proof that the Uzbek people, helped by the socialist system, had advanced and achieved modernity. To foreign visitors, Tashkent was supposedly a city of art and high-technology science. The Soviet Union even opened a nuclear energy research institute in Tashkent, allegedly the first of its kind in the East, to show that Uzbeks, through their membership in the Soviet family, had reached the pinnacle of global innovation.[2] Soviet officials reminded citizens and international guests that non-Soviet Asia remained threatened by British and American "imperialists," who aimed to create postcolonial client states that would depend on Western economic or military assistance. Visitors to the region witnessed the Tashkent model of development—the "postcolonial" transformation of Central Asia into an industrialized state under socialism. The Soviet press and publishing houses highlighted these delegations and their positive impressions of the Soviet achievement that was contemporary Tashkent.

Newspapers published the public and private statements of foreign visitors, particularly their opinions of Soviet success in Asia and comparisons of the prosperity of socialist Uzbekistan versus their more impoverished homelands. Tashkent was no longer just the heart of Central Asia or a "beacon" of light on an oppressed continent, as it was in the 1930s. In the cold war, officials and many visitors argued that Tashkent had become a major economic and industrial center for all of Asia; a book published in 1964 indicated that Tashkent was behind only Beijing and Delhi on the scale of postcolonial development.[3] The new symbol of Tashkent was one of liberation and renaissance, two goals that socialism sought to bring to the impoverished masses worldwide: "The life of the reborn nations and national groups of the Soviet Union serves as a bright example for all workers of the countries of Asia, Africa, and Latin America who fight for their national liberations. In the example of Uzbekistan, they see the future of their countries, they see what a people, liberated from slavery and national oppression, can do in a relatively short period of history."[4] City leaders declared that Tashkent had surpassed even the industrial achievements of Western countries: "Tashkent now is not just the most cultured center of Central Asia and the entire East, but surpasses even many Western European cities in this sphere."[5] Visitors learned that malaria, cholera, and other tropical diseases had been defeated by Soviet science, although, in fact, they had not. The Soviet medical system, with its enormous hospitals, preventive care facilities, qualified specialists, and public health outreach campaigns, had allegedly transformed the Uzbek capital into a vast health-care center with its own research and training institute, the Tashkent Medical Institute (TashMI).

Propagandists informed visitors that these achievements in treating disease were replicated on a smaller scale in towns and villages across Central Asia, and Uzbekistan's medical specialists began to travel the world to train their counterparts in Afghanistan, India, Vietnam, and elsewhere as part of international humanitarian assistance efforts.[6] Tashkent was becoming a scientific research center for Asia, pulling in specialists from abroad via training exchange programs and sending researchers and Soviet technologies overseas to help transform newly independent states in Asia and Africa.

On the literary front, the ancient traditions of Navoi, the Central Asian poet, had been revitalized and transformed into modern art forms (opera, ballet, and drama) that were staged in modern theaters. This new culture meant that Tashkenters knew and appreciated European cultural forms, with Shakespeare, Molière, Pushkin, and Shevchenko becoming as popular as such regional playwrights and authors as Navoi, Oibek, Hamza, and Zulfiya.[7] Soviet and pre-Soviet Uzbek writers were put on the same level as some of the greatest minds of the Western world. Similarly, there existed opportunities for Muslim women to gain education and enter the work force as scientists, technicians, industrial laborers, and government officials. The Gorispolkom chairperson, Halema Yusupova, was a prominent example of this achievement. She frequently met with visiting delegations, an activity that took almost as much time as fulfilling her duties as a city administrator. With such examples of medical, cultural, and gender success, Tashkent was presented as a new, prosperous, and modern city under Soviet power.[8]

In public pronouncements by Party and state officials, Tashkent had become a vibrant city to which "peace-loving" citizens of the world gravitated. With delegations flying in from the East and West, the Tashkent airport replaced the railroad station as the city's main point of entry, its "*vestibul*," with direct airline routes that opened up the region to the outside world, connecting the Uzbek capital to Afghanistan, India, Pakistan, Burma, Indonesia, and what is now Sri Lanka.[9] Both transportation facilities received major overhauls in the late 1950s and early 1960s because they were the primary points for moving visitors into and around Central Asia.[10] Through a one-stop connection at Aeroflot's hub in Moscow, Tashkenters, in theory, could reach any major city of the world in record time. In official discourse, Soviet Tashkent brought Central Asia back to its previous role as a stop on the Great Silk Road, a place where cultures, races, ideas, and languages merged. Prior to the revolution, the cities along the Silk Road had fallen into disrepair and decay, as had great centers of Asian and Islamic culture, including Algiers, Baghdad, and Cairo. With Soviet rule having returned Tashkent, Samarkand, and other Soviet Asian urban areas to their early positions as crossroads of the world, the region became an economic and industrial powerhouse in Asia. Socialist power had effectively transformed the Great Silk Road into an equally impressive Red Silk Road with Tashkent as its major stop. The Uzbek capital was presented as a center of Asia and a point from which positive imagery of socialism could be disseminated.

Soviet officials were well aware of Tashkent's world image and reminded residents and building designers alike of the need to show a positive public face of the city: "The gate to a country is its capital. Therefore, the great interest of foreign delegations in the city of Tashkent is completely understandable."[11] Visible cracks in the region's public face needed repair and, if possible, to be avoided altogether. "Uncapital-like" (*nestolichnyi*) buildings, streets, or tramlines were removed from the city center to provide it with a more modern look. Before international visits, buildings were spruced up with paint, particularly those that were on the main tourist routes. City parks were cleaned, expanded, and planted with additional shrubbery as proof of the thriving nature of Soviet agriculture and the success of water projects in the desert, also highlighted by the proliferation of elaborate fountains in prime meeting places in the city. In fact, Khrushchev himself declared the Uzbek capital to be the Soviet "Gate to Asia" and used the city as a departure point for his Asian tour in 1960.[12] For this reason, local planners announced that the city's reconstruction had the highest-level significance for the entire Soviet state and for Soviet foreign policy. Planning Tashkent was no longer simply important for transforming Central Asians into proper Soviet citizens. Redesigning the city would help bring about fundamental transitions across the globe in colonial and postcolonial societies.

Semyon Tutuchenko, the secretary of the central Architects' Union, admonished his Tashkent colleagues for their failure to build structures that could live up to such high expectations. It was a complaint that underscored the shortage of model buildings spread across an increasingly large city, despite the efforts to build a showcase of socialism. He argued that the renovation of Tashkent was not only for the benefit of the city's residents but also made a political statement to the world at large. He subsequently expressed sharp criticism of bureaucrats and planners who impeded the reconstruction project in the Uzbek capital, targeting the designer of a new "first-class" restaurant for foreign guests and high-level Soviet officials. Although the 480-seat restaurant was a "masterpiece" of architecture, its designer failed to allot enough space for the coat check, a facility that was deemed vital in Soviet public buildings.[13] The eleven-square-meter cloak room was not large enough to hold 480 coats, and it did not provide visitors with space to comfortably remove their outer garments. This oversight allegedly marred the enjoyment of patrons and gave the impression that Soviet architects did not know how to build a cultured dining establishment, particularly for the foreigners, who would have to drape coats over their chair or, worse yet, wear them while eating. Although economizing on construction had become the mantra of the Khrushchev era, cutting costs in public buildings for foreign guests or visiting Moscow officials was considered unacceptable, especially in this case, because checking one's coat before entering a restaurant or theater had become a signifier of Soviet culture's refinement.[14] Once again, Tutuchenko's comments underline the Moscow-centric views of Tashkent's architectural plans. Tashkent's climate, with its hot summers and relatively short, mild winters, makes large cloak rooms unnecessary. In many ways, this "major" flaw in the restaurant's design actually suited the Tashkent environment and the habits of its residents quite well; Tutuchenko, who in the past had called for considering local customs and needs in designing for Central Asians, was guilty of the same mistakes for which he criticized others.

Furthermore, if a poorly planned coat room were not bad enough, Tutuchenko was even more incensed that there were "only two urinals" in the washroom for the 480 diners that the facility could serve at one time. Would the foreigners and visiting Soviet dignitaries have to wait in line to use the bathroom? Architects needed to remember that "Tashkent is the route to India and other countries. Where will our foreign guests go to eat? Of course, to the new first-class restaurant. Or where will members of the government, Nikita Sergeievich Khrushchev go? Of course, he will go to the new . . . restaurant and see how we conserve our money."[15] Cheap and poorly designed buildings were perfectly fine for Tashkenters but not for the Party elite or the city's foreign guests. Although economizing on construction was the mantra of the 1960s, cutting costs in public buildings that showcased Asian socialism for foreign guests was considered unacceptable. Despite the real efforts to bring about a change in the quality of life of Tashkent residents, planners never ceased their efforts to transform Tashkent into an ideal showcase city of socialism.

Tashkent's Cultural Ties

In the Soviet era, Tashkent Radio became an important means of spreading socialist ideology as well as Uzbek identity throughout the Central Asian countryside and even overseas. It helped to connect the villages and cities of Uzbekistan to the capital in Tashkent (which itself was closely tied to Moscow) in the imagined community of Soviet Uzbekistan, to use Benedict

Anderson's phrase.[16] Although Tashkent Radio's domestic programming existed for years, the international service became popular in the 1950s, developing a broad listener base across the world, even possessing one diehard fan in the Bronx, or so Supreme Court Associate Justice William Douglas was told during a trip to Tashkent in 1955.[17] How Tashkent Radio could have beamed its signal directly from the Uzbek capital to distant areas of the globe and connect foreign listeners to Soviet ideology in Central Asia remains uncertain, considering that residents on the outskirts of the city, let alone in Tashkent oblast villages, complained of poor reception.[18] Nonetheless, Tashkent Radio broadcast stories of Uzbek culture, urban renewal in Central Asia, the development of modern industry and economic opportunity in the region, and a variety of other stories that focused on socialism and the new infrastructure that was being built in Tashkent and other areas of Uzbekistan. Despite these stories of Soviet achievements in Central Asia—the content of which Party propagandists rated highly—the radio service came under criticism during the Congress of Uzbek Intellectuals in 1956 for being good "only for Russian speakers" and unable to reach its target groups overseas, namely Hindi-, Pashto-, Punjabi-, Burmese-, and Thai-speaking populations.[19] Tashkent International Radio beamed its signal across the border to India, Afghanistan, and elsewhere but failed to provide programming in languages that its foreign listeners could understand. In other words, propaganda for foreign audiences reached only a small population, namely those who already were inclined to support the Soviet system, indicated by the fact that they knew Russian. Tashkent Radio preached to the choir—to foreign communists and intellectuals on the Left, many of whom had already gone through Soviet educational institutions where they learned the premier language of the Soviet Union. By broadcasting in Russian—not even Uzbek or Tajik, which could at least impact some foreign Turkic, Farsi, and Dari speakers—its programming had little influence beyond elite pro-Soviet groups. This oversight was not surprising, considering that previous "cultural enlightenment" programs in Central Asia had failed because libraries and worker clubs were not provided with Uzbek-language reading material that the population could understand or because Soviet propagandists often would give lectures in Russian to Central Asians who had poor knowledge of the language.[20] Once again following a fairly standard pattern, Soviet officials decreed that Tashkent Radio must provide programming in the foreign languages of its listeners, but Tashkent lacked the infrastructure and a cadre of language speakers to accomplish this task. The Soviet state had elaborate plans to reach out from Tashkent to propagate socialism as a model of development, but it lacked the basic tools in Uzbekistan to implement these public diplomacy projects.

Delegates to the first Congress of Uzbek Intellectuals also criticized the editorial board of Tashkent International Radio for uninspiring programming that did not suit the needs of foreign listeners and ignored listener feedback from distant lands. Additionally, the Uzbek audience of Tashkent Radio's programs showed little "understanding of the life of the peoples of the East."[21] Tashkent Radio should have been a tool to bring together the peoples of Soviet and non-Soviet Asia, but it failed to serve its foreign listeners, providing them with boring and uninspiring programming, much of which focused on technical topics: industrial and agricultural achievement, housing and factory construction, health care, or factory output. Equally troubling was the fact that the domestic service could not interest its local audience in stories and reports on the life of their foreign neighbors, about whom the Uzbek people reportedly were so concerned. The situation had deteriorated so much that delegates to the first Congress of Uzbek Intellectuals in 1956 expressed concern that foreigners were visiting Tashkent in increasing numbers to view the innovations in Soviet Central Asia but that native Tashkenters were not terribly interested in or knowledgeable about the culture, history, and problems of their ethnic neighbors, who still suffered under imperialism but with whom Uzbeks allegedly had so much in common.[22] If Tashkent was to be the center of the postcolonial world, its residents needed to be more aware of Asian, African, and, after the Cuban revolution, Latin American peoples.

Ironically, despite the Soviet Union's offering to provide colonial groups "liberation" and "cultural development," Soviet racial, economic, and cultural attitudes lumped Vietnamese, Cubans, Indians, Sudanese, and Uzbeks into one category when, in reality, there were considerable ethnic, religious, historical, and geographic differences among them. Clearly, Cubans and Algerians were not "neighbors" of the Uzbeks. Besides poverty, what did these national groups really have in common except that the Soviet Union had declared them to be stagnant and oppressed peoples and considered Europeanized Soviet culture to be superior? Soviet leaders did not address or acknowledge major cultural or social differences among those it viewed as "backward." They assumed that such national groups were all alike, shared common interests, and needed the forms of assistance that had been given to the previously "backward" Soviet peoples. This view reflected Marxist theories of history whereby all societies progressed through specific stages of historical development. Officials implied that the "stagnant" cultures of

Asia, Africa, and Latin America had not evolved as quickly along the path of historical development that would lead to communism. They were stuck on a lower level, as the Uzbeks had been before the revolution, and needed similar assistance in transitioning to the next stage. For this reason, the Tashkent model was universal. It was not designed for a specific society or culture but could supposedly be replicated anywhere there were people who had not yet reached a specified level of "modern development."

As the most advanced socialist state, the Soviet Union declared that it had an ideological duty to help other states undergo this transformation to socialism. While on tour in India in 1960, Khrushchev declared that "Lenin, the founder of the Soviet state, said that 'we shall exert every effort to form close ties and unite with the Mongolians, Persians, Indians and Egyptians,' that 'we shall endeavor to render unselfish cultural assistance to these peoples, who are more backward and more oppressed than ourselves.'"[23] Socialism could assist any country that needed to move beyond colonial oppression toward Soviet-style liberation. From the Khrushchev era onward, elite groups of Soviet officials and technicians, armed with this ideology and convinced of their success in transforming Central Asia, were ready to show the colonial world the path to prosperity.

One way they intended to do so was through cultural and sporting events that brought citizens of the postcolonial world to Central Asia to see the achievements of the Soviet Union. Throughout the cold war, Soviet writers, actors, and intellectuals invited foreign colleagues from Asia and Africa to participate in international conferences during which world affairs and decolonization were discussed. *Pravda Vostoka*, in fact, declared Tashkent to be the premier "place for international meetings" because of its sponsorship of academic conferences, international film festivals, healthcare workshops, sports competitions, and literary meetings.[24] On these trips, delegates were given tours of Tashkent and Uzbekistan to learn about the "progress" and "freedom" granted to the citizens of Central Asia. The International Conference of Writers from Asia and Africa, held in Tashkent in 1958, brought cultural figures from fifty-nine foreign countries. Officials decorated the city with colorful flags and multilingual posters to create a hospitable environment for visitors who came dressed in their national costumes. Tashkent frequently celebrated the diversity of socialism and of the states that were positively inclined toward it. The desire to transform the postcolonial world through the doctrine of "national in form, socialist in content" was clearly evident among the delegates who spoke of poverty-stricken and oppressed homelands, all while witnessing the new Soviet culture and civilization that flourished in Tashkent.[25] Visitors marveled at the highly modern and sleek look of the city and compared Tashkent favorably to the squalor of the cities in their home countries.

One Iraqi cultural delegate described his homeland as inferior to the Uzbek SSR in its level of development. He viewed Baghdad and Tashkent as being similar because both possessed marvelous historical monuments and long histories, but he noted that their commonality ended "in the past." More recently, he said, Baghdad had "stagnated," while Tashkent—"liberated" from both its religious and colonial oppression by socialism—flourished to such a point that this Iraqi visitor described his homeland as "backward to" (*ostaly*) or behind Tashkent "just as a donkey cart is backward to a Tupolev 104" airplane, the Soviet aircraft on which foreign visitors arrived in the Uzbek capital.[26] A Chilean visitor similarly stated that Tashkent's transformation into a city with wide streets and heavy industry was the realization of an "Eastern fairy tale," or so Soviet accounts of this foreigner's trip to the city declared.[27] Tashkent became the primary prism through which postcolonial travelers interpreted socialist achievement and how it could be adapted to societies that were trying to move out of poverty and toward modernity. To become "modern" like the Uzbeks, socialist discourse (both inside and outside the Soviet Union) decreed that one should follow the Tashkent path of postcolonial urban development.

Oibek, the famous twentieth-century Soviet writer, invited fellow writers from Pakistan, Nepal, Iraq, Algeria, and Ghana to a private literary "salon" at his home during the International Conference of Writers from Africa and Asia in Tashkent in 1958. In this instance, one again sees a conglomeration of ethnic groups that did not have all that much in common but were grouped together in the Soviet ideological mind. According to published accounts of the meeting, these literary figures needed no help or translators to understand each other's works because they came to Uzbekistan to celebrate the "peace, friendship, brotherhood, and poetry" of Asia and Africa.[28] The Uzbek host told delegates that Tashkenters appreciated high culture. Oibek and other artistic figures of the Tashkent cultural scene read their works to the visiting delegates and explained the various themes that contemporary Uzbek literature explored: Soviet patriotism, bravery, the achievements of national minorities, and the equality of all citizens of the Soviet Union. To mark the visit of these international literary figures, the Uzbek State Publishing House printed *Masters of Literature and Art of Tashkent* (1958) in English. This book included biographies and described the major works of Tashkent cultural figures—writers, poets, playwrights, composers, dancers, and actors.

Although the audience for the book was mostly from Asia and Africa,

Masters of Literature and Art of Tashkent celebrated the city's European cultural forms—symphonies, drama, prose, and opera—all developed under Soviet power and all well represented in the new landmarks of the socialist city, including the Tashkent Conservatory, the Navoi Theater, the Mukhimi Theater, and a variety of other institutions. However, these European art forms had non-European subjects: Oibek's poems "Zafar and Zahkro" and "In Search of Light" were about the "life of the toilers of Pakistan and the growth of progressive forces for peace and democracy."[29] Sharaf Rashidov, writer, poet, and first secretary of the Uzbek Communist Party, used folklore from India to write his "Kashmir Songs."[30] Tamara Khanum, a fifty-year-old Uzbek folk dancer and one of the first Uzbek women to perform unveiled in the 1920s, epitomized the success of the Soviet Uzbek woman, according to *Masters of Literature and Art of Tashkent.* The daughter of a railroad worker, she took advantage of the opportunities that socialism gave to Central Asian women. She rose to prominence and even became a "People's Artist of the USSR." In the book's biographical sketch about her, foreign readers learned that her performances at the Uzbek Philharmonic illustrated how "one can see many colored lines which connect Tashkent with many towns of Eastern and Western Countries." A well-publicized symbol of the liberation of Soviet Central Asian women, this dancer, whose home base was the Uzbek capital, traveled abroad to showcase Uzbek artistry to the people of Afghanistan, India, Pakistan, Indonesia, Burma, Vietnam, and other countries, and she took with her a repertoire of songs in more than fifty languages.[31] The book proclaimed that Soviet liberation and socialism allowed Uzbekistan to develop into a modern, cultured, and almost European-like society, with the city of Tashkent as its anchor.

The book also described Zulfiya, another symbol of Soviet liberation in Central Asia. This celebrated female poet devoted "much of her work to the friendship of nations and the fight for peace throughout the world . . . [serving as] an envoy to such countries as China, India, Yugoslavia, Ceylon, and other countries."[32] Meanwhile, another famous female Tashkenter, Halima Nasyrova, an opera singer from the Navoi Theater, brought the opera *Carmen,* a symbol of high culture, to the peoples of the East and gave tours within the Soviet Union and abroad.[33] This book and the conference highlighted the cultural development of Soviet Uzbekistan and showcased its ties to the outside world, with a particular focus on Uzbek women. *Masters of Literature and Art of Tashkent* celebrated not only the new cultural institutions of the city but also the entire history of female emancipation in Soviet Central Asia, where women now could occupy important cultural roles in advancing the city of Tashkent into the socialist—and ultimately communist—future. With the determination of the Uzbek people, who had been "helped" by the Russian and Soviet people to become the most "advanced" in Asia, Tashkent had become a model of cultural "flowering," even if the flowers planted there were not native to the region. Since, in Soviet ideology, Western European art forms were considered to be more developed, the adaptation of Uzbek traditions to modern Soviet high culture was deemed a natural progression in the Marxist-Leninist understanding of history. Thanks to the success of the Uzbek capital, the Tashkent model already had been replicated across Uzbekistan and soon would spread across the globe.

In fact, in adapting this model to Iraq, Vietnam, or Angola, the Uzbek "little brother" in the Soviet family often was described as assuming the role of "elder sibling" in Soviet relations with the rest of the postcolonial world. Just as they had moved from living in a "backward" desert colony to possessing a "flowering" industrial republic under Soviet power, all "with the help of the Russian people," the Uzbek people were ready and willing to assist their Asian, African, and Middle Eastern friends in making a similar "jump" toward modernity.[34] They would enable their new protégés to move away from American military and financial domination or from the oppressive British Commonwealth, which was publicly identified in Tashkent as a refashioned form of European colonialism.[35] In following the Tashkent model, these countries could skip the capitalist stage of development and move directly into socialism, as Uzbekistan allegedly had. This Central Asian accomplishment of "avoiding" capitalist oppression was so impressive to the vice president of the Indian Committee for Peace that he reportedly stated that Soviet "Uzbekistan is a bright example of the never before quick development of a backwards people, a bright example for people who want to live free without a caste system or exploitation, who want to be equal among equals and to end forever differences according to race and skin color."[36] The Uzbek capital and socialism reportedly offered a roadmap out of poverty, colonialism, and racism. Tashkent, in its role as the center of socialism in Asia, assumed the role that Moscow had previously played in fostering the development of the Soviet Union's "own backward regions." For this reason, the Ministry of Foreign Affairs increased the representation of Central Asian diplomats at Soviet missions abroad, particularly in the Middle East and Asia. Nureddin Mukhitdinov, former first secretary of the Uzbek Communist Party, was elevated to full membership in the Presidium and in the Central Committee Secretariat of the Communist Party of the Soviet Union, the first Central Asian in these positions. In his new role, he was responsible for coordinating the relations of Soviet Central Asia with the postcolonial world.[37] Uzbeks also began to rise in the Soviet bureaucracy in greater numbers at a time when Central Asia was becoming increasingly important for the Soviet Union's drive to expand the global reach of socialism.

On a more practical level, propaganda also spoke of pre-existing ties between foreign states and Uzbekistan, largely through the industrial products that Tashkent factories produced and sent abroad.[38] Tashkent institutions played a significant role in training programs that sought to educate the postcolonial world on the benefits of socialism, and they participated in fulfilling the "international obligations" of the Uzbek people by preparing specialists in agriculture, irrigation, and industry from across Asia. In 1961, Tashkent State University opened a Russian-language program for foreigners and trained Vietnamese, Indians, Mongolians, Afghans, Nepalese, and others.[39] Ironically, the Tashkent education system frequently had been criticized for its inability to teach Uzbeks to be fluent Russian speakers, but suddenly it could train foreigners in a language that was not native to Central Asia. An article in *Pravda Vostoka* also spoke of the important overseas work of Tashkent irrigation experts, energy specialists, and geologists who "trained" the people of North Vietnam in irrigation practices and "left behind good memories of Uzbekistan citizens among the Vietnamese."[40] After forty years of Soviet rule, the Tashkent model and Tashkenters were apparently ready for export on a grand scale.[41]

Guests from the West

Tashkent's dynamic new look also impressed visitors from other parts of the world, not just from developing countries. Holland Roberts, an American from San Francisco, noted that the quickly changing Uzbek capital was a city where "building was in progress on every side, with giant cranes swinging prefabricated panels, sections and beams into place in new apartments, factories and public buildings. As we came up to the newly completed, big modern hotel, I saw the architects had merged classic early Uzbek and contemporary European styles. There was brilliant colorful ceramic work high over the entrance. . . . It was clear that the architectural schools of London, Paris and Moscow would significantly advance their work if their professors and students came here to study."[42] Roberts and other Westerners traveled to Uzbekistan, believing that the West had much to learn from Soviet Central Asia. According to a Soviet published account, foreigners were charmed by Tashkent's beauty and modern feel and often compared the splendor and cleanliness of the Uzbek capital with Afghan, Indian, and

Middle Eastern cities. Two French citizens agreed with Roberts on the miraculous transformation of the city, noting that

Tashkent is an enormous park, planted with a million inhabitants. I do not know another city that is planted with such dense and succulent green areas. Across from each park, one can see another park or a garden [with] beautiful fountains with streaming water. . . . [There are] new regions, just like in Kiev and in Moscow, with the only difference being the decorative motifs here are Uzbek and not Ukrainian as in Kiev and the houses are smaller; in a country where eight months of the year are incredibly hot, each [person] wants to have a balcony and shady garden to be in the fresh air a little longer. Therefore, the number of individual houses, owned by the workers who live in them, is being increased.[43]

Despite continual exhortations that Uzbekistan had been liberated from colonial oppression and allowed to develop its own culture under Soviet rule, these foreign visitors celebrated Tashkent's outward transformation into a European/Russian urban space, just as many Soviet architects had. Socialist liberation brought modernization in its European form, such as the Chilanzar micro-district described previously. Foreign visitors reiterated the official Soviet description of the city to Western audiences just as it had been told to them during their sojourns in the Uzbek capital. Despite their efforts to explore in detail the "freedoms" that Soviet rule gave the former tsarist colonies in Central Asia, many visiting Europeans failed to examine Tashkent's transformation from the perspective of native Tashkenters, instead simply accepting the mantra of rational urban planning, industrial modernization, and gradual Europeanization or Sovietization and disseminating the notion that all these changes were positive developments.[44] In other words, they too viewed the residents of this major Soviet urban center as irrelevant. These Westerners came to the Uzbek capital and saw that Soviet power had given Uzbekistan its own version of Soviet "Moscow," a rationally planned city, and they viewed this new city as a positive development for the Uzbek people and Uzbek culture.

The replication of the metropole across the Soviet Union was considered an achievement by these visitors, as it was by Soviet ideologists. Uzbekistan's success, calculated according to European norms, was proof to foreign visitors that Soviet Central Asia had been "emancipated" from imperialism, even if the visitors measured the achievements of the era against standards that nearly matched those that imperialist observers had used. For the scores of European and American socialists who helped to propagate the Tashkent model in the West, the Uzbek SSR was an example of an egalitarian postcolonial society. In this sense, Soviet modernity in Central

Asia, despite its call for the liberation of oppressed national minorities, was essentially a project of socialist globalization. In the name of anticolonialism, it brought an extreme push toward Europeanization and global uniformity. The end result was to make the outward look of these cities less specifically Asian, more homogeneously "modern," and more uniformly "socialist." Through such orientalist prisms, many visitors saw Tashkent-style urban areas in Africa, Asia, and Latin America as the wave of the future and denigrated traditional ways of life across the globe as backward, even if they did not explicitly say so.[45]

However, the dissemination of the Tashkent model was an exercise in performance art in which local guides carefully choreographed what places foreign visitors would see in Tashkent and with which city residents they would interact. Soviet orchestrators frowned on spontaneous invitations to the homes or workplaces of Tashkenters because these visits often provided outsiders with the "wrong" impression. A slip of the tongue or a drink of alcohol by Muslim officials of the Uzbek SSR could end up in the foreign press in South Asia or the Middle East, providing opponents of socialism with powerful ammunition against the socialist system in Central Asia.[46] Soviet guides sought to prevent unprepared and ill-prepared interactions between their charges and representatives of the model city, although they did not always succeed. Patrick Sergeant, a British journalist, noted how his guide tried in vain to prevent his impromptu meeting with three Uzbek medical students who had been mobilized to work the cotton harvest. Eager to practice their English, they spontaneously invited him to join them at the collective farm. As Sergeant accompanied the students on their expedition, the guide repeatedly insisted that she could and should organize a better, more informative, and more comfortable visit for him to see Uzbek cotton fields.[47]

During this trip to the collective farm, however, Sergeant got a glimpse of the Soviet reality that caused him to question the Tashkent model, especially as it related to gender equity. At the farm, he noted that Uzbek women performed most of the heavy labor, while Uzbek men supervised. He asked two male supervisors why such backbreaking work was not done by men or by mechanized harvesting combines, the pride of Soviet agriculture. The men "gave [him] the look kept by farmers the world over for townsmen asking silly questions. 'Combines are expensive and come out of profits. They break down and need expensive parts and maintenance. These,' the elder said, sweeping his arm across three fields full of the bent backs of women toiling in the sun—'these need no spare parts, no maintenance and work well. Why have the machines?'"[48] In many ways, these liberated

Uzbek women, who had officially been given equal rights and protection against domestic abuse, were no better off than farm animals, according to Sergeant's description. They received little formal training and remained in positions where they were subservient to male relatives and supervisors who were involved in other tasks that "required experience." The "classless" Soviet society in Central Asia had deeply ingrained notions of class, with Uzbeks, particularly women, still on the bottom rungs, a place where gender, class, and ethnicity all converged. Unexpected visits to unsanctioned locations, like Sergeant's trip to the cotton field, were frowned upon by Party minders and official tour guides who only wanted to present the positive aspects of the new Uzbekistan.

Fitzroy MacLean, a British diplomat who visited Tashkent in the 1930s, returned in 1957 and received similarly negative impressions of socialism in Asia. He noted the anger of an ethnically mixed Uzbek-Russian family in a Tashkent restaurant toward the special status that he and other foreign guests received in the Uzbek capital. In sweltering heat, this family lamented that they could not buy beer for their son, on leave from the Soviet navy, because there was none available in the city. They subsequently watched as "trayful after trayful of frosted [beer] bottles were brought to a group of progressive Frenchmen in a corner. Soviet citizens were not duped by the extravagance."[49] This family was a symbol of Soviet achievement in the Uzbek capital in that it was living proof that one of the long-standing goals of creating a new city had been achieved. The couple was ethnically mixed—an Uzbek husband and Russian wife—and thus symbolized the "unification" of the city's diverse national groups. Furthermore, they were celebrating a family occasion in a Soviet institution, not inside the private confines of an enclosed courtyard, which was the traditional Uzbek custom. In addition, the parents marked the achievements of their son in the Soviet navy with an alcoholic beverage, a drink that traditionally is prohibited in Islam. And yet, this very Soviet family appeared to be disillusioned with the Tashkent Potemkin village. Despite being hospitable hosts—as Uzbeks generally are—and opening up their city to foreign guests, Tashkenters at times resented the privileges that many foreign fellow travelers received during their quick sojourns through Central Asia. Many visitors only looked on the surface of Tashkent and did not fully comprehend the enormous upheaval that had taken place and the changes that were continuing to occur in Soviet Uzbek society. These foreigners mostly saw the public successes of Soviet urbanization in the city and viewed them as proof of the successful implementation of socialism in Central Asia without seeing the stress such a transformation had caused in society. On the other hand, many Soviet officials from Moscow—such as architect Semyon Tutuchenko—identified only the cracks in the Tashkent model that caused them privately to question the success of Soviet Tashkent and largely fail to see the tremendous movement of people toward Soviet ideology and ways of life. The Soviet Uzbek people on the ground in Tashkent were stuck somewhere in the middle.

The diplomat Fitzroy MacLean recognized some of these changes, however, and expressed concern over the future of Tashkent. He noted that the new city had increased tremendously in size, taking over parts of the traditional native Central Asian areas. He remarked that Uzbek national dress—not simply the *paranjis* of women but also the *cholpan* or traditional robe worn by men—was less common on city streets than it had been before. He noted that "in Uzbekistan, as in the other more exotic republics of the Union, the standardization and Sovietization of everything is proceeding apace, especially in the towns."[50] Once again, he viewed Tashkent through an orientalist prism and saw traditional Uzbek culture as exotic. By the Khrushchev era, however, MacLean was lamenting that Uzbeks were losing their cultural uniqueness and living normal Soviet lives, in normal Soviet dress, and interacting with normal Soviet institutions. Unlike other foreign visitors, he did not see this change as a positive development or proof of progress but as an indication that socialist modernity was simply bringing uniformity to the region. Time, not the authoritarian pressure from above, was turning out to be an effective way of transforming Uzbek urban space. Tashkent, whether for good or bad, was beginning to resemble any other Soviet city in both form and in content, indicated by the ongoing emergence of "modernity" at the expense of the city's "Asian" uniqueness, even if many Soviet officials still expressed concern over the slow pace of this transformation and the lingering cultural "peculiarities" of Uzbek Tashkenters.

A City Shattered

Despite criticism of the Tashkent model by some foreign visitors, Tashkent officials never stopped their urban renewal program. In the 1960s, progress was evident in improved living standards and the availability of new education, cultural, and career opportunities for the ethnically Central Asian residents of Tashkent. Uzbeks, who had entered the Soviet education system in large numbers in the 1950s, were starting to rise to positions of power in city institutions. After years of playing second fiddle to Soviet officials who came from Russia, Ukraine, and elsewhere, a large Soviet Uzbek elite—many of whom had little knowledge of pre-Soviet life and some of whom were children during the tumultuous Stalin era—was finally emerging in Tashkent. These people were products of the Soviet education system, and the Soviet world was all they knew. They were less religious, less traditional, and better trained in the sciences and technology—the two fields most highly rated by the Soviet system—than the generation before. This group would play an increasingly important role in the city as it moved further into the Brezhnev era.

Furthermore, by 1966, stores, schools, theaters, and other community services had opened in the Chilanzar housing compound, which, with a reported population of 150,000 inhabitants in more than seven hundred buildings, was described as "a city within a city."[51] The Chilanzar housing district's population was larger than that of many provincial cities of the Uzbek SSR; it was three times greater than the population of the Karakalpak Autonomous SSR's capital of Nukus and five times larger than that of the border city of Termez, although it had not yet surpassed its goal of exceeding the population of Bukhara.[52] For Tashkenters, the sight of tall cranes assembling new housing areas became a common sight. The state, if not the residents, described these high-rise structures as "expressions of the party's concern for the people."[53] In official discourse, the taller the construction, the greater the state's purported care for the residents of the city. In 1966, a new sixteen-story tower with sixty-four apartments, complete with balconies, elevators, air conditioners, and sunshades for the windows, was set to open.[54] Tashkent finally was expanding upward, not simply outward, and the housing crunch slowly decreased in severity. The "model" socialist city was taking shape.

That year, 1966, also saw Tashkent step out onto the international stage yet again as the host city for an Indo-Pakistani peace conference that culminated in the signing of the "Tashkent Declaration." In January 1966, the president of Pakistan, Mohammad Ayub Khan, and the prime minister of India, Lal Bahadur Shastri, met in Tashkent for seven days. To mark the importance of the visit, Aleksei Kosygin, chairman of the Council of Ministers of the Soviet Union, Andrei Gromyko, the Soviet foreign minister, and Ia. S. Nasriddinov, chairman of the Supreme Soviet of the Uzbek SSR, met the foreign leaders at the airport.[55] Newspapers reported that the arrival of the foreign leaders drew thousands of spectators into the streets of the city to acknowledge the importance of the summit to Tashkent and to Asia at large. *Pravda Vostoka* chronicled the meeting, dutifully informing the public of world interest in such a high-level meeting in the Uzbek capital. Journalists from Asia, Africa, North America, and Europe allegedly convened at Bulatov's Tashkent Hotel to report on the progress of discussions that were held at the Uzbek Council of Ministers meeting hall in the Government House on Lenin Square and in a suburban retreat center.[56] The Indian-Pakistani agreement, signed on January 10, 1966, thanked the Soviet government, the Uzbek SSR, and the people of Uzbekistan for their "constructive, friendly and noble part" in calling the meeting and in warmly receiving the delegations.[57] Tashkent had become a diplomatic center of Asia, which was one goal of the original Tashkent socialist reconstruction project of 1937. Tashkenters were told—and many believed—that the world was watching them and that, through their membership in the Soviet family of nations, the Uzbeks were playing an important role in the international arena, especially in the postcolonial world.

However, the success of this meeting was dampened by the unexpected death of the Indian prime minister in Tashkent on the evening of January 10–11, 1966. Instead of celebrating the conclusion of the conference and Tashkent's victory on the world stage, the city officially went into mourning for the visiting head of state. Black flags were hung throughout the capital as the body was transported from the conference site to the airport for repatriation, a bad omen as the city began the fateful year of 1966.[58] This death played havoc with Soviet efforts to develop Tashkent's reputation as a regional Asian power center that could bring about peace between its neighbors. With the tragic end to the meeting, the Soviet Union could hardly advertise this achievement in international affairs in Central Asia, and scant mention of the Tashkent summit can be found in subsequent newspaper issues.

And yet, the worst was still to come. At 5:23 A.M. on April 26, 1966, an earthquake rattled Tashkent. Registering 7.5 on the Richter scale, it was followed by a series of smaller aftershocks occurring over a two-month period. The initial tremor brought serious destruction, but the devastating aftershocks caused many Tashkent structures, already weakened, to disintegrate. Tashkent was not leveled all at once but experienced a slow demise as buildings continued to crumble and the city's infrastructure slowly collapsed. The natural disaster wiped out much of the recent achievement in reducing the problem of urban overcrowding. Many of the traditional mud-brick homes in Tashkent collapsed or suffered damage, but the "modern" Soviet construction in the center of the city fared no better. Stepan Polupanov's ever-problematic Government House lay in ruins, and Red (Lenin) Square, with the city's main monument to the leader of the revolution, was piled with rubble. The only solution for cleaning up this area was to knock down these structures and remove the fallen symbols of socialist power.[59] The area of greatest destruction covered a twenty-square-mile radius from the epicenter, which was a few blocks north of Red (Lenin) Square in the heart of the Soviet city.[60] These important buildings for the Soviet state, originally designed to last for centuries, barely stood for thirty years before nature, a force that Soviet technology was supposed to control and architects frequently discounted, demolished them.

With buildings having collapsed or burned, Tashkent immediately lost 2.86 million square meters of living space, leaving 1.02 million square meters of housing space standing but in such a dangerous condition that the structures required demolition. Another 1.1 million square meters of housing space was seriously damaged, requiring major repairs to foundations and support structures. The disaster officially left 300,000 Tashkenters homeless, many of whom were forced to move onto the streets, into tents, or to other cities in the Soviet Union.[61] According to the Tashkent City Health Administration, injury and death tolls from "physical trauma" were not large. Instead, Tashkenters suffered mostly from the psychological stress of a natural disaster and from infectious diseases that spread through the city during the summer months.[62] Sewage and water pipes broke, contaminating the city's drinking water supply. The earthquake severed electrical lines and gas mains, making it difficult to sell, store, and cook food. Communal eating areas—cafes, cafeterias, restaurants, and outdoor food stands— provided homeless Tashkenters with basic sustenance. However, the City Health Administration soon questioned the sanitary conditions of these establishments as the incidence of typhoid, dysentery, and other diseases of the digestive tract increased. Tashkent doctors, many of whose facilities had been damaged, feared for the future of the largest socialist city in Central Asia.[63]

The Ministry of Health and the Council of Ministers of Uzbekistan issued a decree on June 14, 1966, declaring that cleaning the city's drinking water supply and replacing water pipes would be the first emergency projects completed. This task was deemed vital in the hot summer months, when clean water meant survival in the Central Asian desert. Health inspectors closed down eight thousand food service establishments, mostly bakeries, cafeterias, and teahouses, in the city because of unsanitary conditions and contaminated water.[64] Even so, many of the recent construction projects, built with reinforced concrete and located farther from the epicenter, survived the natural disaster with less serious damage than buildings in the center of the city. For this reason, city planners immediately declared Tashkent's high-rise structures to be safe. City officials decided that moving residents into these types of structures was the best way to "liquidate the consequences" of the earthquake.[65] However, in many respects, Tashkenters were back to an era when their basic needs were poorly met.

Furthermore, the destruction gave architects a powerful excuse to

knock down the Old City, rebuild Red (renamed Lenin) Square, and promote apartment construction in place of the traditional single-family
home. Tashkenters were not in a good position to negotiate, as some no longer had a roof over their head. For others, officials declared their homes to
be unsafe and bulldozed them off the map, even those that had not been
severely damaged. The natural disaster thus became an excuse to raze not
only the damaged sections of the Old City but also other areas of traditional
Central Asian–style structures lest they also collapse at some point in the
future.[66] In effect, the earthquake transformed the region into a pseudo-
Magnitogorsk and gave planners the blank slate they always wanted. In the
past, the regime had difficulty reordering the Tashkent landscape, but now
nature stepped in to help. In the "heroic" efforts to rebuild the city, planners would make New Tashkent a city of air-conditioned apartments and
electric stoves. Its residents would move through the urban environment
in a new underground metro system, and the city administrative complex,
to be rebuilt by 1970 at the latest, would center around Lenin Square—an
enlarged square with water fountains and pools, "massive greenery," and
free-standing buildings. The city center once again would reflect "the political importance and greatness of Tashkent" and its role as the focal point of
Asian socialism.[67]

With such devastation and physical loss, the city needed significant
outside help to sculpt its urban space back into shape. Just as Tashkenters
helped to rebuild the devastated city of Kiev in 1945 and Ashgabat in 1948–
1949, Muscovites, Leningraders, Kievans, and others quickly sent "material
support," medical relief, and, most importantly, construction specialists to
help with the rebuilding efforts. "Moral support" flowed into the city from
Uzbekistan's international friends and neighbors via telegrams to express
"solidarity" with the Uzbek people.[68] Since Soviet officials never wasted a
chance to propagandize the strength of the socialist system, this devastating natural disaster became a means to showcase Tashkent's international
ties and the unity of the socialist family. The entire Soviet Union "felt" for
the poor residents of the city. Tashkent children were sent to summer camps
or to live with distant relatives throughout the Soviet Union so as to shield
them from the dangers of living around falling rubble, broken gas lines, and
sharp metal objects lying on city streets. Propagandists even noted that residents of cities in the European parts of the Soviet Union were repaying their
wartime debt to Tashkenters, who had cared for European refugees and orphans from Leningrad, Kiev, and Minsk in the 1940s.[69] In a time of serious
hardship, propaganda declared that the "friendship of the Soviet peoples"
was strong. Unlike before the revolution or during the World War II evacu-

ation period, Tashkent was not a distant wasteland to which travel by train or caravan took months. The Uzbek capital was now seen as a central part of the country and a central concern of all Soviet citizens. In fact, Leonid Brezhnev, general secretary of the Communist Party, and Kosygin, chair of the Council of Ministers, flew to Tashkent within hours of the disaster to inspect the damage and bring aid.[70] With this natural disaster, Tashkent and its residents gained important places in the history of Soviet unity. The government's response showed that Tashkent was not simply the capital of a far-off cotton colony but an essential part of a much larger Soviet state with a population that increasingly identified with that state and expected something from the state, even if they did not always act as central officials thought they should. The Uzbek capital and its people clearly were important to the Soviet polity, and priority was placed on rebuilding the city in record time. In the process, Soviet propagandists created a new myth—that of the earthquake and the unified effort of the Soviet people to raise the Uzbek capital from rubble as fast as possible.

However, the earthquake also prompted a new European migration to the city, as builders from Kiev, Leningrad, Moscow, and Minsk descended on Tashkent to help rebuild it. Many of them never returned home. In the rush to put homeless city residents back into apartments, many of these new non-Tashkent construction experts once again did not consider local customs, climate conditions, or building norms. In the new "Ukrainian micro-district," Ukrainian builders reportedly constructed 70 percent of the buildings with windows on an east/west rather than north/south orientation, causing residents once again to suffer stifling summertime heat inside their new homes.[71] Building standards, lowered a few years earlier, were raised once again. Engineers proposed banning new housing construction and structures higher than nine stories near the quake's epicenter—close to Lenin and Revolution Squares and along Navoi, Uzbekistan, and May 1 streets, main avenues of the pre-earthquake "Soviet City" under which earthquake fault lines ran.[72] Nonetheless, Tashkenters soon would celebrate the opening of a twenty-story skyscraper on Lenin Square.[73] Tashkent was reborn, but the political need to reconstruct the city quickly and to show the strength of Soviet industrial technology of the late 1960s and 1970s forced many planners to repeat mistakes of the past.

In the end, the physical changes that Sovietization brought to Tashkent in the late 1960s were by-products of the Eurocentric convictions of planners, Party officials, and builders alike and of something that the Soviet system attempted to but ultimately could not control—nature. Despite the lessons of Ashgabat in 1948 and of Tashkent in 1966, Soviet technology's attempts at reordering physical spaces and controlling the environment continued to devastate the Soviet landscape until the Soviet state disintegrated in 1991. Chernobyl wreaked havoc over the Ukrainian and Belorussian countryside in 1986. Soviet science and nuclear research decimated an area of northern Kazakhstan near the nuclear testing site at Semipalatinsk, a city with a population of 400,000 people. Water diversion projects to irrigate Central Asian cotton fields drained the Aral Sea, causing enormous health, environmental, and economic problems to this day. In fact, the deadly combination of earthquakes and Soviet cities repeated itself in 1988 when tremors shook Armenia, causing cities, towns, and villages to collapse with a tragic death toll of 25,000. In the end, the Soviet Union attempted but could not successfully use ideology and science to reorder the physical landscape of the country. Officials realized too late that science and ideology cannot solve everything, that humans are not always rational beings, and that nature is unpredictable.

Still, the attempt to create model cities and ideal citizens continued, even after the collapse of the Soviet Union, as the post-Soviet urban renewal campaigns of Moscow, St. Petersburg, Yerevan, Ashgabat, Tashkent, and Astana, the shiny new capital of Kazakhstan, illustrate. However, for the capitals of independent Turkmenistan and Uzbekistan, the same power of nature that devastated these Soviet urban spaces in the twentieth century still lies underneath their city centers and threatens their post-Soviet successors today.

▨ EPILOGUE

It has been more than forty years since the earthquake devastated Tashkent. The city, now the capital of independent Uzbekistan, is by far the largest urban center in Central Asia; as of 2009, it had a population of 2.5 million.[1] The post-earthquake reconstruction campaign of the late Soviet era sparked massive development, population increases, and continued urban growth, with entire new housing districts and satellite cities growing up on the outskirts and alongside Tashkent. In the pressing need to reconstruct destroyed areas, workers from across the Soviet Union had descended on Tashkent—some by direction and others with an eye toward the economic opportunities that the reconstruction project would provide. The city itself expanded by annexing and developing nearby agricultural regions, once again transforming rural residents into Soviet Uzbek urbanites. Just as the wartime stresses helped transform Tashkent into an industrial center, the disaster of 1966 pushed the Uzbek capital farther and faster into the future. It became an increasingly multiethnic, geographically larger, and a much more "modern" city that resembled the architectural ideals of the Soviet Union of the 1960s and 1970s.

After independence, post-Soviet Tashkent began an urban renewal campaign of its own by building tall steel-and-glass structures in the center of the city, replacing dilapidated Soviet buses with Mercedes-Benz versions, and renovating the airport to welcome international visitors, who now arrive on Uzbekistan Airways' new Boeing airplanes. In the best Potemkin village tradition, some Soviet-era buildings have been renovated while others were simply enclosed in an outer layer of reflective glass with little change to their interiors. These "new" structures—whether art museum, government administrative complex, old Soviet hotel, housing compound, or department store—suddenly resembled modern suburban office parks rather than what is typically thought of as Central Asia or even Soviet architecture. A monument to Amir Timur (Tamerlane), disgraced as a despot under Soviet rule, was erected at the center of the former Revolution Square, usurping the spot once occupied by General Kaufman and later Joseph Stalin, to symbolically pronounce that Central Asians have returned to power. Many Soviet-era monuments to socialism have been replaced by symbols of Uzbek nationalism, but Uzbekistan is not only reaching back into the region's distant past in search of its identity. It is also selectively incorporating parts of its recent history, particularly the story of rapid modernization and urbanization, into the new symbolism that it is creating for itself.

Red (Lenin) Square is now called Independence Square and still contains the giant pedestal where the statue of the first Soviet leader once stood, but Lenin was supplanted by a large metal globe with a raised outline of Uzbekistan carved into its center, as if to proclaim that independent Uzbekistan is at the heart of the world, or at least the heart of Central Asia. Tashkent continues to hold international conferences, film festivals, and sporting events, including the annual Tashkent Tennis Open. In an effort to attract foreign investment, the Uzbek government spruced up downtown Tashkent before hosting the 2003 annual meeting of the European Bank for Reconstruction and Development.[2] To mark Uzbekistan's emergence as a regional power after more than a century of Russian and Soviet domination, post-Soviet government officials are attempting to show the best face of the Uzbek state to its citizens and the international community through the urban space of Tashkent.

For better or worse, the Uzbek capital clearly remains a city of political imagery, as it has been since Russian forces first marched into the region in the nineteenth century. Nonetheless, new post-Soviet Tashkent once again focuses on the "outer look" of the city, with districts near the government center, international hotels, and foreign embassies undergoing renovation, while distant suburban areas—far from any point of interest—remain in various states of decay. To mark the tenth anniversary of Uzbek independence, in 2001, the city inaugurated its new metro line, making Tashkent one of the first Central Asian urban centers in the post-Soviet era to rapidly expand its public transportation system. However, workers must have cut corners in their effort to finish the project on time because rainwater started to cascade through the ceiling of the brand new Ming O'rik metro stop, a major transfer station in the center of the city, only a few short weeks after its grand opening. These new "cracks" in Tashkent's public face symbolize the continued duality of the city. Like its predecessors, post-Soviet Tashkent is both an idealized urban space with modern multistory buildings, sleek European cars, and lush parkland as well as a place with dilapidated housing and open *aryks* or drainage canals that become blocked with leaves and garbage. The bifurcated nature of Tashkent, which Soviet planners and administrators tried to eliminate in the twentieth century, lingers, although the signposts and borders of this duality have changed. Tall administrative buildings, fancy restaurants, and new hotels are going up in the center of the city, but average Tashkenters still experience hardship in their daily lives.

Tashkent's modern history and its development into the major city in Central Asia began in 1865. Russian imperial planners attempted to build a modern urban space in Tashkent to mark it as being different from and superior to the existing Central Asian settlement across the Ankhor Canal. The new city was a rationally planned urban environment with important symbols of European-style "modernity," namely gardens, churches, banks, hospitals, schools, and mechanized transportation. These efforts to fashion an orderly and contemporary town were aimed at demonstrating that the tsarist regime could promote development in a harsh desert environment and assist Central Asia in advancing toward the modern world. In the imperial period, Tashkent served as a marker of the power of the tsarist regime, and it stepped onto the international stage as an equal to other European states during the age of imperial expansion. However, the tsarist regime was content to build a Russian settlement in the city and leave the "native" quarter as it was, believing that indigenous residents would eventually see the "superiority" of the Russian and European world and gradually move closer to it.

The subsequent Soviet regime went one step further because its official ideology mandated that nothing be left to chance. Soviet officials worked to jump-start the transformation of Central Asians into "modern Soviet citizens" as a way to push all peoples of the Soviet Union along the teleological course of Marxist-Leninist history that would end with communism. They changed the symbols of twentieth-century progress, with factories, "red teahouses," and sports arenas replacing mosques, madrasas, and banks. Socialist planners brought in important images of modernity—new technology and heavy industry—and used "Soviet" Tashkent in their campaigns for international influence. Socialist Uzbekistan was supposed to prove that the Soviet Union was a dynamic state that could transform a barren desert "wasteland" into a "flowering garden" of Soviet life. A renovated capital allegedly brought both equality and development to the outskirts of the former Russian Empire and symbolically transformed the imperial tsarist regime into a centralized and unified Soviet state. However, creating a new Soviet city in the region not only concerned creating new physical spaces but entailed forging an entirely new socialist civilization by abolishing private trade, nationalizing all property, attacking Islam, and overtly attempting to transform local cultures, of which Uzbek culture was just one of many. The Soviet polity could not and would not settle for the "benign neglect" of Central Asia of which it accused the tsarist regime, just as it would not allow the Russian countryside to remain as it was.

In Uzbekistan, Communist Party officials provided incentives to persuade Uzbeks to join "modern" life, such as Western-style educational institutions, cultural facilities, health-care establishments, and even new housing units. They constructed new industries to entice Central Asians to enter into productive labor. At times, they used more violent and intrusive methods, such as the forced unveiling of women, militant antireligious coercion, political terror, the monitoring and denouncing of marriage and childrearing traditions, and the tearing down of traditional mud-brick homes of Uzbek residents to help create the new Soviet Uzbek citizenry. State officials sought both to create new urban spaces across the Soviet Union and to sculpt the culture that existed within them. In doing so, they actively sought to transform indigenous traditions and make them Soviet. Nonetheless, Soviet officials launched this massive urbanization program in Tashkent at the same time that they promoted collectivization of agriculture and conducted massive industrialization campaigns. These three movements—collectivization, industrialization, and urbanization—were not distinct trends but all part of a titanic state-building process that left no corner of the Soviet Union untouched.

In conducting such a large-scale modernization project, planners ran the risk of antagonizing large sections of the population in Uzbekistan and elsewhere. Soviet officials—armed with ideology—believed the changes that

Sovietization brought would intrinsically improve daily life for the city's residents. However, they frequently failed to understand that their efforts to create modern cities and new urban cultures led to tremendous social displacement, which ultimately complicated their own socialist urbanization projects. This social dislocation was particularly problematic in the non-Slavic regions of the country, where Soviet rule was viewed as both coercive and foreign. Nonetheless, even as state officials encountered roadblocks in their efforts to change the Soviet landscape and its inhabitants, they were not deterred from this massive undertaking. The Soviet system was based on an ideology of total mobilization and was prepared to destroy all that stood in its way, particularly under Stalin, whether the roadblocks were in Russia, Armenia, or Uzbekistan. All peoples and all corners of the Soviet Union had to pass through this socialist transformation process, and Soviet officials were willing to go to extreme lengths to bring this new society into being in Central Asia.[3] The fact that they were adapting a European-inspired ideology to a very different cultural landscape made their task that much more challenging in Uzbekistan and its neighboring republics than it was in Russia or Ukraine, a notion that many understood but few dared to voice publicly.

Creating Soviet Tashkent also was a campaign to forge a city that was worthy of socialism and could represent the Soviet system positively in the foreign policy arena. In many ways, Soviet officials argued that they were reacting to the colonial model that had kept "backward" peoples under oppression, in poverty, and with hunger. In public declarations against colonialism or cold war–era "European/American imperialism," Soviet officials argued that Western powers oppressed indigenous peoples, robbed them of their riches, and left them suffering in "backwardness." For its part, the Soviet state sought to remedy the previous "neglect" of the colonized world through a rapid transformation and modernization project that aimed to include "less developed" peoples in "building socialism." However, Soviet officials did not simply want Russian communists to transform Central Asian society; they wanted Central Asians to do it themselves under the guidance of the Soviet state. Much public effort was made to show that Party officials did not merely impose socialism from above or from outside the region. Instead, as Soviet propaganda declared, the Communist Party and the Russian people, the leading nationality in Soviet society, showed Central Asians the path to prosperity and allowed Central Asians to create their own version of Soviet society, albeit within strictly delineated parameters. This new way of life was meant to showcase the "achievement" of local residents under socialism and the "care" that the state provided to all peoples of the Soviet Union, even those who officially were "less advanced" than its core Russian constituency. By assisting indigenous people in "jumping ahead" to the next stage in the Marxist-Leninist course of history, the Soviet regime strove to show it was providing equality to all groups within its borders. Through Sovietization, Tashkent was to become Moscow's shining star in Asia and the primary "ambassador" of socialism to the people of the East.

Exercising the architectural ideals of the early decades of socialist power, planners initially intended to build a completely modern and functional city, with constructivist buildings, housing communes, and the sleek Government House as the most prominent examples of this trend intended to showcase the revolutionary vision of the Soviet Union in its Central Asian possessions. However, with the terror and after the "successful" completion of the socialist reconstruction of Moscow, planning dictates changed, as they did numerous times throughout the Soviet era. The urban renewal process became much more centralized, reflecting broader movements in Soviet governance, with a Moscow-based organization developing the proposal to transform the ethnically divided Uzbek capital into a "unified" city of monumental public structures. This new Tashkent was to combine classical architectural forms with decorative designs that planners deemed to be "Uzbek." The curved streets of the Old City and the traditional adobe-brick homes became prime candidates for destruction, while Moscow and the rationally arranged pre-revolutionary Russian section of Tashkent served as models for the new Soviet city in Asia. However, population increases, supply problems, and war kept these proposals on the architectural drawing board. World War II forced Tashkent officials to deal with unexpected urban and industrial growth, causing them to once again look toward simple designs, often integrating cost-effective Central Asian construction techniques that they had so recently criticized because Soviet-style building materials and skilled construction workers could no longer be imported from Russia in a time of such upheaval and uncertainty for the regime. The war also led to massive population increases in Central Asia and created in Uzbekistan the new industrial base that socialism had demanded. As the war devastated the European parts of the Soviet Union, it brought unprecedented opportunity and ethnic diversification to Tashkent, both of which helped to solidify the ties between the periphery and the center.

After the war, Tashkent city planners once again returned to the practice of designing monumental public buildings that reflected both the Soviet Union's new status as a victorious world power and Uzbekistan's place as a "postcolonial and liberated" state within the socialist world. Architects focused their energies on a few grand structures—the unfinished administrative center, the Navoi Theater, the Stalin Monument, and the Kuranty clock tower—but did not address the pressing needs of Tashkent residents, thus limiting the construction of housing, hospitals, and schools. With the death of Stalin, planners reverted to modernist and functional city structures, with mass prefabricated housing being an important marker of this change. These new designs, geared for rapid industrial construction, were supposed to quell residents' dissatisfaction over cramped communal apartments, squalid city streets, and collapsing worker barracks. Architects and Tashkent officials, like their counterparts in other Soviet cities, eventually recognized the imperative of addressing the needs of city residents in their designs.

Even so, Party officials clearly had enormous difficulty in bringing their vision of an ideal urban space to Central Asia. The utopian ideology of the revolution, fueled by official declarations of the achievements of socialism, created high expectations among the population. As difficulties occurred and the standard of living of Soviet workers failed to improve, the state identified enemies abroad and treacherous elements within the polity itself as the causes of the regime's problems. Nonetheless, the broader Soviet polity continually reminded the population of the uniqueness of the Soviet project and of the poverty and oppression of workers in Europe, North America, and the colonial world. Leading figures in the Soviet government informed citizens that life was improving by offering bright propaganda campaigns that depicted beautiful cities, large-scale factories, abundant supplies of food, healthy and strong children, and individual apartment units. When local residents complained more loudly that life had not gotten any better, agitators spoke more forcefully of the wonderful future of communism and reminded inhabitants of the oppression and backwardness that they reportedly endured before being liberated by socialism. The vast transformation of the city and the culture that it contained certainly could not occur overnight, but Soviet propaganda created the impression that it would.[4]

Nevertheless, the difference between Soviet claims and the reality of life had enormous political ramifications. During the war, Tashkenters shed their blood for the Soviet state in distant parts of Russia, Ukraine, Poland, and Germany. Many residents of Uzbekistan watched as their family members died of starvation, disease, or physical exhaustion, while others knew they had lost loved ones on the front but did not even have the comfort of knowing when, where, or how they died. Tashkent's urban infrastructure and social safety net broke down under the strain of the more than 2 million refugees and evacuees who passed through the Uzbek capital. When the Nazi-Soviet conflict was over, Tashkenters wanted material improvements in their lives and began to voice a sense of entitlement for their past sacrifices. But the state, with its stress on heavy industry and the need to change the physical landscape of the Soviet Union, still could not meet their material needs. During the political liberalization of society after the death of Stalin, the anger and complaints of Soviet citizens grew more vocal, and Tashkent's Uzbek residents were no exception. The Central Asian population clearly had learned how to interact with the bureaucratic Soviet system and help make it work to their advantage—a phenomenon that occurred across the socialist world. Uzbeks were finally gaining a stake in the system and using whatever power they possessed—including their status as a national minority and the fact that Soviet officials needed a successful Uzbek SSR to propagate socialism abroad—to improve their physical lot and help merge local traditions with Soviet ways of life.

Indigenous Central Asians gradually began to play a much greater role in Soviet society and in building socialism in Tashkent and elsewhere in the region. The Ministry of Foreign Affairs continued to increase the representation of Central Asian diplomats at Soviet missions abroad and in technical assistance projects to newly independent states in Asia, the Middle East, and Africa.[5] Prominent Uzbek figures also gained larger responsibility for refashioning Soviet society in Central Asia, while more and more ordinary Uzbeks became increasingly active in Soviet institutions with the passage of time. World War II opened a new world for many indigenous Central Asians who went off to war either on the front or in factories and were transformed by wartime military or industrial service to become supporters of the Soviet project. When the brutal "Sovietization" efforts of the Stalin era ended, many Uzbek veterans and their children entered the world of higher education in much greater numbers than ever before.[6] As James Critchlow has noted, Uzbek Party members gradually took control over the Communist Party apparatus in the mid-twentieth century. In the 1950s, three-quarters of Party secretaries and department chairpersons in the Uzbek Central Committee were Russian or ethnically European residents of Uzbekistan. However, this figure had reversed itself by 1966, when three-quarters of these top jobs went to ethnically Uzbek Party members, and the overall percentage of officials of Russian/European background in the Uzbek Central Committee decreased from 31 percent to 20 percent between 1958 and 1966.[7] Uzbeks were becoming more "Soviet" in their education and professional levels, and, consequently, the Soviet governing apparatus in the region became more "Uzbek."[8] Time, not coercion, turned out to be one of the most effective tools for Sovietization in Central Asia.

Many of these new leaders—whether they were government or Party officials, factory workers, or Soviet Uzbek intellectuals—were members of the second generation of Central Asians to grow up under Soviet power. Prominent architects, such as Tulkinoi Kadyrova, represented the new Soviet Uzbek woman of the 1960s and 1970s. She designed housing complexes for all of Uzbekistan and became a prominent theorist and historian of Soviet Central Asian urban planning. Aleksandr Kuznetsov, Stepan Polupanov, and other Soviet planners from Russia or Ukraine might have started Tashkent along the path to becoming a Soviet city in the 1930s, but it was Uzbeks themselves who crafted the capital and the entire republic into what it became, particularly as the city grew into the fourth-largest urban center of the Soviet Union. Furthermore, it was Central Asians who helped replicate the "Tashkent model" across Uzbekistan in towns like Navoi, Karshi, and Urgench, all of which grew tremendously in the 1970s and 1980s. Soviet officials from Moscow set the parameters for Uzbekistan and its new Soviet Uzbek culture, but the people of the region over time filled in the content.

The creation of socialist cities was part of the Soviet Union's state- and society-building process. In crafting Soviet Tashkent, political leaders, urban planners, and local officials fashioned images of a Soviet identity—or identities—in the region. With minor variations, Soviet Central Asians were to be full citizens of the Soviet Union and, as such, have the same rights *and* the same responsibilities to the state. They were to act and think according to idealized, secular, and "modern" norms. They were to live in apartments similar to those of their Russian counterparts, enjoy drama performances and operas in the city's new theaters, and participate in productive labor, just like their fellow citizens across the Soviet Union. Tashkenters were to be industrial factory workers, "scientific" researchers, productive agronomists, talented actors, prolific writers, or dedicated medical professionals. In turn, they were to appreciate what the Soviet Union had given them, namely, prosperity and the right to "modernize" their national culture.

In this manner, every major ethnic group of the Soviet Union also had its own geographic area—a national republic or autonomous region—and a modern urban space at the center of its ethnic "homeland." The socialist reconstruction of these regional cities was intended to "improve" them for the greater good of local residents, no matter whether the city was located in Russia, an ethno-national region of the Soviet Union, or, eventually, an independent state in the postcolonial world. Thus, creating a new Soviet Tashkent was not a singular project but part of a large-scale and at times bloody effort to refashion Soviet and non-Soviet citizens into "modern" men and women, no matter where they lived. Tashkent's reconstruction replicated the renovation of Moscow, Kiev, Tbilisi, Baku, Sevastopol, and countless other cities and towns. In this sense, the renovation of Tashkent was not simply the case of a European power building a colonial city in one of its distant possessions. With Soviet Uzbekistan, officials in Moscow spoke of the region as an intrinsic part of the Soviet Union. It was the center of life in Soviet Asia and a city that could be reached by plane in a few short hours and thus could not be "ignored" because of its distance from Moscow, poor communications, or unreliable transportation to the region, as had been the case in the past. The reconstruction of Soviet cities installed a modern socialist infrastructure that would allow cities on the "outskirts" of the nineteenth-century Russian empire to become essential parts of the twentieth-century Soviet state. Likewise, Tashkent residents, formerly imperial subjects of a distant Russian tsar, were transformed into prominent and public members of the Soviet brotherhood of peoples.

While Tashkent's desert location complicated the realization of the Soviet project in the city and created slight variations in the vision of what New Soviet persons wore or ate, the Sovietization of Tashkent was an essential part of an often brutal attempt to transform human nature, one city and one person at a time. Although the twentieth-century authoritarian state that set about creating Soviet Tashkent and governing the city replicated many of the methodologies of imperial control, the Sovietization of Tashkent in fact was as much a lesson in state building as it was a story of empire construction. The Soviet Union was unlike many traditional European empires of the time in that it lacked strict geographic distinctions between the metropole and the periphery. There were no specific boundaries, such as an ocean or large mountain range, to separate the two in the way that so many global empires, such as the British, French, Portuguese, and even American empires had definitive borders. The rapid ethnic diversification of Central Asia in the twentieth century, particularly during the war years, when mass migration to Tashkent was caused by outside forces and not Soviet ideology, further broke down imperial divisions. As a consequence, the psychological distinction of empire that easily separates the outskirts from the center also was largely absent in the Soviet context

Furthermore, there was no legal difference between residents in Uzbekistan and those in Russia proper, with all citizens of the Soviet Union living under the same Soviet constitution, subject to the same laws, falling afoul of similar Party mandates, and coping with the same bureaucratic system. With modern twentieth-century innovations in transportation, newspaper and book publishing, and radio and television transmission, these legal, geographic, and mental distinctions were further distorted as the state was able to tie its outlying regions and their inhabitants much more closely together than ever before, even as it simultaneously sought to create regional and ethnic variations within a new larger Soviet identity across the country. Despite cultural differences from the Finnish to the Afghan border, all Soviet citizens experienced similar deprivation, coped with state-sponsored attacks on traditional belief systems, developed parallel strategies to survive and adapt to the new political realities, and dealt with the same inefficient and often corrupt officials. The Soviet Union at times might have outwardly appeared to be a typical twentieth-century empire, particularly in its paternalistic attitudes toward the Central Asian or Caucasus republics and in its pressing need to adapt the totalizing ideology that originated in Europe to the Soviet Union's non-European societies. However, the Soviet experience in Central Asia in many ways blurs our understanding of colonialism in that the Soviet Union was a polity that was somewhere between an empire and an ultra-centralizing, ultra-modernizing, and extremely powerful ideology-based state.

In an interesting twist, Soviet officials in fact used a similar approach for interacting with, ruling, and exploiting the Russian peasant and countryside as they did Central Asians and Central Asia. The common ideology of total revolution, the agenda of complete physical transformation, and the desire to pull as many resources out of the land and its inhabitants as possible colored Soviet economic policies, social programs, and methods of governance across the country. Therefore, the history of Tashkent in the twentieth century in many ways is not unique but has proved to be a microcosm of the multiethnic Soviet project. Like the union as a whole, the city was both industrial and agricultural. It was ethnic and Slavic as well as being "modern" and "backward." Furthermore, Tashkent was often viewed in Moscow as a "problematic" Soviet city, but, as archives show, no Soviet city or Soviet institution lived up to the high standards and socialist ideals that propagandists, urban planners, and ideologists had created. As a result, the experience of Tashkent under Soviet rule perhaps was more representative of the difficulties in bringing cultural, economic, and social change to such a vast country and diverse population compared to what occurred in Moscow, Magnitogorsk, Novosibirsk, Leningrad, or the rural Slavic landscape.[9] Nevertheless, it was all part and parcel of this large Soviet state-building endeavor.

As John Scott has shown, high-modernist cities were "megaprojects" that made no compromises or concessions to previously existing urban spaces or to local traditions.[10] Cities like Tashkent were envisioned as symbols of the strength of the Soviet polity and were designed for the ease of planning and construction. The needs and desires of the residents of the Uzbek capital were left out of this idealized vision of a socialist urban environment because people were seen as malleable and able to fit into the new urban space. However, building wide avenues, large demonstration squares, Soviet shopping arcades, and massive blocks of prefabricated housing was clearly easier than preserving the Old City's curving roads and shaded pathways or heeding the wishes of inhabitants. Soviet industry created the bricks, mortar, steel, and glass that construction workers needed to refashion the Uzbek capital. Modern technological methods were used in Tashkent to build the outer shell of a city, but, in the end, they could not create an energetic urban community. Soviet demonstration sites certainly were impressive during military parades to mark Victory Day, May Day, or the anniversary of the revolution, but on most occasions, these Soviet public spaces were just large concrete-covered squares that were surrounded by drab administrative buildings.

The lifeblood and vitality of the city came from its neighborhoods—originally the *mahallas* and the traditional Central Asian bazaars, but eventually the shantytowns and single-family housing developments sprouted on the outskirts of the city during the Soviet era, often in response to the disorganized and inefficient manner in which planners went about their urban renewal programs. In building a model city in Uzbekistan, the state frequently destroyed what had made Tashkent both unique and vibrant. The new content of the Soviet space could never quite replace what had been lost, as Tashkent became more modern, nondescript, and standard in appearance. These rationally planned cities of the Soviet Union, particularly the Uzbek capital, are early symbols of the uniformity of twentieth-century globalization. Similarly designed cities across the globe were based on common theories of twentieth-century rationally planned urbanization, and they too—whether Brasilia in Brazil, Chandigarh in India, or even the low-income districts of major American urban areas—largely failed to live up to their promises. The current rapid pace of transformation in such places as Beijing, Shanghai, São Paulo, or Kuala Lumpur is once again dislocating people from their homes and traditional lifestyles all in the name of building modern urban symbols of rising twenty-first century powers.[11] All too often across the globe, urbanites who have little say in their political system are uprooted so that their city officials and planners can create idealized images of the city that they—not the residents—want for the future. The cycle of the Tashkent model continues today in diverse parts of the world.

Sadly enough, much of this socialist transformation in Tashkent also was done in the name of improving the ability of the state to monitor and influence the Soviet Uzbek population. The apartment building was envisioned as a vital tool to control city residents. In constructing these new urban areas, state officials never quite acknowledged that the *mahalla* could also have served this function extremely effectively. In most cases, the structure of the *mahalla* already maintained order and stability in individual neighborhoods. The *mahalla* also curbed inappropriate or unsanctioned activities within the community. Soviet officials never quite trusted this indigenous cultural institution, however, although security and Party officials certainly infiltrated the *mahallas*. In demolishing the mud-brick homes of Central Asians to craft a more modern-looking city, the state tried to eliminate this Uzbek organization of social control instead of co-opting it and making it an integral part of the Soviet project.[12] Nonetheless, while Tashkent certainly got taller, with new apartment buildings going up throughout the city, the *mahalla* concept persisted, likely due to the inefficient ways in which Soviet urban planning was conducted and the fact that the Soviet system in the 1960s and beyond grew more accommodating to local customs and desires.

To solidify Tashkent's place as the leading city of Asia, planners decided to speed up construction of Soviet apartment buildings in Tashkent in the mid-1960s. This progress, too, was part of the effort to banish the traditional Central Asian neighborhood from the Tashkent landscape. That neighborhood, with its serpentine streets, internal courtyards, and local customs, continued to prove much more resilient than many urban planners had initially envisioned. City officials hoped that the mass construction of sleek apartment buildings would finally entice Central Asians to become modern urban apartment dwellers and join Soviet society. However, the manner in which these complexes were built exacerbated the city's problems. Officials proposed that most of these apartment buildings be in the center of Tashkent, usually in the old Uzbek quarter east of the Ankhor Canal, the pre-Soviet boundary between the Central Asian and Russian sections of the city. Under this proposal, however, it was Uzbeks, the long-standing residents of the city, and not the Russians, the more recent arrivals, who had to be displaced from their homes. The need for quick and inexpensive construction led some construction managers to cut corners, and it also mandated the use of reinforced steel and concrete. While this building method was common throughout the Soviet Union and allowed for fast construction, these materials were not necessarily suitable in Tashkent. Not only did most of it need to be trucked in from other parts of the Soviet Union but buildings made out of steel and concrete trapped the desert heat. The small Soviet apartment units also did not meet the needs of the large extended

Uzbek families that had to reside in them. Living conditions across the Soviet Union were less than ideal to say the least, but the new Soviet apartments of Tashkent created even more cramped and uncomfortable conditions, causing residents—including some of the European population—to long for more traditional housing.

Party documents and some published sources detail other problems that were simmering below the surface. Ethnic segregation was increasing in the city, not decreasing, as Russians residents moved into the prefabricated apartments in the city center while displaced Central Asians congregated in developments in the burgeoning suburbs on the outskirts of the city. This segregation developed not only because local Uzbeks were reluctant to move into ethnically mixed apartment buildings but equally because apartments in these new buildings were distributed first to industrial workers, the majority of whom were still Slavic, and not to unskilled laborers, the majority of whom were largely Uzbek. Urban centers might be transformed, but the method of distributing housing in these areas resulted in simply moving Uzbek families to neighborhoods and shantytowns on the outskirts of the city, where traditional community structures were often reestablished. This failure to distribute new factory housing to Central Asian residents undermined one of the overall goals of urban reconstruction, namely, the creation of a unified multinational population, and it disturbed the city's purported ethnic harmony.

Furthermore, the problems of Sovietizing Central Asia often troubled Party officials in both Moscow and Uzbekistan. By the 1960s, Tashkent urban planners and political leaders were complaining that they never had the "blank slate" upon which architects elsewhere built new Soviet cities from scratch. Soviet city planners made numerous attempts to create an "ideal" city for Central Asia that was both socialist and Uzbek. However, neither they nor the residents who had to live in Tashkent liked the results. Sometimes too many Islamic design features were incorporated into Soviet buildings, such as tall towers that supposedly resembled minarets or arched entryways that recalled mosques or madrasas. Some structures appeared so "modern" or "European" that they seemed out of place in the Central Asian desert. Other times, architects promised too much and created an ideal city on paper but could not deliver actual improvements on the ground, leaving local residents dissatisfied with their low standard of living. Still, it was not just the Uzbeks who were troubled by these urban renewal projects. The Russians of Tashkent complained of the "Sovietization" of the city as much as Uzbek residents did, although often for different reasons. Despite the fact that Soviet urban spaces were based on European/Russian norms, they were not universally endorsed by all Soviet citizens, Russians included.[13]

However, by the time the earthquake damaged the city in 1966, many more Uzbeks were working in city planning organizations, and thus more Uzbek-Soviet officials were able to participate in the rapid rebuilding of Tashkent. These local Soviet planners finally had the "blank slate" they had always wanted. After evaluating the devastation caused by the natural disaster, city workers removed the rubble in the worst-hit regions and then went on to tear down some Uzbek neighborhoods and structures that were not severely damaged but were standing in the way of the architects' new vision for the city. The lack of private property in the Soviet Union and the emergency situation after the earthquake facilitated the ability "to start from scratch" and fashion a new symbol of Soviet modernity in Asia. Planners reorganized the city's traffic flow, widened streets, changed the direction of main avenues, built a metro system, expanded parkland, and constructed buildings that were taller than what came before. The Soviet press would later highlight these achievements in housing and urban transportation. The city's metro system, built to mark the sixtieth anniversary of the revolution, was seen as an important achievement. Newspapers noted that it was one of the first such high-tech metro systems in the East, underscoring the fact that Western-oriented Turkey still lacked such a modern and efficient urban transportation infrastructure in its largest city, Istanbul. More importantly, however, the initial sixteen-kilometer metro line pushed commuters off the street and into cool underground tunnels, thereby allowing the Soviet regime to address one of its long-term goals of providing city residents with relief from the brutal Central Asian heat.[14] This relief did not come about by attempting to change the regional "micro-climate" by undertaking water diversion projects or creating lakes in the city center, as was done in the 1930s. Instead, it was a practical application of Soviet technology and a concrete effort to improve the quality of life for average city residents who commuted every day from the Chilanzar housing region to their jobs in the city center.

The Soviet government showed its care for the people of Tashkent in a variety of other ways as well. On his visit to the city after the earthquake, Brezhnev provided psychological comfort to city residents and declared that Tashkent would be reborn "in a new form, one that gives the architectural tone of a massive city of the future."[15] The Communist Party and the government responded quickly and decisively to help the residents of the city and to realize Brezhnev's vision of a new socialist metropolis in

Central Asia. On June 14, 1966, the Central Committee of the Communist Party of the Soviet Union and the Council of Ministers issued a joint proclamation on "the provision of assistance to the Uzbek SSR in liquidating the consequences of the earthquake in Tashkent."[16] New city plans were drawn up—at first to simply clean up after the disaster and then to build for the future. By the 1970s, Tashkent urban designers were no longer planning for the city itself but had expanded the scope of their work to encompass the entire Tashkent region. Little expense was spared on the new housing, schools, hospitals, and roads that were built. Money, building supplies, and construction workers were quickly diverted from other republics to the Uzbek capital. Some of the most prominent Soviet architectural and urban planning experts and institutions were back in Tashkent to design and construct new micro-districts to house homeless city residents. Most of these projects were based on Soviet designs utilizing prefabricated materials that could be assembled quickly, allegedly allowing the city to reconstruct about two-thirds of the destroyed living space by 1968 and fully replace it by 1970.[17] This new housing might not have been beautiful and often lacked adequate balcony space and window shades or shutters, but the rapid completion of these buildings showed that the entire Soviet Union had responded to Tashkent in its time of need. Schools, hospitals, and shopping centers, also built according to existing designs, soon appeared on the scene, allowing life to return more or less to normal within a few short years. The Soviet regime's initial priority was on the structures that city residents needed in the immediate term, and it delayed construction of monuments and public showcase areas, a significant change from the past.

This success in quickly feeding, housing, educating, and finding health care for the city residents in the late 1960s and early 1970s was truly remarkable for a system that traditionally had proven so ineffective and inefficient. The concern shown to the residents of Tashkent and the efforts to rebuild the city likely instilled a sense of loyalty to and pride in the Soviet system. The legacy of the Tashkent earthquake and the reconstruction efforts has since become a well-established part of the city's history. In Soviet times, accounts of the earthquake and the government's response were carefully managed to show the strength and unity of the Soviet people, while also underscoring the resilience of Tashkent as a city reborn. Soviet technology might not have been able to save Tashkent and its people from the destructive power of the 1966 earthquake, but the residents of the city proved they could overcome the disaster and continue their march toward the future. To mark the tenth anniversary of the earthquake, Tashkent opened the Museum of the Friendship of the Peoples, which featured an exhibit highlighting the assistance each Soviet republic gave to Tashkent in the rebuilding effort. Each republic helped to reconstruct particular buildings, many of which were decorated in the "national" styles of the visiting construction workers, so that some buildings had Ukrainian, Belorussian, or Kazakh motifs on the outside. A massive monument of a strong Uzbek man shielding a mother and child was erected near the new museum to symbolize the "perseverance and bravery of the Uzbek people," who had met the danger and challenge of the earthquake.[18] In commemorating the earthquake, Tashkent celebrated both its Soviet multiethnic flavor as well as the heroism of the Uzbek people themselves.

Over time, Uzbek residents of the city gradually moved into newly built housing complexes. Many did so because few other options were available to Tashkenters left homeless by the earthquake, including Uzbek families, whose high birthrates and extended family units meant that more housing space was needed for the additional family members.[19] Toward the end of the Soviet era, apartment building construction in Tashkent soared to new heights, with some structures standing sixteen to twenty stories high in a region where the threat of an earthquake remains on the minds of many city residents. Soviet and post-Soviet leaders continued, however, to reassure the population of the strength of these building designs. Furthermore, large Uzbek families moved into these new Soviet-built sections of Tashkent, although the traditional Uzbek *mahalla*s remain very segregated, with few non–Central Asian residents. Nonetheless, as their city was thoroughly reconstructed along urban planning models of the 1970s and 1980s, more and more Uzbek residents began to live like "normal" Soviet citizens—in apartment units next door to Russian neighbors. The "New City," the traditionally Slavic area of Tashkent, was no longer just a European enclave.

Rebuilding the city center was also a priority. A monument to Karl Marx on the site where Stalin's statue once stood was an easy early addition to Revolution Square in 1968.[20] The street layout of the city around this square was preserved, so that all major Tashkent roads yet again led to a major figure in the history of socialism. The entire area was shaded with trees to help "unify" it with the administrative center being reconstructed on nearby Lenin Square, where a new thirty-meter statue of the first Soviet leader dominated the square, as did the new Tashkent branch of the Central Museum of Lenin. On the southern side of the administrative complex was a new seven-story Uzbek Council of Ministers building, while a reflecting pool with fountains finished off the area. Later, a new skyscraper was added to the complex; it featured twenty floors of office space and a public movie theater. These new administrative buildings of Tashkent were decorated with ceramic panels and sunshades to deflect the light and heat and to provide an "Uzbek" character to the structures.[21] Planners also made special efforts to strengthen new buildings, particularly in these taller structures on the square, to resist seismic activity and protect the employees inside.

The entire square was not brand new, however. The Navoi Library, the premier library of Uzbekistan that was originally built in 1870, survived the earthquake and stands in the square's far corner, its collection of Soviet books and newspapers as well as Central Asian manuscripts still intact. In this ultra-modern Soviet parade ground, urban designers were careful to create a connection between contemporary structures and the historic library building, a symbol of the region's "enlightened" past. Finally, the body of an unknown solider who died in the battle of Moscow was transported from the Soviet capital to Uzbekistan to mark the thirtieth anniversary of the end of World War II. He was reburied in the square on May 7, 1975, at Tashkent's new Tomb of the Unknown Soldier, which has Uzbek- and Russian-language inscriptions declaring "his service to be immortal." Uzbek junipers and Russian spruce trees were planted to "stand guard" at the tomb, while an eternal flame was transported from the Kremlin to sanctify the monument and tie it directly to the central Soviet mythology of World War II.[22] Although they added the supposedly traditional Uzbek water fountains, decorative tiles, and junipers, the imagery of Tashkent's Lenin Square in the 1970s was unabashedly Soviet.

The 1980s saw continued expansion of housing areas, as well as more reconstruction in the traditionally Central Asian parts of the town. The newly designed Chorsu bazaar building opened in the heart of the Oktiabr district of the Old City, as did other, more Soviet-style shopping centers and apartment buildings.[23] However, one of the largest additions to the Tashkent landscape in this decade was the Friendship of the Peoples complex, which included a massive public square, metro station, the largest concert hall in the city, and a monument to the Shamakhmudovs, the Uzbek family that adopted fifteen orphans from war-torn parts of the Soviet Union during World War II. The concert hall, called the Friendship of the Peoples Palace, was built of granite, white-gray marble, and gold-tinted glass windows, while outdoor chandeliers were placed along the entire periphery to illuminate the building from afar. Decorative latticework—in geometric designs to represent the "national" style of the Uzbek SSR—was added to the structure to shield it from the sun and heat. Once again, urban planners in the late Soviet era made an effort to consider the climatic conditions and physical needs of city residents. On the inside of the building, marble and ceramic tiles adorned the walls of the public spaces, while Uzbek stucco and wood carvings were incorporated to give a Central Asian character to the building, recalling a style that dated back to Shchusev's Navoi Theater in the 1940s. The main hall of the Tashkent Friendship of the Peoples Palace could seat forty-one hundred spectators in dark red velour seats with similarly colored carpeting—an interior reminiscent of countless concert halls and theaters across the Soviet Union—for the concerts, films, and political meetings that were held there.[24] Monumental architecture still was clearly at the forefront of Tashkent city planning in the last decade of Soviet power.

The Friendship of the Peoples Square, with its Shamakhmudov "Friendship" monument and ten-thousand-square-meter fountain area with streaming water jets and multicolored lights, is a short distance from both the Old City and Komsomol Park, the massive urban recreation area built in 1939. This entire complex served to unite the indigenous Uzbek past, as seen in the former native quarter, the Uzbek-Soviet past, featuring the Stalin-era park and war monument, and the Uzbek-Soviet future, with its sleekly designed concert hall. The Friendship of the Peoples Square was to be a new unifying center of Tashkent—bringing all ethnic groups of the city together in a complex that theoretically combined the best of the Soviet and Uzbek worlds. By the 1980s, Tashkent had returned to being a symbol of socialist strength, unity and adaptability in Asia. The Uzbek capital likewise reemerged as an international city of peace and friendship, playing host to an annual Asian, African, and Latin American film festival as well as international academic conferences focused on such topics as "Socialist Transformations" and "New Town Planning in Urban Development."[25] Many of these events were appropriately held in the new Friendship of the Peoples Palace. Similarly, numerous "sister city" relationships with municipalities in foreign countries developed at this time, including partnerships with Tunis, Tripoli, Skopje, and Seattle.[26]

Alongside these infrastructure changes, there were clear indications of cultural transformation and acceptance of Soviet norms—some positive and others negative. The veil largely disappeared in Uzbekistan over the Soviet period, particularly after World War II, when the overt violence against the *paranji* was lessened and replaced by the stories of Zulfiya and other Soviet Uzbek women who had risen to positions of power and prominence in Soviet Uzbek society. While the issue of arranged marriages, polygamy, and underage brides persisted in rural areas, the latter two phenomena had become much less common in Tashkent by the 1960s, or so archival documents suggest. Meanwhile, "Sovietization" transformed many "religious" traditions into Uzbek cultural traditions. An aversion to pork is common among both Europeanized and traditional Uzbeks. Some Uzbeks drink alcohol in large quantities, do not identify themselves closely with Islam, and fail to fast during Ramadan. Nevertheless, these same people often explain that eating swine was somehow "un-Uzbek." In many ways, the unwillingness to eat pork has become a signifier of national difference, not solely of religious affiliation. Similarly, circumcision is almost universally practiced among indigenous Central Asian males. But, as scholars have shown, this tradition is also as much of a cultural custom as it is a religious rite. No longer just an identifier of Muslim/Christian difference, the practice serves as marker of distinction between the Uzbek and Russian communities of the republic.[27] Soviet ideology proved incapable of destroying religion and many other local traditions, although it greatly weakened their influence and transformed, secularized, or even "nationalized" some of their meanings. The regime eventually acknowledged that it could accept and tolerate some local "peculiarities," just as locals gradually learned to live with the new socialist culture. This fusion of local traditions with Soviet norms—rather than the destruction of Central Asian culture outright—in many ways helped solidify Soviet mentalities in the region, buttress support for the Soviet regime, and create many of the images of the Uzbek nation that linger to this day.

Russians and Uzbeks also began to marry each other in greater numbers in the late twentieth century, although most of these ethnically mixed unions involved Russian women.[28] However, contrary to Soviet ethnographic claims, these mixed marriages did not necessarily promote Sovietization or the creation of a unified community in Tashkent. Studies on cultural change in Uzbekistan from the 1980s indicate that the Russian and Ukrainian wives in these families believed that their parents were more opposed to these mixed unions than their Central Asian in-laws were. Ronald Wixman notes that children in these Slavic/Uzbek families associated more with Central Asians, not Slavs, who instead rejected or mocked ethnically mixed children. In addition, the European wives of Uzbek men frequently stated that they chose to marry Central Asians because Uzbek men treated their spouses better than Slavic men did. They claimed that Central Asians neither drank excessively nor battered their wives, notions that would have been alien to Soviet ideologists of the 1930s to 1960s, who firmly believed that Central Asians lived backward and uncivilized lifestyles.[29] These studies demonstrate that interethnic marriages in Uzbekistan, a goal of the Soviet regime to bring about the unification of the multiethnic city, frequently led to the "Central Asianification" of these families, not to their Russification, as officials in Moscow had envisioned. As we have seen numerous times before, Sovietization often had remarkably unexpected outcomes.

The campaign to bring water to the parched desert also was deemed an important achievement of Soviet technology and socialist urbanization between the 1930s and 1980s. The area of land under agricultural cultivation increased during the Soviet era, enabling Uzbeks to produce more cotton or "white gold," the purported pride of the Uzbek nation. In fact, Soviet water diversion projects had so much success in "quenching the centuries-old thirst of the Uzbek people" that they disastrously altered the flow of the Amu Darya and Syr Darya rivers. Little water now makes it across Central Asia to the Aral Sea, with devastating environmental and public health consequences. However, Tashkent's green parks remain well watered, fountains flow continuously, city trucks wash down the asphalt streets, and gardens are irrigated with ample supplies of diverted water. The green parks and canals of Tashkent remain important symbols of achievement and have become part of the natural landscape of the city in the minds of many residents.

Soviet engineers tried to save the Aral Sea in the late 1970s and early 1980s with the Sibaral Canal, which was supposed to divert water from the Ob and Irtysh rivers in Siberia to Central Asia in order to "quench" the newly created "Soviet" thirst for water. Known as the "project of the century," this canal sought to reverse the natural flow of water, redirecting it away from the Arctic Ocean and sending it instead toward the Aral Sea. The canal proposal pitted Uzbek officials against their Russian colleagues in Siberia. However, to the dismay of many Soviet citizens in the Uzbek SSR, the plan was shelved in the Gorbachev era under enormous pressure from the "village prose writers," a group of Russian nationalists who saw this large-scale "Soviet" development project as dangerous to the survival of Russian culture and the Russian landscape.[30] The concern over the effects of socialist modernization was universal, not simply an Uzbek phenomenon. This fear of the downsides of modernity and the possibility that technology could and would destroy local cultures—whether Russian or Uzbek—created fissures in Soviet unity and helped weaken state power in many parts of the Soviet Union. In this case, however, it was a group of Russian nationalists who were most suspicious of Soviet innovation and its negative impact on local ways of life in Siberia, while Central Asians eagerly promoted this Soviet project, hoping that modern technology would help them preserve their endangered ways of life.

Russian residents of Tashkent also complained of discrimination and nepotism in the late Soviet era, particularly when it concerned their access to higher education in the Uzbek SSR. Many ethnic Slavs in the Soviet Union believed that they experienced fewer benefits from the Sovietization of Central Asia while the indigenous population had preferential treatment and remained "ungrateful" for the large-scale urbanization and economic development campaigns that the Soviet system brought to the region. In fact, Soviet educational institutions in Tashkent actively tried to increase the numbers of Uzbeks in their student bodies as part of the effort to expand the Central Asian work force. Acceptance rates at some of Tashkent's premier universities in the late 1970s were skewed in favor of indigenous residents, with higher numbers of admissions per Central Asian applicant than for Slavs. Tashkent State University, the Tashkent Polytechnic Institute, the Tashkent Pedagogical Institute, and even the Tashkent Conservatory opened their doors wide to attract more Uzbeks. The increased rates of university acceptance were a clear indication of positive change for the education of Central Asians, particularly Uzbek women, over previous decades, even if such changes caused resentment among some of the Russian population.[31] Similarly, accusations of corruption in the 1980s took on ethnic overtones and led to the discovery of a government scandal, the so-called "cotton affair," which centered on reports of large-scale bribery and the padding of cotton harvesting figures. Uzbek government officials allegedly defrauded the Soviet state of at least 1 billion rubles for Uzbek cotton that was never delivered.[32] Nonetheless, while the revelations were shocking and mostly true, the largely Russian prosecutors and investigators singled out ethnic Central Asian leaders of the republic for cheating the Soviet state even though bureaucratic corruption was endemic across the Soviet Union. In the popular stereotypes held by many Russians, Central Asians were notoriously dishonest, wealthy, and corrupt during socialism. This scandal reinforced the image of criminal Uzbeks hurting Russian-speaking Soviet victims. Once again, the Slavic perception of indigenous residents controlling and profiting from the economic lifelines of the region reemerged during this time of food shortages and economic hardship in the Soviet Union, just as it did during World War II, World War I, and at times of tension during the tsarist period. Despite the rhetoric of friendship and fraternal unity, Sovietization contributed to ethno-national fissures in the Soviet Uzbek capital.

Nonetheless, as Soviet power unraveled in the late 1980s, independence movements in Central Asia were relatively—and surprisingly—weak. Soviet power was much more threatened in the Baltics, western Ukraine, the

Caucasus region, and even Russia. In the end, one of the more "difficult" national groups for Party and state officials to "Sovietize" turned out to be one of the most loyal to the Soviet state. This fact is striking considering that Russia itself "declared independence" from the Soviet Union months before Uzbekistan, which did so only after the failed coup attempt of 1991. The Uzbeks, whom Party officials in Moscow had criticized for years for being backward or uncivilized, remained "Soviet" to the end, even after prominent officials in Russia, like Boris Yeltsin, had dissociated themselves from their Soviet and communist pasts.

The post-Soviet Uzbek state, however, has made public efforts to move away from that past. It has replaced socialism with nationalism as its unifying ideology, but in doing so, Uzbek officials reincorporated many ideas about urban spaces and urban culture from the Soviet era. Independent Uzbekistan has renovated its capital to create an image of a strong government center, like Russian and Soviet rulers historically did with the establishment of St. Petersburg, "Soviet" Moscow, or "socialist" Tashkent. Even the Old City has once again come under scrutiny for its "uncapital-like" appearance and its failure to resemble a "modern urban space." In 1996, the mayor of Tashkent told *Pravda Vostoka* that the post-Soviet urban renovation plan called for the "the renovation of the 'old city' part of Tashkent, which will entail the destruction of entire neighborhoods of traditional Uzbek homes and their replacement with apartment buildings and wide boulevards."[33] Some ethnically Uzbek officials still believe that winding streets and adobe bricks—the symbols of Uzbekistan's history and traditional lifestyle—remain markers of the past. Local residents again began to voice concern over the destruction of their homes but continued to lack the ability to do much about it.[34]

Furthermore, although some monuments to Soviet leaders have been replaced with ones honoring local Uzbek heroes, many "Soviet Uzbek" figures remain. Navoi still possesses his theater, street, library, museum, monument, and metro station. Sobir Rahimov, the Uzbek World War II hero, still has a park, metro stop, and monument in his name. The Rossiya and Moskva hotels, built in 1965 and 1983, respectively, have been renovated but no longer possess their Russian names, while the monument to the wartime Shamakhmudov family near the Friendship of the Peoples Palace—a symbol of multiethnic kindness from the Soviet era—was quietly removed in spring 2008 after the city government decided to rename the adjoining concert hall Independence Palace.[35] Meanwhile, the Russian writer Maxim Gorky lost his subway station, although his Soviet Uzbek literary colleagues, Hamid Olimjon and Gafur Gulom, remain honored with stops on the city's underground public transportation system, despite the fact that after the purges they rose to power over the corpses of some prominent Uzbek cultural and political figures. Tashkent in the early twenty-first century is being rebuilt to suit the image of an independent modern state, but the manner in which this model post-Soviet Uzbek city functions in many ways replicates that very past from which it is trying to escape.

NOTES

Abbreviations Used in the Notes

GARF: State Archive of the Russian Federation

O'zRI-TTHMDA: Central State Archive for Technical Research and Medical Documentation of the Republic of Uzbekistan

O'zRMDA: Central State Archive of the Republic of Uzbekistan

RGAE: Russian State Archive of Economics

RGALI: Russian State Archive of Art and Literature

RGANI: Russian State Archive of Contemporary History

RGASPI: Russian State Archive of Social and Political History

TShDA: State Archive of the City of Tashkent

TVDA: State Archive of the Oblast of Tashkent

Chapter 1. Introduction

The epigraph is from Usman Yusupov, *Izbrannye trudy* (Tashkent: Izdatel'stvo Uzbekistan, 1982), 1:151.

1. "Iz rechi na II s'ezde sovetskikh pisatelei Uzbekistana," April 25, 1939, in Yusupov, *Izbrannye trudy*, 1:65. A *hauz* was a small pond used as a water reservoir for irrigation purposes as well as for cleaning, cooking, and other household needs. European visitors derided these ponds as filthy or stagnant pools.

2. "Komsomol'skoe ozero sozdano!" *Pravda Vostoka*, June 3, 1939, 3.

3. Viktor Vitkovich, *Puteshestvie po Sovetskomu Uzbekistanu* (Moscow: Izd. Molodaia gvardiia, 1951), 32.

4. There are a few notable exceptions to the general lack of scholarship in this area: Timothy J. Colton, *Moscow: Governing the Socialist Metropolis* (Cambridge, MA: Belknap Press of Harvard University Press, 1995); Stephen Kotkin, *Magnetic Mountain: Stalinism as a Civilization* (Berkeley: University of California Press, 1995); and Blair Ruble, *Leningrad: Shaping a Soviet City* (Berkeley: University of California Press, 1990).

5. Benedict Anderson, *Imagined Communities: Reflections on the Origin and Spread of Nationalism* (London: Verso, 1983). More recently, Timothy Snyder has shown how modernization, identified with urbanization, the growth of mass media, population

increases, political ideologies, and mandatory state education, has promoted the creation of national identities in Belarus, Lithuania, Poland, and Ukraine. Central Asia, a region also under Russian/Soviet rule, underwent a similar process of identity creation in the twentieth century. See Timothy Snyder, *The Reconstruction of Nations: Poland, Ukraine, Lithuania, Belarus, 1569–1999* (New Haven: Yale University Press, 2003).

6. Hélène Carrère d'Encausse, *Decline of an Empire: The Soviet Socialist Republics in Revolt*, trans. Martin Sokolinsky and Henry A. La Farge (New York: Newsweek Books, 1979); Gregory J. Massell, *The Surrogate Proletariat: Moslem Women and Revolutionary Strategies in Soviet Central Asia, 1919–1929* (Princeton: Princeton University Press, 1974); Douglas Northrop, *Veiled Empire: Gender and Power in Stalinist Central Asia* (Ithaca, NY: Cornell University Press, 2004).

7. For the process of delineating the borders and determining the national content of the Central Asian (and other Soviet) republics, see Francine Hirsch, *Empire of Nations: Ethnographic Knowledge and the Making of the Soviet Union* (Ithaca, NY: Cornell University Press, 2005).

8. A book on Navoi entitled *Father of Uzbek Literature* was published in 1940, and the following year was designated as the five-hundredth-anniversary year of Navoi's birth. The jubilee year actually was celebrated in 1948, however, probably because of World War II. On the Soviet regime's rehabilitation of Navoi in the 1930s and 1940s, see "Alisher Navoi," *Literaturnaia Gazeta*, May 15, 1948, 1; Edward A. Allworth, *The Modern Uzbeks: From the Fourteenth Century to the Present; A Cultural History* (Stanford: Hoover Institution Press, 1990), 225–31; Svat Soucek, *A History of Inner Asia* (Cambridge: Cambridge University Press, 2000), 135–36.

9. Adrienne Lynn Edgar, *Tribal Nation: The Making of Soviet Turkmenistan* (Princeton: Princeton University Press, 2004).

10. Narrow streets and buildings and poorly constructed tramlines were removed for the sole reason that they were "uncapital-like" (*nestolichnyi*).

11. J. Douglas Porteous and Sandra E. Smith, *Domicide: The Global Destruction of Home* (Montreal: McGill-Queen's University Press, 2001).

12. For descriptions of Samarkand, see Soucek, *History of Inner Asia*, 128–29. For general pre-Russian historic background, see Allworth, *Modern Uzbeks*.

13. Jeff Sahadeo, *Russian Colonial Society in Tashkent: 1865–1923* (Bloomington: Indiana University Press, 2007).

14. Kokand was the last major "Uzbek" city to fall to Russian domination in 1875. It was not until 1884 that Mari, a city now in Turkmenistan, was annexed by Russia. Hélène Carrère d'Encausse, "Systematic Conquest, 1865–1884," in *Central Asia, 130 Years of Russian Dominance: A Historical Overview*, ed. Edward Allworth, 3rd. ed. (Durham, NC: Duke University Press, 1994), 148–49. For background on Russian imperial Tashkent and imperial rule in Central Asia, see Seymour Becker, *Russia's Protectorates in Central Asia: Bukhara and Khiva, 1865–1924* (Cambridge, MA: Harvard University Press, 1968); Robert D. Crews, "Civilization in the City: Architecture, Urbanism, and the Colonization of Tashkent," in *Architectures of Russian Identity: 1500 to the Present*, ed. James Cracraft and Daniel Rowland (Ithaca, NY: Cornell University Press, 2003), 118–25.

15. Robert D. Crews, *For Prophet and Tsar: Islam and Empire in Russia and Central Asia* (Cambridge, MA: Harvard University Press, 2006).

16. Adeeb Khalid, *The Politics of Muslim Cultural Reform: Jadidism in Central Asia* (Berkeley: University of California, 1998); Adeeb Khalid, "Tashkent 1917: Muslim Politics in Revolutionary Russia," *Slavic Review* 55, no. 2 (1996): 270–96.

17. Carrère d'Encausse, *Decline of an Empire*; Edward Allworth, ed., *Central Asia,*

130 Years of Russian Dominance: A Historical Overview, 3rd ed. (Durham, NC: Duke University Press, 1994); Alexandre Bennigsen and Marie Broxup, *The Islamic Threat to the Soviet State* (New York: St. Martin's Press, 1983); Michael Rywkin, *Moscow's Muslim Challenge: Soviet Central Asia,* rev. ed. (Armonk, NY: M. E. Sharpe, 1990).

18. For studies of specific Central Asian peoples, see Martha Brill Olcott, *The Kazakhs* (Stanford: Hoover Institution Press, 1986), and Allworth, *Modern Uzbeks.* Current nationalist historiography of independent Uzbekistan explores the crimes of the Soviet era but pays little attention to Uzbek participation in the Soviet regime. It also fails to provide context regarding the fact that other Soviet peoples experienced similar efforts, both violent and passive, to transform their traditional cultures. See Rustambek Shamsutdinov, *O'zbekistonda sovyetlarning quloqlashtirish siyosati v uning fojeali oqibatlari* (Tashkent: Shark nashriyoti, 2001); *O'zbekiston sovyet mustamlakachiligi davrida* (Tashkent: Shark nashriyoti, 2000).

19. I. M. Muminova, *Istoriia rabochego klassa sovetskogo Uzbekistana* (Tashkent: FAN, 1974); E. Iu. Yusupov, *Tashkent v period razvitogo sotsializma* (Tashkent: FAN, 1983); G. Rashidov, *Sotsialistik Toshkent Tarihi,* vol. 1 (Tashkent: FAN, 1965); G. Rashidov, *Sotsialistik Toshkent Tarihi,* vol. 2 (Tashkent: FAN, 1966). For non-Soviet interpretations of the positive influences of Soviet rule in Uzbekistan, see Shams-ud-din, *Secularisation in the USSR: A Study of Soviet Cultural Policy in Uzbekistan* (New Delhi: Vikas Publishing House, 1982).

20. Massell, *Surrogate Proletariat.*

21. Marianne Ruth Kamp, *The New Woman in Uzbekistan: Islam, Modernity, and Unveiling under Communism* (Seattle: University of Washington Press, 2006); Northrop, *Veiled Empire.*

22. Shoshana Keller, *To Moscow, Not Mecca: The Soviet Campaign against Islam in Central Asia, 1917–1941* (Westport, CT: Praeger, 2001).

23. Cassandra Marie Cavanaugh, "Backwardness and Biology: Medicine and Power in Russian and Soviet Central Asia, 1868–1934" (PhD diss., Columbia University, 2001); Paula Michaels, *Curative Powers: Medicine and Empire in Stalin's Central Asia* (Pittsburgh: University of Pittsburgh Press, 2003); Matthew Payne, *Stalin's Railroad: Turksib and the Building of Socialism* (Pittsburgh: University of Pittsburgh Press, 2001); Yuri Slezkine, *Arctic Mirrors: Russia and the Small Peoples of the North* (Ithaca, NY: Cornell University Press, 1994). Slezkine is the exception. He crosses the 1941 divide and follows the history of Soviet "modernization" efforts in the Arctic through the collapse of the Soviet Union.

24. Kotkin, *Magnetic Mountain.*

25. Andrew Jenks, in his case study of the Russian village of Palekh, shows that "Sovietizing" pre-existing town spaces was exceptionally challenging. Andrew Jenks, *Russia in a Box* (DeKalb: Northern Illinois University Press, 2005).

26. Regarding gender and family dynamics, David Hoffmann focuses on peasant in-migration to Moscow in the 1930s but deals with neither the non-Russian periphery nor the war. See David L. Hoffmann, *Peasant Metropolis: Social Identities in Moscow, 1929–1941* (Ithaca, NY: Cornell University Press, 1994).

27. Most studies of urbanization have focused on the Slavic core cities of the Soviet Union. See Colton, *Moscow;* Ruble, *Leningrad.* Svetlana Boym focuses on urban life in the communal apartment in Leningrad in her book *Common Places: Mythologies of Everyday Life in Russia* (Cambridge, MA: Harvard University Press, 1995). Andrew Day traces urban planning trends from the intellectual debates of the 1920s to the death of Stalin in the 1950s. While he does briefly discuss efforts to adapt the Moscow model for urban planning to national republics, his case studies are Moscow, Sverdlovsk, and

Stalingrad, all Russian cities. Andrew Elam Day, "Building Socialism: The Politics of the Soviet Cityscape in the Stalin era" (PhD diss., Columbia University, 1998).

28. Iu. L. Kosenkova, *Sovetskii gorod: 1940-kh—pervoi poloviny 1950-kh godov; Ot tvorcheskikh poiskov k praktike stroitel'stva* (Moscow: URSS, 2000); Karl Qualls, "Raised from Ruins: Restoring Popular Allegiance through City Planning in Sevastopol, 1943–1954" (PhD diss., Georgetown University, 1998).

Chapter 2. A City to Be Transformed

The epigraph is from Henry Lansdell, *Through Central Asia* (1887; reprint, Nedeln, Liechtenstein: Kraus Reprint, 1978), 171.

1. Joshua Kunitz, *Dawn over Samarkand: The Rebirth of Central Asia* (New York: Covici Freide Publishers, 1935), 204–5.

2. Ibid., 205.

3. See David MacKenzie, *The Lion of Tashkent: The Career of General M. G. Cherniaev* (Athens: University of Georgia Press, 1974).

4. Sahadeo, *Russian Colonial Society in Tashkent.*

5. Allworth, ed., *Central Asia, 130 Years of Russian Dominance;* Elizabeth E. Bacon, *Central Asians under Russian Rule* (Ithaca, NY: Cornell University Press, 1966); Shoshana Keller, *To Moscow, Not Mecca;* Iu. Sokolov, *Tashkent, Tashkenttsy i Rossiia* (Tashkent, 1965), 180–87.

6. On Russia's "special mission" to bring civilization to its Asian neighbors, see Cavanaugh, "Backwardness and Biology," 19.

7. Richard A. Pierce, *Russian Central Asia, 1867–1917* (Berkeley: University of California Press, 1960).

8. Crews, "Civilization in the City," 118–25.

9. Sahadeo, *Russian Colonial Society in Tashkent.* Sahadeo's work has shaped many of my perceptions of the imperial project in Central Asia.

10. See Paul Rabinow, *French Modern: Norms and Forms of the Social Environment* (Cambridge, MA: MIT Press, 1989); Gwendolyn Wright, *The Politics of Design in French Colonial Urbanism* (Chicago: University of Chicago Press, 1991); Nezar AlSayyad, ed., *Forms of Dominance: On the Architecture and Urbanism of the Colonial Enterprise* (Aldershot, England: Avebury, 1992).

11. Count K. K. Pahlen, *Mission to Turkestan,* ed. Richard A. Pierce (London: Oxford University Press, 1964), 7.

12. See Alexander Blok, *The Twelve; and, The Scythians,* trans. Jack Lindsay (London: Journeyman Press, 1982), 69–71.

13. In 1858, before the tsarist conquest of Turkestan, one traveling Russian official complained of unbearable heat in Central Asia. He noted that it was "over 90 degrees in the shade. Occasionally a wind blew, but it was warm and stuffy. At night without mercy mosquitoes and midges devoured us." John Evans, ed., *Mission of N. P. Ignat'ev to Khiva and Bukhara in 1858* (Newtonville, MA: Oriental Research Partners, 1984), 72. See also Eugene Schuyler, *Turkistan: Notes of a Journey in Russian Turkistan, Khokand, Bukhara, and Kuldja,* 2 vols. (New York: Scribner, Armstrong & Co., 1877), 1:79–80.

14. Sahadeo discusses this trend at great length. See Sahadeo, *Russian Colonial Society in Tashkent,* particularly chaps. 2 and 3. See also Edward Said, *Orientalism* (New York: Vintage, 1978).

15. Crews, "Civilization in the City," 126–28.

16. James C. Scott, *Seeing Like a State: How Certain Schemes to Improve the Human Condition Have Failed* (New Haven: Yale University Press, 1998), 53–54.

17. G. P. Fedorov, "Moia sluzhba v Turkestanskom krae (1870–1906)," *Istoricheskii vestnik*, vol. 124, 458–59, quoted in Cavanaugh, "Backwardness and Biology," 81.

18. Victims came down with a horrible disease in which a white worm traveled through the body and caused the infected person's legs to swell. Lansdell, *Through Central Asia*, 394–96; Schuyler, *Turkistan*, 1:147.

19. Lansdell, *Through Central Asia*, 395–96.

20. For example, see F. Kovalev, "Sdelaem Tashkent odnim iz luchshikh gorodov soiuza," *Pravda Vostoka*, February 17, 1938, 3.

21. As Cassandra Cavanaugh has noted, Russian officials viewed European-style medical care as an important way to "improve" the lifestyle of indigenous residents and to build support for the Russian project in Asia among the Central Asian population. Cavanaugh, "Backwardness and Biology," 57–61.

22. However, few memoirists noted the irony that much of Russian medical care consisted of remarkably similar traditions, that infectious diseases rapidly spread through European areas of the empire, or that St. Petersburg and Moscow city workers lived in similarly squalid conditions. Hoffmann, *Peasant Metropolis*.

23. On garden descriptions and European cultural life in Tashkent, see Varvara Dukhovskaia, *Turkestanskiia vospominaniia* (St. Petersburg: Izdaniie t-va M. O. Volf', 1913), 22, 70.

24. On the incorporation of gardens into cities, see the section on Ebenezer Howard and the Garden City movement in Lewis Mumford, *The City in History: Its Origins, Its Transformations, and Its Prospects* (New York: Harcourt, Brace & World, 1961), 514–24.

25. G. M. Shilov, "Traditsii i preemstvennost' v planirovochnoi structure gorodov Tveri (nyne Kalinina) i Tashkenta," *Stroitel'stvo i arkhitektura Uzbekistana*, no. 2 (1983): 23–24.

26. A. A. Ziiaev, "Formirovanie arkhitekturnogo ansamblia ploshchadi V. I. Lenina v Tashkente," *Stroitel'stvo i arkhitektura Uzbekistana*, no. 4 (1983): 27–28; V. A. Nilsen and L. D. Terent'eva, "Iz istorii zastroiki Tashkenta," *Stroitel'stvo i arkhitektura Uzbekistana*, no. 9 (1983): 3–5.

27. For the importance of visual demonstrations of power in imperial Tashkent, see Crews, "Civilization in the City," 125; Sahadeo, *Russian Colonial Society in Tashkent*, 47–56.

28. Ziiaev, "Formirovanie arkhitekturnogo ansamblia ploshchadi V. I. Lenina v Tashkente," 27–28; Nilsen and Terent'eva, "Iz istorii zastroiki Tashkenta," 3–5.

29. Among the pre-revolutionary colonial structures that survived the Soviet era in Tashkent, the state bank and the palace of Prince Nikolai Konstantinovich are the most prominent. Extant buildings, along with pictures of those that were destroyed, recall Moscow structures of the era, such as the State Historical Museum and GUM, the state department store, along Red Square. However, the Tashkent buildings were constructed on a much smaller scale.

30. M. A. Kaiumova, "Osnovnye etapy formirovaniia priemiov ob'emno-prostrans-tvennoi kompozitsii ploshchadei Tashkenta," *Stroitel'stvo i arkhitektura Uzbekistana*, no. 7 (1984): 27–29. There is a discrepancy regarding the introduction of the tram because Tashkent celebrated one hundred years of tram service in 2002. On the symbolic importance of Tashkent architecture, see Crews, "Civilization in the City," 121–25.

31. Joseph Wolff, *Narrative of a Mission to Bokhara in the Years 1843–1845*, ed. Guy Wint (London: Frederick A. Praeger, 1969). This volume, originally published in 1845, recounts Wolff's journey to Bukhara to ascertain the fate of British envoys Charles Stoddart and Arthur Conolly. Stoddart and Conolly were imprisoned, tortured, and

executed by the emir of Bukhara. Wolff described Central Asia as harsh, bloody, and tyrannical.

32. Pahlen, *Mission to Turkestan*, 68.

33. Eugene Schuyler evidently purchased a slave as a servant in the 1870s, much to the disdain of his Russian traveling companions, who believed that Russian rule supposedly had ended the practice. See Schuyler, *Turkistan*, 2:100–104, 108–9.

34. Sahadeo, *Russian Colonial Society in Tashkent*, particularly chap. 1.

35. Cavanaugh, "Backwardness and Biology," 63–66.

36. Schuyler, *Turkistan*, 1:127, 134; Cavanaugh, "Backwardness and Biology," 51. Vasily Vereshchagin, the Russian painter, depicted such themes in his images of Central Asia in the 1870s. His 1872 work, *Selling a Child Slave*, combines many images of deviant behavior. In the painting, elderly Central Asian men examine a naked boy in a dark room before deciding whether to purchase him as a slave. See a description and reproduction of this painting in Daniel Brower, *Turkestan and the Fate of the Russian Empire* (London: RoutledgeCurzon, 2003), 41, plate 1.

37. For a comparison to colonial rule in Egypt, see Timothy Mitchell, *Colonising Egypt* (Cambridge: Cambridge University Press, 1988). See also Nicholas Thomas, *Colonialism's Culture: Anthropology, Travel, and Government* (Cambridge: Polity Press, 1994). Ironically, to describe Central Asian society, many Russian intellectuals used orientalist categories that were similar to those used by British and French writers to portray the Russian autocracy. See Larry Wolff, *Inventing Eastern Europe* (Stanford: Stanford University Press, 1994).

38. Crews, *For Prophet and Tsar*, 241–92.

39. Schuyler, *Turkistan*, 1:118. Count Pahlen also noted the isolation of the Central Asian home life from the "outside" world: "From the street all one sees of a house is a blank wall with a door to one side marking the entrance. When this is opened in response to vigorous knocking one enters a long, covered passage flanked by two high walls." Pahlen, *Mission to Turkestan*, 34.

40. Regarding the strains that immigration placed on Russian society in Central Asia, see Pierce, *Russian Central Asia, 1867–1917*, 103, 135–38, 188–89, 244; Sahadeo, *Russian Colonial Society in Tashkent*, 108–36.

41. Sahadeo, *Russian Colonial Society in Tashkent*, 123–24. See also Lansdell, *Through Central Asia*, 184.

42. For Tashkent and Turkestan during the revolution, see Sahadeo, *Russian Colonial Society in Tashkent*, chap. 8; Khalid, *Politics of Muslim Cultural Reform*, 114–54; Hélène Carrère d'Encausse, *Islam and the Russian Empire* (Berkeley: University of California Press, 1988), 119–92; Allworth, ed., *Central Asia, 130 Years of Russian Dominance*, 189–265.

43. Alexander Neweroff wrote about Tashkent as a haven for refugees from the Russian civil war. See Neweroff, *City of Bread* (New York: George H. Doran, 1927). For the plight of refugees, see F. M. Bailey, *Mission to Tashkent* (London: Jonathan Cape, 1946).

44. V. A. Nilsen and A. A. Ziiaev, "Stanovlenie sotsialisticheskoi arkhitektury Tashkenta," *Stroitel'stvo i arkhitektura Uzbekistana*, no. 8 (1983): 9.

45. Ibid.; *Tashkent entsiklopediia, s.v.* "Leninu, pamiatnik k" (Tashkent: Glavnaia redaktsiia uzbekskoi sovetskoi entsiklopedii, 1983), 188.

46. For creation of national republics and ethnic identities in the Soviet Union, see Hirsch, *Empire of Nations*, 145–227.

47. Visiting Central Asia in the mid-1930s, Rosita Forbes noted that the Sovietization of Uzbeks was largely mechanical. They were without a "Leninesque conception of Communism. They were not even Marxists. Some of them had exaggerated ideas of

the importance of their particular republic." Rosita Forbes, *Forbidden Road: Kabul to Samarkand* (New York: Dutton, 1937), 263.

48. In the 1950s and 1960s, it served as a reception center for the Uzbek SSR Ministry of Foreign Affairs, largely functioning as a place to greet Asian and African delegations. Today, it serves a similar function—as a reception hall for the Ministry of Foreign Affairs of the Republic of Uzbekistan.

49. Nilsen and Ziiaev, "Stanovlenie sotsialisticheskoi arkhitektury Tashkenta," 10–11.

50. T. F. Kadyrova, *Arkhitektura sovetskogo Uzbekistana* (Moscow: Stroiizdat, 1987), 42–43.

51. Ibid., 39.

52. Ibid.

53. G. Rashidov, *Istoriia sotsialisticheskogo Tashkenta* (Tashkent: Izd. "Nauka" Uzbekskoi SSR, 1965), 272.

54. See Northrop, *Veiled Empire,* and Kamp, *New Woman in Uzbekistan.*

55. As Anatole Kopp has noted, Soviet architects saw themselves as social reformers, not simply building designers. Anatole Kopp, *Town and Revolution: Soviet Architecture and City Planning, 1917–1935,* trans. Thomas E. Burton (New York: George Braziller, 1970), 5. For a history of the role of and controversies among Soviet architects, see Day, "Building Socialism"; and Hugh Hudson, *Blueprints and Blood: The Stalinization of Soviet Architecture, 1917–1937* (Princeton: Princeton University Press, 1994).

56. With total control over the land, the state could give architects the ability to refashion entire urban centers, not just individual structures or city blocks, as was the case in most European cities where land remained in private hands. For this reason, modernist architects, of whom the Swiss urban planner Le Corbusier was one of the most prominent, came to work on planning Soviet urban environments in an effort to realize these utopian dreams. See Day, "Building Socialism"; Kopp, *Town and Revolution; Le Corbusier, The Radiant City,* trans. Pamela Knight, Eleanor Levieux, and Derek Coltman (New York: Orion Press, 1967); and Richard Stites, *Revolutionary Dreams: Utopian Vision and Experimental Life in the Russian Revolution* (Oxford: Oxford University Press, 1989).

57. On oppositions to modernist/constructivist architecture and historic architecture, see Day, "Building Socialism," 35–61.

58. Pavlenko was not alone. This belief in the chaotic nature of historical city settlements was a European phenomenon that was voiced most often in colonial contexts. However, the ancient streets of Moscow or Tula were just as crooked and winding as the alleyways of Tashkent.

59. P. Pavlenko, *Puteshestvie v Turkmenistane* (Moscow: Moskovskoe tovarishchestvo pisatelei, 1933), 37.

60. For a description of this urban plan, see "Pervyi proekt pereplanirovki Tashkenta," *Stroitel'stvo i arkhitektura Uzbekistana,* no. 7 (1973): 33–36.

61. Olga Matich, "Remaking the Bed," in *Laboratory of Dreams: The Russian Avant-Garde and Cultural Experiment,* ed. John E. Bowlt and Olga Matich (Stanford: Stanford University Press, 1996), 66; Stites, *Revolutionary Dreams,* 200–204.

62. For biographical information on Polupanov, see T. F. Kadyrova, "Arkhitektor S. N. Polupanov (1904–1957)," *Stroitel'stvo i arkhitektura Uzbekistana,* no. 12 (1973): 26–32.

63. Contemporary authors argued that educational opportunities were off limits to Uzbek women, who were given away in marriage at an early age. Pavlenko noted that the position of women in Central Asia was extremely low, and he recounted tales of women being "bought and sold" and stories of husbands beating their wives to death

without anyone from the community intervening. Soviet ideology declared women to be at the mercy of their husbands and other male relatives behind the confines of the walled Central Asian home. Their traditional position in the family was seen as unacceptable for the revolutionary age, which would instead offer them opportunities to participate in economic life and become full citizens of the Soviet state. Pavlenko, *Puteshestvie v Turkmenistane*, 28–29. Pavlenko does not mention the traditionally low status of women in Russia.

64. However, there is no evidence that these new forms of housing appealed to Uzbeks any more than they did to Russians for whom they were originally conceived. The Tashkent commune was planned to resemble a hotel with long corridors along which individual families would have sleeping quarters.

65. Kadyrova, *Arkhitektura sovetskogo Uzbekistana*, 53–54.

66. The Tashkent Red Square is occasionally referred to as Lenin Square, particularly in the later period of Soviet rule.

67. For a discussion of the decline of constructivist and modern architecture and the purges of architects from the profession and Soviet society, see Hudson, *Blueprints and Blood*, esp. 136–84. See also Day, "Building Socialism," 92–102.

68. Kadyrova, "Arkhitektor S. N. Polupanov (1904–1957)," 28–30; Ziiaev, "Formirovanie arkhitekturnogo ansamblia ploshchadi V. I. Lenina v Tashkente," 28–29.

69. On the transformation of the Voskresenskii Market to Theater Square, see *Tashkent entsiklopediia, s.v.* "Voskresenskii bazar," 71–72.

70. N. Beknazarov, *Istoriia razvitiia Frunzenskogo raiona g. Tashkenta, 1936–1964* (Tashkent: FAN, 1966), 5, 8–9.

71. Usman Yusupov, "Iz otchetnogo doklada VII s'ezdu kommunisticheskoi partii (bolshevikov) Uzbekistana o rabote TsK KP(b) Uz," July 2, 1938, in Yusupov, *Izbrannye trudy*, 1:107; Yusupov, "Rech' na V-oi Tashkentskoi gorodskoi partiinoi konferentsii," March 4, 1940, in ibid., 1:243.

72. L. M. Kaganovich, *The Construction of the Subway and the Plan of the City of Moscow* (Moscow: Cooperative Publishing Society of Foreign Workers in the USSR, 1934), 42.

73. Ibid., 41.

74. *General'nyi plan rekonstruktsii goroda Moskvy* (Moscow: Moskovskii rabochii, 1936), 8.

75. Ibid., 51.

76. *Planirovka i stroitel'stvo gorodov SSSR, materialiy k III plenumu pravleniia soiuza sovetskikh arkhitektorov SSSR, 7–11 iiulia 1938 goda* (Moscow: Izd. Vsesoiuznoi Akademii Arkhitektury, 1938), 50.

77. Kaganovich called for the razing of GUM in order to enlarge Red Square during the reconstruction of Moscow. See Kaganovich, *The Construction of the Subway and the Plan of the City of Moscow*, 51. The building still stands.

78. O'zRMDA, f. 2831, op. 1, d. 18, l. 1. Mention of donkeys can be found in many documents and comes up in conversation with current and former residents of Tashkent. In post-Soviet Uzbekistan, occasionally Russians derogatively use the word *donkey* or *ass* to describe Uzbeks, whom they sometimes believe are not grateful for Russian "help" in the Soviet era.

79. *Planirovka i stroitel'stvo gorodov SSSR, materialiy k III plenumu pravleniia soiuza sovetskikh arkhitektorov SSSR, 7–11 iiulia 1938 goda*, 53.

80. Andrew Jenks, "A Metro on the Mount," *Technology and Culture*, October 2000, 697–724.

81. While visiting Samarkand in the mid-1930s, Rosita Forbes noted that young

Uzbeks were fully aware of the transformation of the Soviet capital even though they had never been there. Uzbek university students were convinced that Moscow was "far ahead of any other capital in science, architecture, civilization, art and the general amenities of life." Forbes, *Forbidden Road*, 263. For visual images, see Matthew Cullerne Bown, *Art under Stalin* (New York: Holmes & Meier, 1991), 71–139.

Chapter 3. Imagining a "Cultured" Tashkent

1. "Mavjuda Abdurakhmanova," *Pravda Vostoka*, December 3, 1937, 2.

2. "Vpered k novym pobedam," *Pravda Vostoka*, November 7, 1937, 2–3.

3. This view of bringing light and air to the working class was not unique to the Soviet system but was a pan-European view of urban development even with respect to colonial Asian or African cities. See Anthony D. King, *Colonial Urban Development* (London: Routledge & Kegan Paul, 1976), 108–13; Le Corbusier, *The City of Tomorrow and Its Planning,* trans. Frederick Etchells (Cambridge, MA: MIT Press, 1971).

4. For descriptions of colonial city building, see King, *Colonial Urban Development;* Michele Lamprakos, "Le Corbusier and Algiers: The Plan Obus as Colonial Urbanism," in *Forms of Dominance: On the Architecture and Urbanism of the Colonial Enterprise,* ed. Nezar AlSayyad (Aldershot, England: Avebury, 1992), 183–210.

5. For declarations that Soviet planning in Central Asia was different from colonial planning, see O'zRMDA, f. 2532, op. 1, d. 10, l. 55. On urban planning practices of colonial powers, see Janet Abu-Lughod, *Rabat: Urban Apartheid in Morocco* (Princeton: Princeton University Press, 1980); Rabinow, *French Modern,* 277–319; and Preeti Chopra, "Pondicherry: A French Enclave in India," in *Forms of Dominance: On the Architecture and Urbanism of the Colonial Enterprise,* ed. Nezar AlSayyad (Aldershot, England: Avebury, 1992), 127.

6. TShDA, f. 10, op. 18, f. 961, l. 67. Rationally planned growth was not unique to Soviet planning. Faith in planned cities was prominent throughout the late nineteenth and twentieth centuries. Le Corbusier, *Radiant City;* Rabinow, *French Modern.*

7. TShDA, f. 10, op. 18, d. 961, ll. 169–70.

8. B. Bezrukov, *Zdravstvui, Tashkent! kratkiy putevoditel'-spravochnik po raionam goroda Tashkenta* (Tashkent: Izd. Uzbekistan, 1970), 5.

9. See statistics from Central Statistical Bureau, RGAE, f. 1562, op. 20, d. 145, l. 197; f. 1562, d. 174, l. 138.

10. RGAE, f. 1562, op. 20, d. 116, p. 222; d. 145, l. 197.

11. O'zRMDA, f. R-837, op. 1, d. 587, l. 12; f. 314, op. 1, d. 3, l. 69; "Eshelon-58: Vladimir Dmitrievich Kim," in *Dorogoi gor'kikh ispytanii* (Moscow: Ekslibris Press, 1997), 71; "Vospominannia spetspereselentsa: Kan San Kho," in *Dorogoi gor'kikh ispytanii,* 189; "Norodnomu kommissaru vnutrennikh del soiuza SSR tov. Yezhovu," *Belaia kniga o deportatsii koreiskogo naseleniia Rossii,* vol. 1 (Moscow: Interpraks, 1992), 97; P. Kim, *Koreitsy respubliki Uzbekistana* (Tashkent: O'zbekiston, 1993).

12. For a personal history of migration to Tashkent, see the memoir of Vasili Stribezhev, a construction worker from Voronezh, in O'zRMDA, f. 2831, op. 1, d. 18.

13. See worker complaints to the factory Party committee in TShDA, f. 231, op. 1, d. 1188, l. 13.

14. For descriptions of young children hawking cigarettes or begging in the city's bazaar, see "Pokonchit' s beznadzornost'iu detei v Tashkente," *Komsomolets' Uzbekistana,* August 6, 1939, 2.

15. Fitzroy MacLean, *Eastern Approaches* (London: Penguin Books, 1991), 76–77.

16. For an example, see "Sud—spekuliaty," *Pravda Vostoka,* June 22, 1937, 4.

17. Rywkin, *Moscow's Muslim Challenge*, 108.

18. Donald S. Carlisle, "Modernization, Generations, and the Uzbek Soviet Intelligentsia," in *The Dynamics of Soviet Politics*, ed. Paul Cocks, Robert Daniels, and Nancy Whittier Heer (Cambridge, MA: Harvard University Press, 1976), 258. The highest level of Uzbek ethnic membership was 63.8 percent in 1934. Kazakhstan had a less dramatic drop in Kazakh ethnic Party membership, from 53.1 percent in 1933 to 47.6 percent in January 1938. Olcott, *Kazakhs*, 220. For a study of Turkmenistan during the purges, see Oleg Hlevnjuk, "Les Mécanismes de la 'Grande terreur' des années 1937–1938 au Turkmenistan," *Cahiers du monde russe*, nos. 1–2 (1998): 197–208.

19. T. H. Rigby, *Communist Party Membership in the USSR, 1917–1967* (Princeton: Princeton University Press, 1968), 229. Rigby notes that the breakdown by social origin of the Uzbek Communist Party changed considerably in the 1930s, from being 25.5 percent white-collar workers, 25.4 percent laborers, and 34.6 percent peasants in 1933 to 54.2 percent white-collar workers, 14.7 percent laborers, and 24.3 percent peasants in 1939 after the purges. This change reflected union-wide trends. Ibid., 229–30.

20. Ikramov's son chronicled his father's trial. See Karim Ikramov, *Delo moego ottsa* (Moscow: Sovetskii pisatel', 1991), 140–66. For an additional account, see MacLean, *Eastern Approaches*, 80–121.

21. Kovalev, "Sdelaem Tashkent odnim iz luchshikh gorodov soiuza," 3.

22. Vasili Stribezhev, a construction worker, recalls having to walk enormous distances to construction sites because the trams worked poorly, if at all. O'zRMDA, f. 2831, op. 1, d. 18, l. 11.

23. "Protsess kontrrevoliutsionnoi vreditel'stkoi bandy burzhuaznykh natsionalistov v g. Yangi-Yul," *Pravda Vostoka*, October 3, 1937, 3.

24. The militarized language used in the show trials, Party plenums, and published descriptions of Tashkent's infrastructure problems underscored for the population the notion that the Soviet Union was surrounded by foreign aggressors and replete with internal foes, even in distant Tashkent. The Resolution of the Seventh Congress of the Uzbek Communist Party expressly declared that the Soviet Union's adversaries had sent agents, diversionaries, and spies far into the Soviet homeland, namely Tashkent. The goal was to create the impression that Tashkent was as close to a hostile border as was Leningrad or Minsk. Descriptions of the city's antiaircraft preparations were published, drills were performed, and Party leaders frequently spoke of Tashkent's vulnerability to attack. European fascism and Japanese imperialism might have been far away geographically, but the language used in the late 1930s was supposed to make Tashkenters fear foreign invasion as much as "bourgeois nationalism" and recalcitrant mullahs. *Resoliutsiia VII s'ezda Kommunisticheskoi partii Uzbekistana po otchetnomu dokladu TsK KP/b/ Uzbekistana* (Tashkent, 1938), 10; "Oborona tyla ot vozdushnykh napadeniyi," *Pravda Vostoka*, May 9, 1937, 3.

25. *Tashkent entsiklopediia, s.v.* "Yuldash Akhunbabaev," 44. For a biography of Yusupov, see B. Reskov and G. Sedov, *Usmon Yusupov: ajoyib kishilar hayoti* (Tashkent: Yosh gvardiia nashriyoti, 1977). For post-Soviet biography, see *O'zbekiston Sovyet mustamlakachiligi davrida*, 325–26.

26. *O'zbek sovyet entsiklopediyasi, s.v.* "Abduzhabar Abdurakhmanov" (Tashkent: O'zbek Sovyet Entsiklopediyasi Bosh Redaktsiyasi, 1971), 1:35–36.

27. See Vadim Volkov, "The Concept of 'Kul'turnost'': Notes on the Stalinist Civilizing Process," in *Stalinism: New Directions*, ed. Sheila Fitzpatrick (London: Routledge, 2000), 210–31; Michael Thurman, "Leaders of the Communist Party of Uzbekistan in Historical Retrospect: The 'Class of '38,'" part 1, *Central Asian Monitor*, no. 6 (1995): 19–27.

28. "Na konferentsii arkhitektorov," *Pravda Vostoka,* April 26, 1937, 3.

29. V. Liudin, "O rekonstruktsii Tashkenta," *Pravda Vostoka,* February 6, 1938, 4.

30. Ibid.

31. Stepan Polupanov, "Zal zasedaniy Verkhovnogo Soveta Uzbekskoi SSR," *Arkhitektura SSR,* no. 12 (1940): 50–51.

32. Greg Castillo, "Cities of the Stalinist Empire," in *Forms of Dominance: On the Architecture and Urbanism of the Colonial Enterprise,* ed. Nezar AlSayyad (Aldershot, England: Avebury, 1992), 269–71. Polupanov's building for the exhibition appears to have been designed before the war but not completed until the 1950s. See Alexei Tarkhanov and Sergei Kavtaradze, *Stalinist Architecture* (London: Laurence King, 1992), 165.

33. King, *Colonial Urban Development;* Mitchell, *Colonising Egypt,* 1–34; Shirine Hamadeh, "Creating the Traditional City: A French Project," in *Forms of Dominance: On the Architecture and Urbanism of the Colonial Enterprise,* edited by Nezar Alsayyad (Aldershot, England: Avebury, 1992), 241–59.

34. TShDA, f. 10, op. 18, d. 14-a, l. 10.

35. TShDA, f. 10, op. 18, f. 961, l. 67.

36. Ibid., l. 171.

37. TShDA, f. 10, op. 18, d. 14-a, l. 21.

38. In order to establish these new industrial institutions, the city was to expand outward through the annexation of 3,730 hectares of collective farmland. Hydroelectric power stations were planned along the Chirchik River to provide for an increasingly industrial urban center. Ibid., ll. 170–71.

39. TShDA, f. 10, op. 18, d. 961, l. 68.

40. O'zRMDA, f. 2532, op. 1, d. 29, l. 19.

41. O'zRMDA f. 2532, op. 1, d. 240, l. 241.

42. O'zRMDA, f. 2532, op. 1, d. 23, ll. 9–11. The resolution from the fourth plenum of the Soviet Architects' Union in Moscow decreed that pre-planned architectural projects were to be adapted across various regions of the Soviet Union. Plans were to be "standardized" and they were to involve the use of "new methods of construction" in order to ensure rapid implementation. In the various republics, these plans were to be adapted to suit national traditions, the local climate, and geographic/geological conditions.

43. TShDA, f. 10, op. 18, d. 14-a, ll. 22–23.

44. TShDA, f. 10, op. 18, d. 14-a, l. 23.

45. See the discussion of Soviet city planners' views of the city and its relationship to Marxist-Leninist ideology in Alfred John DiMaio Jr., *Soviet Urban Housing: Problems and Policies* (New York: Praeger, 1974), 43–46.

46. The continued use of the "radial" street plan in Tashkent was described as necessary primarily because Moscow had a radial plan. O'zRMDA, f. 2532, op. 1, d. 8, l. 240.

47. TShDA, f. 36, op. 1, d. 501, l. 17.

48. Moving city residents into small apartments was supposed to bring about the atomization of the Central Asian family, allowing the state to break down the extended family structure of Uzbek society and decreasing individual efforts to resist Soviet ideology. On the strength of the extended family unit, see Michael Rywkin, "National Symbiosis: Vitality, Religion, Identity, Allegiance," in *The USSR and the Muslim World,* ed. Yaacov Ro'i (London: George Allen & Unwin, 1984), 5.

49. There was no steady supply of wood or water in the Central Asian desert for making cement or building homes. O'zRMDA, f. 2532, op. 1, d. 32, l. 3.

50. On the use of Tatar proxies to represent Russian commercial and financial interests in the eighteenth and nineteenth centuries, see Soucek, *History of Inner Asia,*

196–97. On the Jadid movement, see Khalid, *Politics of Muslim Cultural Reform,* 114–54. Khalid has shown the importance of the Jadid movement, which promoted Muslim cultural reform in Central Asia. In the late nineteenth and early twentieth centuries, the Jadids aimed to promote their program of cultural reform by establishing modern theater, advocating publishing and journalism, and setting up "new method schools" to teach practical literacy.

51. "Pozdravliaem iubiliara, M. S. Bulatov," *Stroitel'stvo i arkhitektura Uzbekistana,* no. 4 (1978): 47.

52. O'zRMDA, f. 2532, op. 1, d. 29, ll. 48–48ob.

53. On Soviet attempts to create "culture" in the 1930s through campaigns to improve hygiene, table manners, and literacy, see David L. Hoffmann, *Stalinist Values: The Cultural Norms of Soviet Modernity, 1917–1941* (Ithaca, NY: Cornell University Press, 2003).

54. TShDA, f. 231, op. 1, d. 1186, l. 13; O'zRMDA, f. 2532, op. 1, d. 29, l. 14.

55. TShDA, f. 10, op. 18, d. 960, l. 47.

56. O'zRMDA, f. 2831, op. 1, d. 18, l. 1.

57. RGAE, f. 1562, op. 20, d. 218, l. 11.

58. "Sanitarnie kody rioia kilish kerak," *Qizil O'zbekiston,* May 13, 1941, 3.

59. O'zRMDA, f. 2532, op. 1, d. 197, l. 163.

60. "Zabroshennye chaikhany," *Pravda Vostoka,* April 10, 1937, 3.

61. See King, *Colonial Urban Development,* 107, 146–48.

62. O'zRMDA, f. 2532, op. 1, d. 197, ll. 162–63.

63. Ibid.

64. Hoffmann, *Stalinist Values;* Volkov, "Concept of 'Kul'turnost.'" For Soviet efforts to civilize the "backward" peoples of Siberia, see Slezkine, *Arctic Mirrors.*

65. TShDA, f. 10, op. 18, d. 960, ll. 46–47. Almazar Trass, a main thoroughfare, was to be built to connect residents of the Oktiabr district in the Old City to the Textile Kombinat.

66. O'zRMDA, f. 2532, op. 1, d. 10, l. 55.

67. TShDA, f. 10, op. 18, d. 960, l. 56.

68. O'zRMDA, f. 2532, op. 1, d. 29, l. 15.

69. O'zRMDA, f. 2532, op. 1, d. 10, ll. 63–64. Red Square in Tashkent is also referred to as Lenin Square in planning documents. By the 1960s, it is almost exclusively referred to as Lenin Square.

70. O'zRMDA, f. 2532, op. 1, d. 10, ll. 55–56.

71. O'zRMDA, f. 2532, op. 1, d. 10, ll. 61–62.

72. Ibid. Kuznetsov did not respond directly to Bulatov's criticism, and Mosoblproekt's final proposal did not fundamentally alter the plan for the city center.

73. King, *Colonial Urban Development,* 172–73; Hosagrahar Jyoti, "City as Durbar: Theater and Power in Imperial Delhi," 102; Paul Rabinow, "Colonialism, Modernity: The French in Morocco," 180–81, both in *Forms of Dominance: On the Architecture and Urbanism of the Colonial Enterprise,* ed. Nezar AlSayyad (Aldershot, England: Avebury, 1992).

74. Ia. G. Karash, "Park Ozero," *Komsomolets Uzbekistana,* July 14, 1939, 3. See also *Tashkent entsiklopediia, s.v.* "Detskaia zheleznaia doroga," 107.

75. O'zRMDA, f. 2532, op. 1, d. 29, l. 190b.

76. Construction began on April 23, 1939, and was completed on June 3, 1939. For descriptions of the building of Komsomol Lake, the park's attractions, and photographs of the area, see "Komsomol'skoe ozero sozdano!" *Pravda Vostoka,* June 3, 1939, 3; "Na

vodnoi stantsii," *Komsomolets Uzbekistana,* July 12, 1940, 4; "Poitakhtimizda," *Qizil O'zbekiston,* January 7, 1941, 2.

77. For a published example of propaganda on the importance of participating in construction projects, see I. Kulganin, "Politicheskaia shkola," *Pravda Vostoka,* August 15, 1939, 2.

78. A. Kuznetsov, "Rekonstruktsiia stolitsy Uzbekistana," *Arkhitektura SSSR,* no. 7 (1939): 6–15.

79. See, e.g., "Toshkent bu yil Toshkent sahar ijroia Komitet raisi urtok Sodik Xusainov bilan suxbat," *Qizil O'zbekiston,* April 16, 1941, 4; "O'zbekiston poyitaxti go'zal bo'lsin!" *Qizil O'zbekiston,* May 13, 1941, 3.

80. TShDA, f. 10, op. 18, d. 14-a, l. 3.

81. O'zRMDA, f. 2831, op. 1, l. 18. In this memoir, Vasili Stribezhev's recounts working on construction projects in the 1930s and 1940s. He notes that the majority of workers were young men from Russia.

82. O'zRMDA, f. 2532, op. 1, d. 31, ll. 48–480b.

83. O'zRMDA, f. 2532, op. 1, d. 8, l. 253.

84. Ensuring that the "flowering garden" of Central Asia kept blooming was difficult. Trees were planted along Tashkent's streets, but once planted, they seemed to have no one to take care of them. The reconstruction plan decreed expanding Tashkent's "green" parkland but did not make any provision to guarantee the survival of the vegetation in these areas. In 1940, the Gorispolkom mandated that all *mahalla* committees and city institutions take care of plants in their vicinity, but it lacked the staff to enforce this regulation. Furthermore, the rush to widen streets and build tall buildings necessitated the destruction of grapevines and fruit trees in the nooks and crannies of the Old City. In creating a "green city" in Central Asia, the Mosoblproekt program actually destroyed the city's existing gardens. Furthermore, despite calls to renovate Tashkent's irrigation canals, many of them were so clogged with refuse that they formed stagnant pools where malarial mosquitoes bred and the water was so polluted that it could kill the plants it was supposed to nourish. Again, the centralization of the reconstruction process did not provide adequate means for its implementation. Local institutions, specifically the Gorispolkom, were given the responsibility for overseeing the realization of the project but lacked the power to compete against central and republic-level institutions and factories. In effect, the centralized system was a two-edged sword for Tashkent. Central planners in Moscow came up with a plan for the city and told local officials and design bureaus to implement it. Local officials, however, lacked the power to go against the needs of industry and research institutions, which had their own agenda, namely, to increase industrial and agricultural production in Central Asia, even if it unofficially meant breaking the "iron law" of reconstruction. TShDA, f. 8, op. 1, d. 1311, l. 11; O'zRI-TTHMDA, f. 1, op. 3, d. 498, l. 35; "O'zbekiston poyitaxti go'zal bo'lsin!" *Qizil O'zbekiston,* May 13, 1941, 3.

85. TShDA, f. 8, op. 1, d. 1311, l. 11.

86. O'zRMDA, f. 2532, op. 1, d. 8, ll. 271–73.

87. O'zRMDA, f. 2532, op. 1, d. 10, l. 55.

Chapter 4. War and Evacuation

1. Richard Overy, *Russia's War* (New York: Penguin Books, 1998), 87–90.

2. L. A. Rybakovskii, *Liudskie poteri SSSR i Rossii v Velikoi Otechestvennoi voine* (Moscow: Rossiiskaia Akademiia nauk, institute sotsial'no-politicheskikh issledovanii,

2001), 42. Overy estimates that twenty Soviet soldiers died for every German soldier killed. Overy, *Russia's War*, 117. On migration figures, see Frederick Kagan, "The Evacuation of Soviet Industry in the Wake of 'Barbarossa': A Key to the Soviet Victory," *Journal of Slavic Military Studies*, no. 2 (1995): 393; Kristen Edwards, "Fleeing to Siberia: The Wartime Relocation of Evacuees to Novosibirsk, 1941-1943" (PhD diss., Stanford University, 1996).

3. John Barber and Mark Harrison, *The Soviet Home Front, 1941-1945: A Social and Economic History of the USSR in World War II* (London: Longman, 1991), 60-61. See also decree published in "Ukaz Prezidiuma Verkhovnogo Soveta SSR o rezhime rabochego vremeni rabochikh i sluzhashchikh v voennoe vremia," June 26, 1941, in *Vstavai strana ogromnaia* (Tashkent: Izd. Uzbekistan, 1990), 14-15.

4. Barber and Harrison, *Soviet Home Front, 1941-1945*, 62-63.

5. The evacuation began almost immediately after the German invasion. The Central Committee of the Communist Party and the Sovnarkom created the Evacuation Council on June 24, 1941, to direct the evacuation of "items of value" from the front lines to the inner regions of the Soviet Union. The evacuation gained in importance and tempo in late summer and autumn 1941 as German troops continued to advance eastward into Soviet territory. See G. A. Kumanev, "The Soviet Economy and the 1941 Evacuation," in *Operation Barbarossa*, ed. Joseph L. Wieczynski (Salt Lake City: Charles Schlacks Jr., Publisher, 1993), 163-93.

6. The net population increase was less, however, considering army mobilization and the movement of people to other regions of Central Asia. TShDA, f. 28, op. 1, d. 6925, l. 5.

7. See Faina Ranevskaia, *Dnevnik na klochkakh* (St. Petersburg: Izd. Fonda russkoi poezii, 1999); Aleksander Topolski, *Without Vodka: Wartime Adventures in Russia* (Ottawa: UP Press, 1999); Mariia Belkina, *Skreshchenie sudeb* (Moscow: Kniga, 1988); Tatiana Lugovskaia, *Kak znaiu, kak pomniu, kak umeiu* (Moscow: Agraf, 2001).

8. In Babi Yar, a suburban area near Kiev, 33,771 Jews were massacred, while approximately 80,000 Jews were murdered in Odessa by Romanian and German troops. See Overy, *Russia's War*, 134, 140-41. See also Gerald Reitlinger, *The House Built on Sand: The Conflicts of German Policy in Russia, 1939-1945* (New York: Viking Press, 1960); Alexander Werth, *Russia at War, 1941-1945* (New York: Avon Books, 1964), 298-342; Lidiya Ginzburg, *Blockade Diary* (London: Harvill Press, 1995); Elena Kochina, *Blockade Diary* (Ann Arbor, MI: Ardis, 1990); Boris Mikhailovich, *Na dne blokady, voiny* (St. Petersburg: Izd. VSEGEI, 2000).

9. See Butov's speech, "Tekushchii moment i nashi zadachi," to the meeting of primary Party organizations of the Central Committee of the Communist Party of Uzbekistan, October 24, 1941, RGASPI, f. 17, op. 125, d. 29, ll. 71-72.

10. RGANI, f. 6, op. 6, d. 667, l. 51; RGASPI, f. 17, op. 22, d. 2784, l. 166.

11. RGASPI, f. 17, op. 88, d. 95, l. 70.

12. Natalia Gromova, *Vse v chuzhoe gliadiam okno* (Moscow: Kollektsiia "Sovershenno sektretno," 2002), 7-8, 162. Confusing rumors about an imminent Anglo-American attack likely occurred because the British and Americans had been identified as potential threats to the Soviet Union, which had a neutrality pact with Nazi Germany. Once Germany broke the pact, Soviet propaganda flipped, transforming Nazis, the former neutral partners, into enemies, while the British, formerly enemies, became allies.

13. See "Postanovleniie TsK KP/b/ Uzbekistana po dokladu sekretaria Tashkentskogo Gorkoma partii o rabote Tashkentskoi gorodskoi partiinoi organizatsii v usloviiakh voennogo vremeni," September 8, 1941, printed in *Vstavai strana ogromnaia*, 30-31. Richard J. Brody notes that political agitation campaigns on the home front

were hampered by the lack of agitators, a lack of newspapers and journals, poor radio transmission, and uninspiring lectures by Soviet agitators. See Richard J. Brody, *Ideology and Political Mobilization: The Soviet Home Front during World War II* (Pittsburgh: University of Pittsburgh Center for Russian and East European Studies, 1994), 9–13, 21.

14. RGASPI, f. 17, op. 88, d. 95, l. 2.

15. RGASPI, f. 17, op. 88, d. 95, l. 18.

16. RGASPI, f. 17, op. 88, d. 95, l. 4; RGASPI, f. 17, op. 88, d. 96. l. 13. No ethnic breakdown for these Samarkand women was documented. Also, it is unclear whether their action was orchestrated from above or was of their own initiative.

17. The number of Tashkent "volunteers" appears to be lower, possibly because of the lack of an immediate threat to the city. In Leningrad, 159,000 people joined the popular militia, the *opolchenie,* to defend the city. For popular reaction and cases of volunteerism in other cities, see Barber and Harrison, *Soviet Home Front, 1941–1945,* 60–63. Casualty rates for the *oplochenie* were extremely high across the Soviet Union, particularly in Moscow, Leningrad, and Kiev. Overy, *Russia's War,* 80.

18. See RGASPI, f. 17, op. 88, d. 95, l. 18; RGASPI, f. 17, op. 22, d. 2884, l. 122.

19. RGASPI, f. 17, op. 88, d. 95, l. 4. Anti-Soviet elements were seen as stronger in Fergana than in Tashkent. While waiting in line for bread at the Fergana Textile Kombinat, Yusup Agadzhanov responded to a plea of Tashkent Textile Kombinat workers to increase production by stating that Russians should be killed or else they would leave Uzbeks to starve. Another said that he thought that the Uzbek people were too clever for Soviet authorities and, therefore, would not fight for the Soviet state. RGASPI, f. 17, op. 88, d. 95, l. 85. See also RGASPI, f. 17, op. 88, d. 96, l. 147.

20. RGASPI, f. 17, op. 88, d. 96, l. 80.

21. RGANI, f. 6, op. 6, d. 667, ll. 47–50; RGASPI, f. 17, op. 22, d. 2786, l. 56; RGASPI, f. 17, op. 88, d. 96, ll. 119, 147.

22. Barber notes that Moscow nurses tried to destroy documents in order to avoid being sent to the front as medical workers. In preparation for the arrival of German forces in the Soviet capital, some Communists and Komsomol members tore up their Party cards and began to wear crucifix pendants or pins to signify that they were Christians and not Communist Party members.

23. The situation of Tashkent men not responding to mobilization and being hidden by their communities caused concern for Gorkom officials in 1941 and 1942. To fight such tendencies, the Gorkom ordered the militia and city NKVD officials to conduct periodic sweeps of all hotels, dorms, collective farms, bazaars, parks, barbershops, and roads leading into the city to find men who refused to join the Red Army. The Gorkom also noted that all Komsomol, Party, factory, and *mahalla* leaders had to conduct propaganda lectures to inform the population of the consequences of failing to complete one's military obligations. RGASPI, f. 17, op. 22, d. 2786, l. 56.

24. Other negative statements reported from the Uzbek capital included: "there are only 13 republics left, and tomorrow we don't know what will happen"; "whoever wins this war, we'll be on their side"; and a statement that Hitler would make "red meat" out of the Red Army. RGASPI, f. 17, op. 88, d. 95, ll. 19, 53, 136, 154, 161, 171.

25. Overy, *Russia's War,* 115.

26. RGASPI, f. 17, op. 88, d. 95, ll. 22, 29, 54, 55; RGASPI, f. 17, op. 88, d. 96, ll. 109, 119; TVDA, f. 652, op. 1. d. 360, ll. 2–3.

27. For wartime identification of Germans as Basmachis, see "Bosmachi gitlerchilar koalitsiiasining emirilishi," *Qizil O'zbekiston,* December 22, 1943, 2; E. A. Voskoboinikov, *Uzbekskii narod v gody Velikoi Otechestvennoi voiny* (Tashkent, Goz. Izd. UzSSR, 1947), 10, 13.

28. *Zhenshchiny Uzbekistana* (Tashkent: Tashkentskaia tipografiia, 1941), 11.

29. "Iz pis'ma Uzbekskogo naroda k boitsam-Uzbekam," *Pravda,* October 31, 1942. Reprinted in *Vstavai strana ogromnaia,* 89–90.

30. The dehumanization of the enemy is a common technique of war propaganda and is not unique to the twentieth century or to authoritarian states. See Sam Keen, *Faces of the Enemy: Reflections of the Hostile Imagination* (San Francisco: Harper, 1991).

31. See RGASPI, f. 17, op. 22, d. 2884, l. 122.

32. For a few examples, see "Alisher Navoii hakida kinofil'm yaratimiz," *Qizil O'zbekiston,* November 23, 1941, 4. See descriptions of wartime work by Oibek, Gafur Gulom, Sheikhzade, and others in RGASPI, f. 17, op. 43, d. 2104, l. 293.

33. O'zRMDA, f. 2532, op. 1, d. 40, l. 10.

34. See RGASPI, f. 17, op. 43, d. 402, ll. 6–9.

35. *Vstavai strana ogromnaia,* 16–18; TShDA, f. 10, op. 18, d. 454, l. 20; RGASPI, f. 17, op. 22, d. 2905, ll. 105, 175; RGASPI, f. 17, op. 88, d. 96, l. 20; TShDA, f. 10, op. 18, d. 454, l. 169. For antiaircraft defense plans of individual Tashkent regions, see TShDA, f. 10, op. 18, d. 49, ll. 28–32. For review of the partial "success" of one air raid drill, see "Toshkenda shaharni korong'ilatish mashqi yakshi o'tdi," *Qizil O'zbekiston,* December 18, 1941, 3. This article notes that the most important institutions of the city—the Textile Kombinat, the Selmash factory, and the Chkalov aviation factory—successfully implemented blackout conditions within the allotted time (five minutes from an air raid warning announcement). However, the Commissariat of Education of the Uzbek SSR, the Tashkent automobile factory, numerous pharmacies, and much of Karl Marx and Pushkin streets remained illuminated. Directors of these institutions were fined for their failure to participate in the air raid drill.

36. See Decree of the Council of Ministers of the Uzbek SSR and the Central Committee of the Communist Party of Uzbekistan, July 2–4, 1941, TShDA, f. 10, op. 18, d. 49, ll. 19–20. See also RGASPI, f. 17, op. 22, d. 2908, l. 106. For military preparedness in Tashkent schools, see TShDA, f. 10, op. 18, d. 49, ll. 91–930b.

37. See RGASPI, f. 17, op. 22, d. 2884, ll. 123–24.

38. See "K zhenshchinam Uzbekistana," in *Zhenshchiny Uzbekistana,* 8–9.

39. RGASPI, f. 17, op. 88, d. 95, l. 50.

40. See "Postanovlenie Tashkentskogo obkoma KP/b/ Uzbekistana o sbore sredi naseleniia teplykh veshchei dlia Krasnoi Armii," September 7, 1941, in *Vstavai strana ogromnaia,* 159–61.

41. See "K zhenshchinam Anglii i soedinennykh shtatov Ameriki," in *Zhenshchiny Uzbekistana,* 13; "Rech' sekretaria TsK KP/b/ Uz po propagande. t. F. Yuldashbaevoi," in *Zhenshchiny Uzbekistana,* 17–23.

42. See "Iz politinformatsii zaveduiushchego orginstruktorskim otdelom Tashkentskogo obkoma KP/b/ Uzbekistana B. Vilcheka v TsK KP/b/ Uzbekistana o vovlechenii zhenshchin v proizvodstvo." This document was reproduced from the Party Archive of Uzbekistan (PA Uz IML, f. 58, op. 17, d. 598) in *Vstavai strana ogromnaia,* 176. The Party Archive of Uzbekistan, now known as the Presidential Archive of the Republic of Uzbekistan, remains closed to researchers. See also RGASPI, f. 17, op. 44, d. 1603, ll. 1–15.

43. RGASPI, f. 17, op. 88, d. 628, l. 131.

44. See RGASPI, f. 17, op. 44, d. 1603, ll. 1–15; RGASPI, f. 17, op. 88, d. 628, l. 131. In addition, the Central Committee report noted that only 9 out of 830 Communist Party member workers at the Rostselmach factory were Uzbek, while only 3 of 288 Communist Party member workers at Tashkent factory no. 735 were Uzbeks. RGASPI, f. 17, op.

88, d. 628, ll. 121–31. High turnover rates persisted in light industry, food processing, and textile refinement as well. See Ibid., l. 81.

45. RGASPI, f. 17, op. 44, d. 1604, ll. 34–35.

46. See "Ko vsem zhenshchinam Uzbekistana: Obrashchenie sobraniia zhenskogo aktiva goroda Tashkenta," reprinted in Grigorii Marianovskii, *Kniga sudeb, dokumental'noe povestvovaniia* (Tashkent: Izd. Literatury i iskusstva im. Gafura Guliama, 1988), 41–42.

47. RGASPI, f. 17, op. 88, d. 95, l. 161. Both husbands were arrested.

48. In May 1945, the mobilization and retaining of Uzbek women in industrial production remained a problem. A report from the USSR Central Committee noted that in 1944, only 15 percent of Tashkent workers were of Uzbek ethnic background and that toward the end of the war Uzbeks deserted the factory in greater numbers than Uzbeks who entered the factory work force. See RGASPI, f. 17, op. 122, d. 95, l. 128.

49. I. Sigalov, *Uzbekskaia delegatsiia na zapadnom fronte* (Tashkent: Gosizdat, UzSSR, 1942), 10.

50. Iu. Akhunbabaev, *Trudiashchikhsia Uzbekistana frontu* (Tashkent: Izd. Profizdat, 1942), 11.

51. "Iz pis'ma Uzbekskogo naroda k boitsam-uzbekam," *Pravda,* October 31, 1942, reprinted in *Vstavai strana ogromnaia,* 89–90.

52. Kagan, "Evacuation of Soviet Industry," 389, 395; Sanford R. Lieberman, "The Evacuation of Industry in the Soviet Union during World War II," *Soviet Studies,* no. 1 (1983): 91–92.

53. *Uzbekskaia SSR v gody Velikoi Otechestvennoi voiny,* vol. 1 (Tashkent: Izd. FAN, 1981), 114. Kagan notes that "the term 'industrial enterprise' is nebulous and does not denote the size or significance of the plant." Kagan, "Evacuation of Soviet Industry," 400.

54. O'zRDMA, f. 88, op. 1, d. 8256, l. 28. In a report dated November 28, 1941, the director of the factory noted that small-scale production had begun in September but that the factory was not fully functional until October.

55. In her dissertation on the evacuation of industry to Novosibirsk, Kristen Edwards states that the two main phases of the evacuation occurred from July 1941 through winter 1942 and from May to October 1942. Edwards, "Fleeing to Siberia," 26. While industrial factories did arrive in Tashkent in the summer of 1941, the bulk of the evacuation arrivals into Central Asia occurred between mid-November 1941 and late March 1942, indicating that the fall of Kiev and the threatening approach of German armies toward Moscow and Leningrad between September and October increased the pressure on the Evacuation Council to speed up the pace of the evacuation. Therefore, for the purposes of studying Tashkent, the first bulk of the evacuation occurred slightly later than in Novosibirsk.

56. Kagan, "Evacuation of Soviet Industry," 392.

57. *Uzbekskaia SSR v gody Velikoi Otechestvennoi voiny,* vol. 1, 115, 121–22.

58. GARF, f. 6822, op. 1, d. 49, ll. 68–70; O'zRMDA, f. R-314, op. 1, d. 33, l. 287; GARF, f. 6822, op. 1, d. 48, l. 36. For example, the Institute of World Languages left Moscow destined for Tashkent but ended up in Alma-Ata. GARF, f. 6822, op. 1, d. 51, l. 94.

59. O'zRMDA, f. 88, op. 9, d. 8255, ll. 1, 17.

60. O'zRMDA, f. 88, op. 9, d. 8255, l. 25.

61. Kristen Edwards discusses the problem of the multiple bureaucratic layers of organizations involved in the evacuation and the difficulty the Soviet state experienced in trying to develop a full-scale union-wide plan to transport industry from areas near

the front lines to the safety of the "deep" home front. See Edwards, "Fleeing to Siberia," 52–85.

62. RGASPI, f. 17, op. 22, d. 2884, l. 87.

63. RGASPI, f. 17, op. 22, d. 2884, ll. 84–85.

64. O'zRMDA, f. 88, op. 9, d. 8256, ll. 27–28. For other examples, see GARF, f. 6822, op. 1, d. 366, ll. 3–6.

65. Unfortunately, the director does not mention how the buildings in question were used before the evacuation. O'zRMDA, f. 88, op. 1, d. 8256, l. 66.

66. On Elektrostanok's transportation problems, see O'zRMDA, f. 88, op. 1, d. 8256, l. 67. The Elektrostanok factory was located more than a kilometer from the nearest tram station on the outskirts of the city. Most workers or visitors to the factory also had to take three trams to get to that stop from other areas of the city. The wartime public transportation system was far from "rational." See ibid. On the mobilization of horses, camels, and donkeys for intra-Tashkent transport, see RGASPI, f. 17, op. 22, d. 2767, l. 41.

67. Of evacuees sent to Uzbek *kolkhozes*, 25 percent reportedly did not participate in agricultural labor, largely because they were unfit for farm work or because, having been urbanites, they were unfamiliar with farming. O'zRMDA, f. 314, op. 1, d. 116, ll. 350b–36.

68. For a breakdown of orphans by social origin and information on where they were placed in Uzbekistan, see O'zRI-TTHMDA, f. 94, op. 5, d. 4261, l. 91.

69. RGASPI, f. 17, op. 22, d. 2884, l. 80. Publishing was important because of the need to produce war propaganda.

70. RGASPI, f. 17, op. 22, d. 2884, l. 80. This statement by the director of a factory was surprising since most factory administrators fought to acquire and keep school buildings and sometimes even refused to return them after the war.

71. RGASPI, f. 17, op. 88, d. 628, l. 56.

72. See "Spisok evakogospitalei po g. Tashkentu i Tashoblasti," TVDA, f. 652, op. 1, d. 262, ll. 2–4.

73. O'zRMDA, f. R-314, op. 1, d. 39, l. 330.

74. O'zRMDA, f. R-314, op. 1, d. 38, l. 1; "Vospityvat' uzbekskie muzykal'nye kadry," *Pravda Vostoka*, June 23, 1943, 2.

75. TShDA, f. 10, op. 18, d. 1029, l. 70.

76. RGASPI, f. 17, op. 3, d. 1043, l. 53.

77. Belkina, *Skreshchenie sudeb*, 304.

78. GARF, f. 6822, op. 1, d. 45, l. 18; GARF, f. 6822, op. 1, d. 266, l. 13; O'zRMDA, f. R-314, op. 1, d. 38, l. 1. The Theater of the Revolution was rerouted from Tashkent to Namangan by order of the Uzbek Sovnarkom. The Evacuation Council revoked this order and returned the theater to Tashkent, where it was placed in the local Theater of the Red Army of the Central Asian Military District (SAVO). GARF, f. 6822, op. 1, d. 50, l. 4.

79. Members of the Union of Soviet Writers, evacuated from Moscow and Leningrad, were given tasks, including "teaching" Uzbek counterparts, providing Tashkent writers with better knowledge of Russian and world literature, and helping them to "improve" their literary techniques. Musicologists were supposed to take over the training of Uzbek musicians through the creation of five-month programs to teach musical theory, the history of Western music, and other topics. TShDA, f. 10, op. 18, d. 36, l. 14. In addition, evacuated architects provided "help" to improve the skills of local urban planners. T. F. Kadyrova, "Puti razvitiia arkhitektury Sovetskogo Uzbekistana," *Stroitel'stvo i arkhitektura Uzbekistana*, no. 12 (1972): 12.

80. See Marianovskii, *Kniga sudeb,* 19; Gromova, *Vse v chuzhoe gliadiam okno,* 39; Belkina, *Skreshchenie sudeb,* 304.

81. On negotiations for evacuation sites for the Academy of Sciences, see GARF, f. 6822, op. 1, d. 351, ll. 1–10.

82. TShDA, f. 10, op. 18, d. 49, l. 271; O'zRI-TTHMDA, f. 1, op. 1, d. 3272, l. 46. Letters containing complaints about forced expulsion were written by both Russians and Uzbeks, but usually in Russian. Those expelled had three days to leave Tashkent. See TShDA, f. 10, op. 18, d. 36A, ll. 4–5, 21, 29, 90, 163, 302. Those with German surnames also were expelled from the city. Ibid., l. 205.

83. GARF, f. 6822, op. 1, d. 49, ll. 68–70; GARF, f. 6822, op. 1, d. 50, l. 55. On Muscovites' dissatisfaction with the Ashgabat university facility, see RGASPI, f. 17, op. 125, d. 85, ll. 42–43, 47.

84. O'zRMDA, f. R-314, op. 1, d. 116, l. 36. Georgii Veniuk, an evacuated writer from Moldova, complained of his placement in Kitab, Bukhara oblast, where he worked at a wine factory. He requested being placed with literary figures with whom he could interact. O'zRMDA, f. 2356, op. 1, d. 94, l. 137.

85. The Tashkent Oblispolkom archival collection contains complaints about hunger in the countryside, including questions over the unequal distribution of food between evacuees and local collective farm members, and reports of citizens in their thirties who died of starvation because they did not receive even "one gram of bread." Many of them attempted to escape into Tashkent. TVDA, f. 652, op. 1, d. 356, l. 192.

86. For the estimate from Tashkent, see O'zRMDA, f. 2454, op. 1, d. 950, l. 82. For the estimate of the Central Statistical Administration in Moscow, see RGAE, f. 1562, op. 20, d. 327, l. 101. According to the Central Statistical Bureau, the prewar figure from 1939 was 584,955. RGAE, f. 1562, op. 20, d. 381, l. 3. The population of Tashkent oblast on January 1, 1940, was reported at 1,241,975. RGAE, f. 1562, op. 20, d. 327, l. 192. This figure for Tashkent oblast as a whole increased to 1,644,455 by June 1942. Ibid., ll. 9, 125. Despite the fact that one should question the accuracy of these numbers due to manipulation of the 1939 census and the difficulties of recording population increases during the war, the tremendous fluctuations indicate enormous population increases into the Uzbek capital region.

87. Yusupov estimated the 1941 population at 600,000, approximately 15,000 more residents than in the 1939 census. At the end of 1943, he estimated the Tashkent population to be "almost up to one million people" ("*pochti do 1 milliona chelovek*"). RGASPI, f. 17, op. 88, d. 628, l. 92.

88. Iu. L. Kosenkova, *Sovetskii gorod* (Moscow: URSS, 2000), 28.

89. Protokol, March 31, 1942, Uzbek Central Committee Meeting, RGASPI, f. 17, op. 43, d. 2105, l. 10.

90. O'zRMDA, f. R-837, op. 32, d. 3514, ll. 3–4.

91. O'zRMDA, f. R-837, op. 32, d. 3514, l. 4.

92. Ibid.

93. Ibid.; O'zRMDA, f. 2532, op. 1, d. 950, ll. 81–91.

94. O'zRMDA, f. R-837, op. 32, d. 3514, l. 40b.

95. See Uzbek Sovnarkom and Central Committee decree "on measures to speed up housing and communal construction and to repair the existing housing fund," August 24, 1942, O'zRI-TTHMDA, f. 1, op. 1. d. 3276, l. 1200b.

96. O'zRI-TTHMDA, f. 1, op. 1, d. 3273, l. 540b–55.

97. RGASPI, f. 17, op. 22, d. 2884, ll. 23–24.

98. O'zRMDA, f. 2532, op. 1, d. 40, ll. 114–140b.

99. V. N. Semenov, "Poselki dlia predpriiatii, evakuirovannykh v Sredniiu Aziiu," *Arkhitektura SSSR*, no. 1 (1942): 20.

100. Ibid.

101. G. Zakharov and Z. Charnysheva, "Opyt proektirovaniia zhilishch dlia Srednei Azii," *Arkhitektura SSSR*, no. 4 (1943): 16, 18.

102. "Ekonomit' vodoprovodnuiu vodu," *Pravda Vostoka*, July 28, 1943, 2; "Ulush-chit' sanitarnoe sostoianie gorodov," *Pravda Vostoka*, April 21, 1943, 1.

103. O'zRMDA, f. R-837, op. 32, d. 3514, ll. 8–10.

104. RGASPI, f. 17, op. 22, d. 2884, ll. 18, 26; RGASPI, f. 17, op. 43, d. 402, l. 11; O'zRI-TTHMDA, f. 1, op. 1, d. 3273, l. 72; TShDA, f. 10, op. 17, f. 53, ll. 35; Kadyrova, *Arkhitektura sovetskogo Uzbekistana*, 70–72. On the search for local energy resources (coal, oil, hydrotechnology), see *Uzbekskaia SSR v gody Velikoi Otechestvennoi voiny*, vol. 1, 122–25; *Uzbekskaia SSR v gody Velikoi Otechestvennoi voiny*, vol. 2. (Tashkent: Izd. FAN, 1983), 45–49.

105. GARF, f. 8114, op. 1, d. 917, ll. 33–34.

106. Document collection in author's possession listing names, work locations, dates of arrival, and deaths of Japanese POWs in Uzbekistan.

107. On the Navoi Theater, see chap. 6 and O'zRI-TTHMDA, f. 1, op. 1, d. 3275, ll. 115–160b. On the Mukimi Theater, see "Stroitel'stvo novogo teatra v Tashkente," *Pravda Vostoka*, July 3, 1943, 1; "Na stroike teatra," *Pravda Vostoka*, November 7, 1943, 4; *Tashkent entsiklopediia, s.v.* "Teatr imeni Mukimi," 332; Kadyrova, *Arkhitektura sovetskogo Uzbekistana*, 74.

Chapter 5. Central Asian Lives at War

The epigraph is from Topolski, *Without Vodka*, 315.

1. RGASPI, f. 17, op. 88, d. 95, l. 177.

2. RGASPI, f. 17, op. 88, d. 95, l. 70.

3. RGASPI, f. 17, op. 88, d. 95, ll. 177–78.

4. RGASPI. f. 17, op. 88, d. 95, l. 178; RGASPI, f. 17, op. 88, d. 95, ll. 177–78. See chap. 4 for additional discussion on the mood of Tashkent at the start of the war.

5. Gromova, *Vse v chuzhoe gliadiam okno*, 7.

6. As part of the German-Soviet nonaggression pact of 1939, the Soviet Union and Nazi Germany secretly agreed to partition Poland. When the Nazis invaded Poland in 1939, the Red Army crossed into the eastern portion of that country and annexed terri-tory. Thousands of Polish citizens—military officers and soldiers, government officials, landowners, intellectuals, those who refused to swear allegiance to the Soviet Union, and countless others—were arrested and deported to Siberian and Central Asian labor camps. After the Nazi invasion of the Soviet Union, the Polish government-in-exile in London and the Soviet Union became awkward allies. The wartime Sikorski-Maiskii pact of July 1941 called for a general amnesty of Polish citizens in Soviet labor camps in 1941 and the organization of a Polish army in the Soviet Union that was to be evacu-ated to Persia. Working with Soviet authorities, the Polish government set up a series of military recruitment camps in Uzbekistan to which thousands of these newly liberated Polish citizens flocked.

7. Aleksander Wat, *My Century* (Berkeley: University of California Press, 1977), 336.

8. RGASPI, f. 17, op. 88, d. 96, l. 119.

9. RGASPI, f. 17, op. 88, d. 95, l. 109.

10. Katherine Jolluck discusses encounters in which Polish women viewed Central Asians negatively, believing them to be uncivilized, lacking in intelligence, and threat-

ening. Katherine Jolluck, *Exile and Identity: Polish Women in the Soviet Union during World War II* (Pittsburgh: University of Pittsburgh, 2002), 227–33.

11. RGASPI, f. 17, op. 88, d. 95, l. 54.

12. Ibid., l. 70.

13. In addition to anti-Russian and anti-Uzbek statements, there were also were numerous anti-Soviet statements. See chap. 4.

14. RGASPI, f. 17, op. l 88, d. 95, l. 80.

15. Dorit Bader Whiteman, *Escape via Siberia* (New York: Holmes & Meier, 1999), 72; interview with Misha Raitzen, 1981, New York Public Library–American Jewish Committee Oral History Collection, Dorot Jewish Division, New York Public Library, Astor, Lenox and Tilden Foundation.

16. RGASPI, f. 17, op. 125, d. 29, l. 74.

17. TVDA, f. 652, op. 1, d. 360, l. 20b.

18. Interview with Misha Raitzin, 1981, Dorot Jewish Division, NYPL.

19. TShDA, f. 10, op. 17, d. 55, ll. 26–28.

20. For impressions that Uzbeks hoarded food, see Whiteman, *Escape via Siberia,* 73. For criticism of local collective farmers for hoarding food to sell at the bazaar, see TVDA, f. 652, op. 1, d. 372, l. 66. Nonetheless, other reports note that Uzbeks were not the only people involved in speculation. It was noted that Russian soldiers were also selling items in Tashkent's bazaars. O'zRI-TTHMDA, f. 1, op. 1, d. 3429, l. 4.

21. Mandel'stam to Kuzin, December 15, 1941, in Boris Kuzin and Nadezhda Mandel'stam, *Vospominaniia, proizvedeniia, perepiska: 192 pis'ma k B. S. Kuzinu* (St. Petersburg: Inapress, 1999), 659.

22. Kornei Chukovskii, as quoted in Marianovskii, *Kniga sudeb,* 19.

23. Wat, *My Century,* 336.

24. Topolski, *Without Vodka,* 345. For other impressions of "exotic" aspects of Central Asian lifestyles, see Topolski, *Without Vodka,* 357; Belkina, *Skreshchenie sudeb,* 305; Lugovskaia, *Kak znaiu, kak pomniu, kak umeiu,* 275.

25. Belkina, *Skreshchenie sudeb,* 304.

26. Aleksei Tolstoi, as quoted in Gromova, *Vse v chuzhoe gliadiam okno,* 39.

27. O'zRMDA, f. R-314, op. 1, d. 38, l. 109; O'zRMDA, f. R-314, op. 1, d. 146, ll. 71, 76; TShDA, f. 13, op. 3, d. 33, l. 33.

28. For the Tatar deportation, see Norman Naimark, *Fires of Hatred: Ethnic Cleansing in Twentieth-Century Europe* (Cambridge, MA: Harvard University Press, 2001); Brian Glyn Williams, *The Crimean Tatars: The Diaspora Experience and the Forging of a Nation* (Leiden: Brill, 2001), 376–82.

29. Topolski, *Without Vodka,* 339.

30. On migration and its correlation with disease rates, see O'zRI-TTHMDA, f. 1, op. 1, d. 3405, ll. 97–990b; O'zRI-TTHMDA, f. 1, op. 1, d. 3584, l. 1; RGASPI, f. 17, op. 22, d. 2786, ll. 132–34.

31. O'zRMDA, f. R-314, op. 1, d. 21, l. 152.

32. TShDA, f. 10, op. 17, d. 14, ll. 2–3.

33. O'zRMDA, f. R-314, op. 1, d. 127, ll. 120–21.

34. Jack Pomerantz and Lyric Wallwork Winik, *Run East: Flight from the Holocaust* (Urbana: University of Illinois Press, 1997), 55.

35. TShDA, f. 10, op. 18, d. 26, l. 363.

36. On conditions of bathhouses and fights inside of them over clothing, see O'zRMDA, f. R-314, op. 1, d. 116, ll. 7, 8, 11, 12; O'zRMDA, f. R-314, op. 1, d. 127, ll. 120–1200b. On clothing shortages, see O'zRMDA, f. R-314, op. 1, d. 116, l. 12.

37. In a letter she wrote to Boris Kuzin in November 1942, Nadezhda Mandel'stam

noted that she was without shoes during winter in Tashkent. Mandel'stam to Kuzin, November 8, 1942, in Kuzin and Mandel'stam, *Vospominaniia, proizvedeniia, perepiska,* 687.

38. TShDA, f. 10, op. 18, d. 36A, ll. 21, 90–91, 96, 175.

39. RGASPI, f. 17, op. 22, d. 2884, ll. 86–87; RGASPI, f. 17, op. 22, d. 2911, l. 4.

40. Belkina, *Skreshchenie sudeb,* 305. For instructions on the placement of unorganized or unskilled workers in the countryside, see TShDA, f. 10, op. 18, d. 49, l. 36.

41. O'zRMDA, f. R-314, op. 1, d. 116, l. 31.

42. D. Khodzhaev, "Za kul'turnyi, blagoustroennyi Tashkent," *Pravda Vostoka,* May 28, 1943, 1; S. Khusainov, "Blagoustroistvo goroda—krovnoe delo vsego naseleniia," *Pravda Vostoka,* June 28, 1944, 2.

43. TShDA, f. 231, op. 1, d. 1505, ll. 68–69, 119.

44. RGASPI, f. 17, op. 43, d. 2104, l. 42.

45. Konstantin Simonov, *Ostaius' zhurnalistom* (Moscow: Izd. Pravda, 1968), 164–65. The actress Faina Ranevskaia purchased two live turkeys for food. She kept them in the basement of her building, where both of them died. Aleksei Shcheglov, *Faina Ranevskaia: vsia zhizn'* (Moscow: Zakharov, 2001), 87–88.

46. Shcheglov, *Faina Ranevskaia,* 87.

47. On the Turman murder, see GARF, f. 8131, op. 23, d. 240, l. 51; TShDA, f. 231, op. 1, d. 1724, l. 32. On petty crime and theft from cafeterias and factory gardens, see TShDA, f. 231, op. 1, d. 1608, l. 11; TShDA, f. 231, op. 1, d. 1724, l. 12.

48. RGASPI, f. 17, op 122, d. 95, ll. 128–29.

49. RGASPI, f. 17, op 122, d. 95, ll. 131, 135.

50. Factories officially were forbidden from hiring deserters, but the need for labor led many directors to overlook this regulation. TShDA, f. 231, op. 1, d. 1656, l. 65.

51. This discussion deals only with the Tatars who arrived in Central Asia, not the reasons for or events that led up to their deportations. It also does not deal with the controversies over the desire to return to the Black Sea region or the extent of Tatar wartime collaboration. For background on the causes for the Tatar deportation, see Naimark, *Fires of Hatred,* 101–2; Williams, *Crimean Tatars,* 376–82; *Crimean Tatars: Repatriation and Conflict Prevention* (New York: Open Society Institute Forced Migration Projects, 1996), 1–28.

52. GARF, f. 9479, op. 1, d. 166, l. 136; GARF, f. 9479, op. 1, d. 179, ll. 241–42. Williams notes that Tashkent oblast had 56,632 Tatar deportees, followed by Samarkand, with 31,540. Williams, *Crimean Tatars,* 393.

53. *Tashkentskii protsess: sud nad desiat'iu predstaviteliami krymskotatarskogo naroda (1 iulia–5 avgusta 1969 g.); sbornik dokumentov s illiustratsiiami* (Amsterdam: Fond imeni Gertsena, 1976), 590. See also Williams, *Crimean Tatars,* 392.

54. GARF, f. 9479, op. 1, d. 180, l. 8.

55. GARF, f. 9479, op. 1, d. 166, l. 156.

56. Ibid.

57. GARF, f. 9479, op. 1. d. 166, l. 112.

58. This specific rumor was reported from Kashkadarya oblast. Another report noted that "the Tatars are coming here, and soon all the Europeans, then the Uzbeks will be expelled from here." GARF, f. 9479, op. 1. d. 179, l. 242. See also GARF, f. 9479, op. 1. d. 180, l. 8.

59. TShDA, f. 10, op. 17, d. 55, l. 10.

60. TShDA, f. 10, op. 17, d. 55, ll. 26–28.

61. TShDA, f. 10, op. 17, d. 55, l. 13.

62. TShDA, f. 10, op. 17, d. 55, l. 21.

63. TShDA, f. 10, op. 17, d. 55, l. 15.

64. TShDA, f. 10, op. 17, d. 55, l. 18.

65. Some Tashkenters expressed anger toward the Soviet state and Soviet allies, whom they felt lied to home-front residents. In April 1943, a woman wrote, "Fedia, do you have any information about the course of the war or do you also want to 'lie' to us like they lie to us on the home front, they walk around and write, but we see no help. You write that in the near future that we will be able to hug you and kiss you, that, Fedia is a self-deception, not happiness. Churchill writes that the war will end in 1944 and 1945. . . . Fedia, we might be on the home front, but we are not idiots. We see everything. Stalin said on May 1, 1942, that the war would be a year. . . . The casualties of this war are not only on the front, but what about on the home front?" TShDA, f. 10, op. 17, d. 55, l. 35.

66. TShDA, f. 10, op. 17, d. 55, l. 15.

67. The Union of Soviet Writers had its own members-only stores and cafeterias. O'zRMDA, f. 2356, op. 1, d. 98, ll. 9–13.

68. TShDA, f. 10, op. 17, d. 55, l. 178.

69. TShDA, f. 10, op. 17, d. 55, l. 13.

70. TShDA, f. 10, op. 18, d. 36A, ll. 205–6, 234.

71. TShDA, f. 10, op. 17, d. 55, l. 20.

72. TShDA, f. 10, op. 17, d. 55, l. 24.

73. TShDA, f. 10, op. 17, d. 55, l. 11.

74. GARF, f. 8131, op. 19, d. 58, l. 19.

75. TShDA, f. 10, op. 17, d. 55, l. 13.

76. TShDA, f. 10, op. 17, d. 55, l. 104.

77. TShDA, f. 10, op. 17, d. 55, l. 206.

78. TShDA, f. 10, op. 17, d. 55, l. 24. Simonov stated that evacuees who formed acquaintances with Uzbek Tashkenters had an easier life. Uzbek residents usually had a larger personal support structure, with relatives in the countryside, and were thus able to get food "from home" when supplies were low in the city. See Simonov, *Ostaius' zhurnalistom,* 166.

79. TShDA, f. 10, op. 17, d. 55, l. 26.

80. TShDA, f. 10, op. 17, d. 55, l. 28.

81. TShDA, f. 10, op. 17, d. 55, l. 10.

82. Rakhmat Faizii, *Ego velichestvo chelovek* (Moscow: Izd. Izvestiia, 1976); Marianovskii, *Kniga sudeb,* 168–70; "Tashkent v gody voiny god. 1942-I," *Vechernii Tashkent,* February 15, 1995, 3.

83. Gafur Gulom, "Ty ne sirota," reprinted in "Gafur Gulom, 1942," *Vechernii Tashkent,* February 15, 1995, 3; Kornei Chukovskii, *Uzbekistan i deti* (Tashkent: Gosizdat, 1942).

84. "Ko vsem zhenshchinam Uzbekistana," reprinted in Marianovskii, *Kniga sudeb,* 41–42.

85. TShDA, f. 10, op. 17, d. 55, l. 42.

86. Ibid.

87. P. N. Pospelova, ed., *Sovetskii tyl v velikoi otechestvennoi voine,* vols. 1 and 2 (Moscow: Izd. Mysl', 1974); *Istoriia sotsialisticheskogo Tashkenta (1941–1965),* vol. 2 (Tashkent: Izd. FAN, 1966); Faizii, *Ego velichestvo chelovek; Uzbekskaia SSR v gody Velikoi Otechestvennoi voiny,* vol. 2. For post-Soviet accounts, see *Fashizm ustidan qozonilgan ghalabada O'zbekistonning tarihi xissasi, 1941–1945* (Tashkent: FAN, 1996); *O'zbekiston sovyet mustamlakachiligi davrida,* 429–98.

88. TShDA, f. 10, op. 17, d. 55, l. 24. People bartered virtually everything down to

their own blood. Others made do with selling their libraries, although they too complained bitterly about their hardship.

Chapter 6. The Postwar Soviet City, 1945–1953

1. On Tashkent's "New Industrial Face," see "Toshkent bu yil Toshkent Shahar ijroiia komitet raisi Sodik Khusainov bilan suxbat," *Qizil O'zbekiston,* April 16, 1941, 4.

2. These veterans specifically complained about the condition of the Kazakh capital, but the Uzbek capital was in a similar condition. Party reports and resident complaints indicate the same sentiment for Tashkent and most other Central Asian urban centers. GARF, f. 8131, op. 25, d. 118, ll. 212–13.

3. See description of this decree in TShDA, f. 10, op. 18, d. 1029, l. 48.

4. TShDA, f. 231, op. 1, d. 2641, ll. 22, 37, 39.

5. M. Zorin, "Dom bez khoziaina," *Pravda Vostoka,* July 21, 1945, 4.

6. TShDA, f. 36, op. 2, d. 7a, l. 78.

7. TShDA, f. 36, op. 2, d. 7a, ll.78–79; TShDA, f. 36, op 2, d. 14a, l. 2.

8. RGASPI, f. 17, op. 48, d. 2034, l. 151.

9. See chap. 4 for details.

10. See Academy of Architecture Protokol of June 13, 1945, RGAE, f. 293, op. 3, d. 171, l. 6.

11. Ibid, l. 19. The architect also cited hospitals in India, Egypt, Greece, Palestine, Algeria, and South Africa as having designs more suitable for southern climates than those in Central Asia. Similarly, he noted that internal canals ran through the territories of Soviet hospitals in Central Asia, thereby promoting infection and disease. Ibid., l. 39.

12. Ibid., l. 44.

13. Veronika L. Voronina, *Narodnye traditsii arkhitektury Uzbekistana* (Moscow: Arkhitektury i gradostroitel'stva, 1951), 117.

14. TShDA, f. 36, op. 2, d. 7a, l. 81.

15. TShDA, f. 10, op. 18, d. 1029, l. 64.

16. See chap. 3.

17. RGAE, f. 9432, op. 1, d. 50, l. 43.

18. TShDA, f. 36, op 2, d. 7a, l. 86.

19. Ibid., l. 89.

20. Karpov proposed that 70 percent of the city's housing should be one- or two-story buildings with the remaining population living in multistory apartment houses. This was a drastic change from the Kuznetsov plan, which envisioned a city where 78 percent of residents would live in apartment houses. With an expansion of small-scale housing, Tashkent's geographic territory would have to double in size, but this size increase, Karpov argued, could be managed through the construction of an efficient transportation system that would connect the city center with suburban outskirts and satellite settlements. Ibid., l. 90.

21. RGAE, f. 9432, op. 1, d. 256, l. 127.

22. Clearly, the cold war had not yet started, and Los Angeles was a still a suitable comparison. Soviet architects rarely mentioned American cities in a positive light after 1946. Instead, they spoke of urban slums in the West. The most frequently mentioned American urban space was not Los Angeles, but Harlem, the African-American section of New York. In Soviet discourse, Harlem was commonly depicted as a place of poverty and urban decay. In Tashkent, propagandists also underscored that it was the home of a large, oppressed American minority. In the Soviet press, Harlem was frequently

presented in stark contrast to Soviet Tashkent. For an example of this trend, see N. Bylinkin, "Arkhitektura stalinskoi epokhi," *Arkhitektura i stroitel'stvo,* no. 11 (1947): 9.

23. TShDA, f. 36, op. 2, d. 7a, ll. 96–97.

24. Ibid., l. 101.

25. TShDA, f. 36, op. 2, d. 7a, ll. 82.

26. Ibid., l. 82.

27. Water and trees were presented as the essential "decorations" of the city, seemingly almost more important than the architectural look of Tashkent. Plans already were under way to build a "Victory Park," which was to include an artificial lake to glorify the defeat of Nazi Germany. These parks had to be located centrally, especially along the city's canals, for both economic and political reasons. Centrally placed parks were more easily accessible to the entire population of the city, while building them along canals and in concentrated areas would make it easier to keep the vegetation alive. In addition, too many of Tashkent's canal embankments were deemed barren. "Naked" canals did not give the city a healthy look but instead imparted a sense of death right alongside the achievement of Soviet irrigation technology. A park built next to water symbolized the dawn of new life in the Soviet Union, as was case with Komsomol Lake in 1939. On Victory Park, see TShDA, f. 10, op. 18, d. 1029, l. 66.

28. RGAE , f. 9432, op. 1, d. 47, l. 23.

29. RGAE, f. 9432, op. 1, d. 47, ll. 24–25.

30. RGAE, f. 9432, op. 1, d. 47, l. 51.

31. On the importance of the Black Sea to Sevastopol's reconstruction, see Qualls, "Raised from Ruins."

32. RGAE, f. 9432, op. 1, d. 50, ll. 51–52. Boris Iofan, a member of the review commission, admitted to not ever having been to Tashkent. See RGAE, f. 9432, op. 1, d. 185, l. 9.

33. RGAE, f. 9432, op. 1, d. 256, l. 56.

34. Ibid.

35. RGAE, f. 9432, op. 1, d. 256, ll. 57–58.

36. RGAE, f. 9432, op. 1, d. 256, l. 61.

37. GARF, f. 5446, op. 74, d. 17, l. 7.

38. Ibid., l. 6.

39. Ibid, l. 7.

40. Ibid. Another earthquake shook Uzbekistan on June 2, 1947, causing the State Architecture Construction Control bureau to inspect buildings. These earthquakes brought to light the need to improve construction quality in the Uzbek SSR. RGAE, f. 9432, op. 1. d. 102, 7–12.

41. GARF, f. 5446, op. 74, d. 17, l. 5. Although, in English, the word *liquidation* seems a strange choice, Soviet officials used the word to indicate state efforts to clean up after natural disasters, war damage, and other forms of destruction that affected Soviet cities and their populations.

42. Kosenkova, *Sovetskii gorod,* 316. See also United States, Department of Interior, U.S. Geological Survey, USGS Earthquake Hazards Program, "Earthquakes with 1000 or More Deaths from 1900," http://neic.usgs.gov/neis.eglists/egsmajr.html (accessed February 13, 2003). The 7.3 magnitude for this earthquake was measured on the internationally recognized Richter scale used at the time, not on the Soviet measurement scale.

43. RGAE, f. 9432, op. 1, d. 176, ll. 6–15. Also published in Kosenkova, *Sovetskii gorod,* 316–17.

44. RGAE, f. 9432, op. 1, d. 176, ll. 6–15; RGAE, f. 9510, op. 4, d. 7, l. 7.

45. O'zRMDA, f. 2532, op. 1, d. 85, l. 7.

46. Tashkent oblast's brick factories continually failed to meet their quotas.

47. See O'zRMDA, f. 2532, op. 1, l. 142.

48. Such cupolas can be seen on Gur-Emir, the mausoleum in Samarkand that contains the tomb of Amir Timur (Tamerlane).

49. RGALI, f. 674, op. 2, d. 280, l. 101. This criticism came during discussions on the Velikaia Druzhba controversy, which involved a campaign against "formalism" and Western influences in the development of Soviet culture, especially with regard to music.

50. RGAE, f. 9432, op. 1, d. 185, l. 2.

51. Ziiaev, "Formirovanie arkhitekturnogo ansamblia ploshchadi V. I. Lenina v Tashkente," 30; Kadyrova, *Arkhitektura sovetskogo Uzbekistana*, 77.

52. Ziiaev, "Formirovanie arkhitekturnogo ansamblia ploshchadi V. I. Lenina v Tashkente," 30. For a picture of the spire, see "Zodchii, uchenyyi, pedagog," *Stroitel'stvo i arkhitektura Uzbekistana*, no. 4 (1978): 46.

53. See S. Polupanov, *Shahar Toshkent* (Moscow: SSSR Arkhitektura akademiiasi, 1949), 33; Kadyrova, "Arkhitektor S. N. Polupanov (1904–1957)," 32.

54. Aleksei Shchusev, "Svodnoe zakliuchenie," April 8, 1948, RGAE, f. 9510, op. 4, d. 70, l. 455.

55. Ibid., l. 456.

56. RGAE, f. 9432, op. 1, d. 185, ll. 11, 15.

57. RGAE, f. 9432, op. 1, d. 185, l. 15.

58. RGAE, f. 9432, op. 1, d. 185, l. 18.

59. See conclusions on the Tashkent city center by Ia. Kornfeld, a corresponding member of the Soviet Academy of Sciences, January 25, 1948. RGAE, f. 9432, op. 1, d. 351, l. 21.

60. RGAE, f. 9432, op. 1, d. 351, l. 22.

61. RGAE, f. 9510, op. 4, d. 70, l. 457.

62. RGAE, f. 9432, op. 1, d. 256, l. 5.

63. For Shchusev's expert conclusions on the city center, see RGAE, f. 9510, op. 4, d. 70, l. 458.

64. P. A. Spyshkov's expert assessment, January 1948, RGAE, f. 9432, op. 1, d. 381, l. 29.

65. RGALI, f. 674, op. 2, d. 280, l. 101.

66. See chaps. 2 and 3. In 1935, Polupanov remodeled the outside of the building with the addition of columns and a review tribunal, allegedly transforming it from a constructivist building into a neoclassical structure. In 1940, he remodeled the main meeting hall, again adding columns, along with balconies and inlaid carvings of cotton plants and geometrical designs. One also should remember that the Government House was simply an adaptation of the pre-revolutionary one-story "White House," the home of the imperial governor-general of Turkestan.

67. "Stroitel'stvo novogo teatra v Tashkente," *Arkhitektura i stroitel'stvo*, no. 7 (1947): 11.

68. RGALI, f. 674, op 2, d. 280, l. 145.

69. The building's size was reduced to 76,000 square meters (but would still occupy a large part of a city block) for an audience of up to fourteen hundred persons. Ia. Kornfeld, "Teatr opery i baleta v Tashkente," *Arkhitektura i stroitel'stvo*, no. 2 (1948): 12.

70. For a history of the theater's construction, see Voronina, *Narodnye traditsii arkhitektury Uzbekistana*, 142.

71. Ia. Kornfeld, "Teatr opery i baleta v Tashkente," 13. Russian colonists established the market during the pre-revolutionary era as part of the effort to create an "ideal

colonial city" that had a trading area of a type familiar to Russian migrants. It quickly declined into a crime-ridden area. See chap. 2.

72. The mountains, unlike water canals, were really part of the city's natural landscape. Ia. Kornfeld, "Teatr opery i baleta v Tashkente," 13. The square still looks rather barren in pictures of the theater from the late 1940s and 1950s.

73. Kornfeld, "Teatr opery i baleta v Tashkente," 14.

74. Ibid., 15.

75. For lancet arches, see Voronina, *Narodnye traditsii arkhitektury Uzbekistana*, 144–45; for sculpture, see ibid., 157.

76. Ibid., 147.

77. "Narodnoe zodchestvo," *Arkhitektura i stroitel'stvo*, no. 6 (1948): 1.

78. Ibid. For further description of the oblast rooms, see Voronina, *Narodnye traditsii arkhitektury Uzbekistana*, 150–55.

79. Similarly, at the All-Union Agricultural Exhibition in Moscow in 1954, there were strict height requirements for the pavilions that represented each region of the Soviet Union. The main pavilion at the exhibition was ninety-seven meters high, the Moscow pavilion was fifty-two meters high, but the Uzbek pavilion was only twenty-seven meters high, underscoring Uzbekistan's low rank in the Soviet hierarchy of nations. See Tarkhanov and Kavtaradze, *Stalinist Architecture*, 165.

80. See Vitkovich, *Puteshestvie po Sovetskomu Uzbekistanu*, 33. Vitkovich notes that Soviet engineers worked alongside Uzbek artist-architects to plan the individual rooms.

81. The praise heaped on the Navoi Theater also can be attributed to the Navoi anniversary. In 1948, Tashkent marked the five-hundredth anniversary of Navoi's birth; the opening of the theater was just one aspect of this national celebration. On the anniversary celebration, see "Alisher Navoi," *Literaturnaia Gazeta*, May 15, 1948, 1.

82. For Kazakhstan, see Kosenkova, *Sovetskii gorod*, 314–15. For the Kazan railway station and Georgia, see Kornfeld, "Teatr opery i baleta v Tashkente," 12. The Kazan railway was built before the revolution; see Brown, *Art under Stalin*, 37. For Moldova, see "Novyi vokzal v Kishineve," *Arkhitektura i stroitel'stvo*, no. 4 (1948): 9–10.

83. This was a common strategy of European powers in designing colonial cities. Mitchell, *Colonising Egypt*, 1–34; Hamadeh, "Creating the Traditional City," 241–59.

84. See Report to the Uzbek Central Committee Division of Literature and Art, 1950, O'zRMDA, f. 2532, op. 1, d. 143, l. 37.

85. RGAE, f. 293, op. 3. d. 15, l. 110.

86. The Kuranty had already been criticized due to delays in its construction and shoddy workmanship. It evidently needed major repairs as soon as it opened. See O'zRMDA, f. 2532, op. 1, d. 110, ll. 34–35.

87. See RGAE, f. 293, op. 3, d. 15, l. 99. For discussion of Soviet historical interpretations of the pre-revolutionary policies in Central Asia from the late 1940s and early 1950s, see Lowell Tillet, *The Great Friendship: Soviet Historians on the Non-Russian Nationalities* (Chapel Hill: University of North Carolina Press, 1969), 148–93.

88. Polupanov, *Shahar Toshkent*, 4, 6.

89. Ibid., 5–6.

90. Vitkovich, *Puteshestvie po Sovetskomu Uzbekistanu*, 23.

91. S. Abduqahhor, *Respublika yuragi* (Tashkent: Q'izil O'zbekiston va Pravda Vostoka birlashgan nashriyoti, 1950).

92. This poem, "Navoi Kuchasi,"written by Iu. Korpiets, was reprinted in T. N. Qoriniyozov, *Sovyet O'zbekistoni madaniati tarihidan ocherklar* (Tashkent: FAN, 1956), 442.

93. On Soviet efforts to use the image of Tashkent in foreign policy, see chap. 9. See also Teresa Rakowska-Harmstone, "Soviet Central Asia: A Model of Non-Capitalist Development in the Third World," in *The USSR and the Muslim World: Issues in Domestic and Foreign Policy*, ed. Yaacov Ro'i (London: George Allen & Unwin, 1984), 181–205.

94. For examples, see "Poitakhtamiz chamazor va obod bo'lsin!" *Qizil O'zbekiston*, April 7, 1946, 2; "Sharqda eng iirik sanoat shaxri," *Qizil O'zbekiston*, April 20, 1947, 2; "Oi-joi qurilishiga jiddii e'tibor berailik," *Qizil O'zbekiston*, June 24, 1949, 1.

Chapter 7. Central Asian Tashkent and the Postwar Soviet State

1. The name Hujum means "attack" in Uzbek and was the same word used for the campaigns to force women to unveil in the 1920s and early 1930s.

2. "S zolotoi medal'iu," *Pravda Vostoka*, August 15, 1946, 2.

3. Ibid.

4. Massell, *Surrogate Proletariat*; Northrop, *Veiled Empire*.

5. O'zRMDA, f. R-88, op. 1, d. 2518, ll. 98–99.

6. Uzbek workers at the Textile Kombinat reportedly received no theoretical training in worker preparation courses. RGANI, f. 6, op. 6, d. 273, l. 160. See also O'zRMDA, f. R-88, op. 1, d. 2518, l. 98.

7. RGANI, f. 6, op. 6, d. 273, l. 158.

8. RGANI, f. 6, op. 6, d. 273, l. 157.

9. Ibid.

10. RGASPI, f. 574, op. 1, d. 7, l. 40.

11. O'zRMDA, f. R-88, op. 1, d. 9363, ll. 37–38.; O'zRMDA, f. R-88, op. 1, d. 9522, ll. 134–36.

12. *Fabkom* Protokol, January 13, 1947, TShDA, f. 231, op. 1, d. 2193, l. 126.

13. TShDA, f. 231, op. 1, d. 2643, l. 22.

14. TShDA, f. 231, op. 1, d. 2194, l. 29.

15. At a plenum of the Central Committee of the Uzbek Communist Party on March 18, 1954, Alimov, a Tashkent Obkom secretary, spoke of the importance of "liquidating the old Uzbek way of life." He described the goals of the Soviet project in Uzbekistan as making "life more beautiful" and giving everyone a "good apartment." Delegates later declared that the state must build "Soviet-style" housing in cities and rural areas, stating, "We must liquidate the mud-brick home, we must liquidate the Old Uzbek way of life. . . . What sort of 'millionaires' would sleep on the naked floor[?]" RGASPI, f. 81, op. 3, d. 240, ll. 110–11.

16. RGANI, f. 6, op. 6, d. 273, ll. 156–57.

17. TShDA, f. 231, op. 1, d. 1729, l. 53.

18. Ibid.

19. Ibid., l. 54.

20. Ibid., l. 57.

21. TShDA, f. 231, op. 1, d. 1729, l. 55. Tashkenters were tired of bringing their personal and family possessions to the bazaar to barter or sell; many had few valuables left to sell after the war. See Yelena Khanga, *Pro vsyo* (Moscow: VAGRIUS, 2001), 79.

22. TShDA, f. 231, op. 1, d. 2838, l. 21.

23. TShDA, f. 231, op. 1, d. 1729, l. 58.

24. RGASPI, f. 17, op. 88, d. 708, l. 28.

25. Ibid., l. 156.

26. For one example of this problem in 1947, see RGASPI, f. 17, op. 88, d. 708, l. 123. Railroad worker theft occurred frequently throughout the Soviet era.

27. RGASPI, f. 17, op. 48, d. 2034, l. 147.

28. RGASPI, f. 17, op. 88, d. 708, ll. 108–9.

29. Among the accusations leveled against teahouses that were insufficiently entrenched in Soviet culture was the charge that some red teahouses were issuing "improper propaganda." See RGASPI, f. 574, op. 1,d. 5, ll. 5–6; TVDA, f. 652, op. 1, d. 1047, ll. 263–64.

30. TShDA, f. 231, op. 1, d. 3410, ll. 165–67.

31. TShDA, f. 231, op. 1, d. 3140, l. 164.

32. Vitkovich, *Puteshestvie po Sovetskomu Uzbekistanu*, 52.

33. The victim had been carrying the money made by his collective farm. TShDA, f. 231, op. 1, d. 3140, l. 164.

34. TShDA, f. 231, op. 1, d. 3140, l. 165. This worker was mostly likely Uzbek. The factory primarily employed Russian women, but male workers were predominantly Central Asian.

35. RGASPI, f. 17, op. 126, d. 626, 7.

36. The annual report on the condition of Uzbek schools in 1948–1949, prepared by the Ministry of Enlightenment of the Uzbek SSR, noted, "At this time, the question of seven years of study for Uzbek girls continues to remain a fundamental problem for the work of the schools in the republic." RGASPI, f. 574, op. 1, d. 21, 42.

37. In the yearly report for 1948–1949, the Ministry of Enlightenment did note a bright side to the continued problems in Uzbek education. Students still dropped out of school and failed at alarming rates, but those Uzbeks who did finish tenth grade in Tashkent oblast were viewed as better prepared to "serve the interests of the Motherland and the people"; they reportedly were more aware of the difference between socialist and capitalist systems and appeared to possess "Soviet national pride." This new affinity for the Soviet Union and Soviet ideas allegedly was witnessed in their reading of patriotic works on the war and active participation in the celebration of the Navoi and Pushkin anniversaries. The interest of Tashkent's Uzbek students in the war and their dual interest in Uzbek and Russian literary figures were seen as positive developments in the creation of a new Soviet identity among the younger generation in the city. See RGASPI, f. 574, op. 1, d. 21, l. 43.

38. RGASPI, f. 17, op. 48, d. 2035, l. 79.

39. RGASPI, f. 574, op. 1, d. 21, l. 74.

40. TVDA, f. 652, op. 1, d. 868, l. 14. With the two alphabet changes (first to the Latin and then to the Cyrillic) since the revolution, one's access to books was further limited by one's familiarity with a particular alphabet.

41. However, it is doubtful that Russian-language schools were able to absorb any more students because they, too, lacked teachers.

42. RGASPI, f. 574, op. 1, d. 21, ll. 2–4, 58.

43. RGASPI, f. 17, op. 48, d. 2035, l. 79.

44. Z. M. Akramov and N. V. Smirnov, eds., *Nauchnye trudy: Tashkent; trudy nauchno-issledovatel'skogo otdela geograficheskogo fakul'teta TashGU* (Tashkent: Tashkent State University, 1964), 148.

45. As late as 1962, the lack of child-care facilities for working mothers was identified as the reason for the state's inability to keep Uzbek women in the workplace. RGANI, f. 5, op. 31, d. 196, l. 188.

46. "Protokol of the general meeting of workers of the cotton refining facility of the Kombinat," February 25, 1949, TShDA, f. 231, op. 1, d. 2641, l. 74.

47. In the archival documents, there is frequent use of the phrase "Central Asian workers" to indicate that not all the workers were Uzbek. Especially when describing Muslim female workers, Party documents often group all Central Asian nationalities (Uzbek, Kazakh, and Tajik) present in Tashkent region together, most likely to make the numbers appear larger. RGASPI, f. 574, op. 1, d. 35, l. 39.

48. M. Mukhamedov and V. Sitov, "Zhivye eksponaty," *Pravda,* October 4, 1953, 2.

49. TShDA, f. 231, op. 1, d. 2841, l. 11; "Rech' stakhanovki Tashkentskogo Tekstil'nogo Kombinata, t. Makhumy Yunuskhodzhaevoi," in *Zhenshchiny Uzbekistana* (Tashkent: Gosizdat UzSSR, 1942), 34. She appears to be the same Nasyrova who traveled to the front as part of an official Uzbek wartime delegation (see chap. 4).

50. The trauma of the war caused a reinvigoration of traditional values in Russia, Ukraine, and elsewhere in the Soviet Union. After the war, the wives of many Soviet leaders reverted from productive labor to traditional female roles. In *Making Sense of War,* Amir Weiner notes how some wives of Red Army officers began to dress more femininely and often ostentatiously. These women frequently were criticized for showcasing their wealth with clothing from the West. However, in Uzbekistan, reverting to traditional female roles was a particular problem because it included not only wives of prominent male officials but also prominent female Soviet officials who had been highlighted as official symbols of female liberation under socialism.

51. TShDA, f. 231, op. 1, d. 2841, l. 11.

52. Ibid.

53. There were 365 abortions reported among Textile Kombinat employees in first six months of 1950. The main reason cited for abortions was the lack of husbands. TShDA, f. 231, op. 1, d. 2841, l. 59. Not all women who had abortions were single mothers. One woman had an abortion because she already had three children; her husband was a driver and was never at home. She did not believe she could handle one more child. Another married woman who already had one child chose to have an abortion because she feared a war would begin soon. She did not want to be left alone again to raise a second child without a husband. See TShDA, f. 231, op. 1, d. 2841, l. 26.

54. RGASPI, f. 574, op. 1, d. 35, l. 97.

55. RGASPI, f. 17, op. 88, d. 708, l. 50.

56. RGASPI, f. 574, op. 1, d. 25, ll. 28, 49.

57. Besides being uncovered, shamed, and possibly excluded from the Party, some of these men and women remained unpunished by the local procuracy, which often did not even record any subsequent conversations with these women that might have given clues as to why the women left public life. Underage marriage or murder was more certain to bring prosecution than breaking the law against polygamy. Furthermore, while Russian men were subject to disciplinary action for "taking advantage" of young Russian workers, an Uzbek man's adulterous affair that led to pregnancy appeared to be a more acceptable ideological "sin" than taking on a second wife. These men were criticized but not necessarily punished by removal from Party ranks as frequently as Russian men were. Perhaps the fact that Uzbeks were not prominently represented in leading positions of Party or government and that the alternate option of taking a second wife was worse than breaking other Soviet sexual or morality ideals gave Uzbeks more leeway in deviating from Soviet codes of behavior.

58. RGASPI, f. 574, op. 1, d. 25, l. 28.

59. Zulfiya, "Vstrecha s zhenshchinoi v parandzhe," *Literaturnaia Gazeta,* April 19, 1950, 2.

60. Ibid. (emphasis added).

61. RGASPI, f. 17, op. 48, d. 2034, l. 144.

62. Ibid.

63. Kamil Faizulin, "Prervannaia svad'ba," *Literaturnaia Gazeta,* December 10, 1953, 2.

64. Another example of an unhappy marriage appeared on the pages of *Pravda* in 1953. Kamal Rahimov, a teacher with a high education level, married a young female student from the Tashkent Pedagogical Institute. Instead of allowing her to continue her education, he forced her to remain in the home. He reportedly never showed *any* form of kindness to his wife or their children, eventually beating her and kicking her out of the home so that he could marry another woman. Thus, he showed himself to be both an abusive Uzbek husband and a polygamist. The district procurator and the deputy minister of enlightenment learned of the case but did nothing. A complaint was even filed against Rahimov for "conduct unbecoming an educator" at the City Education Department, but no action was taken, largely because the official responsible for investigating such claims also was a polygamist, with three wives. See Mukhamedov and Sitov, "Zhivye eksponaty," 2.

65. These examples of evading marriage laws in the Tashkent region can be found in a report to the Uzbek Central Committee, "About the conditions of work among women in Tashkent oblast in 1949." See part 6, "Facts on the appearance of feudal-*bey* relations toward women and the fight against them," TVDA, f. 652, op. 1, d. 1412, ll. 38–45. For additional examples of ingenuity in arranging religious marriage ceremonies, see O'zRMDA, f. 2456, op. 1, d. 331, l. 52.

66. Complaints that such celebrations wasted food are in RGASPI, f. 17, op. 88, d. 708, l. 49. For the Soviet argument that Jewish circumcision was "backward, dangerous, or without medical value," see Joshua Rothenberg, "Jewish Religion in the Soviet Union," in *The Jews in Soviet Russia since 1917,* ed. Lionel Kochan (London: Oxford University Press, 1972), 164–65, 178.

67. Iskanderov, Head of the Council for Affairs of Religious Cults of Uzbekistan, to I. V. Polianskii, Head of Council for Affairs of Religious at the USSR Council of Ministers, July 2, 1955, O'zRMDA, f. 2456, op. 1, d. 174, l. 22. For review of Soviet views on circumcision and the widespread prevalence of the practice in Uzbekistan throughout the Soviet era, see Ewa A. Chylinski, "Ritualism of Family Life in Soviet Central Asia: The *Sunnat* (Circumcision)," in *Cultural Change and Continuity in Central Asia,* ed. Shirin Akiner (London: Kegan Paul International, 1991), 160–70. Chylinski argues that circumcision lost some of its religious connotations during the Soviet era but continued to be a Central Asian cultural expression. It became a signifier of Uzbek identity and a tradition that separated Uzbeks from Russians.

68. For one example in which medical professionals deemed the practice of circumcision to be harmful, see G. P. Vasil'eva and N. A. Kisliakov, "Voprosy sem'i i byta u narodov Srednei Azii i Kazakhstana v periode stroitel'stva sotsializma i kommunizma," *Sovetskaia etnografiia,* no. 6 (1962): 14: "While noting the new and progressive appearances in family relations, one must not, however, ignore the fact that the most stagnant layers of society still are not liberated from the weight of old understandings and religious holdovers, old rites and rituals" (of which circumcision was identified as the primary example).

69. "Fatwa: Publication by the Spiritual Board of Muslims of Central Asia and Kazakhstan," 1963, O'zRMDA, f. 2456, op. 1, d. 477, l. 148–49; O'zRMDA, f. 2456, op. 1, d. 174, l. 20.

70. Rothenberg notes that Soviet officials had more success in stopping the practice among Jews, suggesting that the geographic dispersal of the Jewish minority in the Soviet Union perhaps gave Jews less ability to resist Soviet pressure to end the tradi-

tion, while Muslims, with their own ethnic republics, had more power to resist this campaign. He notes that state harassment against *mohalim* (Jewish ritual circumcisers) impeded the ability of Jews to have the procedure performed, and he estimates that the prevalence of circumcision was low, perhaps occurring among only 10 percent of the Jewish male population of the Soviet Union. Rothenberg, "Jewish Religion in the Soviet Union," 184.

71. Circumcisions were recorded by state authorities either during routine medical examinations or through the monitoring of anyone in the community who sponsored a *sunnat toi*.

72. Amir Weiner, *Making Sense of War: The Second World War and the Fate of the Bolshevik Revolution* (Princeton: Princeton University Press, 2001), 69–70.

73. Vasil'eva and Kisliakov, "Voprosy sem'i i byta u narodov Srednei Azii i Kazakhstana," 14.

74. RGASPI, f. 17, op. 132, d. 29, l. 99.

75. O'zRMDA, f. 2456, op. 1, d. 174, l. 20.

76. O'zRMDA, f. 2456, op. 1, d. 220, l. 88.

Chapter 8. Redesigning Tashkent after Stalin

1. In the 1950s, Red Square frequently was referred to as Lenin Square. The city's monument to Lenin stood at the center of the square in front of the administrative building known as Government House. For reports on the death of Stalin, see "Imia Stalina bessmertno," *Pravda,* March 7, 1953, 3. Unlike *Pravda Vostoka,* on March 6, 1953, *Pravda* published detailed reports on Stalin's death and a medical analysis of his illness. The issue contained a joint declaration of the Central Committee, Council of Ministers, and Presidium of the Supreme Soviet that explained Stalin's importance as an equal of Lenin who was responsible for the success of the revolution, the victory of socialism, and the defeat of the Nazis. The newspaper noted that his death would be deeply felt by all sectors of Soviet society but that the strengthening of the friendship of the peoples and future victories of communism would be guaranteed because Stalin lived on in the hearts of the Soviet people. As usual, *Pravda Vostoka* took its cues from *Pravda* and began to publish similar articles on March 7, 1953. See "Ot Tsentral'nogo komiteta kommunisticheskoi partii Sovetskogo Soiuza, Soveta Ministrov Soiuza SSR i prezidiuma Verkhovnogo Soveta SSSR," *Pravda,* March 6, 1953, 1.

2. "Tashkent v traure," *Pravda Vostoka,* March 7, 1953, 3; "Stalin, znamia nashikh pobed," *Pravda Vostoka,* March 7, 1953, 3.

3. For examples, see Said Nurutdinov's speech in "Vypolnim zavety liubimogo vozhdia," *Pravda Vostoka,* March 9, 1953, 3; Dzhamal Umarova's speech in "Edinstvo," *Pravda Vostoka,* March 9, 1953, 3; "Stalin, znamia nashikh pobed," *Pravda Vostoka,* March 7, 1953, 3; "Po puti, ukazannomu genial'nym vozhdem," *Pravda Vostoka,* March 9, 1953, 3; "Po Stalinskomu puti," *Pravda Vostoka,* March 24, 1953, 3. For student expressions of mourning, see "Tashkent v traure," *Pravda Vostoka,* March 7, 1953, 3. In *Pravda,* the report from the Tashkent Textile Kombinat reported on only one Russian female speaker. See "Imia Stalina bessmertno," *Pravda,* March 7, 1953, 3.

4. Zulfiya, "Samyi rodnoi i blizkii chelovek," *Pravda Vostoka,* March 9, 1953, 2.

5. For a description of the Tashkent wake and memorial service, see "V stolitse Uzbekistana," *Pravda Vostoka,* March 10, 1953, 2.

6. The peasantry was not prominent in the Tashkent "funeral," indicating that the transformation of Uzbeks into Soviet citizens remained a journey that urban residents, not agricultural workers, made more easily. The urban aspects of Uzbekistan were

highlighted in marking the death of Stalin. Those who did not fit this urban image remained excluded.

7. William Taubman, *Khrushchev: The Man and His Era* (New York: Norton, 2003), 241.

8. "V stolitse Uzbekistana," *Pravda Vostoka,* March 10, 1953, 2. For industrial salutes in other cities, see "Poslednii put'," *Pravda,* March 10, 1953, 1.

9. As described by Yevtushenko, the trampling of one hundred people by the mob of mourners in Moscow was caused partly by the fact that militia officers refused to open up barricades, indicating that they had "no instructions" to do so. The failure of Soviet officials to take individual initiative to save lives once again had disastrous results for Soviet citizens. Yevgeny Yevtushenko, *A Precocious Autobiography,* trans. Andrew R. MacAndrew (New York: Dutton, 1963), 84–85. See also Taubman, *Khrushchev,* 244.

10. See GARF, f. 7523, op. 52, d. 71, ll. 1–122 (packet I of this *delo*). The remaining six packets of this *delo* show that the majority of personal letters from residents of Tashkent were written in Russian, while letters from other regions of the Uzbek SSR, including urban areas, were in Uzbek.

11. GARF, f. 7523, op. 52, d. 71, l. 1.

12. In grief, residents evoked a Soviet identity over an ethnic one. The trend of avoiding rhetoric about Uzbekistan's development could also be viewed in collectively signed institutional letters from the Tashkent region. Workers of the Tashkent City Health Administration expressed their appreciation for Stalin, whose "heroism" and "genius" had brought victory in World War II and set the Soviet people on a clear path toward the construction of a communist society. These health-care workers surprisingly failed to mention the construction of hospitals and a Soviet health system in a region where infectious disease had reportedly caused many deaths, a typical motif of Soviet propaganda in Central Asia. Only the chair of the Begovat Gorispolkom directly tied Stalin's wisdom as a military genius to the Tashkent region's development; in the letter he wrote to Central Party leaders in Moscow, he noted that during the "most difficult days" of World War II, Stalin recognized Tashkent oblast's potential in metallurgy and constructed the first metallurgical factory in Uzbekistan, in the nearby city of Begovat. GARF, f. 7523, op. 52, d. 71, ll. 74–75, 106.

13. In 1953, Tashkent had a net in-migration of 41,305 people. Tashkent oblast's population (excluding the city) increased through in-migration by 20,093. Subsequent years saw similar increases. See RGAE, f. 1562, op. 20, d. 1091, ll. 67–68.

14. Of 280 recently demobilized officers' families who still lacked housing in Uzbekistan, 210 lived in the capital. See RGANI, f. 5, op. 31, d. 62, l. 70.

15. "Zabytyi gorodok," *Pravda Vostoka,* April 27, 1956, 3.

16. Ibid.

17. An example of this invisible community network in traditional *mahallas* arose in a state report from 1954 on the "privatization" of state trees in the Old City. Although trees outside of individual courtyards were regarded officially as state property, local residents, of course, knew which family either had originally planted the tree or which community member watered and cared for it, thereby making it de facto personal property in the eyes of many locals. "Zapiski otdelov TsK KPSS sektora Tsentral'noi Azii," RGANI, d. 5, op. 31, d. 72, l. 147. This alternative (non-state) support structure was one of the reasons why transforming the Old Town was so important to Soviet officials.

18. For background on Uzbek *mahallas,* see Eric Sievers, "Uzbekistan's *Mahallas*: From Soviet to Absolutist Residential Community Associations," *Journal of International and Comparative Law at Chicago-Kent,* no. 2 (2002): 91–158.

19. "Stenograficheskii otchet, Tashkentskoi gorodskoi partiinoi konferentsii KP Uz-

bekistana," January 11–12, 1956, RGASPI, f. 17, op. 56, d. 722, ll. 69. On earlier campaigns in Central Asia to get women to use maternity hospitals, see Michaels, *Curative Powers*, 168–73.

20. RGASPI, f. 17, op. 56, d. 722, l. 69.

21. RGASPI, f. 17, op. 56, d. 722, l. 70.

22. For information on hospital waste pollution, see RGASPI, f. 17, op. 56, d. 722, l. 106.

23. RGASPI, f. 17, op. 56, d. 723, l. 125.

24. O'zRMDA, f. 2532, op. 1, d. 212, l. 93.

25. Andrew Day, "The Rise and Fall of Stalinist Architecture," in *Architectures of Russian Identity: 1500 to the Present*, ed. James Cracraft and Daniel Rowland (Ithaca, NY: Cornell University Press, 2003), 190.

26. "Khrushchev's Secret Speech," reprinted in *Khrushchev Remembers*, ed. and trans. Strobe Talbott (Boston: Little, Brown, 1970), 559–618. For Lenin's testament and his letter concerning Stalin's rudeness to Nadezhda Krupskaia, see ibid., 562–63. For a general discussion of the Secret Speech and de-Stalinization, see Taubman, *Khrushchev*, 270–89.

27. RGASPI, f. 17, op. 54, d. 850, ll. 190, 206; RGANI, f. 5, op. 31, d. 72, l. 147. See also RGASPI, f. 17. op. 54, d. 850, l. 259.

28. RGANI, f. 5, op. 31, d. 72, l. 147; RGASPI, f. 17. op. 54, d. 850, l. 259. Amin Niyazov, first secretary of the Uzbek Central Committee, accused Yusupov of hiring inexperienced Uzbek workers in place of Russian employees. Worse still, he was deemed responsible for ethnic animosity at the Tashkent Textile Kombinat by decreeing that the *kombinat* needed to hire more Uzbek women instead of Russian employees, although advancing Uzbeks into production and positions of responsibility had been an official program of Soviet state in the region. The director of the *kombinat* accused Yusupov of failing to promote the "friendship of the peoples" and of actively pitting Tashkent's ethnic groups against each other. Yusupov had decreed that the *kombinat* increase its work force by hiring two thousand Uzbek women per year, a proposal that subsequently led to criticism that Yusupov attempted to rid the *kombinat* of its Russian employees, a difficult proposition considering the overwhelming preponderance of Russian workers at the facility. See RGASPI, f. 17, op. 54, d. 850, l. 347.

29. See Abdurazakov's speech, RGASPI, f. 17, op. 54, d. 850, l. 253.

30. Niyazov to Khrushchev, July 28, 1954, RGANI, f. 5, op. 31, d. 72, l. 147. In his defense, Yusupov responded that while he knew that Tashkent workers waited for months without apartments, he felt that the Council of Ministers' chairman needed a permanent residence. He stated that the Tashkent cottage was necessary because it was incorrect and simply rude for each new chairman to tell his predecessor that he must "get out of this apartment so that he could move in." RGASPI, f. 17, op. 54, d. 850, l. 493. He did not note the discrepancy in his statement that it was improper to evict a former chairman from his residence while at the same time advocating for the construction of a permanent home for the chairman, from which subsequent chairmen ostensibly would evict their predecessors. RGASPI, f. 17, op. 54, d. 850, l. 493.

31. See chap. 4.

32. RGASPI, f. 17, op. 54, d. 850, l. 380.

33. RGASPI, f. 17, op. 54, d. 850, ll. 418–19.

34. Ibid. Furthermore, instead of enclosing the sewage canal, Yusupov proposed widening it for boat travel.

35. DiMaio, *Soviet Urban Housing*, 25.

36. See chap. 3.

37. RGASPI, f. 17, op. 54, d. 850, ll. 326–27.

38. K. A. Zaleskii, *Imperiia Stalina: biograficheskii entsiklopedicheskii slovar'* (Moscow: Veche, 2000), 511.

39. With the fall of Khrushchev, Yusupov's rehabilitation began; new editions of his collected works and biographies were published. Examples include: Usman Yusupov, *Izbrannye trudy;* Reskov and Sedov, *Usmon Yusupov.* For a post-Soviet biography, see *O'zbekistonning yangi tarihi,* vol. 2, *O'zbekiston Sovet mustamlakachiligi davrida,* 325–26.

40. Dissident writers were able to publish accounts of the crimes of the Soviet system, however. See discussion of Yevtushenko's poem "The Heirs of Stalin," in Taubman, *Khrushchev,* 528. See also Alexander Solzhenitsyn, *One Day in the Life of Ivan Denisovich,* trans. Max Hayward and Ronald Hingley (New York: Bantam Books, 1963). On the general literary and artistic thaw, see Taubman, *Khrushchev,* 382–88.

41. DiMaio, *Soviet Urban Housing,* 17–19.

42. RGALI, f. 674, op. 3, d. 759, ll. 85–86.

43. V. A. Lavrov, "Stenogramma," April 14, 1953, RGALI, f. 674, op. 3, d. 759, ll. 155, 165.

44. O'zRMDA, f. 2532, op. 1, d. 212, l. 178.

45. RGALI, f. 674, op. 3, d. 904, l. 15.

46. Stepan Polupanov, the original designer, had already remodeled this structure numerous times, as discussed previously. Ironically, his original design was a simple modernist structure.

47. RGALI, f. 674, op. 3, d. 1024, l. 19.

48. By placing construction projects under the authority of one agency, the creation of new urban neighborhoods having all city services could be organized in a rational and cost-effective manner, at least in theory. However, the lack of an established, technologically advanced building industry that could supply construction sites with pipes, bricks, cement, wood, and reinforced concrete panels kept Glavtashkentstroi from effectively moving to mechanized construction.

49. Housing *kombinat*s originated in Leningrad and Moscow. From these central cities, they were adopted across the Soviet Union, indicating that once again, the center had considerable influence over the creation of the model Soviet city in Central Asia. DiMaio, *Soviet Urban Housing,* 93–96.

50. RGALI, f. 674, op. 3, d. 1805, l. 27. In these plans, Khrushchev-era construction resembled the high-modernist urban planning theories that proliferated in the 1950s and 1960s, particularly those of Le Corbusier. Although Le Corbusier's designs for Moscow went unrealized in the 1930s, he planned Chandigarh, the utopian (and failed) capital of the Indian province of Punjab in the 1960s. His theories later influenced planners of the Brazilian capital of Brasilia. Clearly, the Soviet state was not the only power that attempted (and failed) to construct or refashion urban centers along idealist notions of large-scale, industrialized, and prefabricated city building projects. Scott, *Seeing Like a State,* 103–32; Le Corbusier, *Radiant City.*

51. On Abdurasulov's proposal, see RGALI, f. 674, op. 3, d. 904, l. 170b; RGASPI, f. 17, op. 54, d. 957, l. 255.

52. RGASPI, f. 17, op. 54, d. 957, l. 255.

53. Abdurasulov ignored historical records of devastating earthquakes in the Tashkent region as well as the warnings of the Academy of Sciences Institute of Building Construction and the former head of the State Architecture-Construction Control bureau in Tashkent. Tashkent might have become a "hub" of Soviet science in Asia, but bureaucrats and urban planners, pressed to produce low-cost buildings, ignored the

advice of the city's premier geologists, historians, engineers, and other scientists. See RGALI, f. 674, op. 3, d. 904, l. 170b.

54. T. V. Shakhsuvarian, "Tvorcheskiy put' gosudarstvennogo proektnogo instituta rekonstruktsii i zastroiki goroda Tashkenta," *Arkhitektura i stroitel'stvo Uzbekistana,* no. 3 (1974): 5.

55. O'zRMDA, f. 2532, op. 1, d. 212, l. 7.

56. N. Solov'eva, "Gorod blagoustraivaetsia," *Pravda Vostoka,* April 11, 1956, 3; "Novoe v oblike Tashkenta," *Pravda Vostoka,* December 2, 1956, 4; M. Makhmutov, "Tsentr Chilanzar, interv'iu 'Pravdy Vostoka,'" *Pravda Vostoka,* June 2, 1965, 4. For comparisons to other cities, see Scott, *Seeing Like a State,* 103–32; Norma Evenson, *Chandigarh* (Berkeley: University of California Press, 1966); Lawrence Vale, "Designing National Identity," in *Forms of Dominance: On the Architecture and Urbanism of the Colonial Enterprise,* ed. Nezar AlSayyad (Aldershot, England: Avebury, 1992), 315–38.

57. "Tvorcheskiy otchet arkh. V. A. Malmre o poezdke v Tashkent. 11–31 Dekabria, 1958," RGALI, f. 674, op. 3, d. 1198, l. 2.

58. Leonid Volynskii, "Doroga k novoi zemle," *Novyi mir,* no. 12 (1961): 118–60.

59. Simonov, *Ostaius' zhurnalistom,* 155.

60. Volynskii, "Doroga k novoi zemle," 122.

61. Steven Harris has discussed the problems of constructing prefabricated mass housing at great length. He notes that the state attempted to replace poorly built individual housing with "modern" apartment complexes. In the process of building prefabricated apartment buildings, the state, he argues, destroyed too many individual homes and could not meet the demands of housing large numbers of people, thus leaving residents unhappy with their housing situation. See Steven Emmett Harris, "Reconstructing Everyday Life: Building, Distributing, Furnishing, and Living in the Separate Apartment in Soviet Russia, 1950s–1960s" (PhD diss., University of Chicago, 2003).

62. Volynskii, "Doroga k novoi zemle," 123–24.

63. Volynskii wrote that "the madrasa, built from local bricks, stands for five hundred years, but the houses in Chilanzar, built one and one-half years ago from 'sewing parts together' [*rasshivka*], are disappearing without a trace. Cracks are already appearing between the eroding bricks that are unequal in size and color." Volynskii, "Doroga k novoi zemle," 124.

64. In 1960, 150 elderly Tashkenters were injured in an accident at the Frunze district *ispolkom*'s Department of Social Services. Lacking heat in their homes, these pensioners were forced to wait in line to process their requests for hookups to the municipal heating service. The third-floor veranda of the building, where they were told to wait, collapsed. Of the 150 injured, 48 were seriously hurt and 17 were in critical condition. RGANI, f. 5, op. 31, d. 146, l. 81.

65. Volynskii, "Doroga k novoi zemle," 123.

66. In 1964, Tashkent covered a distance of 220 square kilometers or approximately 85 square miles. This figure, however, did not reflect the continued urbanization of the outer areas of the city. The 220-square-kilometer figure was the entire area that Tashkent State University's geography department considered "urban." Akramov and Smirnov, eds., *Nauchnye trudy,* 17.

67. See Mitkhat Bulatov, *Tvorcheskie zadachi arkhitektorov v Uzbekistane v razvitii zhilischnogo stroitel'stva* (Tashkent: Broshura SSA Uzbekistana, 1958), 8. Bulatov specifically wrote that Tashkent had the largest percentage of individual homes among large cities of the Soviet Union.

68. O'zRMDA, f. 2532, op. 1, d. 212, l. 193. One should recall that the original Mosoblproekt proposal envisioned that 78 percent of Tashkenters would live in multistory

(three- or four-floor) apartment buildings, while only 22 percent would live in one- or two-story homes. See chap. 3.

69. Simonov, *Ostaius' zhurnalistom*, 126–27.

70. Ibid., 127. DiMaio notes that the organization that evicted city residents was required to find them comparable housing. This rule provided city residents with limited control over construction, transportation, and city agencies. DiMaio, *Soviet Urban Housing*, 139–40.

71. RGASPI, f. 574, op. 1, d. 25, l. 149.

72. RGALI, f. 674, op. 3, d. 1806, l. 25. This report estimated that if individual construction continued at the current rate, 70 percent of the city's population would live in private homes, which would cover 90 percent of the urban territory by the mid-1960s. See Ibid., l. 26.

73. RGALI, f. 674, op. 3, d. 1806, l. 26. This report, "Otchet brigady pravlenniia SSA po poezdke v Tashkent," was dated 1961 but included discussion of Tashkent's housing problems for 1955–1961. Unfortunately, it does not give a time frame for the claim that Uzbeks refused to move into apartments. Nevertheless, it proposed that if people wanted to continue to live in the city, they should be required to move to apartments. According to this study, people who wanted individual homes would be required to move *outside* the city limits, not simply to the outskirts of Tashkent.

74. O'zRMDA, f. 2532, op. 1, d. 212, ll. 175–76.

75. Ibid. DiMaio notes that the city architect of Ashgabat, the capital of the Turkmen SSR, made a similar comment. DiMaio, *Soviet Urban Housing*, 72.

76. In emphasizing the need to preserve the old cities of Central Asia, Volynskii noted that the beauty of Tallinn, Prague, and other cities arose from the fact that their streets preserved buildings from the past and had not lost "even one line from their valuable manuscript of the ages" ("*ne uteriano ni odnoi strochki iz dragotsennoi letopisi veka*"). See Volynskii, "Doroga k novoi zemle," 141.

77. He similarly described the courtyards of the city's surviving madrasa buildings, built in the sixteenth century with brick and stone walls rather than the heat-trapping reinforced concrete of the twentieth century. The center courtyard of a madrasa was designed so that the corners of the walls would meet at right angles, creating optimal conditions for changing the "micro-climate" in public buildings by guaranteeing that two sides of the courtyard always would be shaded by the sun, no matter what time of day it was. Volynskii, "Doroga k novoi zemle," 120.

78. Volynskii also compared the monotonous tone of Chilanzar to the ornate Stalinist-era construction, noting that neither fulfilled the needs of a socialist city. Khrushchev-era construction was drab. Architectural details were ignored to enable builders to create uniform buildings that lacked any sort of individuality. However, returning to Stalinist architecture was not the solution. Buildings from that era were simply formulaic, Volynskii argued. If Chilanzar was a sad and depressing part of Tashkent's urban space, Volynskii believed that Stalinist buildings, such as the famed Navoi Theater, provided the city with comic relief. The Navoi Theater had grandiose gold curtains, an enormous chandelier, and flamboyantly carved seats in the shape of lancet arches. At the same time, the building's steam radiators were poorly hidden behind carved plaster wall coverings. In the effort to make Tashkent "Uzbek," Soviet architects went to the other extreme, creating excessively detailed buildings that recalled mosques, madrasas, or palaces but served no practical purpose in improving the lives of the people. Such additions just added to the cost but were unable to hide basic flaws of construction. Volynskii, "Doroga k novoi zemle," 125.

79. Sharaf Rashidov, "Istoricheskie resheniia XXII s'ezda KPSS i zadachi intel-ligentsii Uzbekistana," in *Tretii s'ezd intelligentsii Uzbekistana: stenograficheskii otchet* (Tashkent: Gos. Izdatel'stvo Uzbekskoi SSR, 1962), 49.

80. "Rech' K. M. Murtazaeva," in *Tretii s'ezd intelligentsii Uzbekistana*, 93–94.

81. Ibid., 93.

82. M. C. Bulatov and A. I. Vanke, "Opyt i perspektivy gradostroitel'stvo v Uzbeki-stane," O'zRMDA, f. 2532, op. 1, d. 272, l. 2.

83. RGANI, f. 5, op. 31, d. 146, l. 75.

84. Akramov and Smirnov, eds., *Nauchnye trudy*, 142.

85. Ibid., 143.

86. O'zRMDA, f. 2532, op. 1, d. 272, ll. 7–8. DiMaio notes that this trend was com-mon throughout the Soviet Union. Despite public decrees to curb industrial growth in large cities, individual ministries and enterprises, under pressure from the state to increase production, settled and expanded industries in areas that had the pre-existing industrial infrastructures that made establishing factories cheaper and easier. DiMaio, *Soviet Urban Housing*, 50–52.

87. In addition to overpopulated Tashkent, Samarkand was identified as already meeting its optimal population level in 1962. The populations of Chirchik, Almalyk, and Angren exceeded their limits by factors of 4.3, 2.2, and 2.2, respectively. The Tash-kent agricultural zone, the food-growing region encircling the city, already contained 60,000 residents, equivalent to 7 percent of the urban population. In addition to proposing limits on Tashkent's population, Bulatov also suggested that the city govern-ment forbid development in this agricultural area. O'zRMDA, f. 2532, op 1, d. 272, ll. 6–8. Other figures indicate that Tashkent had a population of 1.5 million people in 1965. "Serdtsa goroda," *Stroitel'stvo i arkhitektura Uzbekistana*, no. 12 (1976): 21.

88. O'ZRMDA, f. 2532, op 1, d. 272, l. 17.

89. Ibid. Bulatov also proposed using sewage water on the city's gardens and park plantings, although this proposal was not new. Dirty canal water had been used for irrigation for years. For discussion of the long-term impact of water diversion and the cotton monoculture on Uzbekistan, see Boris Z. Rumer, *Soviet Central Asia: A Tragic Experiment* (Boston: Unwin Hyman, 1989).

90. Akramov and Smirnov, eds., *Nauchnye trudy*, 209; "Iz pisem v redaktsiiu," *Pravda Vostoka*, June 2, 1965, 2.

91. These achievements began to be made only after the focus of urban design switched from creating model cities that "forged" model citizens to adapting these cit-ies to suit the needs of their residents.

92. While not unconcerned with making Tashkent a monumental regional capital, officials placed more emphasis on providing the city with a modern and technologically advanced look. If the Stalin era attempted to evoke Greece or Rome with a veneer of decoration to pay token tribute to the region's heritage, designers in the 1960s preferred the sleek look of glass, steel, and concrete. The Soviet Union no longer looked to previ-ous empires of the past but meant to impress residents and visitors alike with an image of the modern future.

93. T. F. Kadyrova, K. B. Babievskii, and F. Yu. Tursunov, *Arkhitektura sovetskogo Uzbekistana* (Moscow: Izd. Literatury po stroitel'svo, 1972), 38.

94. Z. N. Chebotareva, "Opyt proektirovaniia eksperimental'nykh mikroraionov-mahallia v Tashkente," *Stroitel'stvo i arkhitektura Uzbekistana*, no. 7 (1968): 11.

95. The reconstruction process would occur in successive stages, whereby evicted residents would be moved a short distance to new state housing. With each successive move, land would be freed up to begin the next phase of the reconstruction project.

In theory, the gradual completion of the new micro-district and the resettlement of entire communities only a short distance from their previous homes would mitigate residents' dissatisfaction over the loss of their homes. Thus, Uzbeks no longer would feel displaced by the urban renewal and reconstruction efforts. This approach mirrored that of Jane Jacobs, who argued that such pre-existing social relationships, not model physical spaces, were the cornerstones of vibrant urban communities. See Jane Jacobs, *The Death and Life of Great American Cities* (New York: Vintage Books, 1961).

96. Chebotareva, "Opyt proektirovaniia eksperimental'nykh mikroraionov-mahallia v Tashkente," 12.

97. A combination of elevators, tall shade trees, air conditioners, ventilation ducts, and outdoor spaces (balconies, roofs, and gardens) would help ensure comfort in extreme temperatures for high-rise apartment dwellers, usually the smaller families of Russians. Chebotareva, "Opyt proektirovaniia eksperimental'nykh mikroraionov-mahallia v Tashkente," 13–14.

Chapter 9. The Tashkent Model

The epigraph, translated by the author, is an excerpt from Khamid Guliam's poem, "Moskvy polpred na vostoke" [Moscow's Ambassador in the East], in *Sovetskii Uzbekistan* (Tashkent: Izd. TsK KP Uzbekistana, 1977), 2.

1. The following is a list of just some of the visitors to Tashkent: Jawaharlal Nehru, Indira Gandhi, President Sukarno of Indonesia, Fidel Castro, Chou En-lai, the shah of Iran, U.S. Supreme Court Justice William Douglas, and the heads of state of Pakistan, Iraq, Finland, Somalia, Afghanistan, Ghana, North Vietnam, and Sudan. In addition, parliamentary delegations from North Korea, India, Cuba, and Angola as well as foreign intellectuals and artists visited Uzbekistan on organized state visits. This list is derived from information in articles published in *Pravda Vostoka* and Tashkent tourist guidebooks between 1953 and 1966. R. G. Gulamov, ed., *Tashkent: kratkii spravochnik-putevoditel'* (Tashkent: Gos. Izdatel'stvo Uzbekskoi SSR, 1957), 98–99; *Tashkent: kratkii spravochnik-putevoditel'* (Tashkent: Gos. Izdatel'stvo Uzbekskoi SSR, 1962), 40.

2. On the nuclear institute, see RGALI, f. 674, op. 3, d. 1808, l. 5; *Pervyi s'ezd intelligentsii Uzbekistana: stenograficheskii otchet* (Tashkent: Gos. Izd. Uzbekskoi SSR, 1957), 22.

3. *Ocharovan toboi, Uzbekistan* (Tashkent: Gos. Izd. Uzbekskoi SSR, 1964), 112.

4. Ibid., 28–29.

5. *Tashkent: kratkii spravochnik-putevoditel'* (1962), 54.

6. *Tashkent entsiklopediia, s.v.* "Meditsinskii institut, TashMI," 195. N. Kravchenko wrote about Soviet efforts to fight smallpox, a disease with "high" infection rates in Asia, Africa, and Latin America, through mass vaccinations and public health campaigns in the factories and worker clubs of Uzbekistan. N. Kravchenko, "Zdorov'ye kruglii god," *Pravda Vostoka,* April 7, 1965, 4.

7. Gulamov, ed., *Tashkent: kratkii spravochnik-putevoditel'* (1957), 74, 94. On art and literature in Soviet Uzbekistan, see *Istoriia uzbekskoi sovetskoi literatury* (Moscow: Nauka, 1967).

8. *Ocharovan toboi, Uzbekistan,* 28–29.

9. Akramov and Smirnov, eds., *Nauchnye trudy,* 138; *Tashkent v proshlom i nastoiashchem* (Tashkent: Znanie, 1968), 20. A picture book of Uzbek architecture published in 1959 highlighted the Tashkent airport. See *Zodchestvo Uzbekistana* (Tashkent: Gos. Izd. Khudozhestvennoi literatury, 1959).

10. *Arkhitektura sovetskogo Uzbekistana* (Moscow: Izd. Literatury po stroitel'stvu, 1979), 61.

11. Ibid., 110.

12. RGASPI, f. 17, op. 56, d. 722, l. 127; *The Awakened East: A Report by Soviet Journalists on the Visit of N. S. Khrushchov to India, Burma, Indonesia and Afghanistan* (Moscow: Foreign Languages Publishing House, 1960), 23–24.

13. RGALI, f. 674, op. 3, d. 1024, l. 17.

14. The fact that limiting the size of the coat check might have made economic sense in a city where outerwear was not necessary for much of the year was not considered. In Russia, all public buildings needed a coat check, an idea that arose in Moscow, where having bulky winter coats in tightly enclosed places was a problem. In creating a model Tashkent, the problem of adapting Russian design norms into the Uzbek environment continued.

15. RGALI, f. 674, op. 3, d. 1024, l. 17.

16. For theories of nationalism and imagined communities, see Anderson, *Imagined Communities.*

17. During that meeting between Justice Douglas and the head of Tashkent Radio, the latter boasted of Tashkent International Radio's broad popularity in the United States but could produce only one fan letter from the United States, from a man in New York City. See William O. Douglas, *Russian Journey* (Garden City, NY: Doubleday, 1956), 237.

18. On poor reception in Tashkent, see "Zabytyi gorodok," *Pravda Vostoka,* April 27, 1956, 3.

19. *Pervyi s'ezd intelligentsii Uzbekistana: stenograficheskii otchet,* 33.

20. A report issued in 1960 reinforced this concern over the inability of Soviet propagandists to use technology (radio, television, film) in a bilingual city. It noted that Tashkent had only one television station, an impediment to the spread of propaganda because city residents were not guaranteed programming in a language they could understand. RGANI, f. 5, op. 31, d. 146, l. 79. See also chap. 6.

21. *Pervyi s'ezd intelligentsii Uzbekistana: Stenograficheskii otchet,* 33.

22. Ibid.

23. Quoted in *Awakened East,* 187.

24. Tashkent played host to the first All-Union Conference of Orientalists (with foreign participants), as well as an international conference to discuss the problems of cotton harvesting, an international film festival featuring films from Asia and Africa, an international health-care workers conference (with participants coming from Asia, Africa, the Americas, and Europe), the Asian chess championship, numerous congresses of Uzbek intellectuals (with foreign participants), an international conference of writers from Africa and Asia, and many others. *Pravda Vostoka* also reported that 874 delegations of 4,716 people and 2,268 tourists, representing 90 countries, visited Uzbekistan to see the "great heights that the Uzbek people have achieved." For their part, the Uzbek people allegedly followed with great admiration the heroic effort people of the colonial and postcolonial world had made in fighting for their national independence and progress. See "Vtoroi s'ezd intelligentsii Uzbekistana," *Pravda Vostoka,* December 12, 1959, 4.

25. *Tashkentskie vstrechi* (Tashkent: Gos. Izdatel'stvo khudozhestvennoi literatury UzSSR, 1960), 7.

26. "Muhammed Saleh-Bakhr Al-Ulum," in ibid., 85.

27. Gulamov, ed., *Tashkent: kratkii spravochnik-putevoditel'* (1957), 100.

28. L. Bat', "V gostiakh u Aibeka," *Kul'tura i zhizn'*, no. 3 (1959): 48–51. Oibek, like Zulfiya, the Uzbek poet, is commonly referred to by only one name.

29. *Masters of Literature and Art of Tashkent* (Tashkent: Goslitizdat of the UzSSR, 1958), 7.

30. Ibid., 29.

31. Ibid., 74–75.

32. Ibid., 44. Other Tashkent authors, playwrights, and actors were involved in popularizing international themes. Aleksandr Ginzburg wrote a play entitled "The Daughter of Ganges." Sara Ishanturaeva presented "Tales about Turkey," and Abrar Khidoatov, an actor, specialized in Shakespearean roles. He introduced Central Asians to *Hamlet* and *Othello*. See *Masters of Literature and Art of Tashkent*, 62, 66, 76–78.

33. *Masters of Literature and Art of Tashkent*, 91–92.

34. On Tashkent's "jump" to modernity and its applications to other Asian peoples, see *Tashkentskie vstrechi*, 209–10.

35. The Somali poet Ahmed Ali Omar al-Azkhari described discrimination in the legal systems of Kenya and South Africa and implied that the British Commonwealth was simply the British Empire with a new name. *Tashkentskie vstrechi*, 72–74.

36. Quoted in Gulamov, ed., *Tashkent: kratkii spravochnik-putevoditel'* (1957), 100.

37. On Mukhitdinov and Central Asian representation in Soviet embassies, see Yaacov Ro'i, "Islam and Soviet Muslims in Soviet Arab Policy, Part One," *Asian and African Studies*, no. 2 (1975): 170–71.

38. Tashkent factories reportedly had sent their finished products to both Western and postcolonial countries, including Brazil, Ethiopia, Cuba, India, Pakistan, Italy, Iran, Indonesia, and others. "Eksport Tashkentskikh izdelii," *Pravda Vostoka*, January 8, 1966, 3; Gulamov, ed., *Tashkent: kratkii spravochnik-putevoditel'* (1957), 85.

39. *Tashkent v proshlom i nastoiashchem*, 28–29.

40. G. Salikhov and A. Bokov, "My s vami, brat'ia," *Pravda Vostoka*, September 2, 1965, 4.

41. This was not the first time Tashkenters were sent abroad as emissaries of the Soviet state. In the late 1940s, Tashkent Koreans, formerly regarded as disloyal deportees, were sent to North Korea as agitators and propagandists in advance of the Korean War. See RGASPI, f. 17, op. 162, d. 39, l. 26.

42. Holland Roberts, "Tamerlane's Uzbekistan Today," *New World Review*, no. 11 (1959): 37. For an earlier example of Europeans disseminating the "Tashkent" model, see General Tubert, *L'Ouzbekistan république soviétique* (Paris: Editions du Pavillon, 1951). For a later example, see Serge Zeyons, *La Révolution des femmes au coeur de l'Asie soviétique* (Paris: Editions Sociales, 1971), 144.

43. Quoted in *Ocharovan toboi, Uzbekistan*, 114–15.

44. Like Party officials and Soviet bureaucrats, Roberts argues that the fact that *Othello* played to a packed audience was a sign of Uzbek cultural advancement. He never questions the fact that Shakespearean drama was not a native art form but a foreign influence imposed by a Russianized/Europeanized Soviet system. Roberts also suggests that Tashkent played the role of San Francisco, a regional center that helped to disseminate culture in an area that was geographically distant from the major urban centers of the United States (New York, Chicago, and Los Angeles). See Roberts, "Tamerlane's Uzbekistan Today," 36–37.

45. Other countries also experimented with planned cities in this era. See Evenson, *Chandigarh;* Heikki von Hertzen and Paul D. Spreiregen, *Building a New Town: Finland's New Garden City, Tapiola*, rev. ed. (Cambridge, MA: MIT Press, 1973); Sten Nils-

son, *The New Capitals of India, Pakistan, and Bangladesh,* trans. Elisabeth Andreasson (Copenhagen: Scandinavian Institute of Asian Studies, 1973).

46. William Douglas noted that Grand Mufti Babakhan, leader of the Soviet-sponsored Muslim Spiritual Board, proposed toasts with wine. Douglas, *Russian Journey,* 197.

47. Patrick Sergeant, *Another Road to Samarkand* (London: Hodder and Stoughton, 1955), 118. Sergeant described his guide's reaction after she learned that he planned to accompany the medical students to the Red Uzbek collective farm outside of Tashkent: "But, Anna was in opposition. 'Mr. Sergeant' (she wasn't pleased again), 'a car is arranged and we will go meet the director, if you wish. Please, you will see the farm comfortably. Do not go in this irregular fashion.'" For description of his entire expedition to the cotton farm and the guide's reaction, see ibid., 118–22.

48. Sergeant, *Another Road to Samarkand,* 121.

49. Fitzroy MacLean, *Back to Bokhara* (New York: Harper & Brothers, 1959), 106.

50. Ibid.

51. "Chilanzarskaia arifmetika," *Pravda Vostoka,* April 12, 1966, 2.

52. Ibid.

53. Ibid.

54. "Tsentr Chilanzara," *Pravda Vostoka,* June 2, 1965, 4; "Polnye glaza Tashkenta u nas v gostiakh zarubezhnye zhurnalisty," *Pravda Vostoka,* August 21, 1965, 3; R. Bulatov, "Legkomyslennaia li rekonstruktstiia?" *Pravda Vostoka,* August 27, 1965, 3.

55. "Pribytie Prezidenta Pakistana," *Pravda Vostoka,* January 4, 1966, 1; "Pribytie Premier-Ministra Indii," *Pravda Vostoka,* January 4, 1966, 1.

56. "Mir polon nadezhd," *Pravda Vostoka,* January 6, 1966, 1; "Na Tashkent smotrit ves' mir," *Pravda Vostoka,* January 8, 1966, 1.

57. See "Tashkent—gorod mirnoi vstrechi," *Pravda Vostoka,* January 4, 1966, 1; L. Stapanov, *Konflikt v Indostane i soglasheniie v Tashkente* (Moscow: Izdatel'stvo politicheskoi literatury, 1966), 7–8.

58. "Tashkent proshchaetsia s drugom," *Pravda Vostoka,* January 12, 1966, 1.

59. RGALI, f. 674, op. 3, d. 1809, l. 7

60. Ibid., ll. 16–17.

61. Ibid., l. 17.

62. No documentation of accurate death tolls could be found. Rumors are that about one thousand people perished, but this figure is not recorded in the U.S. Geological Survey's list of international earthquakes with one thousand or more fatalities. See United States Geological Survey, "Earthquakes with 1,000 or More Deaths from 1900."

63. "Spravka o mediko-sanitarnom obsluzhivanii naseleniia v period likvidatsii posledstvii zemletriaseniia v g. Tashkent," O'zRI-TTHMDA, f. 1, op 5, d. 11, ll. 16–17.

64. Ibid.

65. RGALI, f. 674, op 3, d. 1809, ll. 16–17. Almost immediately, newspaper articles described how moving trucks traveled through the Uzbek capital to transport residents and their possessions from the destroyed regions in the city center to undamaged newly constructed apartment complexes on the outskirts of the city. "Krysha nad golovoi!" *Pravda Vostoka,* April 29, 1966, 4; "Stroim novyi Tashkent," *Pravda Vostoka,* May 4, 1966, 4; "Novye kvartaly na Chilanzare," *Pravda Vostoka,* May 7, 1966, 4.

66. "Ob osnovnykh printsipakh general'nogo plana i kharatera zastroiki goroda Tashkenta s uchetom posledstvii zemletriaseniia," RGALI, f. 674, op. 3, d. 1809, l. 2; "Vtoroe rozhdeniia Tashkenta," *Sovetskaia Bukhara,* August, 19, 1966, in RGALI, f. 674, op. 3, d. 1809, l. 39.

67. RGALI, f. 674, op. 3, d. 1809, ll. 2–6; M. F. Korovin, "Tashkentskii metropoliten,"

Stroitel'stvo i arkhitektura Uzbekistana, no. 9 (1969): 1–4; A. Azimov, "Novye cherty kompozitsionno-prostranstvennykh priemov v arkhitekture tsentra Tashkenta," *Stroitel'stvo i arkhitektura Uzbekistana,* no. 7 (1974): 3–7.

68. "Sochustvie zarubezhnykh druzei," *Pravda Vostoka,* May 5, 1966, 1.

69. See Ivan Orekhov, *Velikii khashar: na zemle Tashkentskoi* (Tula: Priokskoe knizhnoe izdatel'stvo, 1970), the memoir of a construction worker from Tula who assisted in rebuilding the Uzbek capital. See also "Pomoshch' Tashkentu idet!" *Pravda Vostoka,* April 28, 1966, 1; "Vsia strana: my s toboi Tashkent," *Pravda Vostoka,* April 29, 1966, 1; V. Kokushkin, "Leningrad prishel na pomosch,'" in *Tashkent—gorod bratstva* (Tashkent: Izdatel'stvo TsK KP Uzbekistana, 1969), 47–51; Petrus Brovka, "Vspominaia Tashkent," in *Tashkent—gorod bratstva,* 105–7.

70. "L. I. Brezhnev i A. N. Kosygin v golodnoi stepe," *Pravda Vostoka,* April 28, 1966, 1; "V dni ispytanii," *Pravda Vostoka,* May 1, 1966, 2.

71. RGALI, f. 674, op. 3, d. 1809, l. 23.

72. Ibid, l. 19.

73. Azimov, "Novye cherty kompozitsionno-prostranstvennykh priemov v arkhitekture tsentra Tashkenta," 3–7.

Chapter 10. Epilogue

1. Background note: United States, Department of State, Bureau of South and Central Asian Affairs, "Uzbekistan, October 2009," http://www.state.gov/r/pa/ei/bgn/2924 .htm (accessed February 21, 2010).

2. Esmer Islamov, "EBRD Meeting in Tashkent Proves to Be a PR Nightmare for Karimov," *Eurasianet,* May 6, 2003, http://www.eurasianet.org/departments/rights/ articles/eav050603.shtml (accessed May 8, 2008).

3. The desire to change society through art and architecture spanned the Soviet era, as did the willingness to use violence, denunciations, and blood. These trends preceded Stalinist urban planners and lasted well beyond the death of Stalin. See Boris Groys, *The Total Art of Stalinism: Avant-Garde, Aesthetic Dictatorship, and Beyond,* trans. Charles Rougle (Princeton: Princeton University Press, 1992).

4. Boris Groys argues that the boundaries between art and life shifted in the Soviet Union, with art (architecture, literature, theater) often being offered to the public as a more important focus than reality. Groys, *Total Art of Stalinism.*

5. On Central Asian representation in Soviet embassies, see Ro'i, "Islam and Soviet Muslims in Soviet Arab Policy, Part One," 170–71.

6. Between 1963 and 1969, the number of Soviet Muslims in higher education doubled. The number of Soviet Muslim "scientific workers" jumped from seventeen thousand to forty-eight thousand in this period. James Critchlow, *Nationalism in Uzbekistan: A Soviet Republic's Road to Sovereignty* (Boulder, CO: Westview Press, 1991), 28.

7. Critchlow, *Nationalism in Uzbekistan,* 27.

8. This transition occurred at the same time that urban planners began to address Uzbek cultural sensitivities in their city renewal projects, particularly the Mahalla micro-district housing proposal.

9. See Colton, *Moscow;* Kotkin, *Magnetic Mountain;* Ruble, *Leningrad.*

10. Scott, *Seeing Like a State,* 103–4.

11. Ibid., 117–32; Porteous and Smith, *Domicide,* 140–41; Lilian M. Li, Alison J. Dray-Novey, and Haili Kong, *Beijing: From Imperial Capital to Olympic City* (New York: Palgrave Macmillan, 2007), 252–57.

12. On the *mahalla* and its use as an organ of social and state control in Soviet and post-Soviet Uzbekistan, see Sievers, "Uzbekistan's *Mahallas*," 91–158.

13. One also should note that in the 1960s, the "village prose" writers in Russia criticized these same structures and claimed that they were destroying Russian culture. Geoffrey Hosking, *Rulers and Victims: The Russians in the Soviet Union* (Cambridge, MA: Belknap Press of Harvard University Press, 2006).

14. *Po ulitsam Tashkenta* (Tashkent: Izd. Uzbekistan, 1971), 134–36.

15. *Tashkent: kratkii spravochnik-putevoditel'* (Tashkent: Uzbekistan, 1981), 20.

16. T. F. Kadyrova, *Sovremennaia arkhitektura Uzbekistana* (Tashkent: Izdatel'stvo literatury i iskusstva im. Gafura Guliama, 1974), 50.

17. Ibid.

18. Kadyrova, *Arkhitektura sovetsogo Uzbekistana*, 136–37.

19. On Central Asian birthrates in the 1970s and 1980s, see Rywkin, "National Symbiosis," 64–67.

20. *Po ulitsam Tashkenta*, 57.

21. Kadyrova, *Sovremennaia arkhitektura Uzbekistana*, 139–41.

22. V. Tyurikov, *Tashkent: A Guide* (Moscow: Raduga Publishers, 1983), 41–42.

23. Kadyrova, *Arkhitektura sovetskogo Uzbekistana*, 245.

24. Ibid., 260–267; Tyurikov, *Tashkent: A Guide*, 65–66.

25. Tyurikov, *Tashkent: A Guide*, 30–31.

26. Ibid., 29–30.

27. Ronald Wixman notes that the practice is an "*extremely* important part of Uzbek, Tajik and Central Asian Jewish society. Even a number of Communist Party members and intellectuals from these groups maintained that a male cannot be an Uzbek, Tajik or Jew . . . unless he is circumcised" (original emphasis). Ronald Wixman, "Ethnic Attitudes and Relations in Modern Uzbek Cities," in *Soviet Central Asia: The Failed Transformation,* ed. William Fierman (Boulder, CO: Westview Press, 1991), 174.

28. Marriage between Russian men and Uzbek women remained rare.

29. Wixman, "Ethnic Attitudes and Relations in Modern Uzbek Cities," 166–68; Rasma Karklins, "Islam: How Strong Is It in the Soviet Union? Inquiry Based on Interviews with Soviet Germans Repatriated from Central Asia in 1979," *Cahiers du monde russe et soviétique,* no. 1 (1980): 72–73.

30. On the Sibaral Canal proposal, see Philip P. Micklin, "The Fate of 'Sibaral': Soviet Water Politics in the Gorbachev Era," *Central Asian Survey,* no. 2 (1987): 67–88.

31. Rasma Karklins, "Ethnic Politics and Access to Higher Education: The Soviet Case," *Comparative Politics,* no. 3 (1984): 284, 289–90.

32. Critchlow, *Nationalism in Uzbekistan,* 41.

33. "Tashkent to Undergo Renovation . . . " *OMRI Daily Digest,* June 6, 1996, http://www.hri.org/news/balkans/omri/96-06-06.omri.html#02 (accessed July 8, 2003).

34. Ibid.

35. "Monument to Friendship of Peoples Removed in Tashkent," Uznews.net, April 15, 2008, http://www.uznewsnet/article_single.php?ing=en&cid=25&aid=591 (accessed May 8, 2008).

BIBLIOGRAPHY

Archival Sources

Central State Archive of the Republic of Uzbekistan (O'zRMDA), Tashkent

Fond R-88, Gosplan UzSSR
Fond R-314, Plenipotentiary of the Evacuation of the Sovnarkom UzSSR
Fond R-837, Council of People's Commissars of the Uzbek SSR
Fond 2356, Union of Writers of the Uzbek SSR
Fond 2454, Presidium of the Supreme Soviet of the Uzbek SSR
Fond 2456, Plenipotentiary of the Council of Affairs of Religious Cults of the Council of
    Ministers of the Uzbek SSR
Fond 2532, Architects' Union of the Uzbek SSR
Fond 2831, personal archive of construction worker Vasili Stribezhev

*The Central State Archive for Technical Research and Medical Documentation of
the Republic of Uzbekistan (O'zRI-TTHMDA), Tashkent*

Fond 1, Ministry of Health of the Uzbek SSR
Fond 94, Tashgiprogor, 1937–1973

State Archive of the City of Tashkent (TShDA), Tashkent

Fond 8, Council of Workers' Deputies of the Oktiabr District of Tashkent
Fond 10, Tashkent City Council (Gorispolkom)
Fond 36, Architectural Planning Bureau, Tashkent Gorispolkom
Fond 231, Institutional Archive of the Tashkent Textile Kombinat

State Archive of the Oblast of Tashkent (TVDA), Tashkent

Fond 652, Tashkent Oblast Council (Oblispolkom)

State Archive of the Russian Federation (GARF), Moscow

Fond 5446, Council of People's Commissars (Sovnarkom) of the Soviet Union
Fond 6822, Council of Evacuation of the Sovnarkom of the Soviet Union
Fond 7523, Supreme Soviet of the Soviet Union
Fond 8131, Procurator of the Soviet Union
Fond 9479, GULAG Special Settlements

Russian State Archive of Economics (RGAE), Moscow

Fond 293, Academy of Architecture and Construction of the Soviet Union
Fond 1562, Central Statistical Bureau
Fond 9432, Committee of Architecture of the Council of Ministers of the Soviet Union
Fond 9510, Ministry of Urban Construction of the Soviet Union

Russian State Archive of Art and Literature (RGALI), Moscow

Fond 674, Union of Architects of the Soviet Union

Russian State Archive of Contemporary History (RGANI), Moscow

Fond 5, Apparatus of Central Committee of the Communist Party of the Soviet Union
Fond 6, Committee for Party Control

Russian State Archive of Social and Political History (RGASPI), Moscow

Fond 17, Central Committee of the Communist Party of the Soviet Union
Fond 81, op. 3, Kaganovich file
Fond 574, Plenipotentiary of the Central Committee on Affairs in the Uzbek SSR

New York Public Library, New York

Interview with Misha Raitzen, 1981. New York Public Library–American Jewish Committee Oral History Collection, Dorot Jewish Division, New York Public Library, Aston, Lenox, and Tilden Foundation.

Published and Online Sources

Abduqahhor, S. *Respublika yuragi.* Tashkent: Qizil O'zbekiston va Pravda Vostoka birlashgan nashriyoti, 1950.
Abu-Lughod, Janet L. *Rabat: Urban Apartheid in Morocco.* Princeton: Princeton University Press, 1980.
Akhunbabaev, Iu. *Trudiashchikhsia Uzbekistana frontu.* Tashkent: Izd. Profizdat, 1942.
Akiner, Shirin, ed. *Cultural Change and Continuity in Central Asia.* London: Kegan Paul International, 1991.
Akramov, Z. M., and N. V. Smirnov, eds. *Nauchnye trudy: Tashkent; trudy nauchno-issledovatel'skogo otdela geograficheskogo fakul'teta TashGU.* Tashkent: Tashkent State University, 1964.
Allworth, Edward. *The Modern Uzbeks: From the Fourteenth Century to the Present; A Cultural History.* Stanford: Hoover Institution Press, 1990.
———, ed. *Central Asia, 130 Years of Russian Dominance: A Historical Overview.* 3rd ed. Durham, NC: Duke University Press, 1994.
AlSayyad, Nezar, ed. *Forms of Dominance: On the Architecture and Urbanism of the Colonial Enterprise.* Aldershot, England: Avebury, 1992.
Anderson, Benedict. *Imagined Communities: Reflections on the Origin and Spread of Nationalism.* London: Verso, 1983.
Arkhitektura sovetskogo Uzbekistana. Moscow: Izd. Literatury po stroitel'stvu, 1979.
The Awakened East: A Report by Soviet Journalists on the Visit of N. S. Khrushchov to India, Burma, Indonesia and Afghanistan. Moscow: Foreign Languages Publishing House, 1960.
Bacon, Elizabeth E. *Central Asians under Russian Rule.* Ithaca, NY: Cornell University Press, 1966.

Bailey, F. M. *Mission to Tashkent*. London: Jonathan Cape, 1946.

Barber, John, and Mark Harrison. *The Soviet Home Front, 1941–1945: A Social and Economic History of the USSR in World War II*. London: Longman, 1991.

Becker, Seymour. *Russia's Protectorates in Central Asia: Bukhara and Khiva, 1865–1924*. Cambridge, MA: Harvard University Press, 1968.

Beknazarov, N. *Istoriia razvitiia Frunzenskogo raiona g. Tashkenta, 1936–1964 gg.* Tashkent: FAN, 1966.

Belaia kniga o deportatsii koreiskogo naseleniia Rossii. Vol. 1. Moscow: Interpraks, 1992.

Belkina, Mariia. *Skreshchenie sudeb*. Moscow: Kniga, 1988.

Bennigsen, Alexandre, and Marie Broxup. *The Islamic Threat to the Soviet State*. New York: St. Martin's Press, 1983.

Bezrukov, B. *Zdravstrui, Tashkent! kratkiy putevoditel'-spravochnik po raionam goroda Tashkenta*. Tashkent: Izd. Uzbekistan, 1970.

Blok, Alexander. *The Twelve; and, The Scythians*. Trans. Jack Lindsay. London: Journeyman Press, 1982.

Bowlt, John E., and Olga Matich, eds. *Laboratory of Dreams: The Russian Avant-Garde and Cultural Experiment*. Stanford: Stanford University Press, 1996.

Bown, Matthew Cullerne. *Art under Stalin*. New York: Holmes & Meier, 1991.

Boym, Svetlana. *Common Places: Mythologies of Everyday Life in Russia*. Cambridge, MA: Harvard University Press, 1995.

Brody, Richard J. *Ideology and Political Mobilization: The Soviet Home Front during World War II*. Pittsburgh: University of Pittsburgh Center for Russian and East European Studies, 1994.

Brower, Daniel. *Turkestan and the Fate of the Russian Empire*. London: RoutledgeCurzon, 2003.

Bulatov, Mitkhat. *Tvorcheskie zadachi arkhitektorov v Uzbekistane v razvitii zhilischnogo stroitel'stva*. Tashkent: Broshura SSA Uzbekistana, 1958.

Bylinkin, N. "Arkhitektura stalinskoi epokhi." *Arkhitektura i stroitel'stvo*, November 1947, 9–18.

Carlisle, Donald S. "Modernization, Generations, and the Uzbek Soviet Intelligentsia." In *The Dynamics of Soviet Politics*, edited by Paul Cocks, Robert Daniels, and Nancy Whittier Heer, 239–64. Cambridge, MA: Harvard University Press, 1976.

Carrère d'Encausse, Hélène. *Decline of an Empire: The Soviet Socialist Republics in Revolt*. Translated by Martin Sokolinsky and Henry A. La Farge. New York: Newsweek Books, 1979.

———. *Islam and the Russian Empire*. Berkeley: University of California Press, 1988.

———. "Systematic Conquest, 1865–1884." In *Central Asia, 130 Years of Russian Dominance: A Historical Overview*, edited by Edward Allworth. 3rd. ed. Durham, NC: Duke University Press, 1994.

Castillo, Greg. "Cities of the Stalinist Empire." In *Forms of Dominance: On the Architecture and Urbanism of the Colonial Enterprise*, edited by Nezar AlSayyad, 261–88. Aldershot, England: Avebury, 1992.

Cavanaugh, Cassandra Marie. "Backwardness and Biology: Medicine and Power in Russian and Soviet Central Asia, 1868–1934." PhD dissertation, Columbia University, 2001.

Chebotareva, Z. N. "Opyt proetirovaniia eksperimental'nykh mikrorainov-makhallia v Tashkente." *Stroitel'stvo i arkhitektura Uzbekistana*, no. 7 (1968): 11–15.

Chopra, Preeti. "Pondicherry: A French Enclave in India." In *Forms of Dominance: On the Architecture and Urbanism of the Colonial Enterprise*, edited by Nezar AlSayyad, 107–38. Aldershot, England: Avebury, 1992.

Chukovskii, Kornei. *Uzbekistan i deti.* Tashkent: Gosizdat, 1942.

Chylinski, Ewa A. "Ritualism of Family Life in Soviet Central Asia: The *Sunnat* (Circumcision)." In *Cultural Change and Continuity in Central Asia,* edited by Shirin Akiner, 160–70. London: Kegan Paul International, 1991.

Colton, Timothy J. *Moscow: Governing the Socialist Metropolis.* Cambridge, MA: Belknap Press of Harvard University Press, 1995.

Cracraft, James, and Daniel Rowland, eds. *Architectures of Russian Identity: 1500 to the Present.* Ithaca, NY: Cornell University Press, 2003.

Crews, Robert D. "Civilization in the City: Architecture, Urbanism, and the Colonization of Tashkent." In *Architectures of Russian Identity: 1500 to the Present,* edited by James Cracraft and Daniel Rowland, 117–34. Ithaca, NY: Cornell University Press, 2003.

———. *For Prophet and Tsar: Islam and Empire in Russia and Central Asia.* Cambridge, MA: Harvard University Press, 2006.

Crimean Tatars: Repatriation and Conflict Prevention. New York: Open Society Institute Forced Migration Projects, 1996.

Critchlow, James. *Nationalism in Uzbekistan: A Soviet Republics Road to Sovereignty.* Boulder, CO: Westview Press, 1991.

Day, Andrew Elam. "Building Socialism: The Politics of the Soviet Cityscape in the Stalin Era." PhD dissertation, Columbia University, 1998.

———. "The Rise and Fall of Stalinist Architecture." In *Architectures of Russian Identity: 1500 to the Present,* edited by James Cracraft and Daniel Rowland, 172–90. Ithaca, NY: Cornell University Press, 2003.

DiMaio, Jr., Alfred John. *Soviet Urban Housing: Problems and Policies.* New York: Praeger, 1974.

Dorogoi gor'kikh ispytanii. Moscow: Ekslibris Press, 1997.

Douglas, William O. *Russian Journey.* Garden City, NY: Doubleday, 1956.

Dukhovskaia, Varvara. *Turkestanskiia vospominaniia.* St. Petersburg: Izdaniie t-va M. O. Volf', 1913.

Edgar, Adrienne Lynn. *Tribal Nation: The Making of Soviet Turkmenistan.* Princeton: Princeton University Press, 2004.

Edwards, Kristen Elizabeth. "Fleeing to Siberia: The Wartime Relocation of Evacuees to Novosibirsk, 1941–1943." PhD dissertation, Stanford University, 1996.

Evans, John, ed. *Mission of N. P. Ignat'ev to Khiva and Bukhara in 1858.* Newtonville, MA: Oriental Research Partners, 1984.

Evenson, Norma. *Chandigarh.* Berkeley: University of California Press, 1966.

Faizii, Rakhmat. *Ego velichestvo chelovek.* Moscow: Izd. Izvestiia, 1976.

Fashizm ustidan qozonligan ghalabada O'zbekistonning tarihi xissasi. Tashkent: FAN, 1996.

Fierman, William, ed. *Soviet Central Asia: The Failed Transformation.* Boulder, CO: Westview Press, 1991.

Fitzpatrick, Sheila, ed. *Stalinism: New Directions.* London: Routledge, 2000.

Forbes, Rosita. *Forbidden Road: Kabul to Samarkand.* New York: Dutton, 1937.

General'nyi plan rekonstruktsii goroda Moskvy. Moscow: Moskovskii rabochii, 1936.

Ginzburg, Lidiya. *Blockade Diary.* London: Harvill Press, 1995.

Gromova, Natalia. *Vse v chuzhoe gliadiam okno.* Moscow: Kollektsiia "Sovershenno sektretno," 2002.

Groys, Boris. *The Total Art of Stalinism: Avant-Garde, Aesthetic Dictatorship, and Beyond.* Translated by Charles Rougle. Princeton: Princeton University Press, 1992.

Gulamov, R. G. *Tashkent: Kratkii spravochnik putevoditel'*. Tashkent: Gosudarstvennoi izdatel'stvo Uzbekskoi SSR, 1957.

Hamadeh, Shirine. "Creating the Traditional City: A French Project." In *Forms of Dominance: On the Architecture and Urbanism of the Colonial Enterprise*, edited by Nezar Alsayyad, 241–59. Aldershot, England: Avebury, 1992.

Harris, Steven Emmett. "Reconstructing Everyday Life: Building, Distributing, Furnishing, and Living in the Separate Apartment in Soviet Russia, 1950s–1960s." PhD dissertation, University of Chicago, 2003.

Hirsch, Francine. *Empire of Nations: Ethnographic Knowledge and the Making of the Soviet Union*. Ithaca, NY: Cornell University Press, 2005.

Hlevnjuk, Oleg. "Les Mécanismes de la 'Grande terreur' des années 1937–1938 au Turkmenistan." *Cahiers du monde russe*, no. 1–2 (1998): 197–208.

Hoffmann, David L. *Peasant Metropolis: Social Identities in Moscow, 1929–1941*. Ithaca, NY: Cornell University Press, 1994.

———. *Stalinist Values: The Cultural Norms of Soviet Modernity, 1917–1941*. Ithaca, NY: Cornell University Press, 2003.

Hosking, Geoffrey. *Rulers and Victims: The Russians in the Soviet Union*. Cambridge, MA: Belknap Press of Harvard University Press, 2006.

Hudson, Hugh. *Blueprints and Blood: The Stalinization of Soviet Architecture, 1917–1937*. Princeton: Princeton University Press, 1994.

Ikramov, Karim. *Delo moego ottsa*. Moscow: Sovetskii pisatel', 1991.

Islamov, Esmer. "EBRD Meeting in Tashkent Proves to be a PR Nightmare for Karimov." *Eurasianet*, May 6, 2003. http://www.eurasianet.org/departments/rights/articles/eav050603.shtml. Accessed May 8, 2008.

Istoriia sotsialisticheskogo Tashkenta (1941–1965). Vol. 2. Tashkent: Izd. FAN, 1966.

Istoriia uzbekskoi sovetskoi literatury. Moscow: Nauka, 1967.

Jacobs, Jane. *The Death and Life of Great American Cities*. New York: Vintage Books, 1961.

Jenks, Andrew. "A Metro on the Mount." *Technology and Culture*, October 2000, 697–724.

———. *Russia in a Box*. DeKalb: Northern Illinois University Press, 2005.

Jolluck, Katherine R. *Exile and Identity: Polish Women in the Soviet Union during World War II*. Pittsburgh: University of Pittsburgh Press, 2002.

Jyoti, Hosagrahar. "City as Durbar: Theater and Power in Imperial Delhi." In *Forms of Dominance: On the Architecture and Urbanism of the Colonial Enterprise*, edited by Nezar AlSayyad, 83–105. Aldershot, England: Avebury, 1992.

Kadyrova, T. F. "Arkhitektor S. N. Polupanov (1904–1957)." *Stroitel'stvo arkhitektura i Uzbekistana*, no. 12 (1973): 26–32.

Kadyrova, T. F. *Arkhitektura sovetskogo Uzbekistana*. Moscow: Stroiizdat, 1987.

———. "Puti razvitiia arkhitektury Sovetskogo Uzbekistana," *Stroitel'stvo i arkhitektura Uzbekistana*, no. 12 (1972): 12.

———. *Sovremennaia arkhitektura Uzbekistana*. Tashkent: Izdatel'stvo literatury i iskusstva im. Gafura Guliama, 1974.

———, K. B. Babievskii, and F. Yu. Tursunov. *Arkhitektura sovetskogo Uzbekistana*. Moscow: Izd. Literatury po stroitel'svo, 1972.

Kagan, Frederick. "The Evacuation of Soviet Industry in the Wake of 'Barbarossa': A Key to the Soviet Victory." *Journal of Slavic Military Studies*, no. 2 (1995): 387–414.

Kaganovich, Lazar M. *The Construction of the Subway and the Plan of the City of Moscow*. Moscow: Cooperative Publishing Society of Foreign Workers in the USSR, 1934.

Kaiumova, M. A. "Osnovnye etapy formirovania priemov ob'emno-prostranstvennoi kompozitsii ploshchadei Tashkenta." *Stroitel'stvo i arkhitektura Uzbekistana*, no. 7 (1984): 27–29.

Kamp, Marianne. *The New Woman in Uzbekistan: Islam, Modernity, and Unveiling under Communism*. Seattle: University of Washington Press, 2006.

Karklins, Rasma. "Islam: How Strong Is It in the Soviet Union? Inquiry Based on Interviews with Soviet Germans Repatriated from Central Asia in 1979." *Cahiers du monde russe et soviétique*, no. 1 (1980): 65–81.

Keen, Sam. *Faces of the Enemy: Reflections of the Hostile Imagination*. San Francisco: Harper, 1991.

Keller, Shoshana. *To Moscow, Not Mecca: The Soviet Campaign against Islam in Central Asia, 1917–1941*. Westport, CT: Praeger, 2001.

Khalid, Adeeb. *The Politics of Muslim Cultural Reform: Jadidism in Central Asia*. Berkeley: University of California Press, 1998.

——. "Tashkent 1917: Muslim Politics in Revolutionary Russia." *Slavic Review*, no. 2 (1996): 270–96.

Khanga, Yelena. *Pro vsyo*. Moscow: VAGRIUS, 2001.

Khrushchev, Nikita. *Khrushchev Remembers*. Edited and translated by Strobe Talbott. Boston: Little, Brown, 1970.

Kim, P. *Koreitsy respubliki Uzbekistana*. Tashkent: O'zbekiston, 1993.

King, Anthony D. *Colonial Urban Development*. London: Routledge & Kegan Paul, 1976.

Kochan, Lionel, ed. *The Jews in Soviet Russia since 1917*. London: Oxford University Press, 1972.

Kochina, Elena. *Blockade Diary*. Ann Arbor, MI: Ardis, 1990.

Kopp, Anatole. *Town and Revolution: Soviet Architecture and City Planning, 1917–1935*. Translated by Thomas E. Burton. New York: George Braziller, 1970.

Kornfeld, Iakov. "Teatr opery i baleta v Tashkente." *Arkhitektura i stroitel'stvo*, no. 2 (1948): 12–16.

Korovin, M. F. "Tashkentskii metropoliten." *Stroitel'stvo i arkhitektura Uzbekistana*, no. 9 (1969): 1–4.

Kosenkova, Iu. L. *Sovetskii gorod: 1940-kh – pervoi poloviny 1950-kh godov; Ot tvorcheskikh poiskov k praktike stroitel'stva*. Moscow: URSS, 2000.

Kotkin, Stephen. *Magnetic Mountain: Stalinism as a Civilization*. Berkeley: University of California Press, 1995.

Kumanev, G. A. "The Soviet Economy and the 1941 Evacuation." In *Operation Barbarossa*, edited by Joseph L. Wieczynski, 163–93. Salt Lake City: Charles Schlacks Jr., Publisher, 1993.

Kunitz, Joshua. *Dawn over Samarkand: The Rebirth of Central Asia*. New York: Covici Friede Publishers, 1935.

Kuzin, Boris, and Nadezhda Mandel'stam. *Vospominaniia, proizvedeniia, perepiska: 192 pis'ma k B. S. Kuzinu*. St. Petersburg: Inapress, 1999.

Kuznetsov, Aleksandr. "Rekonstruktsiia stolitsy Uzbekistana." *Arkhitektura SSSR*, no. 7 (1939): 6–15.

Lamprakos, Michele. "Le Corbusier and Algiers: The Plan Obus as Colonial Urbanism." In *Forms of Dominance: On the Architecture and Urbanism of the Colonial Enterprise*, edited by Nezar AlSayyad, 183–210. Aldershot, England: Avebury, 1992.

Lansdell, Henry. *Through Central Asia*. 1887. Reprint, Nedeln, Liechtenstein: Kraus Reprint, 1978.

Le Corbusier. *The City of Tomorrow and Its Planning.* Translated by Frederick Etchells. Cambridge, MA: MIT Press, 1971.

——. *The Radiant City.* Translated by Pamela Knight, Eleanor Levieux, and Derek Coltman. New York: Orion Press, 1967.

Li, Lilian M., Alison J. Dray-Novey, and Haili Kong. *Beijing: From Imperial Capital to Olympic City.* New York: Palgrave Macmillan, 2007.

Lieberman, Sanford R. "The Evacuation of Industry in the Soviet Union during World War II." *Soviet Studies,* no. 1 (1983): 90–102.

Lugovskaia, Tatiana. *Kak znaiu, kak pomniu, kak umeiu.* Moscow: Agraf, 2001.

MacKenzie, David. *The Lion of Tashkent: The Career of General M. G. Cherniaev.* Athens: University of Georgia Press, 1974.

MacLean, Fitzroy. *Back to Bokhara.* New York: Harper & Brothers, 1959.

——. *Eastern Approaches.* London: Penguin Books, 1991.

Marianovskii, Grigorii. *Kniga sudeb, dokumental'noe povestvovaniia.* Tashkent: Izd. Literatury i iskusstva im. Gafura Guliama, 1988.

Massell, Gregory J. *The Surrogate Proletariat: Moslem Women and Revolutionary Strategies in Soviet Central Asia, 1919–1929.* Princeton: Princeton University Press, 1974.

Masters of Literature and Art of Tashkent. Tashkent: Goslitizdat of the UzSSR, 1958.

Matich, Olga. "Remaking the Bed." In *Laboratory of Dreams: The Russian Avant-Garde and Cultural Experiment,* edited by John E. Bowlt and Olga Matich, 59–78. Stanford: Stanford University Press, 1996.

Michaels, Paula. *Curative Powers: Medicine and Empire in Stalin's Central Asia.* Pittsburgh: University of Pittsburgh Press, 2003.

Micklin, Philip P. "The Fate of 'Sibaral': Soviet Water Politics in the Gorbachev Era." *Central Asian Survey,* no. 2 (1987): 67–88.

Mikhailovich, Boris. *Na dne blokady, voiny.* St. Petersburg: Izd. VSEGEI, 2000.

Mitchell, Timothy. *Colonising Egypt.* Cambridge: Cambridge University Press, 1988.

"Monument to Friendship of Peoples Removed in Tashkent." Uznews.net, April 15, 2008. http://www.uznewsnet/article_single.php?ing=en&cid=25&aid=591. Accessed May 8, 2008.

Mumford, Lewis. *The City in History: Its Origins, Its Transformations, and Its Prospects.* New York: Harcourt, Brace & World, 1961.

Muminova, I. M. *Istoriia rabochego klassa sovetskogo Uzbekistana.* Tashkent: FAN, 1974.

Naimark, Norman M. *Fires of Hatred: Ethnic Cleansing in Twentieth-Century Europe.* Cambridge, MA: Harvard University Press, 2001.

Neweroff, Alexander. *City of Bread.* New York: George H. Doran, 1927.

Nilsen, V. A., and L. D. Terent'eva. "Iz istorii zastroiki Tashkenta," *Stroitel'stvo i arkhitektura Uzbekistana,* no. 9 (1983): 3–5.

Nilsen, V. A., and A. A. Ziiaev. "Stanovlenie sotsialisticheskoi arkhitektury Tashkenta." *Stroitel'stvo i arkhitektura Uzbekistana,* no. 8 (1983): 8–14.

Nilsson, Sten. *The New Capitals of India, Pakistan, and Bangladesh.* Translated by Elisabeth Andreasson. Copenhagen: Scandinavian Institute of Asian Studies, 1973.

"Novyi vokzal v Kishineve." *Arkhitektura i stroitel'stvo,* no. 4 (1948): 9–10.

Northrop, Douglas. *Veiled Empire: Gender and Power in Stalinist Central Asia.* Ithaca, NY: Cornell University Press, 2004.

Ocharovan toboi Uzbekistan. Tashkent: Gos. Izd. Uzbekskoi SSR, 1964.

Olcott, Martha Brill. *The Kazakhs.* Stanford: Hoover Institution Press, 1986.

Orekhov, Ivan. *Velikii khashar: na zemle Tashkenstkoi.* Tula: Priokskoe knizhnoe izdatel'stvo, 1970.

Overy, Richard. *Russia's War*. New York: Penguin Books, 1998.

O'zbekiston sovyet mustamlakachiligi davrida. Tashkent: Shark nashriyoti, 2000.

O'zbek sovyet entsiklopediyasi. Tashkent: O'zbek Sovyet Entsiklopediyasi Bosh Redaktsiyasi, 1971.

Pahlen, K. K. *Mission to Turkestan*. Edited by Richard A. Pierce. London: Oxford University Press, 1964.

Pavlenko, P. *Puteshestvie v Turkmenistane*. Moscow: Moskovskoe tovarishchestvo pisatelei, 1933.

Payne, Matthew. *Stalin's Railroad: Turksib and the Building of Socialism*. Pittsburgh: University of Pittsburgh Press, 2001.

"Pervyi proekt pereplanirovki Tashkenta." *Stroitel'stvo i arkhitektura Uzbekistana*, no. 7 (1973): 33–36.

Pervyi s'ezd intellitentsii Uzbekistana: stenograficheskii otchet. Tashkent: Gos. Izd Uzbekskoi SSR, 1957.

Pierce, Richard A. *Russian Central Asia, 1867–1917*. Berkeley: University of California Press, 1960.

Planirovka i stroitel'stvo gorodov SSSR, materialiy k III plenumu pravleniia soiuza sovetskikh arkhitektorov SSSR, 7–11 iulia 1938 goda. Moscow: Izd. Vsesoiuznoi Akademii Arkhitektury, 1938.

Polupanov, Stepan. *Shahar Toshkent*. Moscow: SSSR Arkhitektura akademiiasi, 1949.

———. "Zal zasedaniy Verkhovnogo Soveta Uzbekskoi SSR." *Arkhitektura SSR*, no. 12 (1940): 50–51.

Pomerantz, Jack, and Lyric Wallwork Winik. *Run East: Flight from the Holocaust*. Urbana: University of Illinois Press, 1997.

Porteous, J. Douglas, and Sandra E. Smith. *Domicide: The Global Destruction of Home*. Montreal: McGill-Queens University Press, 2001.

Pospelova, P. N., ed. *Sovetskii tyl v velikoi otechestvennoi voine*. Moscow: Izd. Mysl' 1974.

Po ulitsam Tashkenta. Tashkent: Izd. Uzbekistan, 1971.

"Pozdravliaem iubiliara, M. S. Bulatov." *Stroitel'stvo i arkhitektura Uzbekistana*, no. 4 (1978): 47.

Qoriniyozov, T. N. *Sovyet O'zbekistoni madaniati tarihidan ocherklar*. Tashkent: FAN, 1956.

Qualls, Karl. "Raised from Ruins: Restoring Popular Allegiance through City Planning in Sevastopol, 1943–1954." PhD dissertation, Georgetown University, 1998.

Rabinow, Paul. "Colonialism, Modernity: The French in Morocco." In *Forms of Dominance: On the Architecture and Urbanism of the Colonial Enterprise*, edited by Nezar AlSayyad, 167–82. Aldershot, England: Avebury, 1992.

———. *French Modern: Norms and Forms of the Social Environment*. Cambridge, MA: MIT Press, 1989.

Rakowska-Harmstone, Teresa. "Soviet Central Asia: A Model of Non-capitalist Development in the Third World." In *The USSR and the Muslim World: Issues in Domestic and Foreign Policy*, edited by Yaacov Ro'i, 181–205. London: George Allen & Unwin, 1984.

Ranevskaia, Faina. *Dnevnik na klochkakh*. St. Petersburg: Izd. Fonda russkoi poezii, 1999.

Rashidov, G. *Istoriia sotsialisticheskogo Tashkenta*. Tashkent: Izd. "Nauka" Uzbekskoi SSR, 1965.

———. *Sotsialistik Toshkent Tarihi*. Vol. 1. Tashkent: FAN, 1965.

———. *Sotsialistik Toshkent Tarihi*. Vol. 2. Tashkent: FAN, 1966.

Reitlinger, Gerald. *The House Built on Sand: The Conflicts of German Policy in Russia, 1939–1945*. New York: Viking Press, 1960.

Reskov, B., and G. Sedov. *Usmon Yusupov: ajoyib kishilar hayoti*. Tashkent: Yosh gvardiia nashriyoti, 1977.

Resoliutsiia VII s'ezda Kommunisticheskoi partii Uzbekistana po otchetnomu dokladu TsK KP/b/ Uzbekistana. Tashkent, 1938.

Rigby, T. H. *Communist Party Membership in the USSR, 1917–1967*. Princeton: Princeton University Press, 1968.

Roberts, Holland. "Tamerlane's Uzbekistan Today." *New World Review*, November 1959, 33–40.

———. "Islam and Soviet Muslims in Soviet Arab Policy, Part One." *Asian and African Studies*, no. 2 (1975): 157–89.

———. "Islam and Soviet Muslims in Soviet Arab Policy, Part Two." *Asian and African Studies*, no. 3 (1975): 259–80.

Ro'i, Yaacov, ed. *The USSR and the Muslim World: Issues in Domestic and Foreign Policy*. London: George Allen & Unwin, 1984.

Rothenberg, Joshua. "Jewish Religion in the Soviet Union." In *The Jews in Soviet Russia since 1917*, edited by Lionel Kochan, 159–87. London: Oxford University Press, 1972.

Ruble, Blair. *Leningrad: Shaping a Soviet City*. Berkeley: University of California Press, 1990.

Rumer, Boris Z. *Soviet Central Asia: A Tragic Experiment*. Boston: Unwin Hyman, 1989.

Rybakovskii, L. A. *Liudskie poteri SSSR i Rossii v Velikoi Otechestvennoi voine*. Moscow: Rossiiskaia Akademiia nauk, institute sotsial'no-politicheskikh issledovanii, 2001.

Rywkin, Michael. *Moscow's Muslim Challenge: Soviet Central Asia*. Rev. ed. Armonk, NY: M. E. Sharpe, 1990.

———. "National Symbiosis: Vitality, Religion, Identity, Allegiance." In *The USSR and the Muslim World: Issues in Domestic and Foreign Policy*, edited by Yaacov Ro'i, 3–15. London: George Allen & Unwin, 1984.

Sahadeo, Jeff. *Russian Colonial Society in Tashkent: 1865–1923*. Bloomington: Indiana University Press, 2007.

Said, Edward. *Orientalism*. New York: Vintage, 1978.

Schuyler, Eugene. *Turkistan: Notes of a Journey in Russian Turkistan, Khokand, Bukhara, and Kuldja*. 2 vols. New York: Scribner, Armstrong & Co., 1877.

Scott, James C. *Seeing Like a State: How Certain Schemes to Improve the Human Condition Have Failed*. New Haven: Yale University Press, 1998.

Semenov, V. N. "Poselki dlia predpriiatii, evakuirovannykh v Sredniuu Aziiu." *Arkhitektura SSSR*, no. 1 (1942): 17–21.

Sergeant, Patrick. *Another Road to Samarkand*. London: Hodder and Stoughton, 1955.

Shakhsuvarian, T. V. "Tvorcheskiy put' gosudarstvennogo proektnogo instituta rekonstruktsii i zastroiki goroda Tashkenta." *Arkhitektura i stroitel'stvo Uzbekistana*, no. 3 (1974): 5–9.

Shams-ud-din. *Secularisation in the USSR: A Study of Soviet Cultural Policy in Uzbekistan*. New Delhi: Vikas Publishing House, 1982.

Shamsutdinov, Rustambek. *O'zbekistonda sovyetlarning quloqlashtirish siyosati v uning fojeali oqibatlari*. Tashkent: Shark nashriyoti, 2001.

Shcheglov, Aleksei. *Faina Ranevskaia: vsia zhizn'*. Moscow: Zakharov, 2001.

Shilov, G. M. "Traditsii i preemstvennost' v planirovochnoi structure gorodov Tveri (nyne Kalinina) i Tashkenta." *Stroitel'stvo i arkhitektura Uzbekistana*, no. 2 (1983): 23–24.

Sievers, Eric. "Uzbekistan's *Mahalla*s: From Soviet to Absolutist Residential Community Associations." *Journal of International and Comparative Law at Chicago-Kent*, no. 2 (2002): 91–158.

Sigalov, I. *Uzbekskaia delegatsiia na zapadnom fronte*. Tashkent: Gosizdat, UzSSR, 1942.

Simonov, Konstantin. *Ostaius' zhurnalistom*. Moscow: Izd. Pravda, 1968.

Slezkine, Yuri. *Arctic Mirrors: Russia and the Small Peoples of the North*. Ithaca, NY: Cornell University Press, 1994.

Snyder, Timothy. *The Reconstruction of Nations: Poland, Ukraine, Lithuania, Belarus, 1569–1999*. New Haven: Yale University Press, 2003.

Sokolov, Iu. *Tashkent, Tashkenttsy i Rossiia*. Tashkent, 1965.

Solzhenitsyn, Alexander. *One Day in the Life of Ivan Denisovich*. Translated by Max Hayward and Ronald Hingley. New York: Bantam Books, 1963.

Soucek, Svat. *A History of Inner Asia*. Cambridge: Cambridge University Press, 2000.

Sovetskii Uzbekistan. Tashkent: Izd. TsK KP Uzbekistana, 1977.

Stapanov, L. *Konflikt v Indostane i soglasheniie v Tashkente*. Moscow: Izdatel'stvo politicheskoi literatury, 1966.

Stites, Richard. *Revolutionary Dreams*. Oxford: Oxford University Press, 1989.

Suny, Ronald Grigor. *Revenge of the Past: Nationalism, Revolution, and the Collapse of the Soviet Union*. Stanford: Stanford University Press, 1993.

Tarkhanov, Alexei, and Sergei Kavtaradze. *Stalinist Architecture*. London: Laurence King, 1992.

Tashkent entsiklopediia. Tashkent: Glavnaia redaktsiia uzbekskoi sovetskoi entsiklopedii, 1983.

Tashkent—gorod bratstva. Tashkent: Izd. TsK KP Uzbekistana, 1969.

Tashkent: kratkii spravochnik-putevoditel'. Tashkent: Gos. Izdatel'stvo Uzbekskoi SSR, 1962.

Tashkent: kratkii spravochnik-putevoditel'. Tashkent: Uzbekistan, 1981.

Tashkentskie vstrechi. Tashkent: Gos. Izdatel'stvo khudozhestvennoi literatury UzSSR, 1960.

Tashkentskii protsess: sud nad desiat'iu predstaviteliami krymskotatarskogo naroda (1 iulia–5 avgusta 1969 g.); Sbornik dokumentov s illiustratsiiami. Amsterdam: Fond imeni Gertsena, 1976.

"Tashkent to Undergo Renovation . . ." *OMRI Daily Digest*, June 6, 1996. http://www.hri.org/news/balkans/omri/96-06-06.omri.html#02. Accessed July 8, 2003.

Tashkent v proshlom i nastoiashchem. Tashkent: Znanie, 1968.

Taubman, William. *Khrushchev: The Man and His Era*. New York: Norton, 2003.

Thomas, Nicholas. *Colonialism's Culture: Anthropology, Travel, and Government*. Cambridge: Polity Press, 1994.

Thurman, Michael. "Leaders of the Communist Party of Uzbekistan in Historical Retrospect: The 'Class of '38,' Part I." *Central Asian Monitor*, no. 6 (1995): 19–27.

Tillet, Lowell. *The Great Friendship: Soviet Historians on the Non-Russian Nationalities*. Chapel Hill: University of North Carolina Press, 1969.

Topolski, Aleksander. *Without Vodka: Wartime Adventures in Russia*. Ottawa: UP Press, 1999.

Tretii s'ezd intelligentsii Uzbekistana, stenograficheskiy otchet. Tashkent: Gos. Izdatel'stvo Uzbekskoi SSR, 1962.

Tubert, General. *L'Ouzbekistan république soviétique*. Paris: Editions du Pavillon, 1951.

Tyurikov, V. *Tashkent: A Guide*. Moscow: Raduga Publishers, 1983.

United States. Department of Interior. U.S. Geological Survey. USGS Earthquake Hazards Program. "Earthquakes with 1000 or More Deaths from 1900." http://neic.usgs .gov/neis.eglists/egsmajr.html. Accessed February 13, 2003.

———. Department of State. Bureau of South and Central Asian Affairs. "Uzbekistan, October 2009." http://www.state.gov/r/pa/ei/bgn/2924.htm. Accessed February 21, 2010.

Uzbekskaia SSR v gody Velikoi Otechestvennoi voiny. Vol. 1. Tashkent: Izd. FAN, 1981.

Uzbekskaia SSR v gody Velikoi Otechestvennoi voiny. Vol. 2. Tashkent: Izd. FAN, 1983.

Uzbekskaia SSR v gody Velikoi Otechestvennoi voiny. Vol. 3. Tashkent: Izd. FAN, 1985.

Vasil'eva, G. P., and N. A. Kisliakov. "Voprosy sem'i i byta u narodov Srednei Azii i Kazakhstana v periode stroitel'stva sotsializma i kommunizma." *Sovetskaia etnografiia,* no. 6 (1962): 3–16.

Vitkovich, Viktor. *Puteshestvie po Sovetskomu Uzbekistanu.* Moscow: Izd. Molodaia gvardiia, 1951.

Volkov, Vadim. "The Concept of 'Kul'turnost'': Notes on the Stalinist Civilizing Process." In *Stalinism: New Directions,* edited by Sheila Fitzpatrick, 210–31. London: Routledge, 2000.

Volynskii, Leonid. "Doroga k novoi zemle." *Novyi mir,* no. 12 (1961): 118–60.

von Hertzen, Heikki, and Paul. D. Spreiregen. *Building a New Town: Finland's New Garden City, Tapiola.* Rev. ed. Cambridge, MA: MIT Press, 1973.

Voronina, Veronika L. *Narodnye traditsii arkhitektury Uzbekistana.* Moscow: Arkhitektury i gradostroitel'stva, 1951.

Voskoboinikov, E. A. *Uzbekskii narod v gody Velikoi Otechestvennoi voiny.* Tashkent: Goz. Izd. UzbSSR, 1947.

Vstavai strana ogromnaia. Tashkent: Izd. Uzbekistan, 1990.

Wat, Aleksander. *My Century.* Translated by Richard Lourie. Berkeley: University of California Press, 1977.

Wieczynski, Joseph L., ed. *Operation Barbarossa.* Salt Lake City: Charles Schlacks Jr., Publisher, 1993.

Weiner, Amir. *Making Sense of War: The Second World War and the Fate of the Bolshevik Revolution.* Princeton: Princeton University Press, 2001.

Werth, Alexander. *Russia at War: 1941–1945.* New York: Avon Books, 1965.

Whiteman, Dorit Bader. *Escape via Siberia.* New York: Holmes & Meier, 1999.

Williams, Brian Glyn. *The Crimean Tatars: The Diaspora Experience and the Forging of a Nation.* Leiden, Netherlands: Brill, 2001.

Wixman, Ronald. "Ethnic Attitudes and Relations in Modern Uzbek Cities." In *Soviet Central Asia: The Failed Transformation,* edited by William Fierman, 159–95. Boulder, CO: Westview Press, 1991.

Wolff, Joseph. *Narrative of a Mission to Bokhara in the Years 1843–1845.* Edited by Guy Wint. London: Frederick A. Praeger, 1969.

Wolff, Larry. *Inventing Eastern Europe.* Stanford: Stanford University Press, 1994.

Wright, Gwendolyn. *The Politics of Design in French Colonial Urbanism.* Chicago: University of Chicago Press, 1991.

Yevtushenko, Yevgeny. *A Precocious Autobiography.* Translated by Andrew R. MacAndrew. New York: Dutton, 1963.

Yusupov, E. Iu. *Tashkent v period razvitogo sotsializma.* Tashkent: FAN, 1983.

Yusupov, Usman. *Izbrannye trudy.* 3 vols. Tashkent: Izdatel'stvo Uzbekistan, 1982.

Zaleskii, K. A. *Imperiia Stalina: biograficheskii entsiklopedicheskii slovar'.* Moscow: Veche, 2000.

Zeyons, Serge. *La Révolution des femmes au coeur de l'Asie soviétique.* Paris: Editions Sociales, 1971.

Zhenshchiny Uzbekistana. Tashkent: Gosizdat UzSSR, 1942.

Ziiaev, A. A. "Formirovanie arkhitekturnogo ansamblia ploshchadi V. I. Lenina v Tash-kente." *Stroitel'stvo i arkhitektura Uzbekistana,* no. 4 (1983): 26–31.

Zodchestvo Uzbekistana. Tashkent: Gos. Izd. Khudozhestvennoi literatury, 1959.

"Zodchii, uchenyi pedagog, A.B. Babakhanov." *Stroitel'stvo i arkhitektura Uzbekistana,* no. 4 (1978): 16.

INDEX

Stalinism and, 13; sterility of, 268; urbanization campaign and, 47–48

urban planning in Tsarist Tashkent, 10, 19–20, 24–25, 259

urban planning in World War II, 14, 73, 86–87, 262; late war resumption of, 102–4; wartime evacuations and, 96–99, 147–48

urban sprawl, 316n66; Bulatov on, 223, 230; efforts to control, 59–60; industrial development and, 230; municipal services and, 59–60

Uzbek Academy of Sciences, 103

Uzbek Architects' Union. *See* Architects' Union, Uzbek

Uzbek Council of Ministers, closing of red teahouses, 183

Uzbek cultural institutions, Soviet targeting of, 183, 186

Uzbek culture. *See* traditional culture

Uzbekistan: cultural influences, history of, 9; independence, 278–79; influence of Stalinism on, 13

Uzbekistan, post-Soviet: nationalist histories of, 11, 283n18; Soviet past and, 279–80

"Uzbekistan and Children" (Chukovskii), 141

Uzbek language, Soviet revisions to alphabet, 5, 309n40

Uzbek-language schools, 186

Uzbek national identity: as fusion of Soviet and regional identities, 8; as negotiated entity, 6; Soviet remolding of, 4–8, 29–30, 199–200; spread of, through radio, 239–40; Uzbek resistance to, 200–201; World War II and, 11–12, 13. *See also* architecture of Soviet Tashkent

Uzbeks: demands made on Soviet state, 10, 199–200, 225; postwar unrest, 180–81, 203, 208–12, 263–64; purging from government, in 1930s, 52–53; resistance to communal housing, 36–37, 224; resistance to cultural change, 8, 29–30, 286n47; rise within Soviet system, 246, 250–51, 264–65, 323n6; Russian views on, in Soviet period, 30, 50, 64, 121–22, 124, 182, 278; Russian views on, Tsarist period, 21–22, 25; and Stalin, mourning of, 204–8; support for revolutionary ideology, 10; support for Soviet rule, 5, 8, 11–12, 132–33, 264, 276, 278–79; threats of revolt from, 12; traditional clothing, 112, 250. *See also entries under* residents; traditional culture; traditional housing, Uzbek

Uzbek Soviet Socialist Republic, creation of, 5, 10, 29

Uzbek State Philharmonic, 92

Uzbek Statistical Administration, 177

Vatan/Rodina theater, *118*

veiling: disappearance of, 275; forced unveiling campaign (*hujum*), 11, 32, 44, 91, 260; postwar resurgence of, 191–93, 194; Soviet views on, 192–94

veterans: migration to Tashkent, 208; Uzbek, demands made on Soviet state, 199–200

Victory Park, 305n27

village prose writers, 277, 324n13

visitors, foreign, 319n1, 320n24; displays of Tashkent culture for, 237, 243–45; peaks behind official version of city, 248–49, 322n47; privileges of, resident resentment of, 249; Soviet screening of information available to, 235–36, 248–49; and Tashkent as model city, 235–39, 242–43; views on Tashkent, 235, 242–43, 246–50

Vitkovich, Viktor, 2, 170

Volchek, V., 161–62, 169

Volga-Volga (film), 43

Volynskii, Leonid, 221, 223, 227, 316n63, 317n76, 317n77, 317n78

Voronina, Veronika, 149, 167

Voskresenskii Market, 28, 39, 166

Vulkan agricultural machine production plant, 85, 88

wartime industry, in World War II: evacuated workers, processing of, 127–29; impressment of workers, 131–32, 143; Uzbek employment in, 81–82, 131–32, 296n44, 297n48; women in, 81–83, 297n48; worker retention problems, 82, 131–32, 297n48; worker training, 131

wartime industry evacuations to Tashkent, 85–86; disarray of, 86–88; displacement of civilian institutions, 90–91; human life, limited concern for, 87, 89; postwar departures and remaining industries, 103; restarting of production, difficulties in, 87–89. *See also* World War II evacuations

waste removal, ineffectiveness of, 62–63

water, decorative use of: as characteristic of Stalinist urban planning, 13; in city center redesign, 161, 164–65; ideological importance of, 1–2, 66, 67, 155, 161, 305n27; in Khrushchev era Tashkent, 238; in late Soviet era, 274, 275; in post-earthquake reconstruction, 254, 273. *See also* Komsomol Lake

water power, war-era construction of, 103

water supply: in European section of Tashkent, 24; importance of, as display of Soviet power, 1–2, 66, 67, 155, 161, 305n27; limitations of, Soviet recognition of, 230–31; postwar shortages, 180–81, 209; Soviet improvements in, 1–2, 277; Soviet misuse of, 155, 180–81, 256, 277; Soviet postwar reconsideration of, 149; wartime improvements in, 130. *See also* hauz

water supply, contaminated: in Central Asia, 23, 285n18; and city center redesign, 164; earthquake of 1966 and, 253; for plant watering, 318n89; and public unrest, 211; Soviet inability to resolve, 62; Soviet lack of concern about health impact of, 164; World War II industrialization and, 99

Western influence in Uzbekistan, Tsarist Russian rule and, 10

White House (Tashkent), 24, 37

women: as agricultural workers, 248–49; education of, 173–74, 184–85, 186–87, 192, 237, 278,